THE SURVIVOR

THE SURVIVOR

Tony Blair in Peace and War

FRANCIS BECKETT &
DAVID HENCKE

First published in Great Britain 2004 as *The Blairs and Their Court* by Aurum Press Ltd
25 Bedford Avenue, London WC1B 3AT
www.aurumpress.co.uk

This revised and enlarged paperback edition first published 2005 by Aurum Press

A catalogue record for this book is available from the British Library.

ISBN 1 84513 110 X

1 3 5 7 9 10 8 6 4 2
2005 2007 2009 2008 2006

Designed by Geoff Green Book Design
Typeset by M Rules in Monotype Columbus
Printed and bound in Great Britain by Bookmarque Ltd, Croydon, Surrey

CONTENTS

PREFACE

Tony Blair likes to choose his biographers. He has brought to biography the same news management techniques that have served him well with journalists and broadcasters. Co-operation from Downing Street and its friends, plus enticing scraps of information, go to writers thought to be reliable. Levels of co-operation go up and down as a biographer shows himself more or less malleable. A writer can start with prime-ministerial co-operation, and then, as Anthony Seldon seems to have done, step out of line and find himself suddenly banished.

So we take some professional pride in the fact that this is the first of the four biographies of the prime minister for which Downing Street refused all co-operation. Blair and his immediate entourage turned down all our requests for help and interviews, and put pressure on others to do the same, as we know from various scared and whispered telephone conversations.

We are therefore even more than usually grateful to the many people who have talked to us, and told us stories or offered us insights which 'approved' sources might not have given us. Many of them have talked on the record, and their contributions are acknowledged in footnotes or in the text. But many more are anxious for it never to be known that they have talked to us.

Some, perhaps, hope for advancement which can only be given by Blair. A British prime minister has enormous powers of patronage, and Blair, as the reader will discover, has used these powers ruthlessly to reward loyalty and punish dissent. Others are old friends of the Blairs, who value the friendship they once had, even though just now it seems to have been withdrawn, and hope that it may be renewed once Tony ceases to be prime minister. We value their help, and will respect their desire to remain anonymous.

Where our information comes from one of these anonymous sources, you will not find a footnote in the text. We think there is no point in sending the reader on a fruitless mission to the back of the book, only to discover that you are not going to be told the source of the story. Our open sources are acknowledged in the footnotes, and we will not list them here, but they know how much we value their help.

These sources have more than made up for the establishment sources that have been denied to us. We know that some people felt happier talking to us knowing we were entirely 'unauthorised'. Others were delighted to tell us all they knew, partly because they were surprised not to have been contacted by previous biographers. Looking for information sometimes felt like turning on a long-disused tap.

There's a downside, of course. We would have preferred to include the comments of the prime minister or his close confidants on the stories told in this book for the first time, and on many of our judgements. The stories are true, but maybe the prime minister, Cherie Booth, Gordon Brown, Peter Mandelson, Alastair Campbell or Fiona Millar could have pointed us to a more charitable explanation for some of them than the obvious one. Some, like Anji Hunter, his childhood friend, took the view that no book could ever do justice to Blair. 'Any book is bound to be nothing but froth: no one can evaluate him properly,' she said grandly at a recent reception.

Several Blair confidants and members of the government surprised us by their willingness to talk, sometimes anonymously but not always. Those who turned us down often took instructions first. Apart from the best-known courtiers, like Mandelson and Campbell, these included David Triesman, the former Blair-appointed Labour Party general secretary. He told us on the telephone that before deciding whether to talk to us, 'I need to consult one or two people.' Having, presumably, done that, Lord Triesman (as he became recently) wrote to say that it 'would not be appropriate' for him to talk to us.

A much greater loss than Lord Triesman was Carole Caplin, and also her mother, Sylvia. They showed much greater loyalty to Blair than Blair, from what we have discovered, has earned from them. We telephoned Carole's mobile and she said, in an unconvincing Yorkshire accent, 'You've got the wrong number,' and cut us off. We tried again, and before we could speak, she shouted 'I told you you've got the wrong number' — but forgetting the accent that time. Her mother later explained that the Caplins could only talk to us if the prime minister gave permission.

The most surprising refusenik was Ken Livingstone. When we first approached his spokeswoman, she thought he would be glad to talk to us. But then he rejoined the Labour Party, and she told us: 'Things have changed.' She had the grace to seem a bit ill at ease about it.

We want to thank all our sources, those whose names we can give and those whose identity we have to keep to ourselves. We also want to thank our friend Steve Parry, without whom this book might not have been written, or might have been less thorough. At the time of writing, we don't know where Steve is, but he may pick up a copy and see that we value his friendship, enthusiasm and intelligence.

Our researcher, Steve Bloomfield, has made a considerable contribution to this book. Helpful research projects have also been undertaken for us by Peter Beckett, John Booth and Paul Donovan.

We also want to thank our editor at Aurum Press, Piers Burnett; our agent Andrew Lownie; and the *Guardian* newspaper, whose library and other facilities were made available to us, and which made it possible for us to devote the necessary time to the book. For all this we record our gratitude to Alan Rusbridger, Chris Elliott and Matt Seaton.

We would also like to thank people on the *Guardian* who helped us with contacts, facts and sources: Stephen Bates, Paul Brown, Rob Evans, Tom Happold and Will Woodward. Michael White, the *Guardian*'s political editor, and his team uncomplainingly operated one staff journalist short while David Hencke took time off to write the book. Other fellow journalists whose advice and help has been valuable and willingly given include Jef McAllister, London editor of *Time* magazine, as well as Paul Routledge and Peter Oborne.

Our children will have to live with the consequences of Blairism, just as they lived with the family upheavals we caused as we wrote this book in four months, and to them the book is dedicated: Anne McPhail (née Hencke), Peter Beckett and Naomi Beckett; and also David Hencke's grandchildren, Tegan and Leon.

Francis Beckett & David Hencke
September 2005

CHAPTER ONE

THE MAKING OF TEFLON TONY

Memories of the Second World War were still fresh in the minds of the British public when Leo and Hazel Blair's second son, Anthony Charles Lynton Blair, was born early on the morning of 6 May 1953. The nation's wartime leader, Winston Churchill, had been returned to office as prime minister two years earlier. The last vestiges of food rationing had only recently been abolished, and no doubt Hazel retained the frugal habits instilled by the war. Men wore drab grey suits and their hair short; many of them would have been horrified if they could have seen the exotic plumage their sons would be displaying by the time young Blair was a teenager. All young men still had to do three years' National Service in the armed forces – and some of them had, until very recently, been fighting and dying in another war, in Korea.

It was a world of order, discipline, duty. It was the world of Dennis Potter's 'great greyness', the 'flatness and bleakness of everyday England'. A world blown away by the 1960s, and one whose passing Prime Minister Tony Blair often seems to regret. Perhaps, as a *New Statesman* editorial suggested in 2000, that is simply because he does not remember a time when it was illegal to buy *Lady Chatterley's Lover*, to have a homosexual relationship, or to stage a play without consulting the Lord Chamberlain; or where, 'as late as 1957, Malcolm Muggeridge could be sacked from the editorship of *Punch* for printing a mildly facetious poem about the Queen's choice of Cheam prep school for her eldest son'.[1] Perhaps Blair is too young to remember. Or perhaps he does remember, and approves.

On the morning of Blair's birth, newspapers reported a dramatic parliamentary scene. The previous day the Labour Party's deputy leader, Herbert Morrison, made the sensational charge that the prime minister had 'treated Parliament like Hitler had handled the Reichstag'. To our ears this sounds well over the top, but in 1953 reviving the spectre of

Hitler was still part of the small change of political debate. Winston Churchill himself had said, during the 1945 election, that Labour's nationalisation proposals would require 'something like the Gestapo' to enforce them.

As Blair was born, Morrison would have been savouring the headlines his accusation had produced, for he was a newspaper junkie, the sort of politician who was on the telephone to the editor early in the morning if he saw something in a newspaper which displeased him. It would cement his reputation for bashing the Conservatives, and this would help him in his long and bitter battle against the Bevanites, the leftwing of his party led by the charismatic Welshman Aneurin Bevan. It would aid in his plan to 'modernise' (Morrison's word) the Labour Party and turn it into an organisation which appealed first and foremost to the middle classes; and to change the party's name for this purpose.

Of course, he did not know that, in Edinburgh, the Blair family was that morning celebrating the arrival of the baby who was one day to turn his ideas into reality. But he did know that he himself was expecting his second grandson in five months' time. Nearly half a century later, that grandson, Peter Mandelson, was to play a crucial part, as Tony Blair's faithful retainer, in the eventual triumph of the Morrison project.

That morning newspapers also reported the story of an unemployed war veteran, Major Christopher Dryer DSO, aged sixty-one, who had hired a single-engined light aircraft for £5 and flown it under fifteen Thames bridges between Blackfriars and Kew to make a protest about being jobless. The flying club near Luton that hired out the plane denounced his actions as a 'terrifically bad show'.

Agatha Christie's new play, *The Mousetrap*, had recently opened at the Ambassadors Theatre in London's West End, and is still running at the St Martin's Theatre nearby. At the Whitehall Theatre, Brian Rix was starring in *Reluctant Heroes,* which poked fun at service life and was one of the earliest of his famous Whitehall farces. At the Victoria Palace, Bud Flanagan was singing 'Who Do You Think You Are Kidding, Mr Hitler?' in the Crazy Gang's show – one of the few war songs that everyone still knows, for it was later adopted as the theme tune for the TV series *Dad's Army*.

It was not just the last war that was on everyone's mind, but the next one too. Foreign news included an announcement by the United States that it was halving its defence aid to the United Kingdom. Churchill, no doubt, felt he was owed better treatment after Britain had loyally committed troops to fight alongside the American forces in Korea. But in 1953 it was still not clear how subservient a role Britain was to play to the US, even though Churchill's Labour predecessor Clement Attlee had been forced to stave off an economic crisis with an American loan on the harshest possible terms. It would be another three years before the Suez crisis would make the nature of the relationship brutally clear, when President Eisenhower gave Churchill's successor, Anthony Eden, the choice between halting the Anglo-French invasion of Egypt or facing bankruptcy. That humiliating debacle was, however, foreshadowed on the morning of Blair's birth by a report in *The Times* that negotiations between Britain and Egypt over the Suez Canal 'ended in Cairo yesterday without any date being announced for the next session. General Neguib's principal lieutenant, Colonel Gamal Nasser, said that the Egyptian delegates had declined to enter into discussions of detail without agreement on the basic issues of national rights and sovereignty.'

Meanwhile, trade unions were increasing their power, and a pay demand by the powerful engineering union made the front page of *The Times*. The day also provided hope for the Labour Party with the announcement of the urban and district council election results. Labour had gained thirty seats and lost twelve, and took control of Dunfermline from the Progressives – then the equivalent of the Tories in Scotland. The town was later to become the constituency of Blair's greatest rival, Gordon Brown.

Yet despite these successes, Labour would remain in opposition for another eleven years. Although their party was currently riven by a passionate argument between its leadership and the Bevanite left, Labour supporters could take comfort from the fact that Clement Attlee's government, which had lost office two years earlier, had transformed the structure of the country's economy and revolutionised the way in which the needs of its poorer citizens were provided for. The Welfare State which they had created was the basis of a new social consensus which would not be seriously challenged for another thirty-odd years. By creating the National Health Service, bringing in national insurance for all, nationalising great natural monopolies like the railways, and providing the schools to make a reality of the commitment in the 1944 Education Act to free education as of right for all children of school age, all within just six years, the Attlee government had set a standard against which all future Labour governments, including Blair's, were going to be judged.

Leo Blair was working as a law lecturer at Edinburgh University at the time. He and Hazel already had one son, Bill, born in 1950, and a daughter, Sarah, would complete the family in 1956. Just seventeen months after Tony's birth, at the end of 1954, the Blairs sailed for Australia, where Leo was to take up a post as lecturer in administrative law at the University of

Adelaide. Their stay would be comparatively brief – though an acute ear can still detect the hint of an Australian accent in the prime-ministerial vowels – and by 1958 they were back in Britain, settling in Durham, where Leo set up a law practice as well as lecturing at the university and pursuing his ambition to become a Conservative member of parliament.

On the face of it, therefore, Tony Blair comes from a solid, middle-class, professional family. But Leo's background was both poor and exotic.

He had been born in 1923 as the result of an affair between two actors: Charles Parsons (whose stage name was Jimmy Lynton) and Celia Ridgeway, who had been born Augusta Bridson. Celia already had two children by her first husband, who used to beat her up regularly and whom she eventually left. Her second husband divorced her because he knew that young Leo was not his child. At that time, even in the world of the theatre, the birth of a baby outside marriage was still a cause for shame and social disgrace, and Celia decided to foster the baby out to Glasgow shipyard rigger James Blair and his wife Mary, a couple she had met while on tour in Glasgow. Three years later, she married Charles, and thirteen years later she tried to get her son back, but Mary Blair, who was not able to have children of her own, threatened to kill herself if the child was taken from her. She and her husband were the only parents young Leo had ever known, and he wanted to stay with them.

Although he took their surname, Mary and James Blair made no attempt to conceal his true parentage from Leo – he even exchanged Christmas cards with his two half-sisters, the daughters of Celia's first marriage. But when he went away to serve in the army during the Second World War, Mary Blair burnt all the cards and wrote to Celia and Charles to say that he was missing in action, presumed dead. It was not until Tony Blair became Labour leader in 1994 that a newspaper, the *Daily Mail*, found his father's two half-sisters and reunited them with Leo.

The Blairs provided Leo with a warm and loving but poverty-stricken home. The family lived in a crowded Glasgow tenement where five or six families shared one toilet. James Blair was often unemployed and frequently too ill to work even when he had a job; eventually he died young, during the Second World War. Given this background and his experience of growing up in the radical atmosphere of the 'Red Clyde' during the Depression, it was not surprising that young Leo should find himself attracted to the Communist Party.

He was secretary of the party's Govan branch for three years, also working for the Communist paper, the *Daily Worker*, and wanted to become a Communist MP. At that time, when Stalin's Soviet Union was Britain's ally against Hitler and the Communist Party was at the height of its influence and popularity, it was a perfectly realistic ambition: there was already one Communist MP, representing a Scottish constituency, and another, in a London constituency, was to be elected in 1945.

Leo did well in the army. The enormous expansion of the services in wartime meant that officers' messes were no longer the exclusive preserve of the 'officer class', and bright young men like Leo could achieve commissioned rank despite their lowly backgrounds. The future Conservative leader Ted Heath was another example of this new sort of officer. Leo put on his second lieutenant's 'pips' and found that he had joined not just the army but also the middle classes.

He voted Labour in 1945. But by 1947, he had decided that he liked the atmosphere in the officers' mess and went native by joining the Conservative Party, remaining a member until his son was elected leader of the Labour Party.

After his discharge from the army, Leo worked for the Inland Revenue. He studied in the evenings for a law degree from Edinburgh University and, once qualified, worked as a law tutor there. In 1948 he married Hazel McLay, a typist at the Ministry of National Insurance in Glasgow, the daughter of Protestant parents who had moved to Scotland from Ballyshannon, County Donegal. The fact that their two sons were both given the names of Leo's natural father was, perhaps, Leo's final gesture towards a parent who he thought – wrongly, as it turned out – had forgotten all about him.

Returning to Britain in 1958 and settling down into their new home in Durham after their three years in Australia, the Blair family found themselves back in a country which was recovering its self-confidence after the Suez crisis and enjoying a modest economic boom, circumstances which would soon encourage the new prime minister, Harold Macmillan, to tell its citizens that they had 'never had it so good'. Bill and Tony were entered for the most splendid private preparatory school for miles around, while Leo set about turning himself into the sort of man who could afford Durham Choristers School and whose children would fit in there: building up a law business as well as working at the university, lecturing all over the country, and becoming chairman of the local Conservative Association as the first step towards becoming an MP.

At Durham Choristers, since he had an older brother in the school, Tony Blair was known as Blair Two, in the fashion of prep schools in those days. He was by all accounts happy and successful there, playing rugby and cricket in the school team, showing off a lot, acting, spending most holidays near his mother's birthplace in Ireland. He was 'the sort of boy that was the backbone of a school like this' according to his head-master, Canon John Grove.[2] He showed early on the ease and charm he has always had with women by making an ally and confidante of the matron, Rita Jakes. Tony was a day boy; the family lived nearby in the middle-class suburb of Shincliffe. Doreen Gibson, whose son was a con-temporary and friend, remembers him well: 'He liked bananas and KitKats. Canon Grove thought a lot of him because the Canon liked to get debates going and Tony was always the leading light in them.'[3]

But in Tony's last year at the school, Leo Blair suffered a sudden stroke. At first it was thought he might die. That day Tony and Canon Grove knelt down in the headmaster's study together to pray, and Tony Blair later described it as 'the day my childhood ended'. Leo lost the power of speech for three years.[4] It was the end of his political ambitions.

It was a fitting prologue to the unhappiest year the young Blair had known – his first year at boarding school. The Tony Blair we know today is the product of Fettes, a fearsome public school in Edinburgh, founded in 1870 with money bequeathed by a wealthy Edinburgh mer-chant and former Lord Provost of the city, Sir William Fettes. This is where he learned the precious political skills that have served him so well throughout his career. This is where we first hear of the Tony Blair who knows just how close to the edge he can get without falling over it – and amuses himself by balancing on the precipice; the man to whom blame never sticks, who smiles and keeps his own counsel. Successful boarding-school boys learn these skills to survive, and those who fail to learn them are generally very unhappy. That is one of the reasons why the public schools still produce so many of our top politicians.

Two years before Tony Blair entered his new school in October 1966, a new Labour prime minister, Harold Wilson, had entered 10 Downing Street, after thirteen years of Conservative government. Wilson's arrival at Downing Street was not welcomed at Fettes, for public schools in those days still saw the Conservatives as the natural and proper party of government, and they feared that Wilson might plan to abolish fee-charging schools.

Wilson's arrival marks the real start of the sixties, the decade whose freedom, free love and free thought were to be condemned forty years later by Prime Minister Tony Blair. At the time, though, it was Blair's teachers at Fettes who condemned the spirit of the 1960s, while Blair took full advantage of it, making himself a thorn in the side of his teachers.

Although it was not even a hundred years old when Blair arrived, Fettes aped the worst traditions of the ancient public schools. Many public schools founded in the nineteenth century had regimes that were even harsher than those of Eton, Harrow, Winchester and the rest, hoping, perhaps, to make up in brutality for what they lacked in antiquity. Fettes – or so it was said at a nearby rival public school, Daniel Stewart's College – took Scotsmen and turned them into Englishmen; certainly Fettes boys studied for English A-levels rather than Scottish Highers. It is probably best known as the school to which Ian Fleming consigned his hero, James Bond, after he had been expelled from Eton for seducing a college servant. Former pupils include General John de Chastelain, whom Blair was to meet many years later when de Chastelain was in charge of decommissioning terrorist weapons in Northern Ireland, and the Conservative Chancellor of the Exchequer, Iain Macleod. According to the official history of Fettes, Michael Foot once said that Macleod suffered from not having been at Eton – 'I think that he went to some glorified, poshed-up secondary school in Scotland.'[5]

Blair had a miserable first year. He had been taken away from home and from the parents he loved for the first time in his young life and sent to a strange and strictly regimented institution whose life was ruled by unfamiliar codes and rituals and where he was regularly caned by masters and prefects alike. His friend and Fettes contemporary Nick Ryden remembers it as 'a horrible place' where even the towering main building itself, generally shrouded in mist, seemed menacing.[6]

Like all of the younger boys, Blair had to fag for a more senior pupil, in his case a prefect called Michael Gascoigne. Fags had to wait on the older boy they served, making him toast, polishing his shoes, breaking up coal for his fire, cleaning and folding up his mud-caked rugby clothes, and even polishing the studs on his football boots. Gascoigne, now an Edinburgh solicitor, certainly caned his fag; he is said to have demanded that his toast be done just so – a shade too dark or too light and the wretched fag would be in trouble again. Blair and others suffered at the hands of prefects at Fettes who took a run-up with the cane in order to inflict maximum pain, although fortunately that was not Gascoigne's practice. But he was a stout defender of the fagging system.

Blair learned how to survive fast. While Gascoigne reportedly remembers only that his fag was good at making toast and cleaning boots and always appeared willing, Blair was still nursing his burning resentment at the prefect when he was a frontbench politician, and almost certainly still nurses it to this day. He was like E. V. Rieu's lesser lynx:

> So when the Lion steals his food
> Or kicks him from behind,

> He smiles, of course – but, oh, the rude
> Remarks that cross his mind!

This skill of dissimulation is one he has never lost. 'Even if someone was boring the pants off him, he would still appear interested,' Nick Ryden once wrote. 'That is one of his tricks. He was a very good debater, able to express himself very articulately.'[7]

Boys lived and socialised mostly with other boys from their own house, and the strictness of the regime varied according to the views of the head of house. The two original houses, College East and College West, were in the elaborate mock-gothic pile which constitutes the main building. Later, as the school expanded, other houses were built in the grounds.

Blair had been placed in his brother's house, Kingerhame, built in 1928. He slept in a dormitory of a dozen or so boys, divided into cubicles – 'cubes' – just big enough to hold a small iron bed and a tiny wardrobe, and divided from the others by a waist-high wooden partition. It was rather like a stable block. The boys would do their 'prep' – what in a state school would be called homework – sitting around a long, narrow table in the house, presided over by a prefect. Punishments for being late arriving at prep included being forced out to train on Saturday morning at 6.30 a.m. under the tutelage of one of the rugger-playing prefects, who took pleasure in running little boys off their feet.

Blair's misery was increased by a humiliating academic setback. His older brother Bill was then a star pupil at Fettes. Quite soon, in Kingerhame House, a plaque was placed on the wall (it is still there) commemorating Bill's achievement in obtaining an Open History Exhibition to Balliol College, Oxford. The comparison was rubbed into Tony's face at an early stage. He had won a second-rank scholarship in the school's entrance exams; apart from benefiting his parents by gaining them a small rebate on his school fees, this meant that he skipped the first year, and studied with boys who were mostly a year older.

But he must have been crammed for the entrance examination, for he could not keep up at all. One of his contemporaries recalls: 'He struggled to make the grade academically, and after some time, it was probably his second term, he was demoted to the third form and then progressed more normally.' The demotion must have been all the more keenly felt because, as the same contemporary pointed out, 'Tony admired his older brother Bill immensely, particularly his diligent attitude to study.'

No wonder, then, that when it was time to go back to Fettes for his second year, he tried to run away. After his parents put him on the

Edinburgh train at Newcastle station, he walked through the carriages, got off at the other end of the train, made his way to Newcastle airport, and tried to get on a plane bound for some exotic faraway destination, eventually being shepherded off the plane when a stewardess found that he had no boarding card. Next time his parents put him on the train, they waited until it pulled out of the station. One of those who knew him well at the time says: 'Fettes was 100 per cent boarders and 100 per cent male, so that homesickness and general insecurity in the presence of some very bright people could well have been factors.'

The failure of his half-hearted escape bid must have convinced the fourteen-year-old that he was going to have to make the best of it, and he set about doing just that. He made friends with a charismatic and influential teacher, Eric Anderson, who later became headmaster of Eton, but who at that time was setting up a new house at Fettes.

Anderson's new house, called Arniston, was clearly going to be much more liberal than the others. Anderson did not like the dormitory system, and wanted rooms in which not more than four boys slept together. His house members were to experience much less fagging and beating than the other houses. Arniston is a recognisably sixties building, with small, square blue-framed windows and small, square rooms.

There was fierce competition to get in, and many boys failed to do so, but Blair had the precious skill of making himself liked by those who could do him good, and Anderson ensured that he was one of the sixty pupils to transfer to Arniston. He was one of only two who came from Kingerhame, which was, in fact, one of the more liberal of the existing houses, where most of the boys wanted to stay put.

So, while Prime Minister Harold Wilson tried to negotiate the future of what was then called Rhodesia with its Prime Minister Ian Smith, the next Labour prime minister but one managed to make himself more or less comfortable in an alien and forbidding environment.

He showed off a lot, bent the rules to breaking point, and became that well-known public-school character: the loveable rogue. He kept 'dream charts', carefully recording everything he could remember of his dreams as soon as he awoke. He explained to friends that he wanted to know what his unconscious mind was doing, and that if you got into the habit of doing it, your memory became clearer. It's a technique used by psychoanalysts and creative writers. He also kept a guitar in his study and played it at every opportunity.[8]

Just as he had done at Durham Choristers, he put his charm with women to good use by exercising it on the matron, Miss Valentine, who was at Fettes most of her working life, and who took Tony to her heart and listened sympathetically to his complaints. He spent a lot of time in her room, both alone with her and with his friends. There were only three adults in the house – Anderson, Miss Valentine and the house tutor, David Kennedy, who remembers: 'He would place Miss Valentine in a difficult position by trying to get her to take his side against the rest of us.'[9]

In his second year in Arniston, when he was fifteen, Gordon Dowell shared a study-bedroom with Blair. It was a brief acquaintanceship because Dowell was shortly expelled. Today, he concedes that Blair broke the rules more skilfully that he himself did. Nick Ryden noticed the same thing, writing: 'He could talk his way out of situations which probably others of us couldn't.'[10] Dowell adds:

> Tony and I were in a two-man study for one term only. That was my final three months at school, or more accurately I was absent on rustication leave for some of the time and then left for good rather abruptly before Christmas. It was evident even then that Tony was concerned about his image and the effect that he could have on other people. You might say that was common enough for mirror-gazing adolescents but I'd put him into a different category, probably psychologically more feminine in his attitude to image than masculine.

Recently Dowell has read Jon Sopel's biography of Blair, and he says: 'The thing which really hit home for me was the hitherto undiscovered music-hall strand in the lineage. When I read that, a big piece of the jigsaw slammed into place.'

Many of Fettes' rules, says Dowell, 'appeared oppressive to the hormonally imbalanced inmates'. Both he and Blair were infected by the rebellious spirit of the 1960s and loved Lindsay Anderson's film *If*, which is set in a public school not unlike Fettes where the pupils rise in open, armed revolt. The difference was that Dowell himself 'took the whole thing too seriously and failed to grasp the universal truth that "you can't beat the system"'. Blair, on the other hand, was 'an *ersatz* rebel, more concerned with the style than the substance of revolt. He had a talent for sailing close to the wind without badly capsizing, relying on his charm to get him out of trouble.'[11]

When Blair today attacks the spirit of the 1960s, he is attacking the teenager he once was, and the political and social context that gave him the freedom he then enjoyed. He is attacking the *ersatz* rebel who probably cheered from sheer excitement as he watched *les evenements* of 1968 unfold in Paris and almost bring down General de Gaulle's government. He is attacking his rock heroes from the 1960s, the Rolling Stones, who had taught him that the length of a young man's hair was not something that ought to be decided upon by his schoolmasters. He is attacking the sixties generation of leftwing student leaders who thought that a new and better world could be created by the young – including Jack Straw, who later became his foreign secretary. Straw became president of the student union at Leeds University while Blair was at Fettes and was soon afterwards elected to lead the National Union of Students, standing as the candidate of the left. He was seen as the radical young man who would sweep away the fusty, tweedy, reactionary NUS leaders left over from the 1950s.

When he attacks the sixties, Blair is also attacking the system that gave the students of the time their new confidence. They were the first to enjoy the fruits of the Attlee settlement: secondary education for all and free university education. This, and the relative freedom from economic insecurity they enjoyed, gave the sixties generation the confidence to be rebels. And if, like the young Blair, they did not always use that freedom in ways we might consider sensible, what of it? What is freedom for, if not to be used foolishly?

The end of the 1960s was a bad time for schools like Fettes. Created to educate the men who could govern an empire, they had barely noticed (and did not wish to notice) that there was no longer an empire to run. Created to impose rigid conformity in all matters, they stared with incomprehension and indignation at a world beyond their high walls in which refusing to conform had become a virtue. Created to impose an ethical system which no one would question, they had no idea how to deal with a generation of young men who insisted on questioning everything. Created in an age when education was limited to the upper classes, they watched uncomprehendingly as poor families who had benefited from the 1944 Education Act produced children who threatened to compete with their own cherished pupils. They were also beginning to see, dimly, that the new state schools might seem attractive to middle-class parents; Fettes was one of many such schools whose governors were seriously worried about the falling number of applications.

Within their own walls there were a few students who had begun to question the whole public-school ethos and to ask by what right they and friends enjoyed such privileges. Blair, however, seems not to have been much concerned with questioning the existence of the system, more with challenging those aspects of it which he found inconvenient or absurd – such as the stringent dress codes and the refusal to allow him to wear his hair fashionably long.

As they trace Blair's rise through the ranks of the school, it becomes necessary for his biographers to make an attempt to sort truth from spin. He gave considerable help to his first two biographers, and their accounts contain, understandably, the slant he wished to put on his late teenage years. When he became Labour leader in 1994, he very quickly asked Fettes not to release information about him. In particular, Blair's A-level grades were to be regarded as a state secret.[12] The present writers looked at the Fettes old pupils' website and e-mailed several of his contemporaries — and the next time we consulted the website, we found that all e-mail addresses had been stripped out; there was a note saying this had been done because of a 'regrettable security leak'.

It has, nonetheless, been possible to build up a pretty clear picture of the seventeen-year-old Blair, and one that differs in several important respects from the picture he and his friends have given to previous writers.

Just before his last year, Eric Anderson left. The new housemaster, R. J. (Robert) Roberts, known to the boys as 'Ma' Roberts, did not share Anderson's liking for his wayward pupil. In his last year Blair could reasonably have expected to be made a prefect, and his biographers say that this would have happened had Anderson stayed in charge, but Roberts refused Blair this accolade.[13] This is the opposite of the truth. Anderson chose the prefects that year, not Roberts, and, says Roberts, Anderson 'chose not to appoint Blair, presumably because Blair was then too untrustworthy, despite his obvious leadership qualities'.[14]

At the time, Blair felt the rebuff keenly, especially since his brother had been a prefect — so much so that one of his closest school friends believes to this day that Blair was offered an appointment as prefect, but turned it down.

Anderson's decision, according to another teacher, Robert Philp, was the cause of real difficulties. 'A strong character who is not a prefect is a problem,' he says, and Blair was 'more argumentative than most, always demanding to know why we had this or that rule'. The ghost of his older brother Bill came back to haunt him once again, for Bill, says Philp, was 'a model pupil who worked very hard and did not push himself forward'.[15]

Roberts did, however, know a first-rate actor when he saw one, and it was he who chose Blair to play Stanhope — the part Laurence Olivier had played in 1928 — in his 1971 production of *Journey's End*, R. C. Sherriff's play set in the trenches of the First World War.[16] The school magazine, the *Fettesian*, gave him a rave review.

Journey's End was the culmination of a distinguished school acting career, starting with a much-admired performance as a monk in Anouilh's *Beckett* in 1968. This was so successful that, although only fifteen, Blair was given the part of Mark Antony in Shakespeare's *Julius Caesar* over the heads of boys two or three years older than him, which caused some resentment. It would be surprising if, in studying for this role, he did not learn some lessons that would serve him well in his political career, for Shakespeare's Mark Antony is one of the best portraits of a politician in English literature. His famous speech beginning 'I come to bury Caesar, not to praise him' – the opposite of the truth, as we find out a few minutes later – is probably the best demonstration of the art of political spin-doctoring ever presented on a stage. 'Blair emerged,' said the *Fettesian*, 'as a somewhat youthful Antony, but nevertheless a very promising actor who should prove to be indispensable for school productions in the next few years.'

In 1969 he played Drinkwater in Shaw's *Captain Brassbound's Conversion*; again the *Fettesian* was fulsome in its praise, commending his 'superb command of the gestures and mannerisms of the insolent, unscrupulous Cockney'.[17] A fellow Fettes actor, Lindsay Clubb, says: 'He acted throughout his school career and was very competent.' He and Blair appeared together in an evening of three short plays produced by a Fettes society called The Pseuds, Clubb in N. F. Simpson's *Oh* and Blair in Dylan Thomas's *The Return Journey*. The *Fettesian* commented that he 'was only just unsuccessful in capturing the accent of Wales so necessary for the music of the prose'.

Clubb knew Blair throughout his school career. At times they were friendly, and at other times he felt Blair and one of his friends, 'Ellie' Macdonald, 'seemed to be taking the piss out of me'. They were in different houses and moved in rather different circles, and Clubb became a prefect when Blair did not. Clubb says: 'He was a cliquey individual – I was never part of that clique, nor would I have ever wanted to have been, since I delighted in the widest possible range of friends. I did regard the tendency of some people to be cliquey as a weakness or a sign of some insecurity.'[18]

Ellie Macdonald is credited as Blair's research assistant for an article in the *Fettesian* on one hundred years of drama at Fettes, a very proper and respectful, if rather portentous, piece of writing from this youthful rebel, which even includes a genuflection in the direction of his nemesis, Mr Roberts. 'If drama at Fettes is flourishing today,' it concluded, 'it is because it is built on a long and strong tradition, and Fettes and Fettesians are fortunate to have had so many members of the staff who have devoted much time and talent to building up this tradition.'

Ellie Macdonald's real name was Ewan. His sturdy rugby forward's physique earned him the nickname Elephant, shortened to 'Ellie'. Two years after leaving school, in 1973, Ellie Macdonald climbed up on to the

glass roof of Edinburgh's Waverley Station and fell through it to the platform beneath, after, according to other old Fettes boys, 'a bad trip'. He
was certainly close to Blair, both at school and in the two subsequent
years until his death, but Blair has never publicly mentioned him, and has
never provided grounds for the speculation that the Blairs' son Euan
might have been named partly as a tribute to his friend.

The summer of 1971 was the last at Fettes for these seventeen-year-old
boys. Clubb and his friends pub-crawled cheerfully and unsteadily
through Edinburgh, occasionally bumping into Blair and his friends
doing much the same. They all carefully avoided masters when they
returned, for being caught would mean expulsion. Blair was part of a
threesome – Blair, Catto and Macdonald – whom Mr Roberts saw as a
modern-day version of Stalky, M'Turk and Beetle in Rudyard Kipling's
novel *Stalky and Co*: three boys who always pushed disobedience to the
limit but never quite overstepped it, and were thorns in the side of masters and prefects alike. Blair was the ringleader, the Stalky figure, if we
are to judge from Mr Roberts' remark that 'from Stalky and Co to Blair
and Co, schoolboys bent on outsmarting "authority" invariably patrol in
threes'. Perhaps Mr Roberts saw himself as one of the wise masters at
Kipling's school who were remembered with affectionate respect by his
wayward charges in their later lives. If so, he was to be disappointed.
Blair's beatings at Fettes did not leave him feeling as Kipling felt:

> There we met with famous men
> Set in office o'er us.
> And they beat on us with rods–
> Faithfully with many rods–
> Daily beat us on with rods–
> For the love they bore us.[19]

The spirit of the 1960s banished that sort of sentiment from British
public schools forever. And Blair, whatever he says now, was more than
anything a child of the 1960s.

The Macdonald in the threesome was not Ewan, but Alastair Macdonald, now a reinsurance broker who votes Conservative but would vote
Labour if he could only be sure the next Labour leader would be as
responsible as his old school friend. Unsurprisingly, he does not see
things quite as Roberts saw them. He now says:

> Tony tended to see school rules as a challenge. Roberts would get
> tongue-tied trying to justify some of them, like having to have trousers
> with turnups. It was very spartan, a very strict regime, with very little

time off, and you were allowed out on Tuesday and Thursday afternoons only. But around the rules we had a lot of fun going round Edinburgh.

Of Blair he remembers that 'his love was the stage. All the world's a stage to him.' Years later, Macdonald saw Blair on television reading the lesson at the funeral of Princess Diana, and cringed a bit – 'I remembered his tendency to go over the top.'

Macdonald also recalls that Blair 'enjoyed sports, but not team sports that Fettes liked – he liked the minor sports, like basketball, which he was very good at, and soccer, which was not an official school sport, to all our frustration. We played soccer in the field at the back of the house. He was a great person to be around, great company, a great sense of humour, fluent, creative.'[20]

Like most public schools, Fettes preferred rugby – 'a game for louts played by gentlemen', as the saying went – to soccer – 'a game for gentlemen played by louts'. But Blair, despite having been a star rugby player at his prep school, refused to take rugby seriously at Fettes. This did not endear him to the staff of a school where success on the rugby field was seen as a vital sign of distinction, and perhaps he enjoyed provoking their disapproval. His friend and aide Anji Hunter has told one of our contacts that today Blair relishes winding television interviewers up into a froth of fury, and certainly the relationship between the teenage Blair and his housemaster, Mr Roberts, suggests something of the kind. But his refusal to show his prowess on the rugby field may also have been, as with several public schoolboys of the time, a legacy of shivering, miserable afternoons spent on the touchline, in school uniform, being forced to shout 'Play up, Fettes!' at regular intervals.

Fettes was just beginning to experiment gingerly with having girls in the sixth form. (Like most public schools, Fettes has now been forced by economic circumstances to become completely co-educational. Very few expensive schools these days can afford to refuse to admit people who can pay their fees.) Back in 1971 there were only two girls in the sixth form. One of them, Amanda Mackenzie Stuart, was stunningly beautiful and all the boys wanted her for themselves. But it was Tony Blair, the inveterate charmer, who got her.

His main rival for Amanda's affections, a youth called Charlie Falconer, was handicapped by being a hundred miles away at another school, Trinity College at Glenalmond, near Perth. Later, after Blair had departed the Edinburgh scene, Falconer would enjoy more success with Amanda, and he would also in due course become a close friend and political ally of Tony Blair.

*

Somehow, Blair's careful brinkmanship went wrong just a few months before he was due to take his A-levels, and it seemed certain that he would be expelled in disgrace. There is some mystery about exactly what his crime was. Mr Roberts has written a six-page account of his dealings with the future prime minister and deposited it with his will. His solicitor has instructions that, on Mr Roberts' death, one of the two copies should be sent to the then headmaster of Fettes and the other to the archives centre at Churchill College, Cambridge. Until then the contents remain secret.[21]

It seems clear, however, that the headmaster, Ian McIntosh, was determined to expel Blair. As far as we know, he did not accuse Blair of any of the great public-school sacking offences, which generally come under one of three headings – drink, sex and drugs. Blair visited pubs, which was against the rules, but so did most of his contemporaries, and there is no suggestion that his relationship with Amanda Mackenzie Stuart caused the school any concern. The same applied to his other female friend at the time, who was not at Fettes but whom he met up with at parties. Anji Hunter, another remarkably pretty girl, was to play a central part in his later political life.

Fettes was known among other Scottish public schools for the richness of its soft-drugs culture. You were supposed to be able to get anything there, and a couple of boys in Blair's year were expelled for drug-taking. But Blair, according to David Kennedy, 'would flirt with the edges of the drug scene and give the impression he knew all about it, but I think that was all'.[22] Mr Kennedy may be right, though by all accounts Blair would have been perhaps the only boy in his group of friends who did not at least smoke cannabis occasionally. In those days the '*ersatz* rebel' would certainly not have wanted his contemporaries to suppose that he was ignorant of this important part of the sixties scene.

The sudden danger of expulsion seems to have resulted from a build-up of the trivial acts of defiance of an adolescent schoolboy, chafing under pointless rules, irked at not being a prefect and therefore being expected to take orders from people he considered inferior to him – and one with a strong personality and a following. 'Not being a house prefect made him very difficult,' says Kennedy. He refused to get his hair cut. He would arrive late and scruffy for games. He had great influence with younger boys, and he 'made it clear to them that he was against the system'. He annoyed McIntosh by complaining to him that expecting boys to do their prep seated round a big desk was unreasonable, and then making it known that he had complained, which made him a hero to younger boys and a dangerous rebel to McIntosh. He mocked the College

Cadet Force, describing the boys who joined it as 'toy soldiers'. He would refuse to queue for lunch, demanding to know by what right the prefects were given precedence. This would result in him being sent to Roberts, who would notice that he was wearing the wrong tie (there was a tie for weekdays and another for Sundays) or that his hair was too long. McIntosh once bumped into Blair near a barber's shop, and marched him straight inside and stood over him while the cherished locks were reduced to a short back and sides.[23]

On the face of it, it all sounds far too trivial to add up to a hanging offence. But public schools in those days expected absolute conformity. McIntosh and Roberts saw themselves as guardians of the old values in a world that was changing in what seemed to them to be threatening ways and at frightening speed. The student rebellion of the 1960s had appalled them, and they had been horrified by Lindsay Anderson's *If* – all the more so because they knew that boys like Blair had loved it. McIntosh once preached a sermon in which he furiously attacked the sixties satire boom exemplified, to him, by the magazine *Private Eye*. In the view of McIntosh and Roberts, according to Blair's school friend Nick Ryden, 'People who were irritants were of no value to the school, and McIntosh would say he had their tickets [home] in his top pocket.' Fettes, he says, was 'like a penitentiary'.[24] McIntosh, having allowed Eric Anderson to create a more liberal house, had become worried about where it might lead, and had specifically commissioned Roberts to tighten up the discipline there.[25]

Ryden says that he, Blair and their other friends were consciously following in the footsteps of a group of boys a couple of years older, who had tormented McIntosh mercilessly and ignored the rules. These boys were their role models. McIntosh was especially vulnerable to such treatment because he himself was not the product of a public school – he came from a poor family, but fell in love with the public-school system when he graduated and became a teacher, so he had all the zeal of a convert. It made him self-conscious that he had played soccer in his youth, rather than the traditional public-school game of rugby, and he was sensitive to the charge that he was not bringing the school success on the rugby field. Blair's refusal to play rugby and his rebellious pleasure in playing soccer with his friends must have irritated him to distraction, as they were probably intended to do.

Blair's own account of these events, to his biographer John Rentoul, is that he was saved from expulsion by the intervention of Amanda's father, Lord (Jack) Mackenzie Stuart, an old Fettesian, a judge and a school governor, who offered to allow Blair to stay with him for his last few weeks, so that his influence was removed from the school. Rentoul adds that Blair himself suggested purging his offence with some form of social service.

This is not true. It was Roberts himself who saved Blair, with three rather desperate stratagems. First, he made a deal with Ronald Selby-Wright, former chaplain at Fettes and by then the minister of Canongate church in a slum area of Edinburgh. Selby-Wright agreed to take Blair for the week after his A-levels as a helper at his boys'-club camp at Skateraw on the North Berwick coast. 'Blair was not at all pleased with this arrangement,' says Roberts, 'but, as he had made so much of a moral fuss about social service etc., he was in no position to object.'

Second, Roberts caned him. This was very unusual indeed for a boy of seventeen in the second year of the sixth form. But it was not just Blair: Roberts beat all three of his scapegraces, Blair, Catto and Macdonald (the last named claims to have forgotten all about it). Roberts says: 'My beating them saved them from being expelled several months before their A-levels, an altogether preferable alternative.'[26]

Finally, Roberts pushed him off to university as fast as possible. For one final time at school, Blair was made to feel inferior to his older brother. Bill had won a scholarship to the most illustrious of Oxford colleges, Balliol, but Balliol turned Tony down. However, St John's, an academically less prestigious college, but one that was perhaps rather more impressed by former public schoolboys, agreed to take him

Roberts asked if St John's would take Blair at once, so that, as he puts it, 'He would not have to return to Fettes for a seventh term after A-levels, which would not have been in his best interest.' At that time most students applying to Oxford, especially from fee-charging schools, stayed in the sixth form for the first term of a third year to take the Oxford entrance exam in the November or December after their A-levels. But a growing number were applying in the second year of the sixth form, taking the Oxford entrance exam in the same year. This is what Mr Roberts arranged for Blair to do, so that the two would not have to put up with each other's company for another term.[27]

Quite what deal Mr Roberts put together to get his wayward charge into St John's is not at all clear, but it was not a straightforward business. Within days of being elected Labour leader in 1994, Blair asked Fettes never to reveal his A-level results.[28] In 2000 Gordon Brown laid into Oxford University for taking nearly half its intake from the 7 per cent of the population that attends fee-paying schools. Brown cited the comprehensive pupil Laura Spence, who was refused a place at Oxford despite getting five As at A-level. Blair was embarrassed and furious with Brown.

Whatever his own results, we know they were not a patch on Ms Spence's – for a start, he took three A-levels, not five. Never an outstanding scholar, he was certainly not doing a lot of work in his last year at Fettes.

The *Daily Mail* recently claimed to have discovered that Blair got two As and one C at A-level, though its source for this remains obscure. Blair's results are unlikely to have been better than this, though he may have done well in the Oxford entrance exam, which was generally thought to favour public-school pupils. The well-connected housemaster Mr Roberts admits to have negotiated with St John's over Blair's admission, and it looks as though he got Blair in with A-level results that would not have earned a place for a comprehensive-school pupil.

Mr Roberts went on to be headmaster of another public school, Worksop. Years later, in retirement in 1995, he watched the new leader of the opposition in action on television. Afterwards he sat down and wrote a poem, which he called 'Opposition Spokesman'. Part of it reads as follows:

> … You've flourished as a wild sport should:
> You learnt to plead your case at school,
> To act a part, to mock, disarm,
> Make fun of things for which we stood,
> Pretend compassion, play the fool,
> All injured innocence and charm.
> Your front bench indignation now
> At Government's action just the same
> As when you sensed you'd proved our weak
> Dissembling and at once knew how
> To cry hypocrisy – your game
> Of merry moral hide-and-seek …
> … You smile and talk away out there
> Just as you did when you had me
> To check your facts and trim your wings;
> But now you're free and on the air,
> I've no more opportunity
> To expose your specious arguings.[29]

McIntosh's farewell to his troublesome charge was both prompter and more abrupt. Before Blair left, he was persuaded to go to see the headmaster to apologise for his behaviour, and McIntosh responded gracelessly, simply saying: 'Don't let me see your face again.'[30]

Today, when invited to Fettes, Blair goes if he can, and when the present headmaster, Michael Spens, wrote congratulating him on the birth of his youngest child, Leo, he wrote back a friendly letter showing interest in what the school was doing. But his real feelings about the school are indicated by his closest school friend, Nick Ryden, who is young Leo's godfather. 'He might write them nice letters,' says Ryden, 'but I bet they haven't got a cheque out of him for the school appeal.' (Like many such schools, Fettes puts much effort into contacting success-ful old boys and asking them for donations.)

When Blair was a member of the shadow cabinet, Ryden asked him to be the guest speaker at an Edinburgh dining club he then ran. Blair was visibly upset to see, among the thirty or so assembling guests, anoth-er Edinburgh solicitor, Michael Gascoigne, for whom he had fagged in his first year at Fettes. Conspiratorially, while they were together in the gents, Blair told Ryden: 'The last time I saw him he was flogging me.' It upset Blair so much that he could not help mentioning his canings in the course of his speech, though without naming Gascoigne. When it was time for questions, Gascoigne put his hand up, which enabled Ryden to introduce him as 'the man with the cane'[31] – something Blair the politi-cian would have been too cautious to do, but which he was glad to see his old friend doing.

For just as, in politics, people like Peter Mandelson and Alastair Campbell have acted as lightning conductors for Blair, lobbing a propos-al or an innuendo into the public arena and then taking the return fire when critics respond, so Nick Ryden, a clever, cautious, thoughtful Edin-burgh lawyer who Blair knows can be trusted with journalists, gives us Blair's real, but unattributable, views on the subject of Fettes. This frees Blair himself to respond to an invitation to write a foreword to the offi-cial school history, as he did in 1998, and then feed biographers like Philip Stephens (whose uncritical biography for the US market had Blair's co-operation) this line: 'When he was asked as prime minister to write the Foreword to the school history, he felt obliged to agree. But there was no warmth to his words.'

Actually, there was a lot of warmth in his words. Blair's foreword expressed the '… hope that the boys and girls of Fettes reading this his-tory will be proud of their school and carry into the future the torch of liberal values, duty and open-mindedness first lit back in 1870 … its values go back to the first headmaster … His humanity, his powerful sense of duty and his inspirational teaching shaped a tradition …' And so on.

It was at Fettes that Blair learned how to have his cake, eat it, and then pretend it never existed.

Fettes must also have played some part in giving Blair the social ease and the elaborate courtesy which have served him so well. It was probably at Fettes (but probably also from his father) that he learned always to write the thank-you letters which are a Blair trademark: always, however busy he is, handwritten, in fountain pen. Their recipients appreciate the gesture. Roy Hattersley says he has spoken for literally hundreds of by-election candidates, but only Blair ever wrote him a thank-you letter for doing so.

After Blair visited Fettes in 1991 to talk to some sixth-formers, the teacher who invited him, Mark Peel, received one of these letters. 'I was delightfully surprised at how much I enjoyed re-visiting the old school!' wrote Blair. And this illustrates the other skill he learned at Fettes: the precious ability to say one thing while almost certainly feeling another; the skill to dissemble, to ensure that no bad thing ever stuck to him. Teflon Tony was born at Fettes.

An excellent illustration of this skill is the way in which he has chosen to sanitise his time there. It does not suit Blair any more to appear a rebel, but he was one. It certainly does not suit him to be seen as a child of the 1960s, whose spirit of freedom and political radicalism he has condemned, but that is what he was. Nor does it suit him any more to attack his *alma mater* in public; it would be bad public relations. But Ryden can. Ryden – like Peter Mandelson, like Alastair Campbell, like half a dozen others in Blair's life – can fire the bullets Blair wants fired, and they can never be traced to Blair.

Within days of Blair's election as Labour leader in 1994, batteries of press officers were on the telephone to all his and Cherie's old friends telling them what to say to journalists – and what not to say. They had a 'line' for every part of his life. The 'line' on Fettes was that Blair's unhappy final year was all the fault of the narrow-minded pedagogue Roberts. If only the wise old patriarch Anderson had stayed, everything would have been fine. Things were painted in stark black and white: Anderson, good cop; Roberts, bad cop. It was Roberts (and the headmaster, McIntosh) who had made his life a misery over such trivial matters as the length of his hair, and his near expulsion was due to Roberts' exaggerated concern for such things. Eric Anderson was sanctified. As prime minister, Blair even used him as an example of a great teacher in a government recruiting advertisement for the teaching profession.

Of course, Blair himself was never to be heard peddling the line: that was left to Nick Ryden, who did so quite honestly because he has scant respect for Roberts. It is the line accepted by all his biographers until now. And it is not true.

Anderson was only slightly more liberal than Roberts, and it was Anderson, not Roberts, who refused to make Blair a prefect. Anderson felt just as strongly as Roberts and McIntosh about the length of a boy's hair. 'When Eric found Blair with longer hair than regulations allowed, he put him in his car and drove him to a barber, and stood over him while Blair wept real tears as his locks were cut off,' recalls David Kennedy. The truth, as is usual with Blair, is more multi-layered than the spin.

CHAPTER TWO

OXFORD, ROCK AND RELIGION

Roberts may have gone to considerable lengths to get the young Tony Blair out of Fettes and into Oxford as rapidly as possible, but Blair himself had other ideas. He asked St John's College to defer his admission for twelve months so that he could enjoy what would now be called a gap year. He apparently hoped that he could use this time to seek his fame and fortune as a rock star – or if not a star, then at least a band manager. And the place to do that was, of course, London, still swinging well into the 1970s.

He arrived in the capital, like hundreds of young public-school rebels, with no job and no money, just a guitar, a change of clothes, the names of friends of friends who might give him a floor to sleep on, and shoulder-length hair which would have given Roberts a seizure. He worked his way through the list of people he could stay with quite quickly – 'He was only supposed to be staying a night while my parents were on holiday and he ended up staying two weeks,' one of them told John Rentoul. There was at least one night when he slept under the stars in a London park. He had come out of the stifling atmosphere of an English public school; it was like escaping from something like a prison into a world of sunshine – freer, fresher, fairer and infinitely more fun.

It was 1971. Harold Wilson's government had fallen just as Blair left Fettes. The new Conservative prime minister, Edward Heath, would pin his place in history on his ambition to take Britain into the European Community and on a battle to curb the trade unions. He was to fail in both these objectives. But he remains the only post-Second World War prime minister who thought Britain's key relationship lay with Europe rather than with the United States, which places him well to the left of Tony Blair.

Eventually, Blair managed to find temporary accommodation with the parents of Alan Collenette, a fellow public-school boy – he had just left St Paul's – and a fellow wannabe rock mogul. Together they decided they were going to discover and manage the next big group, and naturally they looked for talent among the recent alumni of the most exclusive public schools. They found one quite quickly: a band called Jaded, led by Adam Sieff, who could not play the guitar, but who had been at Westminster and whose father, Edward Sieff, chairman of Marks & Spencer, was extremely rich.

Blair could hardly lodge with the Collenettes permanently. Once he had overstayed his welcome, he found a Richmond vicar who was able not only to give him lodging, but also to let the bands play in his church hall, Vineyard Congregationalist Church. Blair and Collenette brought in the bands and attracted a reasonable audience by leafleting outside schools. Blair's attraction for women came in useful again, as it had done with the matrons at Durham Choristers School and at Fettes. Collenette told John Rentoul that when they leafleted outside the girls' schools, the first question to Blair was: 'Will you be there?' Sometimes Blair, who usually supervised the lights, took the stage to sing Rolling Stones numbers – a particular favourite was 'Honky Tonk Woman'. In an effort to expand the scale of their operations they bought an old Ford Thames van for £50 to carry their bands and equipment round London.

Since the bands were not making them enough cash to live on, they started working on hare-brained money-making schemes, like using the van for making deliveries, or trying to sell Collenette's mother's lemonade recipe to Beecham's. But eventually they had to face up to reality and get proper jobs, shelf-stacking in the food hall at Barkers in Kensington. One lunchtime Blair paid a visit to Kensington Market, where he made a significant addition to his wardrobe with the purchase of a pair of white flared trousers, so tight that he had to hold his breath to get them on, with lace-up flies. They went well with his purple-and-blue-striped jacket – Collenette's father's old blazer from his own public school, Radley.

It could, of course, only be upmarket Kensington, which in 1971 was as trendy as London got, with legions of upper-middle-class youth trying to out-sixties the sixties by having longer hair, stranger clothes and more cannabis than old fogies from 1968 ever dreamed of, and by saying outrageous things in languid public-school accents. It was the location for the trendy young shops of its day – Biba was in Kensington, and so were a host of bars and restaurants patronised by the young, one of which had a clock face painted on the wall with the words 'no tick' written inside it.

It was a haven for people like Blair – *ersatz* rebels filling in time before turning their minds seriously to respectable careers. And if you needed work, naturally you went to one of the three department stores that huddled around High Street Kensington tube station, of which Barkers was one. The food-department manager liked Blair and Collenette and told them that if they worked hard, there might be a career for them at Barkers. How they laughed! Sad little careers in department stores were not for the likes of them.

After six months of putting on discos and gigs at the church hall, they tried to move onto bigger things, booking the Queen Alexandra Hall in Kensington. But it did not work. Far too few people turned up, and that was the end of Blair's career as a rock promoter. There was time for a few summer weeks serving behind a bar in Paris before he packed himself off to Oxford to study law.[1]

Music was to be one of Blair's main interests throughout his time at Oxford. He became the lead singer of a rock group called the Ugly Rumours, and that is what he is chiefly remembered for at St John's. Fellow student David Haines remembers 'Tony doing the most atrocious Mick Jagger impressions with his band at a JCR [Junior Common Room] gig'.[2] He played tennis, ferociously and competitively, and was envied for the ease with which he picked up women.

It seems certain that he was already sexually experienced, though his more slavish biographers try to imply some sort of monkish abstinence to the young Blair. When the college authorities discovered a lipstick in his room and accused him of having a woman in there overnight, he said quickly and smoothly: 'Oh, that's mine.' When Blair became Labour leader and the spin machine got to work ringing round everyone he had known and asking whether they had any dirt on him, and what they would do with it if a journalist asked, Blair's St John's room-mate Duncan Foster simply replied that he had 'nothing printable'.

Throughout the three years he was never short of girlfriends. One of them, Mary Harron, later became a film director. When her film *American Psycho* opened in Britain in 2000, she told a newspaper: 'I always thought of Tony as the only nice person I went out with at Oxford. He was very good looking in a kind of sweet way, and wasn't at all predatory.'

He also renewed his friendship with Anji Hunter. Anji was a lively, attractive girl whose middle-class background was given an exotic twist by the fact that she had spent much of her childhood in Malaysia, where her father managed a rubber plantation. Like Blair, she had been a rebel at her exclusive girls' school, St Leonard's in the cathedral city of St

Andrews; but for her there had been no last-minute reprieve, and she was expelled for insubordination. Now she was studying for her A-levels in Oxford, not at the university but at St Clare's College, an exclusive finishing school for young women whose pupils did something to level up the imbalance between the numbers of male and female undergraduates, which at that time still left Oxford men chronically short of female companionship.

Although there was a mutual attraction between the two of them, both Hunter and Blair insist that they never went out together. Instead, Anji's best friend, Suzy Parsons, became one of Blair's girlfriends during his first year at St John's.

All in all, Blair seems to have had an enjoyable and successful social life during his three years in Oxford. St John's provided rooms in college for all its undergraduates for their first two years, but in his final year, 1974–5, when he had to move out of his college, he and a friend, fellow St John's lawyer Marc Palley, went to share a house in Argyle Street, off Iffley Road, with three female undergraduates from St Anne's College whom they had known since they first went to Oxford. The Argyle Street house seems to have been a happy one. One of the three St Anne's women, Laura Mackenzie, says: 'We all got on and we didn't get entangled with each other. Feminism was an issue in those days and Tony was very good at taking his turn with the Hoover. The men cooked for us as much as we cooked for them. [Tony] had a lot of energy, well above the average.'

Blair has said that he wished he had studied history at Oxford, like his brother Bill, instead of law. It is reasonable to suppose that his choice of law owed something to his father's influence, but the choice may partly have been dictated by the fact it was then, as it is now, easier to get a place at Oxford to study law than to study history. Any regrets he had about his choice of subject were not evident at the time to those who taught him, one of whom says that he had 'a real aptitude and enthusiasm for the subject'.[3] But he already had a strong feeling, certainly by his third year at Oxford, that he was not going to spend his whole working life as a lawyer and might well move into politics. 'I think he was finding law pretty dull,' says Laura Mackenzie.

One of the alternative career choices available to lawyers, as Blair would certainly have been aware, is parliamentary politics – even today the House of Commons is packed with lawyers. And one of the many myths that have grown up about Tony Blair, with or without his help, is that he was not much interested in politics at Oxford. His chief interests were music and religion – of which more later. (Interestingly, he never seems to have sought to continue his acting career after he left Fettes, despite the promise he had shown there.)

Peter Mandelson, who was at St Catherine's College, Oxford, when Blair was at St John's, did not know of Blair's existence, and he has attributed this to the fact that 'I was interested in politics'.

But, in fact, so was Blair. Oxford in the early 1970s, with the Vietnam war at its height, was a hotbed of political activity, much of it leftwing. Many young leftwing people had abandoned Harold Wilson's Labour Party because Wilson failed to condemn the Vietnam war, even though he did keep Britain out of it, and Blair at least appeared to be one of them; certainly Laura Mackenzie thought her housemate was either in, or close to, the International Marxist Group – one of the most ideologically rigorous of the Trotskyist groups, founded at Oxford by Tariq Ali a few years earlier.[4] She was mistaken, but understandably so: Blair met and talked to several IMG people and already possessed the political trick, so evident in the Blair we know today, of leaving everyone with the impression that he agreed with them. Colin Meade, a fellow St John's undergraduate who was a member of the IMG, once told a newspaper dismissively: 'He would dress up in silly clothes and hang around with Lefties.' But, says Meade, he also had an eye to his legal career too: 'He always went to dinners with visiting judges.' Blair himself once said he 'went through all the bit about' reading Trotsky and attempting a Marxist analysis, and Laura Mackenzie is sure he was much more leftwing in those days than he is now.

In fact, whatever impression he may have given, Blair's political interests were never going to be in a small splinter group that never had any chance of attaining power. A regular visitor to the Argyle Street house – a young London journalist whose girlfriend lived there – remembers that Blair lapped up any piece of political gossip he could provide. He once asked, out of the blue: 'What's the Gay Hussar like? You're an journalist, you must have been there.' The Gay Hussar is a Hungarian restaurant in Soho, then, as now, much frequented by politicians and political journalists. As it happens, the journalist had at the time never been there, and was not able to satisfy the young lawyer's thirst for knowledge.

Blair was not taking the conventional route followed by politically ambitious students – standing for student union posts, joining political groups, speaking in the Oxford Union – but he already knew that his future might well lie in politics. What he did not know was what he wanted to go into politics for.

But he did find two things at Oxford: God and a guru. God was far and away the most significant discovery of his life. But Blair is the sort of Christian who is looking to religion for a complete answer to every ethical decision you may be called upon to make, and for that you need more than God: you need a philosopher upon whom you can rely for a philosophical system which answers all the difficult questions. Blair's, he told the world when he became leader of the Labour Party in 1994, was 'a guy called John Macmurray'. He added: 'It's all there.'

Macmurray was first recommended to Blair by Peter Thomson, an Australian priest who befriended Blair at Oxford. Thomson was a mature student, seventeen years older than Blair. He had been chaplain at Timbertop, the outward-bound section of a private fee-charging school in Victoria, Geelong Grammar School, until he went to Oxford in 1972, and he returned there after Oxford in 1975 as head, before becoming head of St Mark's Anglican College, University of Adelaide, in 1983, and retiring in 1991 aged fifty-five. He is energetic, talkative and charismatic, and is a modern sort of priest, wearing his religion with fashionable informality. At Oxford Thomson gathered around him a coterie of fellow undergraduates who listened with respectful attention to the ideas of the older man. One of these was Blair, who was received into the Church of England in the St John's College chapel before he left Oxford – though the Church of England was not to be his final religious home. In the end, though he has not admitted it, he has ended up in the very un-Macmurray-like arms of Rome – but that story is for the next chapter.

The Tony Blair we know today has lived in the pragmatic, day-to-day world of a top politician for many years, and Macmurray's work no longer has the resonance for him that it once did. But Blair's apparent acceptance of Macmurray's ideas is worthy of some discussion, if only because it is the nearest he has ever come to embracing a philosophical system, in the way that other political figures have embraced the thoughts of Karl Marx, Robert Owen, John Stuart Mill or Adam Smith.

Certainly Blair has no interest in the thinkers who have shaped the British labour movement. When he was opposition leader, Roy Hattersley, knowing Blair's interest in education, mentioned Michael Young, the socialist educationalist whose work gave rise to the Open University and the University of the Third Age. Hattersley was shocked to the core by Blair's reply: 'Who's Michael Young?' For a Labour leader who said his priorities were 'Education, education, education', this was indeed extraordinary.

Hattersley recalls an even more startling instance of Blair's lack of interest in the people and ideas upon which the Labour movement was founded, when Blair accused him of being a Marxist determinist.

Hattersley, who is neither a Marxist nor a determinist and could only be mistaken for one by someone who did not understand the words, asked what he meant by the expression. Blair said: 'Well, it means if you've got a poor background you're bound to fail.' It does not, of course, mean anything remotely like that. Hattersley's conclusion is that Blair sees no point in spending time finding out about the labour movement when he could spend the time getting on in it.[5]

Nor is Blair interested in contemporary English philosophy. When he was at Oxford, philosophy's best-known figure was still A. J. Ayer, who thought that discussing religion was useless because you cannot prove the truth or falsehood of a religious belief by logical means. Macmurray, who died in 1976 and was a contemporary of Ayer's, is outside the mainstream of twentieth-century English philosophy. Until Blair mentioned him, you could easily find university lecturers in philosophy who had never heard of him. In 1968 the vast *Routledge Encyclopedia of Philosophy* did not include an entry for him.

But although Blair enthusiastically adopted Macmurray as his guru, his precis of Macmurray, quoted by Anthony Seldon, does not make the philosopher's thought sound exactly rigorous: more like a soundbite, full of feel-good words. 'What he was on about was community. It's about fellowship, friendship, brotherly love.'[6]

In fact, Macmurray thought that you discovered God through knowing other people: 'Until we can be acquainted with a particular person and say of him that his personality is the revelation of God's personality ... we can have no knowledge of God ...' Ayer would have asked impatiently for a definition for the words 'God', 'revelation' and 'knowledge'.

However, there are gaping differences between Blair's view of the world, as we understand it from his speeches and his actions, and Macmurray's. According to the philosopher Dr Sarah Hale, who teaches at Portsmouth University and has made a comparative study of Macmurray and Blair's 'Third Way' speeches, Macmurray 'was very scathing of the established church and the church establishment, and had a pretty idiosyncratic take on Christianity which led him to refuse involvement with any church or denomination until he became a Quaker at the end of his life'.[7]

Quakers insist that there is nothing special about Christianity, and will take in other faiths as well as Christians. This is not Blair's position at all. Blair's Macmurray thinks that religions other than Christianity are imperfect lights, groping after the complete truth which can be found in Christ. This, though his early writing betrays some signs of it, is not the real Macmurray, according to Dr Hale.

Blair, unlike Macmurray, seems to have grown closer to established Christianity with each passing year. In 1998, Blair's second year as prime minister, the religious journalist Clifford Longley wrote an article saying that Christianity had become enlightened and had adopted democracy and human rights; he hoped, he wrote, that Islam might one day imitate this. Longley was surprised to get a handwritten letter, written in Blair's usual fountain pen, to say how much the prime minister liked the article and agreed with what it said.[8] The superiority of Christianity over other religions is not something Blair seems ever to have doubted.

This helps explain why Blair has been the most bellicose prime minister for fifty years, committing troops time and again in what he saw almost as holy wars, and, at the time of the Kosovo war, unblushingly using the word 'crusade'. Unlike President George W. Bush, he had learned more tact by the time it came to Iraq.

In fact, Blair has misunderstood Macmurray's views about politics and society even more completely. The political idea he claims to have taken from Macmurray is that of community, and ever since he became Labour leader, intellectual London has been full of people talking learnedly of 'communitarianism'. Blair himself defined it in a speech to the Women's Institutes' Triennial General Meeting in June 2000: 'At the heart of my beliefs is the idea of community. I don't just mean the villages, towns and cities in which we live. I mean that our fulfilment as individuals lies in a decent society for others ... The renewal of community is the answer to all the challenges of a changing world.'

But this is exactly what Macmurray did *not* mean by community. Dr Hale says: 'Blair's "philosophy", as reflected in both his words and his deeds, is markedly different from Macmurray's and frequently in stark opposition to it, with very little common ground; and only an extremely superficial reading of Macmurray could have led commentators – and Blair himself – to believe otherwise.'

The problem is that Macmurray draws a distinction between what he calls 'communal' human relationships, and 'social' ones. The relationships that he considers vital to human progress are communal relationships. In a communal relationship 'we can be our whole selves and have complete freedom to express everything that makes us what we are' and people 'find joy and satisfaction in living together, in expressing and revealing themselves to one another'. A happy marriage might be one example of what Macmurray means by communal relationships.

Blair and New Labour mix up Macmurray's 'communal' relationships with his 'social' ones. Therefore, says Dr Hale, they 'reject the distinction at the very heart of Macmurray's work, and negate everything he has to say about the desirability of community ... Blair's position is almost diametrically opposed to Macmurray's.'9

Macmurray never met Blair, but he worried about people like him. The philosopher wrote in 1971 to someone who wanted to set up a John Macmurray society: '... I have perhaps become too suspicious because I have suffered most from people who thought they understood me but didn't. From a few things that pleased them they took it for granted that I agreed with them on all points.'10 That is just what Dr Hale thinks Blair must have done.

Old Labour people, whom Blair despises, believe we have rights, as citizens, to the benefits of the Welfare State. They believe people should be able to depend on rights, not charity. They are ferociously opposed to the idea that a person's morality should play any part in deciding how far he or she should benefit.

Macmurray is with them all the way. He has little time for conventional morality and had himself what is called an open marriage, happily accepting his wife's lover as a guest in the home. 'Macmurray,' says Dr Hale, 'talks about rights far more than he talks about duties.' Contrast that with Blair, his supposed disciple, a politician for whom the phrase 'family values' could have been created: 'A decent society is not based on rights; it is based on duty,' he told the Women's Institute. Dr Hale concludes: 'It cannot be argued that New Labour's conception of responsibility is anything like Macmurray's.'

For Blair, charity is the highest good. This is the opposite of traditional Labour thinking, summed up by Clement Attlee in 1920: 'Charity is only possible without loss of dignity between equals. A right established by law, such as that to an old age pension, is less galling than an allowance made by a rich man to a poor one, dependent on his view of the recipient's character, and terminable at his caprice ...'11

Macmurray is on Attlee's side, not Blair's. He would have been as fiercely opposed as any Old Labour relic to the idea that community service should buy the right to the benefits of the community. Macmurray, says Dr Hale, 'sets out in detail the kind of morality currently espoused by Blair, only to condemn it as false and evil'.12

Two weeks after Blair graduated, his mother Hazel died, aged fifty-two. She had been suffering from throat cancer for four years. In her last months the family had kept the seriousness of her condition from Blair, for fear of distracting him during his finals. 'I felt,' Blair told a journalist two decades later, 'not so much a sense of ambition as a consciousness that life is short. My life took on an urgency which has probably never left it.'[13] He seems to have drawn closer at this painful time to Anji Hunter, whose mother had died in a car crash when she was eleven.

CHAPTER THREE

GOD, CHERIE AND THE LAW

'Blair's interest in political philosophy was limited. His interest in religion and comparative religions was inexhaustible,' wrote John Kampfner in 2003.[1] Religious ideas interest him far more than political ones. That is the key to understanding his politics. So it is hardly surprising that religious faith was the mainspring of the woman he met and fell in love with in 1976, a year after he completed his degree.

Cherie Booth is a working-class Liverpool-born Catholic with Irish ancestry – a type well known among Catholics for their unswerving loyalty to the Church. She is the sort of Catholic to whom the Church is a bedrock, an institution she would never abandon, whatever criticisms she might make of it privately. It's a mindset she inherited from her father's family.

Her father is the actor Tony Booth, who achieved fame as the 'Scouse git' in the television series *Till Death Us Do Part*. Booth was himself the product of a staunchly Catholic home – his uncle was the parish priest – and as a child he saw the dark side of Catholic education. Born in a flat in a tiny back-to-back Liverpool terraced house, he was, as his daughter would also prove to be, a very clever pupil, passing the eleven-plus a year early and going to a Christian Brothers school, St Mary's College in Crosby. The Christian Brothers had a well-deserved reputation for beating the boys in their care unmercifully, and some of them sexually abused boys as well. One of Tony Booth's favourite stories is of how, while he was up a ladder, one of the Brothers put a hand up his shorts, and he kicked out and broke the man's nose. His mother had to rescue him from expulsion. Booth does not know quite how she did it, but it sounds as though she discreetly threatened the head with exposing the Brother responsible.

His parents could not afford the textbooks or uniform, because his father had had an accident at work and his employers had dismissed him without compensation. So Booth paid for them himself with a daily paper round before going to school, and his burning anger over his father's treatment made him a lifelong socialist and trade unionist.[2] For him, as for his daughter Cherie, Catholicism is the faith of their fathers, and socialism is the faith they learned from the privations of their fathers.

So Cherie is what fellow Catholics call a 'cradle Catholic'. In the eyes of many members of the Church this somehow makes her a more 'real' Catholic than a convert, in some indefinable sense that only Catholics themselves perceive. She was born on 23 September 1954 in Bury, an old northern textile town between Manchester and Liverpool, while her father was a struggling actor playing in the farce *No Time for Sergeants* at the local theatre. Two years later, Tony Booth and her mother Gale had a second daughter, Lyndsey. When Cherie was five, her father moved out to live with another woman, and Tony's parents took in Gale and her two daughters while Tony Booth enjoyed himself for many years with a large number of women and far too much drink.[3] Gale took a job in a fish-and-chip shop to help eke out her husband's wages.

Years later, by which time she was the prime minister's wife, Blair's old school friend Nick Ryden asked her to speak at a charity dinner his Edinburgh solicitors' firm organised in Scotland for Barnardo's. Cherie told the assembled diners, simply and straightforwardly, what motivated her to be there: 'I came from a home that was destroyed by alcohol.'[4]

Alcohol was certainly one of Tony Booth's vices. He seems to have spent most of his adult years, until the age of fifty-two, more or less permanently drunk. Very little of the money he earned as an actor found its way back to any of the three women whose children he had fathered; nor did it stay with him, for he was permanently broke. Cherie has one full sister and six half-sisters, including one she only heard about for the first time when she visited Australia in 2004.

Cherie has a fiercely powerful intellect. She was a star pupil at Seafield Convent Grammar School in Crosby, where every lesson began with a prayer and the girls were taught that you should work hard for the glory of God. Tony Blair, starting at Fettes a year ahead of his age group, had to be demoted because he could not keep up; Cherie Booth was put up a year because it was the only way to keep her satisfied with her own progress, and she stayed there. By common consent one of the cleverest pupils the convent ever had, she left with four A-grades at A-level. She joined the Labour Party at sixteen – it was almost as natural to her as being a Catholic.

In the early 1970s the Liverpool Labour Party was one of the first to be taken over by the extreme leftwing Militant group and Cherie watched their antics with horror.[5] The Militant Tendency was a new and frightening phenomenon. The Labour Party has always been under attack from Communist and Trotskyist groups to its left, but the Militant Tendency did not seek to attack Labour from outside, but to subvert it from within. It placed its people inside constituency parties and urged them to fight their way to the top and, like cuckoos, drive out of the nest those who did not adopt Militant policies and Militant discipline.

Labour has always feared this strategy, which was deployed with lethal success in the 1930s by the Communist Party to destroy the once-mighty Independent Labour Party. Communists toyed with the idea of using it against the Labour Party itself, but never set about the task seriously. So the Militant Tendency was the stuff of Labour's worst nightmares. Its takeover of the Liverpool Labour Party enabled it briefly to control Liverpool City Council in the 1980s.

Before Cherie left school she gained a place at the London School of Economics, where she was principally noted for her hard work. There were no rock groups and not a lot of play in her undergraduate years. But she was a loyal, thoughtful and noticeably leftwing member of the university Labour Club. John Carr was its chairman and spearheaded the running battle against Militant, both at LSE and in the National Organisation of Labour Students. He knew he could rely on Cherie in a crisis.

'She would always turn up if there was an important vote, especially if she was needed to vote against Militant. She had seen what damage they did in Liverpool,' he says. He was especially grateful for her support after Militant had succeeded in getting its people to fill all five of LSE's places on its delegation to the NOLS conference. Carr maintained that the election had been done unconstitutionally, and called a meeting to reverse it. It was a tight vote, and Booth responded to Carr's plea, coming to the meeting herself and bringing others with her. Carr's coup worked: 'We deselected the five Militants and elected five reliable delegates.' It made a difference: Carr's margin of victory at the subsequent NOLS conference was less than five.

But apart from helping to win votes she believed to be crucial, Cherie was not especially active in Labour student politics. Anti-Militant though she was, her politics were far to the left of conventional Labour loyalists like John Carr. One LSE contemporary, journalist Martin Whitfield, who knew the Blairs later in Hackney, often talked politics with her and assumed she was in one of the serious Trotskyist groups, either the International Marxist Group or the Socialist Workers Party. He was probably mistaken, because if she had been a open member of these organisations, she could not have joined the Labour Party, but it's still an indication of the sort of views she held at the time.

Cherie had been brought up in hardship in Liverpool, and she carried with her to London the sense of injustice, of conspicuous wealth rubbing shoulders with soul-destroying poverty, that makes someone a socialist. She had clear socialist convictions, based on what she had seen rather than on what she had read. It is something her husband cannot understand to this day.

Nevertheless, it is clear that in her student days politics took a poor second place to work. She was a clever working-class girl, very conscious of having the privilege of higher education denied to her ancestors, and at university she got her head down and worked. All her friends were fellow law students. 'Everyone knew she was Tony Booth's daughter and very bright, though she wore both these things lightly,' says Carr. Her tutors confidently predicted that she would win a first-class degree, but did not see her as a future QC, much less a politician. She was nervous, hesitant, brittle. 'I saw her as a future academic, not as an advocate,' says one of her tutors. 'She had a nervous delivery. If she practised at the Bar, I would have expected her to write opinions rather than appear in court.' In the event, she obtained the best first-class law degree of her year, and a better one than LSE had awarded to anyone for many years.

When Cherie first knew Tony Blair, he was living in a basement flat in Fulham, which he shared with his old Oxford housemate Marc Palley, and had just completed the one-year full-time course at Bar School, which all aspiring barristers have to pass before they can practise. They met when they both sat for a scholarship to see them through their pupillage. One of the reasons the bar is still dominated by former public-school boys and girls is that you have to study and then work for years without payment; it is a system that favours those with wealthy parents. Cherie Booth won a scholarship; Tony Blair did not. There was some justice in that. She had a better legal brain than he had, and she needed the money – he didn't.

Cherie came top in that year's bar exams and went to do her pupillage with Derry Irvine QC. She was selected because her lecturers at LSE told Irvine she was outstanding. She was told that she was to be Irvine's only pupil, and was disappointed to find out there was another. She had reckoned without the well-connected Blair, who achieved only a third-class pass in the bar exams: at a friend's twenty-first birthday party at Beaconsfield Golf Club he met a leading QC, who recommended him to Irvine. Irvine liked him and agreed to take a second pupil.[6]

Cherie began her pupillage straightaway, while Blair spent the summer working as a waiter in the splendid Frantour Hotel in Paris, near the Eiffel Tower, and teaching English to managers at a Paris insurance company, and then spent the money he had earned on a cycling tour of the Dordogne.[7]

They both knew that, at the end of their year's pupillage, only one of them would be taken on as a tenant. They both knew Cherie was the better lawyer. Today, one of Blair's oldest friends, Nick Ryden, himself a lawyer, says: 'If I had to be cross-examined by one of them, I'd far rather it was Tony. Cherie has a very analytical mind.'

Irvine, too, knew Cherie was a better lawyer, but he chose Tony for the tenancy, explaining years later to a friend that Tony was much easier to get on with. It was a common perception. 'Cherie seemed nervous, but Tony always managed to sound pleased to see you,' says a barrister who knew them both well. At the Bar, being clubbable, especially if you went to a public school, often matters much more than being good at the job.

The kind of relaxed affability which comes so easily to Tony Blair has never been Cherie's forte. She is, according to someone who knows her well, 'very intense, her eyes always focused and you can see the brain working behind them'. He says that she photographs very badly (and, it has to be said, some newspapers take pleasure in printing the most unflattering photographs of her). In the flesh, he says, 'she's very nice-looking, though her smile is a little cold'. She is very good with people, so long as they want to talk properly: 'She's no good at small talk, doesn't see the point of it; she wants to know what makes you tick.' She lacked, in other words, all the talents that Blair possessed in abundance – and that make him the most accomplished politician of his generation. Cherie would probably not have been a successful politician.

Cherie got another tenancy, in the chambers of George Carman, a celebrated libel lawyer, which did not suit her anything like so well, because she had been doing mostly family and employment work and was not interested in being a libel lawyer. By then, she and Tony Blair were an item – she dumped a previous boyfriend for him.[8]

Tony Blair joined the Labour Party by getting in touch with the head office, which passed his application on to Sandy Pringle, the ward secretary in Fulham where he was living. He was probably persuaded to join by Cherie, for he almost certainly did not do so until after he met her. We say 'almost certainly' because the records of the ward Labour Party, and its minute book, were lost at around that time. They were mislaid by the new ward secretary who took over from Pringle – Tony Blair. There is probably nothing sinister about this. The basement flat which Blair shared with Marc Palley was 'seriously untidy', says Sandy Pringle. The influence of Laura Mackenzie and her two friends from St Anne's College was clearly sadly missed.

Pringle's recollection is that Blair joined the party in late 1976, when he started his pupillage. Around this time he also discovered that his old rival for the affections of Amanda Mackenzie Stuart, Charlie Falconer, was working as a barrister in the building where Derry Irvine had his chambers. The two men quickly became, and still remain, firm friends; Falconer, too, was a Labour Party activist and shared Blair's interest in rock music. Unlike Blair, he has never played in a band, but he was extremely knowledgeable – even today he will boast that he can tell you the titles of the B-sides of almost every hit single from the 1960s. When Blair left his Fulham flat, he and Falconer decided to share a new flat in Wandsworth.

Blair stayed in the Fulham Labour Party for about eighteen months. 'Cherie was more politically committed that he was,' says Pringle. 'I have no recollection of his political opinions, though they seemed to be mostly anti-establishment. But we found him a most agreeable young man.' Another lawyer in Blair's chambers at the time says: 'Cherie was very left-wing, Tony much less so – I saw him as middle of the road, a Labour man who would not rock the boat.'

It seems clear that, despite her support for John Carr's anti-Militant campaign, Cherie was not in those days the sort of person Carr and his friends would have regarded as entirely politically reliable. She seems to have been a supporter of the Campaign for Labour Party Democracy, which would have made people like Carr nervous of her, for the CLPD was a thorn in the Labour leadership's side. It campaigned for power in the Labour Party to be spread more widely, and for new systems for the election of Labour's leader which would take the choice out of the hands of Labour MPs, where it rested in those days. It had a kind of rigid, self-righteous spirit, condemning its opponents in the most extreme terms, and was the cause of much of the bitterness amid which Labour Party politics were conducted in those days. Years later, as we shall see, Neil Kinnock was to worry about the awkwardly leftwing reputation of Blair's wife.

Cherie had some contacts Carr would have regarded as dubious – and which have melted away over the years. Sandy Pringle recalls that some time after Blair had joined his ward party, he met Blair at a public meeting and was introduced to Cherie. 'She said "Come on, Tony" and whisked him away. She wanted to introduce him to the speaker, who she obviously thought was a more important person than me, and she was probably right. It was Jeremy Corbyn.' Corbyn was, and is, a far-left Bennite Labour MP.

Tony and Cherie became engaged during a two-week holiday in a rented apartment in Italy in 1977. They were married in the chapel at St John's College, Oxford, in 1980. Later that same year, Cherie's father's life changed forever. Ferociously drunk one night, Tony Booth (or some companions he had met in a pub) set his North London flat on fire, and he suffered horrific burns from which he nearly died. Family members remember with gratitude that Cherie's new husband was always around when needed at this difficult time.

Cherie had grown up with an understandable resentment towards her father, who had drunk away the money that would have made her childhood easier and more pleasant. But after the fire, according to one of her sisters, 'she realised she did not want to lose her father, and he started to make an effort with her and with others'. He also gave up alcohol for good. So after her marriage, Cherie, for the first time since she had been a little girl, stayed in regular contact with her father – who was later to play his own part in her husband's rise to power. At the wedding, in Tony Booth's absence, and the absence of Blair's father, who had suffered another stroke, Derry Irvine made the necessary speech giving the bride away.

The newlyweds lived together in Hackney. Blair worked at the chambers where he had been a pupil to Derry Irvine, led by Michael Sherrard QC at 2 Crown Office Row. He was a tenant – that is, a barrister for whom the chambers and its clerk arranged work – between 1977 and 1981. But in 1981, his fourth year at Sherrard's chambers, he was involved in an acrimonious professional split.

Derry Irvine suddenly announced that he was leaving to form a new set of chambers with himself at the head, at 11 Kings Bench Walk; and he was taking seven other members of chambers with him – almost half the members. This came as an unpleasant shock to those left behind, who had not been invited to go along with Irvine. One of Irvine's seven was his young protégé, Tony Blair.

Irvine's decision to break away tore the heart out of the existing set of chambers, says one observer. There was, at least in the short term, bitterness and recrimination, because those remaining had to try to keep the chambers afloat on a radically reduced income. The reason for the split seems to have been that the Irvine-Blair faction, who did almost exclusively civil work, no longer wanted to be tied to barristers who did a lot of criminal work; civil work is much better paid than criminal work.

'It came to me as a complete surprise,' says one of those who stayed with Sherrard, and who had been a friend of Blair's.

> I didn't see anything on the horizon to suggest it was coming. Even today I can't see what the real reason was, but I assume it was because Derry wanted a completely civil-oriented set rather than a mixed one. I think there must also have been some irritation between Derry Irvine and Michael Sherrard. At that time employment law was important – it's less so now – and Derry Irvine was at the forefront of employment law.

Sherrard is said to have felt betrayed by Irvine, whose career he had always encouraged.

Ironically, after the departure of the Irvine faction, Sherrard's set at 2 Crown Office Row became more and more a civil rather than a criminal chambers, until within a few years there was only one barrister in it who was doing mostly criminal work.

Much of Blair's own work was for the trade unions – either advising them himself, or acting as junior to Irvine in court. Richard Rosser, then general secretary of a small trade union, the Transport Salaried Staffs Association, remembers being taken by his solicitor to hear an opinion from Tony Blair. 'He explained crisply in about ten minutes why he considered we would be wasting our money if we went to court,' he recollects.

But his was by no means an exclusively employment-law practice. There were several trips to the United States, most frequently New Orleans, for shipping arbitrations. These, according to a lawyer who knew Blair at the time, were 'easy and very well-paid pieces of work which went to bright young lawyers'. Sometimes Cherie accompanied her husband on these American trips.

Irvine was, in any case, moving away from employment to the better-paid commercial and civil work, and lawyers who knew them at this time say that this was the clear direction in which Irvine and his protégé were going until Blair left the law to enter Parliament in 1983. The unions had hoped that Irvine's would be a labour-law specialist chambers, at a time when the Thatcher government was changing labour law hugely to the unions' disadvantage, but it was already apparent to them that Irvine himself had different ideas.

Just as Cherie brought her husband to Labour politics, so also she brought him to the Catholic church. Tony Blair today is effectively a Roman Catholic, though he has not yet, as far as we know, been formally received into the church.

The odd thing is not that he has embraced the Catholic church, but that he chooses to hide it. When asked directly, he replies evasively: 'Surely being a Christian is what is important.'9

But the evidence is conclusive. It is not just that the entire Blair family has always attended Mass together every Sunday. That could be explained by the fact that Cherie would have had to promise her priest before her marriage that the children would be brought up as Catholics. Nor is it just that Blair was regularly receiving Communion during Mass until told to stop doing so by Cardinal Basil Hume, for this by itself isn't incompatible with Blair still being an Anglican.

After the Blairs started their family and moved from Hackney to Islington, Tony Blair always went up to receive Communion with his family at the St Joan of Arc church in Islington, right up to the point when he became Labour leader. But then, when he was a public figure, a new priest in Islington asked for guidance from the Cardinal.

Cardinal Hume would have preferred to go on ignoring the situation, but when it was drawn to his attention, he had to make a ruling. He could not afford to let people think there was one rule for a prospective prime minister and another for everyone else. The result was a letter to Blair from the Cardinal, asking him to desist from taking Communion. In his reply, Blair promised he would not do so again, but added: 'I wonder what Jesus would have made of it.' His old friend Peter Thomson has told friends that Blair felt far more angry than his letter suggested.

Hume was enforcing the rule that Blair, who had been received into the Anglican church at Oxford, should not take Communion in a Catholic church. Now the Prime Minister is forced to sit at the back of the church every Sunday while his family go up for Communion. Shortly after the Cardinal's decision, he met a Roman Catholic priest and joked: 'If you give me Holy Communion, I'll make you Bishop of Liverpool.'

These things in themselves do not prove he is a Catholic. He could have been telling the whole truth when he said: 'My wife is Catholic, my kids are brought up as Catholics. I have gone to Mass with them for years because I believe it's important for a family to worship together.' But Blair was doing much, much more than simply going to Mass to be with his family. Before he became prime minister, he regularly attended Mass at Westminster Cathedral, more often than not by himself, and always took Communion. The priests there knew him well. He would normally attend either the 9 a.m. Mass with his family, or the 5.30 p.m. Mass by himself.

Noticing this, the Anglican Archbishop of Canterbury, Dr George Carey, wrote to him: 'There are many who are deeply troubled by a view being disseminated by the press that you are about to "convert".' Dr

Carey asked him to 'be seen, occasionally, at an Anglican or free church act of worship'. Blair replied that he had attended Mass by himself just once, and the reason was that he expected his family to join him and they were delayed.[10] This was quite untrue. He had been for several years a regular part of the congregation at Mass every Sunday, whether his family was with him or not.

In Islington, he was one of those who regularly performed the readings during Mass. Today he takes full advantage of the oddity in the Catholic rules that allows him to take Communion in a Catholic church when he is abroad. In many countries that he visits, there is no easily available Anglican church, and therefore the local Catholic church is not obliged to turn him away. So each Sunday when abroad, he goes to Mass and takes Communion – and, according to our Catholic sources, derives great spiritual comfort from it.

He no longer goes to Westminster Cathedral, because of security considerations. 'He used to stop and talk to us after Mass, but after he became prime minister he was rushed straight to his car,' says a priest. Sometimes, without notice, he will turn up at a country parish, where the local priest will suddenly realise he has the prime minister in his congregation.

In 2003, when Tony and Cherie visited the Vatican, apart from the well-publicised formal meetings with the Pope in which the latter argued against attacking Iraq, there was one utterly private meeting. The Pope's secretary, Bishop Stanislaw Dziwisz, said a Mass just for the two of them, and both received Communion from him. The Pope would not have allowed that unless he was sure his visitor was, in his heart, a Roman Catholic.

'The question of Tony's faith is dormant by decision,' says a prominent Catholic who knows the Blairs well. 'They have decided not to let news of his Catholicism break while Tony is prime minister.' That decision does much to explain Alastair Campbell's well-known retort to a journalist who asked about Blair's religion: 'We don't do God,' he said. (It's a common turn of phrase among the Blair entourage, one of whom once told a trade unionist dismissively: 'We don't do collective bargaining.') Campbell was not, as has always been thought, simply avoiding an appearance of piety that might turn voters off. He was protecting a secret: the secret of the prime minister's Catholicism.

What has made him into a Catholic? And why does he hide it?

The answer to the first question begins, but does not end, with Cherie. Her Catholicism is described by a priest who knows her well: 'She's an old-fashioned Northern Catholic from poor Irish roots in Liverpool. She wants that faith for her children.'

For her, as for many people from Catholic families, going to Mass on Sunday is as natural as breathing. A man who wanted to share her life, but could not share the Mass with her, would not really know her. He would not know the mystical moment of transubstantiation, when Catholics believe that the bread and wine become the body and blood of Christ. To a Catholic, only a Catholic priest can give Communion.

Cherie was taught at her convent, and in her home, about hellfire, and the eternal damnation that inevitably follows if you die in a state of mortal sin, and how Catholicism is the only true faith, though today the Catholic church has retreated a little from all that. Blair seems to have craved that sort of absolute certainty. In the days when the Communist Party was still some sort of force in the land, it used to be said, with just a little exaggeration, that it was full of ex-Catholics, for only Catholicism and Communism offered a complete answer to all life's dilemmas. You can only get that from a political or religious faith. Blair seeks it from a religious one.

The Catholic faith, even today, is harsh and prescriptive in its fundamental beliefs. Marriage is good and right; single-parent families and abortion are bad and wrong and to be condemned. Blair approves of all this, and each month he seems to become bolder in proclaiming it – though without, so far, feeling able to proclaim his own Catholicism.

In 1993 John Smith, then Labour leader and open about his own Presbyterian faith, published a book about Christianity and socialism, and Blair wrote the introduction:

> Christianity is a very tough religion. It may not always be practised as
> such. But it is. … It is not utilitarian – though socialism can be
> explained in those terms. It is judgemental. There is right and wrong.
> There is good and bad. We all know this, of course, but it has become
> fashionable to be uncomfortable about such language. But when we look
> at our world today and how much needs to be done, we should not hesi-
> tate to make such judgements. And then follow them with determined
> action. That would be Christian socialism.

It sounds like a Catholic sort of Christianity, and no sort of socialism at all.

So why does the prime minister hide his Catholicism? The political commentator Anthony Howard, who knows Blair and is writing a biography of Cardinal Hume, says: 'I think he feels he cannot announce his conversion because of the situation in Northern Ireland. I think he will formally join the Catholic church when he ceases to be prime minister.' No doubt Northern Ireland is part of the explanation. But Blair was committed to Catholicism well before he was prime minister: definitely when he was opposition leader, and almost certainly before that. And it is many years since a prime minister had to be, or pretend to be, a member of the established church. Today, opposition leader Michael Howard is an active member of his synagogue, while Charles Kennedy is a practising Catholic.

It is more likely due to the instinct for secrecy, which, as we shall see, grips Blair the politician and grips the Blair court. Religion has become, with every passing year, a bigger part of the Blairs' life and their thinking. Everyone the authors have spoken to who knows the couple at all well says they get steadily more religious and more wrapped up in religion. In the last few years, the essential religiosity of both the Blairs has taken new, unorthodox and unexpected turns – but that is for a later chapter.

CHAPTER FOUR

RISING THROUGH THE SNAKEPIT

Tony Blair often points out how bad a mess the Labour Party was in during the years of the first Thatcher government from 1979 to 1983, when he was active in Hackney Labour Party. He is right, so far as it goes, though, as we shall see, Blair's role in making things better is at least open to debate.

During this period the Labour Party tore itself to pieces, not, ostensibly, over high matters of policy, but over such things as the way in which the leadership should be elected. In fact, of course, the conflict about these constitutional issues was merely a façade which disguised much more profound ideological divisions within the party.

The last Labour prime minister before Blair, James Callaghan, lost office at the 1979 general election, amid furious accusations from certain party members that the government's defeat and Margaret Thatcher's victory were the direct result of Callaghan's policies. The former minister Tony Benn and his supporters argued that a more radical approach would have enthused Labour supporters. So far, this simply means a traditional Labour Party battle between left and right. What made it poisonous – so poisonous that it was fatal to Labour's electoral chances and consigned the party to opposition for the next eighteen years – was the bitter, grinding, personal, sectarian quality of the Bennite campaign.

They believed that a different way of choosing Labour's leader, taking it out of the hands of Labour MPs, would produce a more leftwing candidate. The effort to secure this was led by the Campaign for Labour Party Democracy (CLPD), and key figures in this campaign recall clearly that one of their supporters was the young, radical lawyer Cherie Booth.

The CLPD's campaign was successful. The 1980 Labour Party conference agreed that a new system, which included constituency Labour parties and trade unions as well as Labour MPs, would be introduced. But it failed to agree on the relative weightings that should be attached to the votes of each of these three groups, so the details were left to a special conference to be held in 1981.

In the meantime, Callaghan resigned. The left bitterly attacked him for resigning at once – meaning that his successor would be elected by Labour MPs – instead of waiting until the new system was in place. Michael Foot narrowly defeated Denis Healey for the vacant leadership, and soon afterwards four key Labour Party figures – Roy Jenkins, David Owen, Shirley Williams and Bill Rodgers, the so-called 'Gang of Four' – announced that they were leaving Labour to form the Social Democratic Party (SDP).

At the special conference, after a bitter battle it was eventually agreed that in future the leader and deputy leader should be chosen by an electoral college composed of 30 per cent MPs, 30 per cent constituency Labour parties, and 40 per cent trade unions, and that Michael Foot should continue as leader for the time being. The party then started to tear itself into yet smaller pieces over the election for the more or less meaningless post of deputy leader.

Foot begged for a period of peace, which in 1981 meant electing Denis Healey unopposed as his deputy. Tony Benn's friends insisted that the machinery needed to be 'tested'. Neil Kinnock, then shadow spokesman for education, thought this was 'a bit like Christmas morning when a kid's given a watch and starts taking it apart to see how it works'.

But arguing against an election was dangerous. Benn's coterie, whose methods were remarkably unfastidious, would at once accuse you of being anti-democratic: 'Don't you believe in elections, then?' Jon Lansman, Benn's chief fixer and cheerleader, would say, leaving opponents floundering in the quicksands of political philosophy. Many of the methods used today by the Blairites are, as we shall see, remarkably similar to those of the Bennites – and many of the fiercest Bennites of those days are today among the fiercest of the Blairites.

A young Scottish MP, Robin Cook, spent the whole of an all-night Commons sitting on 2 April 1981 gathering signatures of leftwing Labour MPs for a petition asking Benn not to stand. 'The party needs an election for deputy leader like it needs a hole in the head,' he said to anyone who would listen. But at 3.30 a.m., while Cook was still collecting his signatures, word of his activities reached Benn's supporters, and they persuaded their man to make his announcement straightaway, before the petition could reach him.

The six-month campaign centred on how the big unions were going to vote. Outside the Labour Party, people saw the battle for what it was:

a fight for union patronage. Labour's popularity plummeted, and so did trade union membership. But inside the Labour Party, supporting Tony Benn was quickly turned into a litmus test of whether or not you were really committed to socialism. The miners' leader, Arthur Scargill, was only summing up a common opinion when he told the Scottish Miners' Gala that anyone who criticised Benn was 'sabotaging ... the principles of socialism which are basic to our movement'.

The anti-Bennite left, the so-called 'soft left', cast around for a third candidate, so as to block Benn without having to incur the wrath of their activists by voting for Healey. But none of them wanted to be the candidate, for they feared the consequences. A vengeful rumour mill stirred up by the Bennites was not something any politician wanted to live with for the rest of his or her career. At first, the veteran leftwinger Eric Heffer agreed to stand, but a weekend in his Liverpool constituency, listening to the activists on whose support he depended, changed his mind. He returned, said colleagues, a changed man, quiet, thoughtful, almost shy, and no one ever heard him say an unkind word about Tony Benn again until his dying day.

With considerable courage – and at enormous cost to his career and personal happiness – the former agriculture minister John Silkin picked up the poisoned chalice. Of course he knew he could not win. Privately he said: 'I shall come third. I hope to make it not too bad a third.' Publicly, of course, he proclaimed his confidence of victory, so as to provide cover for his colleagues to vote for him as an alternative to Benn. It was, in its Byzantine way, the most selfless gesture any modern politician has ever made.

This set the scene for a dreadful summer for Labour, with all three candidates appearing at union conference after union conference. By the end of the summer, when Healey squeaked home, the next general election had been effectively lost. The Bennites took their revenge on Silkin by making life hard for him in his Deptford constituency. Silkin and the Bennites entered into a meaningless but newsworthy battle for control of the small-circulation leftwing weekly magazine *Tribune*. The Bennites' frontman for this was *Tribune*'s editor, Chris Mullin, who embarked on a speaking tour of Deptford to persuade the local Labour Party to deselect Silkin. Mullin is now a strong Blair supporter.

By 1982, the Labour Party was in a state of civil war. Bitter battles to deselect MPs thought to be hostile to Benn were fought all over the country. In Hemel Hempstead the longstanding Labour MP, Robin Corbett, was ousted after a brutal and bruising two-year campaign by a young Bennite, Paul Boateng – now another convert to Blairism.

The recruitment of party members almost ceased. The balance of political power within the party seemed much more important than getting new people in: moreover, if a constituency Labour party got a new member, who knew whom he or she might side with? The playwright Steve Gooch tells a story of his attempt to join Southwark Labour Party after the 1979 general election. He telephoned and left a message for his local party secretary, and heard nothing for several months. When the European elections were called, he telephoned again to offer help with canvassing. There was a long pause. At last a voice, bristling with suspicion, said: 'Are you a friend of Eric's?'

Hackney Labour Party was in the front line of the battle. Charles Clarke, the former President of the National Union of Students, Cherie Blair's old mentor John Carr, the historian Ben Pimlott, the journalist John Lloyd (then industrial correspondent for the *Financial Times*), Tony Blair and Cherie Booth led the fight to recapture the constituency from the Bennites. Carr's wife, Glenys Thornton, however, was working for Tony Benn – a source of some marital disharmony at the time. Cherie already knew both the Carrs well, and it was she who introduced her husband to them and to the Hackney political scene.

On the deputy leadership the Blairs both followed the line adopted by the up-and-coming star of the soft left, Neil Kinnock, which was to vote for Silkin and then, if there was a runoff after Silkin was eliminated, to abstain. It was a bruising battle, but they and their friends eventually persuaded Hackney to adopt this position.[1] It was a pretty feeble approach, and if he had not had a political future to consider, Blair might have pressed for a vote for Healey; but he never even mentioned Healey's name, only saying that he would not under any circumstances vote for Benn.[2]

It was Carr and Clarke, not Blair, who led the infighting in Hackney and earned the hatred of the Bennites. 'Tony was a toff and sounded like one,' says John Carr, 'so people were a bit sceptical about him. He didn't make concessions, didn't start dropping his aitches or anything like that.' Everyone knew that both Tony and Cherie were looking for parliamentary seats to fight, and both were in the Labour Co-Ordinating Committee (LCC). Cherie, according to a politician who knew the couple well (and who later served in Blair's cabinet), was 'highly respected in left-wing circles in those days'. Blair was not, for it seemed less clear what he believed in.

The LCC had been formed in the last days of the Callaghan government, before the left irrevocably split into the Bennites and the soft left. Its launch brought together Benn's old researcher Frances Morrell, by this time the leader of the Inner London Education Authority, with such mainstream figures as the white-collar union leader Alan Fisher and former cabinet minister Peter Shore. Veteran Bennite Michael Meacher was the committee's first chairman. After the 1979 election it became an ideological battleground, according to its secretary, Nigel Stanley. It voted to support Benn for deputy leader, but only by a majority of two to one. Slowly the soft left gained ground, turning the instrument the Bennites had created against them. Carr puts it this way: 'At first we were all in the LCC together, Bennites and others from the left. As time went on it became clear that the Bennites had another agenda.'

Short, stout, jovial and, when you got to know him, unexpectedly clever, Carr was a member of Ken Livingstone's Greater London Council. He had a huge office in County Hall which the LCC used for its strategy meetings, and which the Blairs got to know well.[3]

Back in 1981 Charles Clarke was a big, thickset, heavily bearded young man, three years older than Blair and, like Blair, a product of a public school, in Clarke's case Highgate in North London, where he had been head boy. Clarke already had his eyes set on a political career when he was a student, and was elected president of the Cambridge University Students Union (not to be confused with the Cambridge Union: even as a student Clarke wanted to do things, not talk about them). He followed this with the high-profile presidency of the National Union of Students, and when Neil Kinnock became education spokesman early that year, he asked Clarke to come and work for him.

Unlike Blair, Carr and Clarke knew what they were up against. (So did Cherie, who, as we have seen, had stood shoulder to shoulder with Carr against Militant in the Labour Party's factional fights when they were students together at the London School of Economics.) They had been involved in politics since they were teenagers, and had sat together on the executive of the National Union of Students. In the Hackney party's internecine warfare they were senior partners to the Blairs. That suited Blair fine. All his political life he has had a talent for placing others in the frontline, a talent he would hone to perfection in Downing Street.

But Blair did put his head far enough above the parapet to stand, early in 1981, against the Bennite branch secretary Mike Davis, and to beat him by 17 votes to 15. Later the same year he joined Solidarity, the anti-Bennite group set up by Roy Hattersley and Peter Shore.[4] Its secretary was Mary Goudie, whose husband, James Goudie QC, shared a chambers office with Blair. Already Blair was quietly making himself a known and trusted figure on the rightwing of the Labour Party.

The point inevitably came when Blair's name was put forward for a council seat. The branch met to choose its candidate from among those who had been nominated – and Blair was not there. He was, explained Cherie, away on a legal case. What she did not say was that he was on one of his many trips to New Orleans to do a shipping arbitration.[5] She spoke for him, but, unsurprisingly, the members were not happy about choosing someone who was not there to speak for himself. Almost certainly this came as a relief to Blair, who did not want to get his hands dirtier than necessary at the rough end of Hackney Labour Party politics.

Already it was clear that Blair hoped for a parliamentary career. And he was far more likely to achieve his goal with the help of the political contacts he had made at the Bar than with that of the bruisers of Hackney Labour Party. In his own chambers, both James Goudie and Derry Irvine had the best possible Labour contacts, and Blair got to know well their fellow barrister, Labour MP and former minister John Smith. Joining Solidarity, though a step into controversy, helped too: Smith was also a member, and the organiser was Labour's most ruthless and effective rightwing fixer, John Speller of the electricians' union EEPTU. Nonetheless, Blair hedged his bets by joining the Campaign for Nuclear Disarmament at about the same time, though nothing he is ever recorded as having said would identify him as a supporter of unilateral nuclear disarmament.

Blair's first forays in quest of a parliamentary seat took place in the North East. His first unsuccessful attempt was in Middlesbrough in 1980. He was one of seventeen candidates listed for the seat – having got a nomination from the local branch of the right-leaning EEPTU. But he didn't have a chance against fellow barrister Stuart Bell, who already had the seat sewn up. Bell had the backing of Tom Burlison, the regional secretary of the General and Municipal Workers' Union – later the GMB – one of the two most powerful union powerbrokers in the North East. Behind Blair's back, Stuart Bell made sure that while the EEPTU would nominate Blair, they would vote for Bell. Blair didn't even make the short list. Bell says in his book, *Tony Blair Loves Me*: 'I knew this particular candidate had no hope of winning the nomination and persuaded the GMB and the EETPU to switch their votes to whichever candidate stayed in the race.' Burlison, however, was impressed with Blair: 'He was quite a charismatic character, but he was young, pretty fresh looking. I didn't think he was going to get a northern seat.'[6] Neither of them would in the future have cause to regret this brief initial encounter, but Blair learned some lessons about the rougher side of Labour politics which soon came in useful.

Blair tried to get selected for two other seats. He received a nomination for Teesside Thornaby — now Stockton South — but the 'Southern smoothie', as he was dubbed locally, could not convince the constituency party that he was a left-leaning candidate. Frank Griffiths, the successful candidate who went on to lose to SDP defector Ian Wrigglesworth, recalls Blair protesting 'in a friendly but firm way' to a group of members in Teesside Thornaby that he was on the left of the party because he was a supporter of *Tribune*.[7] They were more perspicacious than they realised, as Blair had successfully managed to conceal the fact that he was a member of Solidarity. He tried later to get selected for Stockton North, but he couldn't even get nominated there.

His chances of getting noticed on a wider political stage appeared to have reached a dead end, until events that had nothing to do with him gave him the first step on the ladder to Parliament in 1982.

If it had not been for the fatal sexual peccadillo of a Tory MP, Tony Blair would probably not be prime minister today. For his first foray into national politics, standing as a 'no hoper' by-election candidate in the Tory stronghold of Beaconsfield in the Chilterns, was courtesy of a Westminster sex scandal that has been kept quiet for twenty-two years. Without Beaconsfield, Blair would probably not have got a safe seat in the 1983 general election.

The trigger for the by-election was the death of Sir Ronald Bell, a rightwing Thatcherite Tory who had extreme views on immigration and was a self-appointed guardian of family values. The MP — known to colleagues as 'Pac-a-Mac' because of a fondness for wearing a cheap proprietary brand of plastic fold-up mackintosh — had a guilty secret.

In the Commons he made coruscating attacks on gays, lesbians and trade unions and highlighted the soaring divorce rate among the young. In one speech he ranted against Britain becoming 'a second-class nation riddled with tribal dissensions, class warfare and degenerate practices', citing 'degenerates practising buggery and lesbians flaunting their vice under the impudent banner of gaiety'. But on Saturdays he played away, so to speak. Every Saturday afternoon he could be found in his office, situated along a corridor in the gothic splendour of Norman Shaw North (the Old Scotland Yard building on the Embankment, which had been turned into MPs' offices), where he was supposed to be dictating urgent correspondence to his secretary. In fact, he was entertaining a longstanding mistress behind a locked office door.

On 27 February 1982, a cold but bright February afternoon, he left an anti-Common Market meeting of MPs addressed by his friend Enoch

Powell for his usual rendezvous in his Commons office. The building was nearly empty, though on the floor below some Labour MPs were holding a meeting with trade unionists. In the midst of energetic sexual relations, the sixty-seven-year-old MP suffered a heart attack, literally 'on the job'. The mistress calmly put on her clothes, tidied up the room, searched in his pockets for the key to open and close his office door, and left the dead and near-naked MP slumped among his constituency files. The Commons security staff found her a few minutes later unsuccessfully trying to find a way out of the now-deserted building. Her cool broke and she told them what had happened.

Since his death occurred on a Saturday afternoon, it was barely reported in the press, although he did receive a few glowing obituaries. The police and Commons decided to hush up the incident – which would have been highly embarrassing to his family, friends and, indeed, the strait-laced burghers of stockbroker-belt Beaconsfield, who saw him as a right-thinking local hero. The atmosphere in the Commons at that time was not conducive to publicising such stories. It predated by a decade the spate of Tory sex and sleaze scandals that were to help bring down John Major.

The story that Sir Ronald had expired while dictating a letter to his secretary led to at least one misplaced condolence from a fellow MP. A Labour backbencher, whose office was in the same building, proffered his sympathies to Bell's secretary when he saw her in the Norman Shaw photocopying room. He said: 'It must have been awful for you, a man collapsing with a heart attack, while you were in the middle of dictation.' According to the MP, she 'immediately puckered up' and responded: 'It wasn't me, it was another woman,' obviously horrified to think that this must have been a polite way of linking her to the unreported scandal.

A week later, the Labour Party's magazine, *Labour Weekly*, dubbed Sir Ronald a 'neo-Nazi' in its obituary. Tory whips were furious at this posthumous mudslinging and threatened to take out a writ against the magazine. The attack was reported in the local newpaper, the *Slough Observer*, on 12 March. The paper got Bell's elder brother to denounce the 'slur' and to point out that Bell had fought against the Nazis and had taken part in the famous Dieppe raid – the dry run for the D-Day landings.

Harold Frayman, the chairman of the Slough Labour Party, a journalist who worked on *Labour Weekly* at the time and who was to become Blair's by-election campaign press officer, distanced himself from the report. He told the *Slough Observer* that he had had nothing to do with it.

Blair himself decided to apply for Beaconsfield after taking advice from both John Smith and Tom Pendry, a senior Labour MP who had been a junior minister in the Wilson and Callaghan governments. Pendry is said to have told Blair: 'It is only twenty-five minutes down the road, you'll have a high-profile campaign – and what is more an old girlfriend of mine is the local party secretary.'[8] In fact, Blair's profile during the campaign was anything but high.

The by-election was conducted in the shadow of the opening stages of the Falklands War, and political and press interest in Beaconsfield was focused on whether the SDP and their Liberal allies would snatch this safe Tory seat – just as one of the original Gang of Four, Shirley Williams, had grabbed Crosby from the Tories.

Understandably, when the Labour Party sought a parliamentary candidate for Beaconsfield, there was not exactly a stampede to gain the nomination. Blair was one of only four candidates who went through to the selection process. His main rival, John Hurley, Labour leader of Slough council, performed less well during the selection meeting – being floored by Blair over the latest research on housing policy, which was rather embarrassing for a local council leader.

Blair's success in securing the nomination was marred (for him) by a damning local press headline. The *Slough Observer* and its sister paper the *South Bucks Observer* both reported his selection under the headline 'Benn-backing Barrister is Labour's Choice'. The two papers went on to deplore the fact that the London lawyer who had 'all the right credentials for a such a stockbroker seat' was, reportedly, a supporter of unilateral disarmament (those were the days when Blair still boasted of his CND membership), an opponent of the Common Market, and generally an exponent of leftwing views.

Blair replied the following week, taking particular offence at seeing his name linked to Benn's and – rather ironically, given his own future – to the whole idea of personality politics. 'I am emphatically not a Benn-backer,' he wrote. 'Alliteration is a poor substitute for accuracy.' (Perhaps this is why, in his maiden Commons speech the next year, he said that socialism 'stands for co-operation, not confrontation, for fellowship, not fear' – probably the least accurate, but most alliterative, description of socialism ever recorded.) He went on:

> The support or lack of it for [Benn's] personality dominates so much dis-
> cussion about the Labour Party in the press. I do not support some of
> Tony Benn's policies, I support the Labour Party policies. Just so as
> there is no further misunderstanding, I support the Labour Party's pres-
> ent leadership; Labour's plans for jobs; withdrawal from the EEC (cer-
> tainly unless the most fundamental changes are effected); and nuclear

disarmament, unilaterally, if necessary; in particular I intend to campaign against Trident and American-controlled missiles on our soil. I do so as a Labour Party man, not as a 'Bennite' or any other 'ite'.

His tactic worked. The next by-election story in the *Slough Observer* was headlined 'Labour Moderates are Backing Blair' and reported that Denis Healey, Merlyn Rees and Gwyneth Dunwoody were coming to town to speak on his behalf. But he also had support from Stan Orme, Peter Shore and Fenner Brockway, the veteran CND campaigner. Tony Benn, unsurprisingly, was not invited. Other speakers included Neil Kinnock and John Smith. Kinnock recalled later that Blair 'couldn't have picked a better place to cut his teeth – right down to the gums as the result turned out'.

The Labour Party leader, Michael Foot, made a personal appearance in Beaconsfield and gave a prophetic quote to the BBC's *Newsnight* and regional television. Coming out of a fish-and-chip supper at the Stag & Hounds pub, he told waiting reporters: 'We're proud of everything he's been saying here and, whatever the result, we believe he's going to have a very big future in British politics.'

Cherie Blair – as she unusually called herself for the purposes of fighting an election in a traditional Tory stronghold – came to give him support. She tried to attract interest by asking the *Coronation Street* mega-star Pat Phoenix (who played Elsie Tanner in the soap) to do the rounds of Beaconsfield to help her husband. Pat Phoenix and Cherie's father, Tony Booth, who was later to marry Pat on her deathbed, were unilateralists and therefore happy to back Blair on this issue. Cherie also put out a personal leaflet supporting her husband, aimed at working wives who might be losing their jobs and other women suffering from government spending cuts.

Paul Tyler, the Alliance candidate in the by-election, remembers that Cherie had independent views on the tactics used in the Beaconsfield campaign and was in favour of playing to Labour's strengths in the poorer parts of the constituency. 'She was the one saying to him he should concentrate on the traditional Labour working-class vote.' This was, and is, the opposite to Blair's view of Labour campaigning, as the Beaconsfield campaign made clear.

Although Harold Frayman was well aware that Cherie, too, had political ambitions, he was convinced that she did not have 'the same steel as Blair' and would not stay the course. 'I knew there was an understanding that they were determined they were not both going into Parliament.'[9]

But there was another aspect of Blair's campaigning that showed where his real loyalties lay – even at this early stage in his political career. John Rentoul's biography highlights Blair's early interest in law and order. He distributed a leaflet to the wealthy but nervous householders of Beaconsfield saying: 'The decision to put police "back on the beat" is a welcome move back to closer contact with the public and in the right direction to help to reduce crime.' He also tried out another initiative that showed what he saw as the way ahead for the Labour Party. Harold Frayman recalls that the local party produced a poster headed 'Why Conservatives are voting for Tony Blair' as part of a charm offensive intended to persuade the owners of Beaconsfield's often palatial homes to switch their allegiance. It is clear that a decade or more before Labour became New Labour, and even when saddled with leftwing party policies, Blair was already set on wooing *Daily Mail* readers.

Paul Tyler, who had the strong backing of Roy Jenkins and the recent Crosby by-election victor, Shirley Williams, in his campaign to win Beaconsfield for the Liberal/SDP Alliance, remembers clearly Blair's wooing of wealthy Tories.

> He used the campaign to fight plans to infill gravel pits to woo the wealthier Tory voters. It was like a Liberal Democrat 'pavement politics' campaign, concentrating on a local issue. And the voters were wealthy in that area. I remember going up large drives with people telling me they had purchased a third car – so they always had one on the drive to deter burglars when they were out.[10]

Harold Frayman, the press officer supplied by Labour Party headquarters, thought Blair should be seen to be backing local nurses and porters who had gone on strike at Wexham Park hospital – a major medical centre on a site just outside Slough. The strike, which had high-profile coverage in the *Slough Observer*, was part of a national campaign by the National Union of Public Employees for a 12 per cent pay rise for low-waged workers. On 19 May the union called a one-day strike and put picket lines outside the hospital. At least fifty nurses and porters walked out and local bus drivers refused to cross the picket lines.

But Blair adamantly refused to go to the scene to be photographed supporting the strike. It was, says Frayman, the only serious disagreement they had throughout the campaign. Most of the time Blair was 'a perfect candidate', which is the party official's traditional way of saying that he did what the agent and press officer told him to do. 'He did what he was told by me and the agent, Tony Beirne, the southern regional organiser who came in to act as agent. He was pliant and well behaved. He threw himself into campaigning with no sense that it was a lost cause.' But on the issue of the striking nurses, Blair was immovable.

Frayman then suggested that if the candidate was unwilling to put in a personal appearance he should at least issue a press statement in support of the strikers. 'He was very careful about the wording of the statement of support,' says Frayman. 'He insisted on seeing and changing it. This was unusual. With all other statements, he just let me put them out. It was the only real disagreement we had.'[11]

In retrospect, Blair's attitude towards the strikers was highly significant. There was no chance of Labour winning Beaconsfield, and there were few votes to be lost, and perhaps some to be gained, by being seen alongside the nurses. Blair was already thinking not of his by-election result, but of his future in the Labour Party. He was already committed to a political career, already grooming his image for high office, already concerned about giving hostages to fortune which might be exploited by those who would write about him in the future. He also has a lifelong distaste for people who go on strike.

Blair was similarly careful in the phraseology he used to back Labour's opposition to the Common Market, leaving nothing on the record that might prove embarrassing if he decided to support European integration at a later date.

Out on the campaign trail he cracked the occasional weak joke. The patriotic fever aroused by the despatch of the Falklands task force, which the Tories were eager to exploit, had led Captain Anthony Wilkinson, the Tory agent, to reissue pictures of himself in his Second World War khaki shorts, in the hope of reminding the electorate of past British glories. Blair told meetings: 'It wouldn't be so bad if he had good knees.'

But, for all the hype about Blair's first venture into electoral politics, Labour did not set much store by the result. Labour HQ at Walworth Road was much more worried about a forthcoming by-election in Mitcham and Morden, where the sitting Labour MP had defected to the SDP.

This lack of interest is illustrated by the fact that Harold Frayman took on the job of press officer. The party's two senior press officers who normally handled by-elections, Monica Foot and Min Birdsey, were engaged elsewhere. Press conferences were not held every day, and when they were, they were held at 11.30 in the morning. If Labour had been really serious, there would have been a daily press briefing at an earlier time, aimed at evening papers and broadcasters, and at setting the day's agenda.

For the Tories and the Alliance it was a different matter. While Labour had only four applications from potential candidates, the Tories had no fewer than a hundred people vying for the blue-chip seat, with its 21,000 majority. They ranged from Sir Ronald Bell's eldest son, Andrew, a twenty-eight-year-old City stockbroker, to at least two men who would later become well-known MPs, Bill Cash and Edward Leigh. The Tories' selection ballot attracted nearly 400 votes and ended up in a tie, with Tim Smith and Edward Leigh each getting 184 votes. The chairman, Lord Burnham, had to use his casting vote. Tim Smith was chosen. He had already sensationally won a safe Labour seat during Callaghan's premiership at a by-election at Ashfield in Nottinghamshire.

On the morning of the poll, Harold Frayman gave Blair two alternative speeches. 'Here's the speech if we come third and here's the speech if we come second,' he said. 'Where's the speech if we win?' quipped Blair. 'I think there was a bit of him that thought in his heart he might make it,' says Frayman.[12]

In fact, Blair had no chance of victory whatsoever, and he must surely have known it. Despite making a solid local issue his own – the issue of infilling gravel pits – and despite the carloads of people from Hackney whom John Carr brought to canvass for him, he was on a hiding to nothing. Even before the announcement of the result, Tim Smith, sensing victory, placed a story in the London *Evening Standard* diary saying that, once he had won, he planned to run a charity marathon with Jonathan Aitken MP, across Beaconsfield and two neighbouring Tory constituencies. He had also briefed the *Slough Observer* on the times and venues for his 'thank-you' speeches across the constituency, so the details could be published on the Friday after the result was declared overnight.

Blair's hopes of a big turnout – already hit hard by saturation coverage of the Falklands War – were finally doomed by an attraction that soccer-loving Labour supporters would find it hard to resist. The previous Saturday's FA Cup final between Tottenham Hotspur and Queen's Park Rangers had been a draw – and polling night had been chosen for a televised replay. Barney Tinn, a Labour activist, told the *Slough Observer*: 'There are so many QPR and Spurs supporters around here that we are going to have a job getting them out.' Blair referred to the football coverage after the result was declared. Paul Tyler, the Alliance candidate, remembers him fretting that the match had dented his vote and damaged his showing in the seat.

Harold Frayman says: 'On polling day the only thing worrying me was whether we were going to lose our deposit. We didn't talk about it. I went with him that day on the loudspeaker van and we went back to our house for tea. After the result we went for a drink at the NGA office we had used as campaign HQ.' The result was as bad as it could be. The Labour vote dropped from 10,443 in the general election to 3,886 – and it did indeed cause Blair to lose his deposit. The Alliance came a respectable second; Alliance candidate Paul Tyler later went on to become Liberal Democrat MP for North Cornwall in 1992. He is now a peer.

The triumphant Tory Tim Smith appeared to be set for a glittering career, and he did rise to be a junior minister and vice-chairman of his party before becoming the second Beaconsfield MP in succession to have his career was prematurely ended by a scandal. This time it was financial rather than sexual, but he was forced to resign in circumstances that helped Blair win a landslide majority in his first general election as Labour leader.

Blair was despondent at his poor showing. Harold Frayman remembers: 'He sent me a very nice handwritten note. In it he said he despaired for the future of the Labour Party unless it could stop the infighting.' Frayman says that Blair asked him whether he should stay and fight Beaconsfield at the general election. 'I said stay in Beaconsfield and prove yourself there and go for something winnable next time round. I said a bit of loyalty to Beaconsfield would do him no harm.'[13]

In fact, as Jon Sopel's biography records, Blair had already taken other advice from his friend and boss, Derry Irvine. 'I advised him that sometimes amazing things can happen in politics and persuaded him to ride his luck,' said Irvine. The truth was that, by the time he spoke to Frayman, Blair had already decided to sever his connections with Beaconsfield in the hope of finding something better.

Harold Frayman kept in touch with Blair and Cherie for some time afterwards but eventually lost contact. He recalls: 'I wrote to him when he became leader and said "Not only are those who praise you not always your friends, but those who criticise you are not always your enemies."' Blair never replied, and does not seem to have taken any notice of the advice either.

Two postscripts to the Beaconsfield by-election are worth recording.

Sixteen years later, in 1998, when the leftwing Labour MP Joan Lestor died, Prime Minister Blair turned up at her memorial service and explained to the chairman, Bob Hughes, and to veteran leftwing Labour MP Tam Dalyell, that he felt he had to be there because she had been the first senior party figure to come and support him in Beaconsfield. 'She gave me confidence for the first speech I ever made in public,' he said.

Dalyell could hardly believe what he was hearing. A Labour parliamentary candidate who had never in his life spoken on a public platform – had never fronted a campaign, or spoken to a trade union gathering, or enthused the troops during a strike, or even tried to influence a party meeting, before standing for Parliament – seemed a very strange, alien and not very appealing life form to him. Dalyell was in politics to campaign for things he believed in. What, he wondered, was Blair in politics for?

And twelve years after the by-election, in the *Spectator* magazine, Blair airbrushed his valuable experience in Beaconsfield by trying to present it as a daft move: 'Believe me, fighting the '82 Beaconsfield by-election for Labour was hardly seen as a smart career move. Michael Foot was struggling with the problems of leadership, Tony Benn was in charge of policy, Arthur Scargill was leading the trade unions and we were in the middle of the Falklands War.'

This was all self-serving rubbish. Benn was not in charge of policy, Scargill did not lead the unions, and fighting a hopeless seat was the traditional first rung on the ladder in a parliamentary career – Blair's coup in getting a safe seat the next year would have been impossible without it. Many young politicians who aspired to a luminous political career would have gratefully seized the chance to fight Beaconsfield in 1982, as Blair did. He would calculate that by the time he was experienced enough to be considered for his party's frontbench, the poisonous times would be over.

Though he was determined to desert Beaconsfield, there was never any doubt that he would stay in the Labour Party, if only because he had worked out that deserting to the Social Democratic Party would be a poor career choice. In a seminar in August 1981 in Australia, where he was visiting his old Oxford friends Peter Thomson and Geoff Gallop, and which was not reported in Britain, he said frankly: 'The Social Democrats haven't a hope of winning a general election' because the unemployed and low-paid made up '40–50 per cent of the entire country's workforce' and 'under the present electoral system, they will provide Labour with a solid 200-seat base'.[14]

Within the Labour Party, indeed, he had pulled off a remarkable political trick. Not only did he now know pretty well everyone worth knowing, but also, and even better, everyone thought he was his or her friend. Michael Foot desperately needed good legal minds to help fight Militant, and he had clearly identified Blair as a man he could work with. Foot's intervention on his behalf nearly a year later was to prove crucial to Blair's future career. Meanwhile, on the right of the party, John Smith and Roy Hattersley knew something Foot did not: that Blair was a member of their pressure group, Solidarity. Roy Hattersley had telephoned the leftwing Michael Foot and teased him by saying that Solidarity had achieved a coup in getting one of their own men selected as candidate for Beaconsfield. 'He's not one of yours, he's one of ours,' said Foot.

CHAPTER FIVE

BLAIR WINS AS LABOUR LOSES

Knowing everyone who mattered in the Labour Party was what secured Tony Blair a safe seat to fight in the 1983 general election.

Sedgefield was a new constituency created by boundary changes. Bordering both Durham and Darlington, it consists of several villages, most of them former mining communities. It was clearly going to be a safe Labour seat and was therefore much in demand in 1983, when Labour under Michael Foot had poll ratings so bad that a candidate in anything other than a rock-solid seat was likely to lose.

Sedgefield Labour party was caught out when Margaret Thatcher announced a snap election in May 1983. The active Labour Party members were still getting used to each other. With that most precious thing, a safe seat, to bestow, they all wanted to delay until they could see the lie of the land, and they had put off selecting their candidate as rival factions jockeyed for power. The timetable they eventually set meant selecting a candidate on 20 May. As it turned out, the general election was well underway by then, and polling day was less than three weeks away.

Other constituency Labour parties were much better prepared – like Thanet, whose candidate, Cherie Booth, was already in place when the campaign began. But Thanet was as safe a Conservative seat as Sedgefield was a Labour one. The best Cherie could hope for was to put up a good fight and fare better than her husband had done in Beaconsfield.

Blair's feat in snatching the Sedgefield nomination at the last moment, solely by means of his own heroic efforts and those of his five obscure supporters in the little village of Trimdon, led by the ever-loyal Trimdon Village branch secretary John Burton, all alone against the powerful party machine, has become part of the Blair mythology. John Rentoul paints an affecting picture of a lonely young lawyer going to Trimdon because it was the one branch of Sedgefield Labour party which had not nominated anyone for the candidature, and sitting outside in his car for a long time wondering what he was doing there, before thinking: 'I've come all this way, I might as well go in.' He went in, he watched the European Cup Winners' Cup final with the five leaders of Trimdon Village branch, and then he persuaded them he was the man of destiny. They fought for him, they even prayed for him, and this plucky little team, with no other support, won their place in history. They have even become known in Blair mythology as the 'famous five' – a phrase which owes its currency to Enid Blyton's series of children's books.[1]

Blair himself has written 'It was in [John Burton's] home that night that I met the handful of people who convinced the local party to take a chance on me as their parliamentary candidate.'[2]

But this is all a useful and sentimental fiction. Long before Blair went to Trimdon, a classic trade union fix was underway to secure him the nomination.

Shortly after the Beaconsfield by-election, Blair started telling his Hackney friends that there was a new seat being created as a result of boundary reorganisation in Durham, and he thought he had a good chance of being selected because of his connections with the GMB and the TGWU, then the two most powerful trade unions in the country. He had, he pointed out, done a good deal of legal work for the GMB, and knew its northern regional secretary, Tom Burlison, well.[3] Burlison was one of two powerful trade union fixers in the North East, with parliamentary seats more or less in his gift; the other was the Transport and General Workers' Joe Mills.

The unions were still the real seat of power in Labour politics. At about that time John Mortimer interviewed Arthur Scargill for the *Sunday Times*, and found the miners' leader almost offended to be asked if he wanted a seat in Parliament. 'I was asking King Arthur if he'd care for a post as a corporal ... Why should he forsake the reality of union rule for the pallid pretensions of Westminster?' Trade union officials had always tended to see the Labour Party as the junior branch of the labour movement. Sometimes the party might entice a union leader into government as a matter of duty, as had happened with Ernest Bevin in Attlee's government and Frank Cousins in Wilson's, but generally they preferred their union offices, where they believed the real business of the working class was done. They tended to think of politicians as grubby chaps who had their occasional uses, a bit like journalists. They also believed that it was the unions' solid good sense, as well as their money, that had kept the Labour Party on the right road.

Tony Blair dislikes unions and their leaders, but he knows a stark political reality when he sees one. A young man who wanted a safe Labour seat in 1983 could hardly do better than to find a union-dominated seat and ingratiate himself with the leaders of whichever union had the most votes. He never seems to have minded that he obtained his big chance to become an MP aged only thirty thanks to trade union fixers.

The two North Eastern union barons, Mills and Burlison, were both approached by both Neil Kinnock and Roy Hattersley and asked to do their best to get the nomination for Blair.[4] Since everyone knew that the general election would be lost, that the Labour leader, Michael Foot, would resign afterwards, and that the next leader was going to be either Kinnock or Hattersley, this meant that the plea for Blair came directly from Labour's next leader. Mills even found that the national leader of his union, TGWU general secretary Moss Evans, had been roped in to lend a hand, and that Evans wanted Blair.

Blair was also able to boast of several glowing tributes from Michael Foot for the way he had handled Beaconsfield, and of Foot's wish to see him in the House of Commons.

Part of the reason that Foot, Kinnock and Hattersley were so keen to see Blair in the seat was that they seem to have thought the only alternative was that it would go to Les Huckfield. Huckfield was MP for Nuneaton, which he had chosen to leave because he thought it would fall to the Conservatives in the atmosphere of 1983. (He was right: it did.) The three Labour grandees wanted Huckfield out of the House of Commons because he was a Bennite. The leaders therefore wanted a 'stop Huckfield' candidate, and thought that only Blair was available. They were quite wrong.

The trouble with plotting, when there is a lot of it about, is that the plotters start to fall over each other's feet. In the case of the Sedgefield nomination there were plots and plotters galore. Michael Cocks, the chief whip and another GMB fixer with influence in the North East, was busy organising for seats to fall into safe (that is, not Bennite) hands, and had already made other arrangements. Cocks was planning to beat Huckfield by lining the seat up for a former cabinet minister, Joel Barnett, who had also been displaced by boundary changes.

And if Barnett had not been available, Michael English was. Cocks would have been perfectly happy with English. He was another long-serving MP, a pleasant, clubbable man, popular among fellow MPs, who had been in Parliament for nineteen years and had many years of quiet House of Commons committee service behind him. His seat had disappeared and he was casting around for another. He, too, was a longstanding GMB-sponsored MP and could probably have beaten Huckfield to the nomination, particularly if Burlison and Mills had supported him. But before applying he spoke to his friend Michael Cocks. 'Don't touch Sedgefield,' said Cocks. 'It's being lined up for Joel Barnett.' So he didn't.

After Blair's selection, English ran into Joyce Gould, a top Labour Party official, on a London underground train. English expressed surprise that Blair had the seat. 'I'd been told it was lined up for Joel Barnett,' he said. Gould claimed that she was personally responsible for Blair getting the nomination. This almost certainly means she persuaded Foot to support Blair, for she was close to Foot. She had, she told English, got to know Blair very well in the months before the general election. She liked him and was pleased to find that he was apparently pro-choice on the matter of abortion. English, on the other hand, was known to be anti-abortion.[5]

Ben Pimlott, the distinguished historian and one of Tony Blair's Hackney friends, was also after Sedgefield. He did the rounds of the branches, but he came in a little late, when most of them had already made their nominations. Pimlott eventually found his way to the one branch which had not nominated anyone, Trimdon Village, and he saw the secretary, John Burton. Burton thought him a highly intellectual man but did not take the matter any further. Trimdon remained the one branch without a nominee.[6]

Another contender was Sid Weighell, a major national trade union figure recently retired as the rightwing leader of the railwaymen's union. He was a heavyweight candidate who had to be taken seriously, even though his image at the time was a little dented as the result of some dubious block votes he had recently cast at the Trades Union Congress.

Other people who could have fronted a 'stop Huckfield' campaign included sitting MP David Watkins and rising young star Hilary Armstrong, the daughter of a respected local MP, Ernest Armstrong. Sixteen people were nominated altogether.

But it suited Blair to give the impression that the constituency was sewn up for the leftwing candidate, Huckfield. It was not, and the left knew it. At one crisis meeting they decided they could not be sure of fixing it for either Huckfield or the other leftwinger in the frame, Pat McIntyre. The left in the constituency was split, for McIntyre also had a good deal of support. She was a postgraduate student at Durham University, who was finishing her PhD on Durham politics 1918–39, and had just missed out on other local seats.

Divided, and uncertain of success with either Huckfield or McIntyre, the Sedgefield leftwingers resolved to offer their wholehearted support to Tony Benn, behind whom they could unite, and with whom they were confident they could win. Benn had also been affected by boundary changes. His seat had disappeared, and of the two seats it left behind, one was safe and the other marginal. He had lost the nomination for the safe one to Michael Cocks – the same Michael Cocks who thought he had fixed Sedgefield for Joel Barnett. When his Sedgefield supporters telephoned Benn, he asked for a couple of days to think about it. He duly came back and said he felt obligated to his Bristol constituency, even though he risked losing it. (He did lose it.) It is an odd irony that had Benn, of all people, been a little less principled about deserting an unsafe seat for a safe one, Tony Blair would not be prime minister today.[7]

While Blair was quietly lining up the union barons behind him, the unfortunate Les Huckfield spent a month before the election staying with a sympathiser in Sedgefield. He came straight from an unsuccessful attempt to capture Wigan, and was driven across the Pennines overnight by his aide Alan Meale (later to become MP for Mansfield). In Sedgefield he went out every day to a branch or a local trade union with delegates at the selection conference to ask for their support.[8] It soon became clear that his hard work was paying off, especially with the TGWU branches. Unless the trade unions moved to squash his campaign, he looked like a winner. The fear of the left was that Burlison and Mills might start putting pressure on local activists to switch from Huckfield to Joel Barnett, or perhaps to the council leader, Warren McCourt. They had not yet heard of a young lawyer called Tony Blair. But Mills and Burlison had.

Alan Meale thought that the main rival would be Sid Weighell – being blissfully unaware that, as we shall see, steps had already been taken to derail Weighell. The man whose sophisticated wheeler-dealing with *Tribune* to get Campaign Group members elected in the shadow cabinet elections later led to the coining of the phrase 'the Meale ticket' admits now: 'I was beat fairly and squarely by Joe Mills.'

Blair has told his biographers that when he went to canvass for Labour during the Darlington by-election, just weeks before the general election, he telephoned the party secretary in Sedgefield and was refused any help. He said he got the impression that the seat was stitched up for Huckfield. That, certainly, was the impression he gave Foot, Kinnock and Hattersley.[9] But he must have known that the story was not true.

The first potential candidate to fall by the wayside in the political manoeuvrings over Sedgefield was David Watkins. It was his third and final doomed attempt to remain in the Commons. His Consett constituency was to be abolished in the boundary reorganisation and most people expected Ernest Armstrong to agree to switch seats to help Watkins. The idea was that, in that group of County Durham seats, if all the sitting MPs moved round one, there would have been no need for any fresh blood in the new Sedgefield seat. But there had been bad blood between Armstrong and Watkins in the Commons and Armstrong was determined to stay in the seat he held, Durham North West. (Later, it turned out that his aim was to keep the seat warm for his daughter, Hilary.) Watkins then tried unsuccessfully to challenge Giles Radice in Durham North.[10] In Sedgefield he secured nominations from the engineering union AEU, only to lose them the moment Les Huckfield dramatically turned up on the scene.

Joel Barnett, who thought he was a frontrunner, had expected to get Burlison's support. He didn't. Blair had already made a striking impact on Burlison when he failed to get the parliamentary nomination in Middlesborough – and Burlison, lobbied by the Labour leadership, decided that he preferred this time to give his union's backing to a young, energetic candidate rather than a Commons retread, no matter how distinguished.

Sid Weighell fell victim to a very clever 'dirty tricks' campaign by another young and energetic GMB union official, Nick Brown. Today, Brown, an ex-minister and MP for Newcastle-upon-Tyne East, is regarded as the authentic voice of Gordon Brown, so much so that the well-known chronicler of the Blair–Brown relationship, journalist Andrew Rawnsley, quips that they even share the same surname. But in 1983 Nick Brown had never met Gordon. He was a good friend of Blair who was a regular visitor to Newcastle.

Brown was regularly teased by his Geordie mates about Blair – 'You're all right but if we'd known about Tony, we'd have had him instead,' they used to say. They also used to boast about the time Blair was sent out by Willie Allen, a local GMB activist, to a rough Newcastle chippie to get fish and chips for his mates. The story of Blair with his posh Oxbridge accent being sent trudging through the alleyways among the back-to-back terraces in Nick Brown's constituency to a very down-at-heel chippie gained in the telling as Blair became more famous.

A friend of Burlison, Brown was only too willing to help Blair in Sedgefield, and was told to make sure other candidates did not prosper. When Weighell came into the union's offices in Newcastle to try and get a list of local members to canvass for support, he couldn't understand why there was so little information available in party files. But there was a very good reason. Tipped off about his visit, Brown had deliberately misfiled the data. So Weighell went away empty-handed. Blair, of course, already had the list. The 'black arts' that would later make Brown a respected government whip were already in evidence. Even today, Weighell's old friends are still puzzled about why he couldn't get any support.

Joe Mills — no fan of the candidate favoured by local TGWU branches, Les Huckfield — had been approached by Giles Radice, the former GMB head of research and now an MP, who had urged him to support Blair. Radice had dined with Blair and was impressed with his abilities. Radice's intervention led to Mills ringing Roy Hattersley to check him out. Hattersley says: 'Joe Mills telephoned me and John Smith and said, "What is Tony Blair like?" We said: "Do your best for him, he's good."'

Blair, meanwhile found Trimdon, the one branch in Sedgefield Labour Party which had not nominated a candidate. This is where the authorised version of his selection begins. He telephoned the Trimdon branch secretary, John Burton. Burton arranged for Blair to come to his house on an evening when four other key people in the branch were going to be there. He had made no such thoughtful arrangements for Pimlott. He must have known that Blair already had the powerful backing of the union barons, for Burton was not some innocent abroad in the murkier depths of Labour politics. He was a county councillor, and he knew the regional union barons Mills and Burlison well.

The Trimdon five liked Blair, decided to back him, and planned a campaign. 'Here was this young public-school and Oxford lawyer coming to an area that had always had a mining MP,' says Burton. 'But the pits had closed and people were travelling to factories in Hartlepool and Aycliffe.'

Burton's deep local roots compensated for Blair's lack of them. (Blair's early childhood in an affluent Durham suburb, and his attendance at the very splendid Durham Choristers School, hardly counted as local roots in Sedgefield.) Burton is a stout, comfortable, sociable, pipe-smoking teacher, then aged forty-two and head of physical education at the local comprehensive school. Hail-fellow-well-met and popular with everyone, he is a talented folk musician who plays the banjo and likes a pint or several in local pubs. His father had been a county councillor before him. Local Labour party meetings were always full of people whom he had taught, or played football with, or who remembered his father.

Even so, the key man was not Burton, but the chairman of Trimdon branch, Micky Terrens, who was also chairman of both the council and the constituency Labour party, a TGWU man and the real fixer in the constituency. He was an old friend, not only of Burton's, but of Burton's father too. Micky Terrens (his real name was George, but everyone called him Micky) has been virtually written out of the authorised version of the selection, but it was his various posts, and his skill at manipulating procedure, that delivered Sedgefield for Blair.

Terrens was the sort of chairman who knows procedure inside out and uses it to get what he wants. Terrens and Joe Mills are both now dead, and Blair and Burton aren't saying, but there is little doubt that Terrens and Mills had already hatched a secret plot to deliver the seat for Blair.

Burton, in haste, convened a meeting of Trimdon Village branch for that Saturday so that Blair could be nominated. Other candidates had to be invited too, and several, including Les Huckfield and Hilary Armstrong, turned up. But when it came to the votes, Micky Terrens, in the chair, blithely disregarded the proper procedure in order to get Blair the nomination. Instead of putting all the names of the candidates who wanted a nomination to a vote, which is what Labour Party rules prescribed, he simply asked members to vote on whether they wished to nominate Blair. Blair spoke briefly, he seemed a nice young man and, almost absent-mindedly, Trimdon Village branch kick-started the most remarkable political career of modern times by 12 votes to 4.[11]

Terrens came out to where the other candidates were waiting and said: 'We've decided to nominate young Blair because he's the only one of you lot that hasn't got a nomination.' This was being economical with the truth.

Blair slept at Burton's house, and on Sunday Paul Trippett, one of the five who had been at Burton's house that first night, drove him round to visit as many as possible of the delegates to the selection conference. Blair knocked at every door, cold-calling – a remarkable thing to do, and the sign of a really determined politician. He did not ask for support, for he knew that most of them had nominated one of the other candidates. He just asked them to vote to put him on the short list.[12]

On 18 May, in the middle of the general election campaign, while Michael Foot, a month away from his seventieth birthday, bravely hauled himself round a schedule that would have exhausted a thirty-year-old, the executive of Sedgefield Labour Party drew up its proposed short list of six from the sixteen candidates who had nominations from one or more of the branches. Blair's name was in front of them thanks to that last-minute nomination from Trimdon Village branch. But the left-dominated executive decided on a short list which included neither Blair, nor Weighell, nor Joel Barnett. It did include both Huckfield and Pat McIntyre, but also rightwingers such as Warren McCourt, the council leader.[13]

The next day, the general committee – a much bigger body than the executive, with 111 delegates – met to approve the short list. Once again, even more than in Trimdon, Terrens' strong chairmanship was the crucial factor working for Blair. Blair by then had a second nomination, from a TGWU branch, fixed for him by Joe Mills.

The meeting, held at Spennymoor town hall, had the right to add any of the nominated names it wished to the six-strong short list submitted by the executive. Candidates were not allowed into the meeting. The names of those not short-listed were put to the meeting in alphabetical order, so Hilary Armstrong was put first, then Joel Barnett. No one proposed that either of them be added, so the chairman moved on quickly. This must have come as a nasty shock to Barnett. He never knew that the trade union fix he was promised had by then been transferred to Tony Blair. The reason Barnett never made the short list, according to those who remember the meeting, was that he had only one nomination; but then Blair originally had only one nomination, too. What Blair had was the support of the regional trade union barons. By then, Joe Mills had telephoned several of the TGWU people and told them they ought to support Blair.

Then came Tony Blair. John Burton had been lobbying people as they walked in. Now he proposed that Blair be added to the shortlist: 'I have here a letter from Michael Foot thanking Tony for his performance in the Beaconsfield by-election and stating that he would like to see him in the House of Commons as soon as possible.' Of course, as a Huckfield supporter pointed out, this was a standard letter; the leader sent something similar to most unsuccessful by-election candidates.[14]

After a short debate, Terrens put it to the vote, and announced in firm tones that the addition of Tony Blair had been carried by 41 votes to 40. What he did not say – and what has been kept secret until now – was that these figures were given him by just one of his three tellers. Another teller said it was a tie, 41–41. And the third had Blair defeated by 41 votes to 40. Terrens, loyal TGWU man that he was, was doing all he could to deliver the nomination to Mills's man, by choosing to announce only the figure which favoured Blair.[15] Bill Waters, the teller who had given that figure, said to John Burton afterwards: 'You owe me a pint.'[16]

Burton has a slightly different version of these votes. Years ago, he told John Rentoul that there were two tellers who came up with slightly different figures, but that both gave Blair victory. Today, Burton has remembered that there was a third teller and says this third teller gave the vote as a tie – which would have meant that two tellers had votes in favour of Blair being added to the shortlist, and one had a tied vote. But the embarrassing truth is that Blair might not have got the Sedgefield nomination if the chairman had not suppressed an unfavourable result. ·

A lesser chairman would not have got away with it. One leftwing delegate, Brian Gibson, had an inkling what was going on and tried to challenge Terrens' ruling. There was ten minutes of angry debate, while the Fire Brigades Union delegates, who had their own candidate, started chanting: 'Recount! Recount!' Terrens blustered his way through. Gibson talked quickly to Huckfield's aide Alan Meale and said there should be a legal challenge. Meale said it did not matter; he was sure the real threat was Warren McCourt. But Gibson, who knew a political machine cranking up when he saw one, told him: 'No it isn't. The danger's Tony Blair.'[17]

For Blair, there was everything to play for.

The day after the general committee had approved the short list, extended from six names to seven to include Blair, the full selection meeting was held. As the 119 delegates were getting ready to leave their homes and go to the meeting, Joe Mills was working the phones. One TGWU branch secretary took a call from Mills as he was about to leave his house and get into a minibus to take him and seven other voting TGWU delegates to the meeting. 'If Joe had phoned five minutes later he'd have been too late and we'd all have voted for Huckfield,' he said later. At the same time Burton and Terrens were lobbying their council colleagues hard. It is fairly reliably estimated that twenty branches switched to Blair from Huckfield or McIntyre in the twenty-four hours before the vote.[18]

Each of the seven candidates on the short list spoke for ten minutes and then took questions. Questions at these meetings are often placed by your opponents to embarrass you and have been carefully researched for this purpose, so Blair cannot have been surprised when a leftwing delegate pointed out that his wife Cherie was standing for a Southern seat; if they were both elected, where would the family live? It was important to several delegates that their MP should live in the constituency. He replied that, regardless of anything that happened down south, he would live in the constituency; something which he has never done and can hardly have had any intention of doing. He also confirmed unblushingly that he was a member of the Campaign for Nuclear Disarmament, though he later denied ever having been a member.[19]

Les Huckfield was asked why he had not stayed to fight the good fight in his former constituency of Nuneaton. This question had been provided by Joe Mills – and he in his turn had been given it right from the top, in a telephone call from his own boss, TGWU general secretary Moss Evans. John Burton says: 'I was given three questions for Huckfield and they all came from Moss Evans.'

After three ballots, only four of the seven candidates remained. Blair led with 51 votes, followed by Huckfield with 32, McIntyre with 20, and McCourt with 16. McCourt was eliminated, and nearly all his second preferences went to Blair. On the next ballot McIntyre was eliminated, and on the final ballot Blair beat Huckfield by 73 votes to 46.[20] 'No, I haven't got Sedgefield,' Hilary Armstrong snapped to a councillor in a neighbouring constituency. 'Some bloody lawyer from London's got Sedgefield.' Now the bloody lawyer from London is prime minister, Armstrong serves him faithfully as his chief whip.

Blair and his wife Cherie accepted a post-selection dinner invitation from Pat McIntyre and her husband Vin. Blair's precious ability to be all things to all men served him well again, for at the end of the evening the McIntyres were sure he was not really, as Pat puts it, 'of the right'. 'How wrong we were,' she says now. Vin thought he was 'more interested in politicking than politics'.

Outside Sedgefield, there was only one other equally late selection. That, too, had its own long-term significance. Robin Corbett had been driven out of his seat in Hemel Hempstead, where he had been an MP for several years, by a particularly sharp-toothed Bennite, Paul Boateng, for denying the gospel according to Tony Benn. At the last moment, Corbett was selected for Birmingham Erdington, where he ran an energetic campaign and won the seat against the swing. His Hemel Hempstead supporters, disgusted by Boateng's behaviour, deserted their town to come and canvass for Corbett. Boateng came a poor third in Hemel Hempstead. 'Me? Gloat?' said Corbett privately afterwards. 'Not half.' But Boateng had his revenge. He got into Parliament at the next general election, and when Blair became Prime Minister, Corbett was considered too Old Labour for government office. Boateng, on the other hand, did a swift somersault and became, like many Bennites, an enthusiastic Blair supporter. He now sits on the frontbench and pours the same vitriolic abuse on those who deny the gospel according to Blair.

There was never any chance of Labour losing Sedgefield. All the same, just as he had done in Beaconsfield, Blair insisted on canvassing the Tory areas just as hard as Labour's heartlands. It was a revelation to Burton, who had once joked that the way to handle the Tory areas was not to tell them that the election was on. He remembers Blair saying: 'We've got to win villages and towns in the South of England that are even more affluent than this if we are ever going to form a government.'

During the campaign, the proprietor of a Trimdon taxi firm, Mr Elliott, placed a £10 bet with a local bookie that Blair would be prime minister one day. It eventually won him £5,000. Today, Mr Elliott explains why he placed the bet: 'He was a Labour man but unlike the other Labour men, he dressed right and he spoke well.'

Meanwhile, back in London, the Labour Party headquarters was beginning its long autopsy of the most incompetent general election campaign ever run by a major political party.

Michael Foot and the deputy leader Denis Healey were given long, punishing schedules in which they addressed audiences of the faithful, because that was what Labour's national organisers, David Hughes and Joyce Gould, thought would work. The campaign was frozen into inaction by a vast and unwieldy campaign committee which met every morning. Jim Innes from Labour's London media office, who kept a diary of the campaign, recorded the following account.

> Average attendance at this decision-making committee is between thirty and forty. There are not enough seats in the general secretary's office, so our leaders are perched on tables or lined up along the walls. One chap was in there for the first two days and nobody recognised him. On the third day someone asked who he was.

He turned out to be the Special Branch officer assigned to Foot.[21]

Innes and senior press officer Monica Foot were given the task of dealing with television and radio, but had to queue up behind regional organisers whenever they wanted top politicians to perform. Innes described how this worked in practice:

> I go to Healey's people and say I think he should do such and such a programme. If his diary's got a gap he may do it. If my powers of persuasion are working, he may do it. If not, he won't. I fight for Healey's time and my opponents in this fight are the national or regional or constituency agents. It means that for the next few weeks I work for the radio stations. The Tories manipulate them and then they manipulate me. The Labour Party just pays my wages.[22]

Even worse, it meant that when Foot, Healey and other shadow cabinet members did go to a radio or television studio, they came straight from their gruelling schedule, tired and with no time to prepare or even think.

Joyce Gould once rang the media office in a towering rage because one of the regional organisers had complained that he had waited several hours for an answer to an enquiry. The press office explained they had been inundated with media calls, and Gould replied icily: 'Yes, but it's a matter of priorities.' It was; and Labour had the wrong ones.

That is why, afterwards, the new leader, Neil Kinnock – and later Blair and Peter Mandelson – were so determined to change the balance of power within the party so that the media had greater priority. The trouble was that their cure was in some ways worse than the disease. Asked during the 1983 campaign to allow the media people more leeway, Joyce Gould had memorably said that Labour was not going to be 'sold like soap flakes'. But selling it like soap flakes did not work either.

The campaign sometimes descended from the incompetent into the absurd. When a political party which is critically split has to decide on an election slogan, the key consideration is how to invent one without alienating either faction. That is how Labour ended up in 1983 with the rightly derided slogan: 'Think positive, act positive, vote Labour.'

The worst spinoff from this slogan was kept from public gaze: a dreadful campaign song built around it, which went, in part:

> If you and me
> Believe in democracy
> We're going to put
> Michael Foot
> In the league where he belongs.

The media team's one success of the 1983 campaign was to suppress this song. Just six copies of the lyrics were made, and one was kept as a memento by each of the six press officers who, as the campaign progressed on its dreary way, tried to revive their flagging spirits by dancing round the press room, singing the whole song at the tops of their voices under Jim Innes' energetic direction.

As the scale of the disaster became obvious, Gerald Kaufman approached Foot and asked him to stand down in Healey's favour. Foot refused. One of the present authors, Francis Beckett, was a Labour press officer, and approached Kaufman soon after this meeting, to ask him to do an interview. 'Fuck off,' said Kaufman. When you are a press officer on a temporary contract and a leading member of the shadow cabinet tells you to fuck off, off you fuck. Only Michael Foot and Roy Hattersley managed to maintain their thoughtfulness and courtesy throughout

The result, as everyone knew it would be, was a landslide for Thatcher. Labour was lucky not to be beaten into third place by the SDP/Liberal Alliance. As dawn broke on 10 June, Foot and Healey addressed their headquarters staff, after Foot had been driven back to London at breakneck speed from his Welsh constituency where he had conceded victory to the Conservatives. Foot spoke with courage and dignity, and the hundred or so people in the room, even those who had opposed his leadership, felt nothing but affection and respect for this decent, intelligent, elderly man who had driven himself so hard for a hopeless cause.

Healey, also dignified but looking pinched and ill, struck a critical note. The leaders, he said, must never again be given such a ridiculous schedule. Foot said nothing, but as he left the room he made a point of embracing Joyce Gould, who had devised the schedule. Gould was another apparatchik who would later stand on her head as the Blair star rose, and enthusiastically endorse the new media-centred strategy.

Soon after the election, just after the state opening of Parliament, there was a long-planned public meeting in Sedgefield. Veteran leftwinger Dennis Skinner had been booked as a visiting speaker. Brian Gibson, who chaired the meeting, still shivers as he remembers it.

> The first speaker was from Militant. Then there was Pat McIntyre, who was as always calm and measured. Then Blair got up, talked about the splendour of the state opening of Parliament, said: 'By the way, did you know the queen wore glasses?' Then about how we've got to modernise, change, forget all the things you learned at your mother's knee. And as he was speaking I saw Dennis Skinner frown and tear up all his speech notes. I thought, 'Oh dear, what's coming?'
> Then Skinner got up, said to the audience, 'I apologise for turning sideways to you but I've got something to say to the person beside me.' And he turned to Blair and says: 'Don't you ever tell me to forget what I learned at my mother's knee,' and he lectured Blair for what seemed like an hour. After the meeting Blair went to Vin McIntyre at the back of the hall and said 'I think I've been set up.' And Vin said: 'No, you set your-self up.' Vin told me about this conversation, so I wrote to Blair after-wards saying we didn't set him up.

A few days later, Blair telephoned Gibson and asked to meet him for a pint at the Labour Club. Gibson, among other things, was secretary of the local trades council, and to his amazement Blair asked him what the trades council was. Gibson said: 'Don't say I've got to start from scratch with someone like you.' He explained that it was the local branch of the Trades Union Congress, and he talked Blair through the structure of the TUC. After that, says Gibson, people from Trimdon started appearing at trades council meetings, and within a year one of Blair's Trimdon sup-porters had displaced Gibson as trades council secretary.

A couple of weeks after the election, Blair was in London, in the then rather gloomy basement of St Stephen's Tavern, opposite the House of Commons, a favourite MPs' watering hole, with his old Hackney friend Charles Clarke. 'I do recognise,' he said with that becoming boyish mod-esty he does so well, 'that I'm the luckiest person here.' But luck, as Mae West might have put it, had nothing to do with it.

CHAPTER SIX

THE EARLY KINNOCK YEARS

For Charles Clarke there was a purpose to that apparently chance meeting with Blair in St Stephen's Tavern. As Neil Kinnock's political adviser, he was charged with the task of getting Kinnock elected as Labour leader to replace Michael Foot. He wanted the newly elected MP's vote.

Clarke might have expected an uphill struggle to wean his prey away from the candidate of the party's rightwing, Roy Hattersley. Blair was a member of Hattersley's organisation for the Labour right, Solidarity. Hattersley was the Solidarity candidate, Kinnock the candidate of the soft (that is, anti-Bennite) left. Blair knew Hattersley and had far more in common politically with him than with Kinnock. And Hattersley's campaign manager was Blair's closest friend among Labour's top brass, John Smith, the Scottish lawyer who was close to Blair's old pupil-master at the Bar, Derry Irvine, and with whom Blair had frequently dined.

But Clarke found that he had only to ask the question to get Blair's pledge for Kinnock. This came as a mildly unpleasant surprise to Hattersley, though he retained his affection and respect for Blair for many more years (he has completely lost it now). He compares Blair's behaviour unfavourably with that of John Smith, who 'stayed with my campaign even though it was obvious we were going to lose. When the general secretary of the GMB trade union, David Basnett, wanted to back out of my campaign. Smith went to see him to tell him he had a duty to his members.'[1]

A third candidate, Peter Shore, was pleased when Sedgefield's new MP turned up to his campaign meeting. Shore's campaign manager Bryan Gould observed at the time that Blair 'obviously thought the House of Commons was like going up to university – you went to the Buddhists and you went to the Communists and you picked up their literature and you decided which of the clubs you'd join.'[2] Gould, who years later, after leaving politics, admitted to having been a rather naïve politician, had no idea that Blair had already pledged his vote to Kinnock. Like many others, he was taken in by Blair's ingénue act. Attending the meeting was Blair's way of putting himself about, quietly, modestly, discreetly, but so that he would be remembered kindly.

In fact, neither Shore nor Hattersley had a chance of getting Blair's vote, because neither of them was going to win. Right from the start, the Kinnock bandwagon was unstoppable. Blair, like many another ambitious politician, quickly hitched himself to the winning candidate.

Briefly, after he had entered the Commons, Blair found himself sharing a small office with Dave Nellist, one of the two Labour MPs who were members of the Militant Tendency, but swiftly found someone more congenial to share with – Gordon Brown, the newly elected young Scottish MP. Brown, as everyone now knows, was a crucial friend and mentor to Blair in those early days. Though the two men tended to agree about most things, Brown, unlike Blair, knew, understood and cared about the Labour Party, its history and its curious traditions. He had been a student politician, elected as the first student rector of Edinburgh University, and chairman of the Scottish Labour Party. His PhD thesis was on Jimmy Maxton, the romantic Labour Party hero of the first half of the twentieth century.

Unlike many barrister MPs, Blair did not continue his career at the Bar; he focused completely on his career as a politician. Tom Sawyer, then leader of the public-sector trade union NUPE and later to be Blair's choice as the Labour Party's general secretary, recalls him as 'unusually ambitious. He looked for people with influence in the party. I am sure I was one of a long stream of people who got a call from his office. "Would you like to come and have a cup of tea with Tony?"'[3]

Cherie, who had come third fighting the hopeless seat of Thanet, abided by the bargain she made with her husband and has made no further effort to make politics her career. She may already have known, while fighting Thanet, that she was pregnant with their first child. She seems to have accepted quickly that Tony was to be the politician in the family, and to have acquiesced to her role as the MP's wife as gracefully as she could manage, while continuing her career at the Bar. It was probably the right decision. Although she has a more powerful brain than her husband, she does not have his precious political skill of never making an unnecessary enemy. Moreover, she can be abrasive and occasionally short-tempered.

Cherie did get herself elected to the Labour Co-ordinating Committee, on a slate put forward to ensure that the rightwing of the party stayed in control of that organisation: the Bennites were trying to take it back. But after three years she quietly dropped out even of that, and she has not been actively involved in politics since then. She spent weekdays as a barrister and weekends in Sedgefield. On those weekends, the Blairs always took metropolitan friends with them: neither of them seems to have wanted to be stuck all weekend with the locals.[4]

One of the most frequent visitors was the journalist John Lloyd – now an ardent Blairite. A highly intellectual, rather pompous and humourless one-time communist, Lloyd was then industrial editor on the *Financial Times*. He was immersed in Labour politics in a way that Blair was not. He at first thought Blair was not sufficiently committed to the rightwing of the Labour Party, describing him as a 'trendy lefty'.[5] As he got to know Blair, he became an uncritical admirer, and today gets unaccountably upset at any criticism of his hero – his indignant denunciations of the prime minister's critics became angrier and more frequent after the Iraq war. Blair has that effect on some people.

On those weekends, Cherie would organise general-knowledge quizzes with visiting journalists and local party luminaries, and she always won: she possesses an amazingly well-stocked mind and instant recall. One local Labour party member has noted: 'Tony won't join [in] quizzes because he is not as good as Cherie.'[6]

Blair was also the only MP among his Hackney group. John Carr had unsuccessfully fought Hertford and Bishop's Stortford, and his career today is outside politics. Ben Pimlott, beaten to Sedgefield by Blair, eventually returned to his history books. Charles Clarke still saw his future not in Parliament, but as the power behind a Kinnock premiership.

Supporting Kinnock in 1983 was a good career move. It's hard today to recall what an exciting politician Neil Kinnock once was. Those who remember only the damaged, diminished, defeated, demoralised figure who gave up the party leadership in 1992 can have little idea of the passion and promise of Labour's forty-one-year-old star of 1983.

Short and sturdy, with thinning red hair and an air of permanent excitement, a man who genuinely could not stand still, Kinnock regularly had huge audiences laughing and crying with him. He had the burning socialist passion that came from a poor but secure South Wales mining childhood, together with an ear for a soundbite: 'Now, the cabinet wets – by the way, you know why they call them that?' he asked an enraptured audience in Darlington in 1983. 'It's because that's what they do when she shouts at them.'

Kinnock was young and very human. He wore his heart on his sleeve. He struggled unsuccessfully to give up cigarettes (and continues to do so). He had the air of the great political leader whom the generation that had been students in the sixties were waiting for. He seemed, as Tony Blair seemed a decade later, untainted by the compromises, vendettas and manoeuvrings of the past.

He had the quick wit and the confidence to take on and beat the old bruisers of the day. Confronted on television by Norman Tebbit, who sneered that Labour had 'lurched' to the left, he jabbed back: 'Parties do change. If they didn't, we'd still have nice old Ted Heath instead of this gang of barbarians.' The word 'barbarians' came from his close friend and father figure Michael Foot (Kinnock's own parents were dead), who regularly used it to describe the Thatcher government. Kinnock was the Aneurin Bevan of his time: a man of the left imbued with the revivalist socialism of the Welsh valleys. Foot was Bevan's biographer and Kinnock's mentor.

Kinnock was untainted by the Bennites. Repelled by their vindictive, sectarian methods, he had broken with them conclusively over the deputy-leadership election in 1982.

He had been sharp enough to see that the 1983 general election campaign was a shambles, and he arranged his own programme and his own press conferences without reference to the party machine. He showed that he knew a good story when he saw one. One of the present authors, Francis Beckett, a Labour Party press officer in 1983, received a leak from the National Economic Development Council, a minute quoting the CBI chairman as saying that anyone who knew the truth about Britain's industrial situation would want to take the first boat out of the country. The party was frightened of using the quote, so Beckett offered it unofficially to Kinnock, who employed it to score one of Labour's few election successes.

Two days before polling day, his voice almost destroyed by three weeks of non-stop campaigning, he told an audience in South Wales, and a much wider one through national television: 'If Mrs Thatcher wins on Thursday, I warn you not to be ordinary, I warn you not to be young. I warn you not to fall ill. I warn you not to get old.'

But the Kinnock leadership had potential weaknesses. A remarkably prescient memorandum written jointly on 24 June 1983 by Nigel Stanley and Peter Hain (the latter had been brought over into Labour by Kinnock from a high-profile role in the Liberals and suffered the humiliation of having pennies thrown at him at his first appearance at a Tribune rally) summed them up:

Neil's leadership will either act as a midwife to the rebirth of the party as a mass force in British politics again, or preside over its collapse into a totally marginal force. The alternatives, we feel, are as stark and as serious as that …

Neil's leadership must help bring about the quickest transformation the party has ever experienced, by providing the direction needed to reverse a decline dangerously close to terminal.

Everyone knows [Neil] is the party's best platform orator, that he is excellent on TV, that he can rally the party faithful and provide a basis for internal unity. They are his existing strengths. But they are not sufficient for winning power.

The problem with this was that Kinnock himself took this sort of talk too seriously, and thought it required him to develop an entirely new persona, with disastrous results.

Such was the man who became Labour leader in October 1983. The runner-up, Roy Hattersley, became deputy leader – largely out of loyalty to the party and a sense of duty, for he knew that the deputy leadership was a miserable task. Kinnock and Hattersley set about the task of saving the Labour Party from itself. It wore them both out, Kinnock especially.

No one yet knew that the main beneficiary of all their expenditure of energy, enthusiasm and reforming zeal would be a young man of just thirty called Tony Blair, one of only thirty-two newcomers to the Labour benches in the House of Commons. Most people had never heard of him, although he had ensured that the people who mattered in the Labour Party – Kinnock, Hattersley, John Smith, Bryan Gould – knew exactly who he was.

Kinnock and Hattersley made Blair's 1997 election victory possible. The coalition, and the circumstances, that were to make Blair prime minister just fourteen years later came together in those first two years of his parliamentary career, 1983–5. They were the years when Kinnock and Hattersley took their party by the scruff of its neck and taught it some of the basic facts of life. They were the years during which the party accepted the need to employ professional marketing techniques. And this transitional period culminated in 1985 with the appointment of Peter Mandelson as Labour's director of campaigns and communications. If Mandelson had not got that job in 1985, Blair might well not have won the leadership in 1994.

During those two years, Kinnock had the bounce kicked out of him. He had his fingers burnt in newspaper interviews a couple of times, and vicious attacks from rightwing tabloids punctured his skin – a relatively thin skin for a top politician. The magic went out of his relationship with journalists. A few days after his election he told a broadcaster: 'Don't tell me how to do television – I became leader by being good on telly'; but his sure broadcasting touch started to desert him as he began weighing every word and waffling to conceal policy divisions. The long war of attrition against Militant and the Bennite left sucked his strength and enthusiasm from him. The little Welsh magician in the loud hound's-tooth jacket who had taken his party by storm and looked set to win over the nation started to wrap himself up in grey flannel suits and grey woollen phrases.

It happened for several reasons – and one was the emergence of what we now know as the Blairites. Neil Kinnock suddenly, perhaps for the first time in his adult life, felt unsure of himself.

He knew that he was young and inexperienced for the job of leader. He could have become the first person since Ramsay Macdonald in 1924 to become prime minister without ever having served in a government. And he was made, quite unjustly, to feel intellectually inferior. Hugo Young wrote in the *Guardian* that he had 'a pass degree in Industrial Relations from Swansea University on the second try in a bad year'. It was a snobbish jibe but 'it haunted Neil', according to Roy Hattersley.[7] Kinnock knew that every prime minister since 1945 had been an Oxford graduate, except for Churchill and Callaghan, neither of whom had been to university. He happened to have a few senior colleagues who were politicians of great intellectual distinction, such as Hattersley, John Smith, Denis Healey and Michael Foot. 'If only he could have got over his sense of intellectual inferiority,' says Hattersley.

In fact, Hattersley may, without intending to, have contributed to the problem. The two never quite clicked. Kinnock appreciated his older deputy's unwavering loyalty, but never seemed sure what he was thinking. Hattersley admired his leader's courage and determination, but was privately sure that he had the more powerful intellect (he probably has). 'Neil and I got on,' he wrote years later. 'We were never soul mates. Perhaps we were not even "pals" – Neil's definition of the proper relationship between leader and deputy,' he added, rather loftily.[8] Even today, the interplay between them when they meet is forced, with clumsy attempts at playfulness. But to the great credit of both men, they made an effort in public, and the obvious strains that characterise the present relationship between Blair and Gordon Brown were never in evidence.

Kinnock had a personality that people instinctively trusted; that was what got him elected as leader. But instead of building on this, he listened to advisers who assured him that what he needed was political and intellectual gravitas. Cambridge graduate Charles Clarke became his chief of staff and persuaded him to bring in Clarke's college friend Patricia Hewitt as his press officer. Hewitt, like Mandelson, had no experience with the media, but Kinnock was told that he did not need that – he himself could provide the media experience. Hewitt would contribute political and intellectual sophistication.

Clarke was Kinnock's most loyal lieutenant, and Kinnock has always returned Clarke's loyalty in full measure; however, Hattersley says: 'Charles did Neil great harm. He always thought he had to protect Neil from situations which in fact Neil could handle perfectly well.'9 A lobby journalist who is close to Clarke echoes this assessment: 'I think he was bad for Kinnock. Charles was so tense himself, he created a lot of tension in Neil. Charles is sometimes boorish and sounds like a thug, though he's not a thug.'

Hewitt, meanwhile, erected a barrier between Kinnock and the lobby journalists and stopped him from taking on television interviews in which she feared he would be nailed on policy. It started in her very first week in the job, when she abruptly cancelled the leader's appearance on *Weekend World* because, according to Kinnock's biographer Martin Westlake, 'She believed Kinnock needed more time to prepare for what would have been a searching interview by Brian Walden, especially after the programme failed to undertake not to question him on policy matters.' It is not clear how she thought a serious political programme could possibly give such an undertaking. She told the Westminster lobby correspondents, who were used to the old, genial, witty Kinnock, that all contact with him had to go through her. And she phased out Kinnock's own lobby briefings.10

Kinnock himself remembers a meeting with some local activists in Liverpool where, as he talked, Patricia Hewitt kept looking at him hard. Eventually she disappeared to the ladies', emerging seconds later to push a piece of lavatory paper into his hands, on which was written in lipstick: 'They are Millies' (that is, supporters of the Militant Tendency).

Hewitt even tried to keep the Labour leader from making faux pas among his own shadow cabinet. Kinnock recalls a visit to Glasgow with Donald Dewar during which the former spent a lot of time in the back seat of the car extolling the virtues of Derry Irvine, Blair's legal mentor and friend: 'Great man, Derry, he's doing a splendid job giving us legal advice on how to defeat Militant.' He couldn't understand why he kept getting black looks from Hewitt. When they got to the destination she took him aside and whispered: 'Don't you know Donald's wife has just gone off with Derry? It is not very tactful, all that.' 'How was I supposed to know about that, I'm not expected to know who's sleeping with who, am I?' was Kinnock's response. But he didn't raise the subject again with Dewar after that.[11]

It is hard to resist the conclusion that the so-called Kinnockites did not trust their man not to bungle things if let out without his leash. They never felt that way about Blair. And they were wrong in their assessment of Kinnock. Sadly for Kinnock, he started to accept their worst estimate of his abilities.

It was Clarke who persuaded Kinnock to back the appointment of Oxford graduate Peter Mandelson as Labour head of campaigns and communications in June 1985.[12] It is one of New Labour's most enduring myths that their hero Mandelson single-handedly turned round the party's communications after 1985. The truth is that Mandelson came to the job knowing next to nothing about public relations, marketing or journalism. All the means of making Labour electable again were in place by the time he arrived. All he had to do was to take credit for them, which he did very efficiently.

For example, Mandelson is often credited with having set up the famous Shadow Communications Agency, but its first meeting took place months before his appointment and he had absolutely nothing to do with it. On 21 March 1985 Robin Cook, the shadow cabinet member with responsibility for campaigning, wrote to a few experts in public relations and marketing. They included Chris Powell, managing director of the advertising agency Boase Massimi Pollitt, who had worked on Ken Livingstone's highly praised 'Save the GLC' campaign; Bob Worcester of MORI, Labour's pollsters; Labour communications director Nick Grant; Colin Fisher of the strategic marketing company SRU (who was to play a crucial but shadowy part in Mandelson's political rise); as well as one of the authors of this book, Francis Beckett.

'On Thursday next [28 March] at 7.30 p.m. I am holding a brainstorming session with a few people in the marketing business to work out a strategy for Labour to the next election, and would like you to come,' Cook wrote. 'It is being held in Colin Fisher's office at 78 St John Street, London EC1.' At that first meeting the concept of the Shadow Communications Agency emerged.

Later that year, Nick Grant announced his resignation. Grant wanted to go – he had experienced a searing couple of years in the communications job – but his wishes also coincided with those of his senior colleagues in Labour's headquarters, Joyce Gould and David Hughes, who were anxious to find a scapegoat for the dreadful 1983 election campaign, and had selected Grant for the role. Grant had in fact been appointed a matter of weeks before the general election and had had no chance at all to affect the strategy – unlike long-serving top officials Gould and Hughes. 'Nick Grant carried a can he did not deserve,' says Bob Worcester of MORI. 'Labour headquarters tried to pin the result on him.'[13]

The myth of Grant's incompetence suited not only Gould and Hughes, but also several Labour politicians; and later on it suited Peter Mandelson. At the time even Robin Cook was heard to squeak indignantly in a Westminster restaurant: 'Are you seriously suggesting we could ever win a general election with Nick Grant in that job?' Grant became public affairs adviser to Robert Maxwell, and later founded a successful media research company, Mediatrack.

Jim Mortimer, the party's general secretary, retired and was replaced by Larry Whitty, head of research at the General, Municipal and Boilermakers trade union (GMB). Whitty was Kinnock's key lieutenant in the process of turning Labour into an election-winning party, staying in the job until he was abruptly fired by Blair in 1994.

With Grant and Mortimer gone, Gould and Hughes were able to pretend that the party had been purged of the men of 1983, and they were themselves appointed to two of the three new 'directorates' being created in Labour headquarters. The search was on for the head of the third directorate – a new director of campaigns and communications to replace Nick Grant.

Kinnock at first backed the *Scotsman* journalist David Gow, and then Denis MacShane, at the time the Geneva-based head of communications at a trade union international and a former BBC journalist. But Blair's old Hackney friend Charles Clarke persuaded him to back Hattersley's candidate, Peter Mandelson.

Mandelson inherited not only the Shadow Communications Agency, but also a pretty clear consensus about what needed to be changed. The outgoing deputy leader, Denis Healey, had sent Kinnock a terse and forthright paper:

> We did not properly appreciate the importance of the media ... . The travelling and speaking programmes of the leader and deputy leader should be more restricted, allowing more time for food, rest and thought ... Control far more tightly the occasions at which top politicians appear before the news cameras ... Leaders should get better constituency briefs – I got none at all, and was once sent to a factory which made parts of Argentinean warships ... Better facilities for radio and TV ... Did we really advertise in the *Economist*?[14]

The press officers for the 1983 campaign had written collectively to Kinnock immediately after the election:

> The Conservatives are skilled at news management. We were not organised even to attempt it ... Press conferences were chaired in the plonking style appropriate to trade union meetings. The chairman sat in the middle, instead of at the side, thereby denying television and photographers of human shots of shadow cabinet members together as a team ... . The campaign slogan was placed out of camera view (perhaps wisely in view of its unparalleled awfulness) ... . Party leaders arrived at press conferences with no proper briefing, and it showed. They had spent the previous hour in a large meeting at which the morning's press conference was just one item ... . The press office had the skills and facilities to help, but was not enabled to do so – no function had been contemplated for us other than that of keeping the press off everyone else's back ...

Similar comments came from other key officials. Graham Allen (later to become a government whip) wrote, in a failed application to become head of fund-raising in March 1983, 'The immense reservoir of goodwill and generosity within the movement is the party's most precious resource. That resource is presently mismanaged and squandered.' Frank Dobson – later to become health secretary – wrote in perhaps self-mocking tones: 'Melodrama is not my strong point but it is fair to say the future of our party as a major political force is in the balance.'[15]

There were very few places in the party, except perhaps for the wilder shores of the Bennite left, where this sort of thinking was not accepted after the 1983 debacle. When Kinnock became leader and told the party conference to remember how they had felt on election night and promise themselves they would never feel like that again, he was responding to a mood, not creating one.

So Mandelson did not have to create the mood for change – it was already there. He did not have to find the techniques or the experts – Cook had already done that. Not for Mandelson the business that had so wearied Nick Grant, of persuading top officials and politicians to take the subject seriously. Not for him the doorstepping of his own leaders, the process that Jim Innes had found so frustrating. Mandelson was pushing at an open door.

Now the party had decided that communications mattered, Mandelson was in a position of great power. He used it, vigorously and ruthlessly, to promote his friends in the party through the media, and to frustrate his enemies. He chose to promote two young men, about his own age, with whom he believed the future to lie, Tony Blair and Gordon Brown, as well as one rather more senior figure, Bryan Gould. He pruned the Shadow Communications Agency down to a steering committee of six: Chris Powell and two of his colleagues from BMP; Bob Worcester and his colleague Brian Gosschalk from MORI; and the ubiquitous Colin Fisher, whose firm, SRU, Mandelson was already familiar with, and who was to play a key part in the development of New Labour. Mandelson's own contribution to the team was his friend Philip Gould, whose star was to rise alongside Mandelson's.

By the time Mandelson arrived at Labour Party headquarters, Blair had already taken the first step up the ladder. In November 1984 Neil Kinnock sent for him and asked him to join shadow chancellor Roy Hattersley's frontbench team as its most junior member. (Kinnock had seen another promising young newcomer, Gordon Brown, twenty minutes earlier, and offered him a place in the Scottish office team, which Brown turned down because he did not want to be typecast as a Scottish politician. He joined the trade and industry team the following year.)

At the meeting Blair was modest, flattered, all downcast eyes and humility. 'Tony came in, he thought he was being called in for a bit of a wigging,' says Kinnock, but he was surely taken in by Blair's mock naïveté. Blair would have known that if he was to be ticked off, then the whips, not the leader, would send for him. 'I said, "I want you to go on the frontbench." He said, "Do you really mean it?" One of the women in my office told me he walked down the corridor in a daze.'[16] A politician who knew Blair well at the time says: 'I always think of Tony as wet behind the ears, so today I find the world figure hard to believe in. He was like a puppy dog.' He was not the only one to misjudge the future leader so entirely.

There is incontrovertible evidence that Blair was dissembling at that interview. He knew exactly why his leader had sent for him. Stuart Bell was offered an appointment by Kinnock at the same time and, days before, Kinnock's aide, Dick Clements, had tried to contact both of them – saying that they were about to be offered junior jobs. Blair, who was on holiday with Cherie in Normandy at the time, had been told by Bell that they were both likely to get posts.

Blair's new job was not that important in itself, but it was a remarkable promotion for a man of thirty-one who had only been an MP for seventeen months. Peter Hain, speaking for many on the soft left of the party, where Kinnock's support had come from, was upset at the contrast between the rapid promotion of the young lawyer and the exclusion of the experienced leftwinger Clare Short. He saw the hand of Roy

Hattersley – then still seen as a rightwinger – behind the appointment, and he was partly right: Hattersley had identified Blair as one of the party's brightest hopes.

But it was Kinnock who launched the meteoric parliamentary career which saw Blair become prime minister aged only forty-four. Without Kinnock's patronage, then and later, Blair would never have succeeded. However, the commentators who make the leap from this fact to the idea that Blair was Kinnock's ideological soulmate, the inheritor of the Kinnock mantle, are quite wrong. Blair has nothing at all in common with the political tradition from which Kinnock sprang and to which Kinnock remains true. Today, it is only by stretching his loyalty and discipline to the limit that Kinnock manages to avoid saying so publicly.

Blair, as we now know, admires the then prime minister, Margaret Thatcher; Kinnock loathes her and everything she stood for. Asked in a television interview in 1985 what three things he admired about her, he replied: 'Well, frankly, it might seem very uncharitable to you, but there aren't any.' This response was not broadcast: the passage was shot again, and this time Kinnock managed to come up with the answer that she had reached the top in a male-dominated world.[17]

By the time Blair joined his frontbench team, Kinnock was deeply enmeshed in the worst crisis of his leadership: the 1984–5 miners' strike. Margaret Thatcher had won the tactical battle with miners' leader Arthur Scargill before the strike even began, for Scargill led the miners out on strike during the summer, when industrial action would have least effect, and without a ballot of his members. Kinnock could hardly condemn the miners, but neither could he wholeheartedly support them. It was a personal misery for Kinnock, too: his was a mining family and some of the Labour leader's relatives were themselves on strike. The best possible outcome for him would have been a negotiated settlement, but both Thatcher and Scargill were determined that there should be no such thing. The strike ended, as it was bound to do, in humiliating defeat for the miners, on 5 March 1985, a year to the day after it began.

Tony Blair was not required to do much in this battle, and he shared none of Kinnock's personal feeling of involvement with the miners, but the strike certainly consolidated his thinking. Blair has the public-school boy's instinctive distrust of trade unions going on strike. The miners went down to a crushing defeat, and there was a lot of real hardship in mining communities as a result. You did not have to be a Scargill supporter to find it heartbreaking. But there is no doubt that even the cautious Kinnock line seemed to the young Tony Blair to be far too sympathetic.

The miners' strike was the main, but not the only, factor in making the mid-1980s the worst period of Kinnock's nine years as leader. He was also embarrassed by Ken Livingstone's reign at the Greater London Council, for 'Red Ken', as the tabloids had christened him, seemed to symbolise all the leftwing Labour tendencies that Kinnock wanted voters to forget.

On Clarke's advice, Kinnock threw away the chance to reach some agreement with Livingstone. Livingstone himself seems to have left the door open for some accomodation; he warned the left at the 1985 Tribune rally that 'we can't win by denouncing Kinnock'.[18] But for Clarke, the struggle with Livingstone was just another battle in the long war against 'the Trots', which he remembered with a shudder from his days as a student leader and from the time when he and Tony Blair were young Hackney politicians. A couple of months later, Tony Benn recorded in his diaries that Livingstone was now 'pessimistic about Kinnock'. Benn's hope was that after the next election, when Livingstone was expected to become an MP, the new intake 'would push him and David Blunkett to the forefront'. Blunkett at that time was identifiably on the Bennite left; he did not join the unseemly scramble of the Bennites to embrace Blairism until some years later.

Margaret Thatcher also provoked a battle with Labour-led councils on her own territory, by capping their rates and threatening to abolish the GLC. Kinnock was stuck in the middle again. He needed, and wanted, to support the councils, but he thought Livingstone's leadership played into Thatcher's hands. In some councils (though not Livingstone's GLC) Labour councillors voted to set an illegal rate, and Kinnock knew it would be electoral suicide to support them in this. Kinnock was also forced to spend valuable hours every week overseeing every aspect of his party's long battle to expel members of the Militant Tendency.

Liverpool Labour party, along with Liverpool city council, had fallen into the hands of Militant, and the council was effectively led by its flamboyant, sharp-suited deputy leader, Derek Hatton. At Labour's 1984 conference, Kinnock made one of the best, the most important, and the bravest speeches any Labour leader has ever delivered to conference. Three days before the conference opened, the Militant Liverpool councillors, starved of money by the government because of their defiance of its rate-capping measures, sent out redundancy notices to all their 31,000 staff.

Kinnock's speech could only have been made by a man with deep roots in the Labour Party. It is a speech that Blair could not have made. 'I'll tell you what happens with impossible promises,' Kinnock said. 'You start with far-fetched resolutions. They are then pickled into a rigid dogma, a code, and you go through the years sticking to that – outdated, misplaced, irrelevant to the real needs – and you end in the grotesque chaos of a Labour council – a *Labour* council – hiring taxis to scuttle round a city handing out redundancy notices to its own workers.'

It was, and it was intended to be, a declaration of war on the Liverpool Militants, a war Kinnock could have won quickly – except that David Blunkett, former leader of Sheffield council and a member of Labour's national executive, snatched near defeat from the jaws of Kinnock's victory. Blunkett, without telling Kinnock, did a behind-the-scenes compromise deal with Hatton. Hatton would withdraw his motion demanding support for the Liverpool councillors in return for a public pledge that the Labour leadership would visit Liverpool and try to find a way through the crisis.

When Blunkett came to sum up for the executive, instead of doing what Kinnock wanted, which was to nail Liverpool council, he publicly offered the deal, and asked Hatton to withdraw. Blunkett is blind and could not see what was going on in the hall, but a colleague whispered that Hatton was running to the platform. Alarmed that his deal would be torn to shreds by a rant from Hatton, he called out desperately: 'No, Derek, not a speech, just yes or no.' Hatton reached the microphone and said: 'Yes, in the interests of unity, Liverpool will withdraw its resolution.'

Blunkett had kept his credibility with the Bennite left for the time being. Kinnock was furious. Of course the proposed investigation produced a scheme that Hatton would not accept, as Kinnock knew it would. The stage was set for the long, grinding process of expelling Militant members from the Labour Party.

Blunkett's was the sort of lukewarm support that Kinnock was getting in those days from many of his colleagues, including Blair. Bob Worcester of MORI, Labour's pollsters since Harold Wilson's day, told the government frontbench that it was vital for them to continually reinforce Kinnock in every public statement they made. Kinnock's image, he told them, suffered because he was not perceived as capable or understanding of Britain's problems. With the sole exception of Roy Hattersley, they took little notice of this advice, says Worcester.[19] In March 1984 Worcester wrote to Kinnock:

> You may be interested to know that following my presentation to the
> shadow cabinet and my comment to your colleagues that they could
> help the effort by referring to you as 'capable', 'understanding of
> Britain's problems', etc, I was subject to criticism for my lack of political
> sensitivity, nous etc.[20]

Where was Blair in all this? His frontbench duties did not bring him into the frontline of the titanic struggle Kinnock was waging, and he did not seek to place himself there. He certainly approved, but the idea that he was one of those who buttressed Kinnock and tried to make his position more bearable is pure myth. He and Blunkett seemed, as they seem today, to be in the same camp, watching Kinnock's efforts with approval and interest, but not doing much to help. Nigel Stanley, who was Robin Cook's political adviser until 1986 and then adviser to Bryan Gould, says Blair was 'a non-practising Kinnockite'.[21]

So it seems that Blair was trying to keep his head down. He did, however, have an old debt to pay, and it was called in during 1986, the year after the miners' strike. That year, the general secretary of the GMB trade union, David Basnett, took early retirement. Tom Burlison, who had played such an important part in getting Blair the Sedgefield nomination, was a candidate for the job and now he wanted his protégé's help in getting elected. Blair did his best, among other things persuading his London contacts to invite Burlison to address meetings so that Burlison could make his mark in the South.

Burlison was not elected, but his campaign for the GMB leadership marked the start of a significant feud. During the campaign, Blair formed a fixed dislike for the other main candidate, national official John Edmonds, whom he seems to have regarded as a dangerous leftwing intellectual. The dislike was mutual. Edmonds won the election, and their antipathy contributed to a dramatic public falling-out after the 1992 general election. Today, Edmonds and Burlison have both retired; Burlison is now Lord Burlison.

The same year, 1986, Robin Cook lost his seat in the annual election for members of the shadow cabinet. Mandelson and Kinnock decided that Bryan Gould should take over the campaign brief from Cook, and Cook's adviser Nigel Stanley moved over to work for Gould, so as to ensure continuity. Gould, like Cook, was to find his role in making Labour electable again expunged from the authorised version of history. Nigel Stanley says: 'Mandelson wrote both Cook and Gould out of their role as the real creators of the Labour Party media strategy.'

By 1986, the future Blairites had coalesced as a force, though as yet without a leader. Charles Clarke, Patricia Hewitt, Peter Mandelson, John Reid (who also worked in Kinnock's office) – the people the party later called 'the Kinnocracy' – only came into their own under Blair. But in 1986 they were already in place around Kinnock.

That same year, Blair brought his old friend Anji Hunter into his office as a part-time researcher. Since their Oxford days, Anji had married and resumed her education at the age of thirty as a day student at Brighton Polytechnic. She started working for Blair in her vacations. According to Mandelson's special adviser, Derek Draper, Anji's husband was 'a dead ringer for Blair'. 'If you saw him in a restaurant, you'd think "What's Blair doing here?"' he says.[8] Draper was not the only person to notice this, or to speculate on the nature of the friendship between Tony and Anji. Cherie was never at all comfortable with Anji being so close to her husband, and, as we shall see, this contributed to a spectacular falling-out some years later. The team that would surround Prime Minister Blair was starting to take shape.

And what of Blair himself? Polite, diffident, bright, he impressed everyone and seemed to threaten no one. He was, however, moving silently into the confidence of everyone who mattered, and he became Bryan Gould's chief lieutenant in the task of preparing for the next general election campaign. He was, though, increasingly concerned that he might be wasting his time. 'To close friends,' writes Anthony Seldon, 'he would confide that he did not feel his career or the party were making the progress he had hoped for, and he had thoughts of looking elsewhere.'

Gould valued him, though fearing him to be shallow. 'I always saw him as young for his age,' Gould told us. 'He was very presentable and articulate and bright but I never saw him as a towering intellect. He was a performer rather than a thinker. There was not much substance but a lot of talent.' In his relationship with Gould he showed once again that valuable aptitude for being all things to all men. Gould, a New Zealander, was as near as a top Labour politician got in those days to being a Eurosceptic. Today, Gould says:

> Throughout the time I knew him, he seemed to be pretty agnostic on Europe. I'm surprised today to find that he was always thought to be pro-Europe. He gave no sign of that in my hearing. So he was a longer-term planner than we thought. He revealed of himself what he judged to be appropriate to the person he was with.[22]

Stuart Bell observes:

> Tony would speak from the back of the Commons as far away from the front bench as he could get, and at the back of meetings of the Parliamentary Labour Party held on the Wednesday morning, and at the back of the meetings of the regional conferences of the party held at different venues in the North East. He showed no eagerness to put himself forward.[23]

But he was carefully making the right connections. He had a well-established and well-known friendship and political partnership with the other rising star of the 1983 intake, Gordon Brown. He had got to know the right journalists, in particular Alastair Campbell, political editor of the *Daily Mirror* and the journalist who was closest to Kinnock. Bob Worcester of MORI remembers meeting him for the first time:

> It was in a debating club in the House of Commons in the Grand Committee Room. I'd been asked to oppose the motion that publication of opinion polls should be banned during general elections. Bryan Gould was campaign director and I worked with him on a day-to-day basis doing private polling for Labour Party. I'd asked Gould to speak with me but he was arriving back from New Zealand from a long flight that morning. He said he had a bright new young man called Tony Blair who he was sure would love to do it.
>
> Blair agreed at once and came round to our Old Queen Street office and I gave him his brief, first ascertaining he believed in it. He asked questions like a barrister would and we next met on the evening of the debate. I was Mr Nasty and he was Mr Nice and we wiped the floor with the opposition, which consisted of George Foulkes MP and journalist Eric Jacobs. We won 80–20 or so. I found him enormously likeable, clearly a trustworthy sort of guy.

There was just one thing that threatened to hold Blair back: his wife. Neil Kinnock confided privately that she worried him: he thought she was too leftwing. The news seems to have reached Blair and given him the first hint that his wonderful, intellectually high-powered wife, who had shown him the way in the Labour Party, who had the Labour roots and the understanding of what Labour was about that he himself lacked, might also be a political liability.

At about the same time, he was picking up stories of her prickliness in dealing with political colleagues. Bryan Gould still recalls with a slight shiver how irritable she was when she met him for the second time and he failed to remember who she was. (Gould insists that it was his fault really: he should have remembered.) Blair himself once talked about her 'Liverpool chippiness'. She certainly lacked the public-school graciousness that he himself brought to a frequently graceless Labour Party.

Blair started to fear that Cherie's family might be something of an embarrassment, too. Her famous father, Tony Booth, whose endorsement had been so useful in Beaconsfield and Sedgefield, had leftwing views that Blair the MP started to find irksome, while he was permanently worried about what Cherie's tall, willowy, articulate and independent-minded half-sister Lauren Booth might say.

In subsequent years, as we shall see, Blair and his advisers displayed an almost obsessive determination to keep Cherie and her family out of the limelight, and to put all possible obstacles in the way of writers who wanted to find out something about her.

The Blairs' first child, Euan, was born in January 1984; the second, Nicholas, two years later; and the third, Kathryn, after another two-year interval. Blair was present at the birth of Euan and Kathryn, but missed that of Nicholas because the baby was born early, while Blair was in Sedgefield. The family moved in 1986 to 1 Richmond Terrace, one of the elegant Georgian townhouses in fashionable Barnsbury, at the wealthy end of Islington in North London, with, on the ground floor, a big living room and a small den where Tony could work. The house was carefully furnished in a style described by a frequent visitor as 'very chintzy'. For a constituency base, they bought a large, comfortable old house in Trimdon, called 'Myrobella'.

Blair was definitely on the way up. Everyone liked him, everyone was impressed by his charm, his studied moderation, his hard work. His boss in the treasury team, shadow chancellor Roy Hattersley, liked him very much – the years of their bitter estrangement were yet to come. Hattersley still remembers with some embarrassment the day that Blair brought his father to meet him, for Hattersley told Leo Blair that if his son continued to work hard, he might do quite well in politics. Tony Blair, of course, looked humbly grateful.[24]

He made his first appearance on the BBC's *Question Time* in May 1985, reinforcing his growing reputation as a safe pair of hands. He made a respectable showing on the treasury team, even when pitted directly against experienced big-hitters like Chancellor Nigel Lawson.

Bryan Gould had learned the lessons of the 1983 general election disaster. For the 1987 election, he reduced the election management committee to just seven people, including Gould himself, Mandelson and Larry Whitty. In effect it was only six, because Charles Clarke was usually out on the road with Kinnock. Party political broadcasts made by Hugh Hudson successfully projected the attractive character of the Labour leader. The party's senior figures were all under strict central control – there was no inspired freelancing of the type that Kinnock himself had undertaken in 1983. It was a slick, professional, well-run campaign, probably the best that Labour has ever mounted – for the party's campaigning skills declined sharply afterwards.

But it did not succeed. The result was not as bad as in 1983, but it was bad enough. Four years of Kinnock's relentless battle with the left and the divisions created by the year-long miners' strike were capped just before the election by two disastrous by-elections, in Southwark and Glasgow Govan, in which Labour fielded Bennite candidates whom its leaders found it hard to support without embarrassment. The party's divisions were exposed yet again at a crucial time, and a slick and effective campaign could not save it from defeat.

Kinnock and Blair drew the same lesson from the result: that Labour policy needed to move yet further to the right. But the difference between them was that Blair welcomed it and had believed it before the election, while Kinnock was driven unwillingly to this conclusion by the scale of the defeat.

Even then, the natural conservative in Tony Blair was starting to be detected – not by his Labour colleagues, but by the Tories. Nigel Lawson later said that he was 'slightly surprised that he was in the Labour Party at all'. Other leading Conservatives were taking an interest in him, inviting him to their dinners – and afterwards feeling puzzled that he was not in their party.[25] Partly, no doubt, it was that extraordinary capacity he has to be all things to all men and always to leave people thinking that he agrees with them. Partly it was that, as a member of the present government puts it, 'He would be at least equally at home as a European Christian Democrat.' A senior Eurocrat disagrees: 'No, he's too rightwing for the European Christian Democrats.'

In 1985 he had joined the Tribune group, once Labour's leftwing and now the centre left – supporters of Kinnock. But this, like his one-time membership of CND, was not a decision made out of conviction but out of expediency. One senior Tribunite of the time has said: 'He played the part of someone on the left mainstream of the party. But he was never ideologically of the left. He was never properly committed to our camp.'[26] He himself confirmed as much in private immediately after the 1987 election.

Deputy leader Roy Hattersley had had enough of the job and wanted out. Kinnock badly wanted him to stand again and sent Blair and Gordon Brown to persuade him to stay. They told Hattersley that they had just attended a meeting of the Tribune group and could promise Hattersley the group's support. 'They were all prepared to vote for you,' said Blair. 'I mean real Tribunites, not people like Gordon and I, who felt we had to join.'[27]

CHAPTER SEVEN

THE DECLINE OF KINNOCK AND THE RISE OF BLAIR

Peter Mandelson was the chief beneficiary of the 1987 election defeat. Afterwards, his power increased enormously until, within months, he was single-handedly making and breaking careers. He quickly used his position to push forward the two men whom he backed to lead the party after Kinnock: Tony Blair and Gordon Brown. In order to do this, he hastily disentangled himself from the politician whose career he had previously nurtured, Bryan Gould. That is one of the main reasons why Tony Blair and not Bryan Gould rose to the top.

Mandelson's greatly increased power was partly the result of a post-election meeting between Charles Clarke and Neil Kinnock. They decided that if it was to get elected, Labour needed dramatically to change both its policy and its communications. So far, both men believed the party had made no significant progress in either of these two key areas. They were agreed that Labour needed a great policy renewal. But so far as communications was concerned, although they felt no progress had been made, the media seemed to think they had made great strides. The consensus in the press seemed to be that Labour had lost the election but won the campaign. So the score was zero out of two but they were being credited with one out of two. They decided, therefore, to go along with the myth that their communications and presentation had been wonderful.

It was an extraordinary conclusion. Most close observers would have judged it to be the other way round. Martin Linton, then a *Guardian* journalist and now a Labour MP, had written a paper after the 1983 election which put that savage defeat down to the hostility of the press and questioned whether Labour could ever win against such united media hostility. And Geoffrey Goodman, industrial correspondent on the *Daily Mirror* and a friend of Kinnock's, pointed out in 1987 that not one single national newspaper gave its full support to Labour. But such was Clarke and Kinnock's assessment, and it had its own inexorable logic. It required them to build up the Mandelson myth. That was the thinking behind their decision to keep Mandelson and boost his profile. Clarke is reported to have said: 'All we have to do now is transform our policy and everything will be fine.'

This all sounds like pure Clarke, and it probably was, because after the 1987 defeat, Neil Kinnock was in the blackest of depressions. It took him a good year to recover fully. Indeed, there is a sense in which he has never recovered. The wounds of his long and bitter battle with the Bennites, and of the ferocious media campaign waged against him, went very deep in this complex and sensitive man, and the ebullience which came naturally to him in 1983 was starting to look very forced by 1987; it still does, just a little, today. But he forced himself to do what he believed to be his duty, which was to change the party's policies thoroughly enough to make Labour electable again. In particular, he was convinced that he needed to get rid of three cherished policies: unilateral nuclear disarmament, public ownership of key industries, and the commitment to repeal all of Margaret Thatcher's anti-trade union laws. And he believed he had to build up Peter Mandelson's undeserved reputation.

But Kinnock and Clarke were handing power over people's careers to a man who longed for that sort of power, and Mandelson quickly became the most feared person in the party. This is borne out by almost everyone who watched the process at close quarters. Mandelson's shadowy influence, they say, cannot be overestimated. His decisions on who was in and who was out had a cruel finality about them. Without that decision by Kinnock and Clarke, Tony Blair would probably not be prime minister today.

Mandelson is an extraordinary man. People think of him as a great communicator, but in fact that is one skill he lacks. His writing is poor – turgid and self-indulgent. His television appearances, though articulate, sound smooth and insincere: he has not been able to develop either the practised spontaneity of Blair or the gravitas of Brown. So, far from being a public asset, he is a liability. 'When we do surveys Mandelson is always bottom of the poll for trust,' says Bob Worcester of MORI. 'He is the least trusted senior person in the Labour Party.'[1] And he was the first Labour image-maker – Alastair Campbell was the second – to commit the elementary PR blunder of letting himself, rather than his boss, become the story.

His real skill lies in what most of us know as office politics. In most workplaces there is someone who always seems to have the boss's ear, whose unseen hand is always believed to be behind every decision, who is always thought to know who is on the up escalator and who on the down one, and to be able to make or break careers. In the Parliamentary Labour Party that someone was, until 2004, Peter Mandelson. Like his famous grandfather Herbert Morrison, he knows the Labour Party inside out and knows how to make it do the things he wants it to do. And, like his grandfather, he found that this skill bought you influence, but seldom love and friendship. Unlike his grandfather, he craves love. That is his tragedy.

Blair knew very well that the director of communications was a very powerful figure. So he turned on Mandelson all the winning charm that had gained the patronage of the matrons at Durham Choristers School and at Fettes, and had won the prettier of the two girls in the Fettes sixth form. It was at about this time that women in particular started noticing something special about Mandelson's attitude to Blair. One woman, a former senior official in Labour's Walworth Road headquarters who knew both men well, says that she frequently saw Mandelson watching Blair with what she could only describe as adulation. She says she thought that Mandelson was in awe of Blair. She describes occasions over the years when Blair gently put him down, or told him to be quiet, and Mandelson looked utterly crushed. On those occasions Blair would call Mandelson 'Pete' – no one else called him that, and it seemed to soften the blow. She claims that there is, and always has been, an element of hero-worship in Mandelson's attitude to Blair. Blair, she thinks, knows it: it is part of his power over his mentor.

Other sources describe an extraordinary personal closeness and understanding between the two, greater than Blair has with anyone else – even Cherie. Until Mandelson resigned his seat to become Britain's European Commissioner in July 2004, they would be seen sitting talking for hours, secretively, head to head, on long train journeys to their northern constituencies. Mandelson still rushes to Blair's side at times of trouble. 'It's called being Peter,' he says as he walks through the door to sort out a problem which has spilled over from the professional to the personal.

Mandelson is one of the most prominent gay men in British politics. Their relationship has never been a sexual one, but one of Blair's frontbench colleagues says that at this time 'Blair and Mandelson used to strut about Westminster like a gay couple.' Blair the inveterate charmer had scored again.

'Seduction is what Mandelson is about,' says Bryan Gould. 'If you're in favour with Mandelson you feel the glow of goodwill, as I did. But in 1988 he decided that, having backed me as the next leader, he would switch his affections to Brown and Blair.'[2] But in Blair, Mandelson had met his match in the seduction stakes.

Blair performed the same trick, with modest variations, for a different but equally insecure character, the aggressive and rather macho political editor of the *Daily Mirror*, Alastair Campbell. Campbell's biographers, Peter Oborne and Simon Walters, describe Blair at this time as 'almost giving the impression that he was flattered that a man of the stature of Alastair Campbell was ready to give him the time of day'.[3] Gordon Brown, too, gained the mistaken impression that Blair looked up to him. Brown and Blair shared a tiny, windowless office. Brown, said Blair later, taught him how to write press releases, how to structure his speeches, how to sum up a complicated idea in a single phrase. 'My press releases used to read like essays before Gordon showed me how to write them,' Blair has said.[4]

In 1987, immediately after the general election, Blair asked Bryan Gould whether he should stand in the election for the shadow cabinet. 'He wasn't interested in my view, it was his way of canvassing support,' says Gould. Gould advised him to stand. It would be putting down a marker for the future, even if he did not get elected. Blair said: 'I'm frightened I might get found out.'[5] Few people do humility as well as Blair.

To get elected, you had to be on a slate, and Blair and Gordon Brown both got on the Tribune slate. (To get on the slate, they had to get on a slate for the slate, organised by their friend Nick Brown. The idea of this was to go to the Tribune meeting with a slate, and persuade the Tribune group to adopt it as their slate. Politics is like that, sometimes.) There were fifteen to be elected. Blair came seventeenth, which was a good result for a first attempt, but placed him behind his friend and fellow star of the 1983 intake, Gordon Brown, who was elected and given a job as Bryan Gould's deputy. Gould would have liked to be shadow chancellor – economics was his field – but the job went to John Smith, and Gould had to make do with the second-ranked economic post, shadowing trade and industry.

Although not in the shadow cabinet, Blair was given responsibility for relations with the City of London and for consumer affairs, and did his usual thoroughly competent job. But he was after much bigger fry now, and Mandelson was becoming hungrily ambitious for his new protégé.

By this time, Anji Hunter had completed her course at Brighton Polytechnic, graduating with a first-class honours degree in history and English, and was employed full-time in Blair's office as a political adviser.

She was busily establishing herself in the role that was to make her a key figure in both Blair's government and his personal and political life for more than a decade.

There is some evidence that Cherie was starting to fret about the demands her husband's political career were likely to make. Colin Byrne, who worked as press officer under Peter Mandelson, was assigned to Blair to look after his media work (itself a sign that Mandelson was backing Blair's career). Byrne never much liked Cherie (he is a New Labour type through and through, and New Labour people tend not to like Cherie, feeling, rightly, that she is Old Labour at heart). He told us how he once telephoned Blair at home one Sunday with a press query. Cherie answered the telephone and bit his head off for interrupting the family Sunday. 'It's my Sunday too,' protested Byrne. 'Yes, but I'm not married to you, am I, Colin,' snapped Cherie, and handed the telephone to her husband, who apologised to Byrne.

The next year, in the shadow cabinet elections in November, Blair was actually elected, coming ninth. It was pretty impressive for a thirty-five-year-old, but Brown had done a lot better. He came first, having made a fine job of standing in as shadow chancellor while John Smith recovered from a heart attack.

Blair became energy spokesman, responsible for opposing the government's plans for electricity privatisation. This brief required him to say, with conviction and a straight face, a great many things which we can now be quite sure he has never believed. A month after his appointment he was telling the House of Commons: 'We are proud that we took the industry into public ownership. When we come to power, it will be reinstated as a public service for the people of this country, and will not be run for private profit.'[6]

Despite the fact that he was promising things he certainly never intended to deliver, there is no doubt at all that he fought a skilful parliamentary campaign, and he had one great success. The government abandoned the sale of Nuclear Electric. It was eventually privatised a year before Blair became prime minister, and remains in private hands.

In the meantime, the skids were under Blair's old boss Bryan Gould in his post as shadow trade and industry spokesman. One of the policies that Kinnock and Clarke had determined to ditch was the pledge to renationalise British Telecom, but the policy review group for that area, for which Gould was responsible, was not coming to the conclusion Clarke and Kinnock wanted.

One day, Gould had two surprise visitors. Gordon Brown and Tony Blair were there to tell him he had given too much ground to the trade unions. They told him they wanted more fundamental policy changes than were being proposed, and Gould told them, politely, to mind their own business. After the meeting, according to Gould, 'Brown and Blair said to Kinnock: you have to get rid of Gould'. It was a matter of months before Gould was moved to environment, and Brown inherited his trade and industry brief.

Gould had been the party's rising star during the 1987 election, when he had basked in Mandelson's favour. But after he was moved out of trade and industry, he says, 'My vote in shadow cabinet elections started to decline because Peter Mandelson was briefing against me. I was seen as an obstacle.'[7] There were other signs that Gould had fallen into disfavour. Before 1988, when the formal picture of the shadow cabinet was taken, Mandelson ensured that Gould was placed at Kinnock's right hand. In 1988 he found himself exiled to the back row, and Blair and Brown were placed beside the leader.[8]

As Gould's stock began to fall, Blair's was rising, and for the same reason. In the 1989 shadow cabinet elections he came fourth, behind Brown, John Smith and Robin Cook. It was confirmation that Blair and Brown had replaced Gould in Mandelson's, and therefore Kinnock's, affections.

By the next year, 1990, Gould, now environment spokesman, knew for certain that he was out in the cold, for he saw his efforts to attack Margaret Thatcher's poll tax deliberately undermined by Mandelson. The poll tax could, and should, have been the downfall, not just of Thatcher, but of the Conservative government she led. She proposed to replace the rates, paid to local councils and set at a rate which reflected the value of your property, with a tax which would be the same however rich or poor you were. It was a drastic way of redistributing wealth from the poor to the rich, quickly dubbed the 'poll tax' by its opponents, after the hated fourteenth-century poll tax, a major cause of the Peasants' Revolt. The plan was widely unpopular and 1990 became a year of violent protests and demonstrations. It was a huge electoral liability for the Conservatives, but Labour's attempts to attack it were blunted by the party's internal politics.

Gould explains that 'people were concerned about what we would put in the place of the poll tax'. He therefore constructed an alternative and planned to launch it at a press conference. But, he says, 'Peter Mandelson was determined this should never see the light of day.'[9] Mandelson insisted, unusually, on holding the press conference at Labour's Walworth Road headquarters, which made it harder to get journalists to come along; and then seems to have forgotten to invite the press. One journalist came. Gould attended with his deputy, David Blunkett, and the press conference was memorable principally because Blunkett's guide dog was sick on the floor.

Gould had been warned of his impending eclipse as a future leader of his party, though cryptically. 'Mandelson told me in late 1987 that he was under some pressure to swap horses. But he gave the impression that he was being asked to give his support to John Smith rather than to me.' In fact, Gould thinks a deal was struck the next year: 'The three of them, Mandelson, Blair and Brown would go on working for Kinnock until Kinnock stepped down, and then the time would be right for Brown and Blair. By 1992, Mandelson had undermined the generation of political leaders who might have replaced Neil.'[10]

Mandelson's patronage was in the currency most valuable to ambitious MPs: television appearances. He could, by and large, choose which MPs got on which programmes. Brown and Blair put themselves in his hands. He promoted them, he sent them to television studios, he rang them after each performance and gave them his appraisal. It was also at this time that Mandelson developed his own policy of seeking a 'tame journalist' on every national paper so that he could promote his protégés. Not only would he seek favourable coverage – he would also want the article skewed in their favour, preferably with a couple of bitchy quotes about their detractors. Journalists who declined to take up his offer found themselves victims of Mandelson's cold shoulder and were kept permanently out of the loop.[11]

One of those who noticed what was going on was the shadow chancellor, John Smith, who was known to feel little affection for Mandelson. So Mandelson had to hope that Kinnock would stay on long enough to stop Smith succeeding him. 'It was very bad news for the three of them that Kinnock resigned in 1992,' says Gould, who adds: 'Peter is intensely personal. His technique is to bind people to him.'

Michael Meacher, who was in the shadow cabinet at the time, says: 'I realised that year that there was a gang of three.' And he noticed the same characteristics: 'Mandelson's technique is to get close to the leader, to become associated with the leader, to make sure that the press knows that what he says carries the leader's imprimatur. He's devilishly clever, and it's attractive for a politician to have someone like that who's 100 per cent on your side.'[12]

Of course, there is always more than one way of looking at the same facts. Colin Byrne became Mandelson's deputy in the mid-1980s. He now heads Britain's biggest public relations consultancy, Weber Shandwick. Mandelson is still perhaps his closest friend; he was best man at Byrne's wedding. To his mind, Mandelson is the man who has selflessly done the dirty work for Kinnock and then for Blair. 'He has done them a great service by drawing fire to himself,' says Byrne. 'He is a kind of lightning conductor.'[13]

This is exactly right. Mandelson became, and remained, a man who took the flak on Blair's behalf. The prime minister who became known as Teflon Tony is a bit like T. S. Eliot's 'Macavity the Mystery Cat' – a point noted as far back as his Fettes days by the wife of his housemaster Mr Roberts:[14]

> And when you reach the scene of crime Macavity's not there!
> You may seek him in the basement, you may look up in the air
> But I tell you once and once again, Macavity's not there!

To emulate Macavity, you need the assistance of people like Mandelson and Alastair Campbell. Blair's personal responsibility for many of the shady dealings generally put down to Mandelson and Campbell is greater than people think – as we shall see later.

By the time of the 1987 election, Mandelson had decided that the future lay with either Blair or Brown. He had not yet decided which one, but television appearances were ruthlessly employed as an indication of Mandelson's favour, and we know that Blair appeared on the BBC's *Question Time* three years before Brown had his chance to do the same, and before the 1987 election. This might be an indication of the way the master manipulator's mind was working at that time.

During the period after 1987, Mandelson recreated his communications team in his own image. The most significant change was the departure of Labour's pollsters, MORI, and its charismatic chief Bob Worcester. Mandelson felt threatened by Worcester, who had a high public profile which competed with Mandelson's own, and who was also a rival for the leader's attention: Worcester had had the ear of every Labour leader since Harold Wilson. Worst of all, his advice was sometimes the opposite of the advice Mandelson and his protégé Philip Gould gave. In the run-up to the 1987 election, Worcester had advised Neil Kinnock to be himself. He had also predicted, embarrassingly, that Labour would not improve its position in the polls until Kinnock's shadow cabinet colleagues started going out of their way to express confidence in their leader. He wrote immediately after the election in the *New Statesman* that bridging the gap 'will take more than being packaged like soap powder or dog food'.

Worcester was less keen on focus groups than Mandelson. MORI conducted both quantitative polling, which gives you figures reflecting what the public thinks, and qualitative polling, commonly known as focus groups, which gives you a much less tangible feel for public opinion. Mandelson and his friend Philip Gould wanted less quantitative research and more focus groups. Many pollsters believe that focus groups can be manipulated to give you any results you want. Certainly much of the evidence from them is purely anecdotal. That would have suited Mandelson, for whom polling data was another source of power. If you could tell the leader that this or that policy, or this or that politician, was an electoral liability, you could get the person or the policy changed.

The sort of thing focus groups were telling Labour in 1987 was summed up in a memorandum to Neil Kinnock from Gould's assistant Deborah Mattinson: 'Top of mind are the "loony" lesbian/gay issues. In fact, however, extremism links to everything else – it's an umbrella for all Labour's negatives: trade unions, mismanagement of the economy (local council experience), defence.'[15] No statistical evidence was offered for this huge generalisation. All Mattinson needed to provide by way of evidence was a couple of short quotations from things individuals had said in her focus groups. Her report gives every impression of being about as scientific as reporting the conversation in the snug bar of a stockbroker-belt pub. It's hard to avoid the conclusion that Mandelson, Philip Gould and (crucially, though more quietly) Blair were trying to change the Labour Party and persuade it to adopt their views by passing them off as the views of the electorate.

The first shots had been fired in Worcester's direction as early as 1983, when Mandelson's friend Colin Fisher wrote, in a letter copied to Neil Kinnock, that Worcester was no good at running focus groups.[16] But Worcester only became aware of what was happening when Mandelson suddenly turned on him after a meeting before the 1987 election, at which Patricia Hewitt and Worcester's colleague Brian Gosschalk were also present, in a restaurant in Buckingham Gate, near the House of Commons. Worcester was amazed to hear Mandelson say there should be no questions on the party's election broadcasts in MORI surveys. Worcester protested that the party would then have no way of knowing whether its broadcasts were working. But Mandelson insisted, saying: 'I want no information before the campaign strategy committee which will enable them to deviate from what I know the election broadcasts should be.'

Worcester decided this was so extraordinary an instruction that he had to know whether the leader agreed with it. So, two months later, at a meeting of the campaign strategy committee, Worcester again questioned his instructions. Kinnock, surprised, said: 'Of course we want questions about the PPBs.' Worcester caught a look from Mandelson which said: 'I'll get you.' From that day on, says Worcester, 'I do not recall Mandelson ever speaking to me again except on business through clenched teeth. From that minute on he was out to get me.'

He succeeded. For nineteen years Worcester had reported direct to the party leader, but in 1989, during one of their regular quarterly meetings, Kinnock said this was to cease. Worcester was to report instead to a committee chaired by Mandelson. Worcester replied, as Mandelson knew he would: 'I don't believe you will get an honest report of my work from Peter Mandelson.'[17] And that was the end of his association with Labour. Philip Gould took over as Labour's pollster.

Worcester had been preceded to the exit door by Mandelson's deputy, John Booth. A journalist and former National Union of Teachers publicity chief, Booth had joined Mandelson's office in 1985. Mandelson told him he had no experience with the press himself and therefore wanted as his deputy someone with a strong background in both the Labour Party and the media. Booth recalls Mandelson asking him to meet Tony Blair in the spring of 1986. Afterwards, Mandelson asked him to share his thoughts about Blair. They were not favourable:

> I'd not met Blair before. I knew his constituency well, having being a local reporter there, but Blair didn't seem to want to talk about it. I tried other topics: the miners' strike, unemployment, education, the United States – about which I knew quite a bit, having worked there – but he didn't seem to have any serious political interest I could engage with, or practical union or Labour experiences to share.
>
> The other thing that put me off him was the rictus grin. I'd been brought up to believe that people who smiled that much either had something wrong with them or had something to hide. I couldn't get any sense of who he really was or why he was a Labour MP at all. He seemed to me then like a glove puppet who'd perform according to whoever manipulated him.[18]

Shortly afterwards Mandelson effectively fired Booth. According to Booth's shorthand note of his conversation, Mandelson told him: 'If we have to terminate your contract, I will make any fabrication of the truth and stick by it faithfully.' Booth also claimed in a *New Statesman* article that Mandelson told him that if he ever was to raise his dismissal in public, he might never work in Britain again.[19]

Mandelson made no comment about this article and has declined to discuss anything with the present authors. What was presumably his account of the dismissal was given in *Mandelson: The Biography*, a sympathetic account by Donald Macintyre published in 1999. Booth issued libel proceedings, as a result of which Macintyre apologised and paid substantial damages and HarperCollins pulped the book. Booth reported in his *New Statesman* article: 'Within weeks, my regular freelance work for two national newspapers sympathetic to New Labour ended.'[20]

The image-makers had already forced Kinnock to give up the simple, direct, passionate language that won hearts. More and more, the Labour leader was delivering his thoughts in vast, shapeless bundles of words. They told him that, when asked a difficult question on television, he was to flannel until the time ran out, and he would follow their instructions, though he felt foolish doing so. (Kinnock loyally insists that he himself felt the need to be packaged in this way, and that it was not the fault of his advisers.)

Yet the new Kinnock still did not attract public confidence. During the 1992 election, only 36 per cent of voters thought Kinnock was a capable leader, compared with 52 per cent for the Conservative prime minister John Major, and if the communicators had understood their trade, they would have known why. You can build on the product you have, but you can't pretend that it is a completely different product. They seem dimly to have recognised that they might be making a mistake: in 1990, Philip Gould suggested at a top-level internal meeting that they should 'let Neil be himself'. But by then it was too late.[21]

After Worcester's departure, Labour's leaders were getting much less hard statistical polling evidence and much more data from focus groups, whose findings could be seen through the prism of Peter Mandelson's own views and preferences. And one of Mandelson's main preferences was for Tony Blair, who became the key beneficiary of his patronage.

Blair, for his part, had been showing that he possessed that most valued of political assets: a safe pair of hands. He was devoting a lot of time to impressing his leader, but there was a wide and growing gulf between the Northern Labour habits of his local party members and Blair's sophisticated metropolitan lifestyle, as was apparent when Sedgefield council's chief executive, Alan Roberts, came down to London with the then leader of the council, Brian Stevens, and another councillor to see their local MPs.

They were taken to the crowded and smoke-filled Strangers' Bar in the Commons to have a few pints of cheap Federation bitter and rub shoulders with some well-known figures. The job of hosting them was shared somewhat unenthusiastically between Blair and an MP from a neighbouring constituency, Derek Foster. Foster asked his political adviser, Roger Pope, to join them. It must have been a remarkable scene as the teetotal Foster and the occasional drinker Blair reluctantly joined the councillors and officials for round after round. As Pope remembers it: 'Suddenly Blair turns to me and asks me to come outside the bar, and makes his excuses to the Sedgefield councillors. We get outside and he gets his wallet out, pulls out a fiver and gives it to me. He says: "Go and buy them a round. I'm off. I can't stand these people."'[22]

Kinnock regularly had Blair's virtues impressed on him by both Clarke and Mandelson. Since these two advisers never agreed about anything else (privately they were growing to loathe each other), this must have had a great impact on Kinnock. He started to rank Blair among his key advisers – a remarkable compliment. It was a position of enormous power: working alongside a leader who was in a black depression, who was starting to withdraw from his other colleagues, and who needed, more and more, to be reassured by his friends that he was on the right track. 'Tony's a great consulter,' says Kinnock, who, like many others before him, seems to have assumed that when Blair asked advice, he genuinely wanted it.

Moreover, he valued Blair's loyalty. Blair supported him enthusiastically when Tony Benn challenged for the leadership in 1988. More importantly, Blair had no connection with another, quieter but much more serious, threat the same year, of which the public never heard. In summer 1988 Kinnock says, 'There was a plot against me run by Donald Dewar. I had a system of intelligence and I found out about it.'[23] Dewar, the shadow Scottish secretary, may have wanted to replace Kinnock with his old undergraduate friend and fellow Scottish lawyer John Smith.

Blair already shared Mandelson's low opinion of Smith, considering him an old Labour Party type who had no place in the modern party. Kinnock did not share Blair's view, irritated though he sometimes became with Smith; and Smith did not encourage anyone to promote him as a replacement for Kinnock. The deadly 'Old Labour' charge could be used against Kinnock, too. There is no record of Blair using it, but Mandelson did. The man whom Kinnock thought was indispensable and loyal was writing privately to Hattersley that Kinnock's 'values and rhetoric are still tied strongly to the "have-nots". He cares too much. He's too much of a socialist and hates the idea of being seen as anything different.' Voters, Mandelson claimed, 'don't want to be inspired as much as led'.[24]

As one of Kinnock's trusted favourites, Blair was placed on the group set up to review the party's stance on trade union law. He was now a key figure in the rewriting of Labour's policies on two out of Kinnock's three key areas. And he was also involved in the third, as one of the few people

Kinnock consulted before ditching the party's commitment to unilateral nuclear disarmament.

In 1989 there were county council elections and European elections. Shadow ministers competed hotly for appearances on party political broadcasts. A PPB is a wonderful opportunity to shine and to show that you are an electoral asset. These appearances were in Mandelson's gift. And in the summer of 1989 he pronounced the verdict of the focus groups: it had to be Tony Blair. Older colleagues could fret and fume, John Prescott could complain impotently about the promotion of the 'beautiful people', but there was no chance of appeal against the decision of the director of communications.

Just as, when Mandelson spoke, journalists were sure they were hearing Kinnock's voice, so it started to be understood that when his two young protégés, Brown and Blair, spoke, MPs were hearing their leader's voice and ought to listen.

Their first recorded mission to tell an older colleague to pull his socks up had been the occasion when the two of them turned up in Bryan Gould's office. The next shadow minister to get the treatment was Michael Meacher at employment. What Kinnock, Mandelson, Brown and Blair wanted here was the wholesale abandonment of Labour's pledge to make a bonfire of Margaret Thatcher's anti-trade union legislation.

This, in 1989, was a tall order. Unions had watched, helpless, as the government sequestrated the assets of the print union NGA, of the seafarers' union over its dispute with P&O Ferries, and of the miners' union. 'Sequestrated' is a legal euphemism; what they actually did was to take away all the money and assets to which generations of union members had contributed. It was not just the members of those unions who considered it unjust and believed the balance of power between employer and employee had been shifted far too far towards the employer. The Thatcher government was revelling in the chance to rub the face of its old enemy, the unions, in the dirt.

But Mandelson, backed up by the focus groups, considered the commitment an electoral liability, and it had to go – all of it. Meacher was not going to oblige, so he would have to be replaced by someone who would. That someone was Tony Blair.

The change was predicted in the *Sunday Times* by the paper's political editor, Andy Grice, who has always been close to Peter Mandelson. Meacher is still sure he knows who was responsible: 'The whole thing was orchestrated by Mandelson,' he says.[25] But he is wrong. It was Kinnock's chief of staff, Charles Clarke, who telephoned Blair's press officer, Colin Byrne, and said: 'I want you to "assassinate" Michael Meacher.' It was Byrne who then telephoned Grice, among other journalists. Mandelson was told what was going on later in the day.[26]

Meacher could not believe that he had lost the confidence of his leader: 'I had not changed my view in the years 1987 to 1989. Kinnock knew my view when he appointed me in 1987. If he had wanted a different policy then, he would have appointed someone different.'[27] But Kinnock did want a different policy, and Tony Blair became employment spokesman with a brief to deliver it. He did so, and faster than Kinnock himself believed possible.

It was in those few months after his appointment that Blair turned himself from a promising young man into a potential party leader. He threw away the most cherished policies of a party that had been created by the trade unions as a voice for the working class in Parliament. And he did it almost without any trouble – certainly without the anguish it had cost Kinnock to convince himself of the need for it. Blair was not handicapped by the emotional attachment to the labour movement that would have inhibited most of his colleagues.

It was in those months that he revealed himself to be, as Roy Hattersley put it years later, 'The soldier who crossed a minefield in confident safety because he did not know that the mines were there.'[28]

He prepared the ground quickly and thoroughly. Before abandoning Labour's support for the closed shop, he went to see everyone who mattered in the trade unions and said that it was impossible to support both the closed shop and the social chapter which had just been published by the European Commission, because the social chapter would outlaw the closed shop. He made sure of his political ground, telephoning Roy Hattersley for advice on what to do about the closed-shop issue, even though Hattersley now says: 'He'd already made up his mind.'[29]

The union leaders succumbed to Blair's blandishments far more rapidly than Kinnock imagined possible. Bill Morris, head of the Transport and General Workers Union and the first black general secretary of a major trade union, said there were not many black people in closed shops. Brenda Dean, head of the print union SOGAT, suddenly remembered that there were not many women in closed shops. Initially, Blair did not speak to John Edmonds at the GMB, who was furious when he heard about the discussions with his colleagues. The next move was pure Blair. He did not contact Edmonds. Instead, he asked Peter Mandelson to do so. Mandelson was already generally identified as Blair's messenger. Mandelson telephoned Edmonds and said Blair was anxious for a talk and could Edmonds phone him. Edmonds made the call and was mollified.[30]

Within days the only major union figure who remained unconvinced was Tony Dubbins, leader of the other main print union, NGA. The NGA's industrial strength had always relied on the closed shop, and Dubbins's union had been all but destroyed by a succession of disputes with big newspaper owners. According to John Rentoul, when Blair went to see Dubbins he was subjected to 'a one-sided screaming match'. But Dubbins was isolated. Blair had persuaded the people who mattered: Morris, Dean, Edmonds, and John Monks, who was the TUC's deputy general secretary and soon to be its general secretary. Monks explains what happened:

> In the debate in Parliament he repudiated the closed shop and got away with it. He'd handled the politics well, prepared the ground well. When the press phoned up expecting an angry response, we said, yes, we know about that and we know why he did it. That was the day he arrived as a frontline politician.[31]

He may have handled the unions adroitly, but when it came to the words he would use to abandon Labour's commitment to the closed shop, Blair turned to his real confidantes. His speech to Parliament was drafted one weekend in Sedgefield. Colin Byrne, Peter Mandelson, Gordon Brown, Anji Hunter and Alastair Campbell (still at that time the *Daily Mirror*'s political editor) crammed into a tiny room in Blair's Sedgefield home and produced it.[32]

Blair had only been employment spokesman for three months when Harriet Harman heard Kinnock say, perfectly seriously, as Blair entered the room: 'Here comes the next leader of the Labour Party.'[33]

The union leaders might have been less easy to deal with if they had known the contempt Blair felt for them. They certainly know now. Even at the time there were signs that he shared with Margaret Thatcher the view that the whole practice of industrial bargaining between management and unions was out of date.

That opinion was at the root of his long, long feud with the media's industrial correspondents, which continues to this day. In the 1970s being a labour and industrial correspondent was a prized job on national newspapers. First Thatcher, and then Blair, worked successfully to change this. As soon as he became employment spokesman, he several times asked the BBC's labour correspondent, Nick Jones, 'why I persisted in reporting the progress of what he thought were pretty pointless trade union motions at Labour's annual conferences'.[34]

Groups of specialist journalists tend to take on something of the outward character of the people on whom they report. Religious correspondents tend to be devout men and women. Royal correspondents are frequently tweedy, with plummy voices. Lobby correspondents mutter to each other secretively and think of each other as being attached to one or another of the cabinet factions.

Industrial correspondents have always unconsciously aped trade union officials. Even those who worked for very rightwing papers could be mistaken for trade union officials if you met them at a union conference. They drink hard and talk tough, they award each other the 'Golden Bollock' for the member who has made the most embarrassing error of the year, and their most revered colleague in those days was Mick Costello of the Communist Party's *Morning Star*, because he was considered (rightly) to know his way round the trade unions as well as anyone alive.

Blair's first informal meeting with this hard-bitten group of journalists was not a success, and it must have confirmed his worst prejudices. One day in Blackpool during the TUC's conference in 1990, after a press briefing, Labour's new employment spokesman asked the *Independent's* labour correspondent, Barry Clement, whether the journalists were going back to their hotels. No, Clement replied, they were off to the pub. Blair suggested he should come too. Clement tried to put him off: he and his colleagues went, he said, to a shabby working-class back-street pub called the Empress, which he did not think Blair would like. But Blair persisted, so Clement gave him directions to the Empress, and later on, well into the evening, after several pints of beer had found their way into the journalists, Blair turned up. Into this noisy, pubby group, with crumpled suits and leftwing instincts, even if not leftwing views, walked the fastidious young lawyer, in his beautifully cut suit, with his quiet voice, understated public-school charm, and smooth manners.

He spoke to Clement for a few minutes, but then, says Clement, 'He decided to do the cocktail party thing and network, but the Empress near closing time isn't a place for networking, it's a place for boozing.' Blair went over to the *Daily Mail*'s David Norris and said: 'Hello, David.'

Norris looked up balefully from his pint and said: 'You're that fucking freelance from Berkhamsted who owes me twenty pounds.'

'No, no, I'm the Labour Party employment spokesman. Don't you remember, we had lunch with [*Mail* editor] David English....'

'No, you're not, you're that fucking freelance from Berkhamsted.' (There is, or was, or may once have been, a freelance journalist in Berkhamsted who bears a passing resemblance to Blair.)

Unable to make further progress with Norris, Blair went to (of all people) Mick Costello, who was talking to someone else. He tapped

Costello on the shoulder. Costello, whose views about Blair's trade union reforms are unprintable, said, 'I don't know who you are. Fuck off,' and returned to his conversation.

The industrial correspondents often took their sources – union leaders, even politicians, even Conservative politicians – to the Empress, but they took an instinctive dislike to Blair overtly using their pub as a networking opportunity. A politician with a common touch could have got away with it. Blair left shortly afterwards, and ever since then, says Clement, 'He's hated us. He sees us as Old Labour rude mechanicals. He's made at least two references as Labour leader in conference speeches to the industrial correspondents, saying what a rotten lot we are.'35

The evening must have confirmed all Blair's worst suspicions. Here was a group of journalists who had got close to the trade unions, who considered them important and reported their activities. Blair already knew in his heart, with the clarity that came from not understanding Labour's history, that the unions had to be marginalised if the party was to have the future he dreamed of. From that day on he knew that, in order to achieve this, he had to marginalise the industrial correspondents. Years later he was still harping on the same theme, saying to Nick Jones in 1996, when he was Labour's leader and about to become prime minister: 'Look, it must be very sad being a labour correspondent, reporting all those meaningless resolutions. I do wish you could find a different agenda.' 'I realise,' writes Jones, 'how my enthusiasm as a labour correspondent must have grated on him and other like-minded young reformers.'

Blair, according to a union leader who knew him well at that time and admires him, 'has a very low opinion of unions and union leaders', though this has not stopped him, throughout his political career, from making ruthless use of old-fashioned trade union fixers when it suited him.

With the Conservatives in power, Kinnock leading Labour and Blair as employment spokesman, Nick Jones says:

> The union movement was in retreat, and the labour and industrial staff lost their prominent place in the hierarchy of most newsrooms, finding that the space and airtime they had once commanded was increasingly being filled by business and financial correspondents, to whom we rather mockingly referred as the 'footsoldiers for popular capitalism'.

Like Blair, Jones continues, Peter Mandelson 'was intent on doing all he could to thwart attempts by journalists like myself to report Labour's affairs from a union perspective'. When Jones moved from industry to politics and joined the Westminster lobby, Mandelson told him: 'I don't trust you. Once a labour correspondent, always a labour correspondent.'[36]

By helping Blair in his dealings with the unions, as in so many other things, Mandelson was doing exactly what his friend Colin Byrne describes: doing the dirty work for Blair, acting as Blair's lightning conductor. Jones described to us how this worked in practice. After Blair had announced the change of policy on union laws to the House of Commons, he came out to College Green, just outside Parliament, where television interviews are conducted, to do an interview with Jones. He stood, smiling in a friendly manner, while Mandelson bullied and abused Jones. Once the tirade was over, Blair agreed to answer one question, and one only. He ignored the question that Jones asked and said the one sentence he wished to say, then watched, still smiling, while Mandelson resumed the business of berating Jones. Blair and Mandelson knew, of course, that if Jones only had one sentence in the can, he would have to broadcast that one sentence.[37]

Mandelson may have been a master of this kind of manipulation but the trouble was that he was growing discontented with his role. He wanted to be a serious politician in his own right as well as remaining a friend and confidant of the powerful and a backstairs fixer. In the end the two roles would prove incompatible; but he did not foresee that in 1989, when he told a horrified Neil Kinnock that he wanted to stand for Parliament. Kinnock felt betrayed. He should not have been surprised, of course. Mandelson is an ambitious man, and was bound to want to move on. He wanted to be a politician by profession, and professional politicians are bound to want to get into Parliament.

Blair knew his man better, and helped line Mandelson up for the nomination in the safe Labour seat of Hartlepool, next door to his own Sedgefield constituency. There was a moment of awkwardness at the start, for when Blair asked John Burton, his lynchpin in Sedgefield: 'What do you think about Peter Mandelson for Hartlepool?' Burton replied: 'I was thinking of having a go at Hartlepool myself.' But it was swiftly overcome: Blair withdrew deprecatingly, telling Burton he should go for it if he wanted to, and Burton, as Blair probably knew he would, said: 'No, no, Peter's good, he should have it.' Burton explains now: 'I wanted to be a part of Tony's future. And I was fifty. So when he said he wanted Peter, I was quick to say, yes, it should be Peter. And anyway it would have been harder to get it for me because I was the local councillor.'

Burton knew Peter was good because Blair had told him so. He once asked why, and Blair replied: 'A good press officer will tell you what the headlines will be tomorrow, but Peter Mandelson will tell you what they will be in three days' time.'

There was another awkward moment to come. Burton trotted off to do what Blair wanted, and tell the constituency chairman in Hartlepool that he had a wonderful, whizzy candidate for the seat, only to be told that the Hartlepool chairman had a candidate of his own – the famous actress Glenda Jackson. Burton, a bit crestfallen, reported back, but was cheered to hear Mandelson himself, on one of his regular weekend trips to the Blairs' Sedgefield home, say: 'Don't worry, I'll phone Glenda up and we'll sort it out between us.' He did, and persuaded Jackson to settle for the rather less safe seat of Hampstead.[38]

Mandelson was selected as Labour candidate for Hartlepool on the same day as Tony Blair ditched the closed shop, 17 December 1989. Neil Kinnock, by then fatally emotionally dependent on Mandelson, felt as if his right arm had been cut off. Mandelson seems to have thought he could carry on being director of communications – an extraordinary assumption, for how could you have a director of communications who, as soon as the election is called, would have to rush off to Hartlepool to fight his own seat? Back in 1982, Labour's national executive had been foolish enough to ask its then communications director, Max Madden, to stay on even though he was a parliamentary candidate. Madden had had the sense to refuse.

Kinnock saw that Mandelson's idea was absurd. Charles Clarke told Mandelson: 'You'll have to decide immediately when to leave your job … Neil is so angry he cannot bring himself to talk about it. I have never known him so furious about anything. We'll want you to go straight-away.' Clarke added that if it were up to him, Mandelson would clear his desk that day.[39] To understand his fury, you have to consider that Clarke was starting to realise that continuing his loyal service to Kinnock was not as good a career move as he had once believed. If Kinnock never became prime minister, Clarke would be left out in the cold. Mandelson's successor, John Underwood, says: 'Kinnock's closest aides, Clarke and Patricia Hewitt, both wanted to go for parliamentary seats in 1992, but decided to stay with Kinnock. So they and Kinnock felt Mandelson had ratted by going for a seat.' But Blair, who had fixed the Hartlepool seat for Mandelson, escaped all censure. As usual, all the resentment was focused on Mandelson, Blair's lightning conductor.

Mandelson agreed to leave in the autumn of 1990. All the same, his friend and deputy Colin Byrne was furious that Mandelson was, as he puts it, 'hastily forced out'. The real trouble, though, was that he never really left. Between partners at the time, he was sharing a house with Byrne and Byrne's fiancée Julie Hall, who was also Kinnock's press secretary. As if that did not make the whole operation of the leader's office incestuous enough, a way was quickly found for him to become the leader's behind-the-scenes fixer. On 26 March 1990, six months before Mandelson's departure, the management consultant Colin Fisher, a Mandelson confidant at least since 1983, wrote to Neil Kinnock. He had, he said, been talking to Mandelson and had a suggestion to make:

> Peter is so good – as I think you know – that to lose him would be a great mistake. My business – SRU – which is a strategic management consultancy, will take Peter under its wing for a while, so he will be economically secure, but in an arrangement which would give him time to be helpful to you personally. Either way Peter is going to come and work for us, but would you like us to make it possible for that to happen?[40]

Unwisely, Kinnock said yes, thereby ensuring that Mandelson would be in a position to second-guess his successor and persuade the leader to overrule him – unless that successor was Mandelson's bosom pal Colin Byrne.

Mandelson pressed Byrne's case to be his successor. Kinnock accepted Mandelson's advice and voted for Byrne in the meeting of the national executive. But Byrne was so closely identified not just with Mandelson, but with Mandelson's two protégés Blair and Brown as well, that even Kinnock's loyal deputy, Roy Hattersley, did not for once feel able to support his leader. Behind the scenes, Hattersley was becoming impatient with Kinnock, and he voted for his old adviser, the calm and experienced (but, in today's terms, rather Old Labour) David Hill. But the executive, normally by this time inclined to follow Kinnock's lead, followed neither Kinnock nor Hattersley. The job went to the broadcaster John Underwood.

Underwood now says:

> I got the job without the leader's or the deputy leader's vote, but to do the job, you need the leader's support. On my first day in the job Neil Kinnock called me in and said, I didn't vote for you but we're together now. He said he would work with me, but over the next few days it became clear that Peter Mandelson was determined not to help me at all. He did not want anyone to eclipse him in the spin stakes when he moved on.

It was the last time the NEC chose a communications chief. From then on, the job was effectively in the gift of the leader.

Just for a day or two, it looked as though a split might occur in the old alliance of Mandelson, Blair and Brown. 'Tony Blair and Gordon Brown tried hard to work with me and make me their friend,' says Underwood. Blair in particular knew how important the director of communications was. He once approached Underwood in a corridor:

> His eyes lit up as we came towards each other, he put his hand on my shoulder, and he said: 'John, what's going on?' I said: 'You should know, Tony, you're in the shadow cabinet.' Blair said: 'I'm just a member of the shadow cabinet, you're the director of communications.' [Blair was always] very hail-fellow-well-met, very keen to be on good terms with anyone of influence.[41]

Underwood inherited Byrne as his deputy – always a classic prescription for friction. Byrne wanted Underwood's job and bitterly resented both the fact that the executive had appointed Underwood over his head, and the fact that his best friend and housemate Peter Mandelson had been forced out. Byrne went home every night to listen to Mandelson stoking up his grievances. Mandelson, paid by SRU, was given all the time he wanted to tell the receptive leader of the party what ought to be done. Meanwhile, according to Byrne, 'Underwood was being badly wound up about me by Robin Cook.' Byrne adds: 'Underwood could not take the pressure.'[42]

In these circumstances Underwood couldn't survive, and he didn't. He felt himself undermined at every turn. Charles Clarke tried ineffectually to stop the rot. He told Byrne and Hall that sharing a home with Mandelson was a mistake. In a paper for Kinnock, he wrote of his concern about Mandelson's continuing strong relationship with Brown and Blair. This, he wrote, 'has led to the specific allegations ... that Peter, Gordon and Tony are plotting a new post-Kinnock leadership of themselves'. Which, of course, is exactly what they were doing.

Underwood's broadcasting officer, Sally-Anne Lomas, left after only a month because the atmosphere was so unpleasant, writing to her bosses: 'The Directorate of Campaigns and Communications is divided against itself. It cannot communicate and its campaign victories are internal ones. One of the losers seems to be the director himself.' She added presciently: 'The over-promotion of some younger shadow spokesmen seems to have more to do with the post-electoral reorganisation of the party after a further defeat, rather than in winning the election with the team we have.'[43] She was referring, we may assume, to Gordon Brown and Tony Blair.

Later, Clarke seems to have tried to give the impression that he was really on Mandelson's side all along. Kinnock felt that Mandelson had totemic value to the Labour Party. Kinnock's view, according to Under-wood, was: 'He frightens the Tories because they think he has magical powers that will bring them down.' Underwood's view, which he tried to convey to Kinnock, was: 'Mandelson was such a divisive influence in the Labour Party, and of such value to the Tories, that if he had not existed, the Conservative Party would have had to invent him.'[44]

For the moment, Kinnock's view prevailed. So when a by-election in Monmouth came along, Kinnock and Clarke instructed Underwood to send Mandelson. In the past the communications director had always either gone himself to run by-election campaigns, or sent a trusted subor-dinate.

Writing from Monmouth in May 1991, Mandelson addressed Clarke in typically emotional and disingenuous terms. He had, he said, a lot of sympathy with Clarke 'in handling what I had not realised was such a difficult situation'. He said he was 'trying to put my bruised feelings aside after another evening of press calls'. And he put in his bid to be placed, over Underwood's head, in charge of future by-election battles:

> I just wanted to say this. Obviously my first priority is to win Hartlepool
> where I am facing pressures from my political opponents and the press.
> But working in Monmouth gave me real pleasure ... . I think I can con-
> tribute more in the same way, in a quiet, tactful, reasonable way. I would
> like to do so and I find it perplexing that, with victory so close for us,
> some people would prefer not to use all we've got.

It did not take a man as clever as Clarke to work out that 'some people' meant Underwood.[45]

Underwood, as all his predecessors would have done, interpreted Kin-nock's decision to send Mandelson to Monmouth as a sign of lack of confidence in himself. The next month he told Kinnock that Byrne had to be shifted, or he would resign. Kinnock refused; Underwood resigned.

Mandelson still might have wanted Byrne in the job, but this time Roy Hattersley got his way, and David Hill was given the job of steady-ing Labour's communications before the general election. Steadying the ship seems to be Hill's forte: he has recently been brought back once again, this time by Blair, to steady Downing Street communications after Alastair Campbell's incandescent departure. Soon afterwards Colin Byrne left – another 'terrible blow to the campaign' according to Philip Gould, though it is unlikely that David Hill saw it that way.[46] The problems had been patched over, not resolved.

Clearly, the party's campaigning and communications operation was in no state to fight a general election, and neither was the shadow cabinet. What seems to have happened next is that Gordon Brown and Tony Blair sabotaged the regular Monday strategy meetings with shadow cabinet members organised by Hill and Hattersley. Of the shadow cabinet, only Hattersley and Gerald Kaufman turned up regularly. Others appeared from time to time. But Blair and Brown came once, together, and never came again. Charles Clarke told Hill that it was asking too much to expect Kinnock to attend regularly, in addition to the burdens he already carried. So the meetings withered and died.[47]

In September 1991, three months after Underwood's departure, Roy Hattersley tried to get the strategy meetings going again. He had been complaining on and off ever since 1987 about how hard Kinnock's staff made it for the leader and the deputy to have a meeting. Now he wrote to Kinnock:

> We have had a very bad summer – only partly as a result of bad luck … .
> We have done little or nothing to keep domestic politics on the agenda.
> As far as I can see we had no strategy for doing so. You will recall that
> at the last of our 'regular' meetings (held during the second week in
> July!) we both agreed that summer campaigning was essential but that it
> would not go on unless someone took charge of arranging rotas of
> speakers and special opportunities for publicity … . Nothing happened
> throughout the summer.

Prime Minister John Major and Liberal Democrat leader Paddy Ashdown were appearing regularly on television, Hattersley continued; not so Kinnock. And 'senior members of the shadow cabinet are simply not working hard enough'. In January 1992 he wrote again: 'The risk that you will imagine I am panicking after one weekend of moderate opinion polls is one that I will have to take.' He wanted a clearer statement of the party's financial proposals, which Kinnock and Blair believed could only damage the party. And he wanted

> a more effective command structure. Too many decisions are still taken
> by individual shadow ministers – date of initiatives, reaction to Tory
> proposals …
>   I have, on and off for nine years, suggested regular meetings of a
> small group under your chairmanship and guidance. I now believe the
> creation of such a group to be essential for our success. It can only oper-
> ate with your presence and therefore your authority and I urge you to set
> it up and arrange for its regular meetings at the earliest opportunity.[48]

All this time, the Conservative government's popularity was declining. In 1989 Margaret Thatcher ended her first decade as prime minister, and she was no longer looking impregnable and invincible. Labour's poll ratings were better than those of the Conservatives, but not sufficiently high for comfort. The party's by-election results were improving as Kinnock exercised his power to impose approved by-election candidates on local Labour parties. The results in the European elections of 1989 were a triumph, leaving Labour with 45 MEPs as against 32 for the Conservatives – an 8.8 per cent swing to Labour compared with the 1987 election, and a result that, if repeated at a general election, would give Labour a parliamentary majority of about twenty seats. The hard left was in full retreat, with Ken Livingstone losing his place on Labour's national executive in 1989, to Kinnock's unrestrained delight.

The poll tax, introduced in 1990, was immensely unpopular, with even many Conservatives hating it, though Labour's attack on it was, as we have seen, blunted by the party's internal jealousies. The economy was no longer a key Conservative strength, as inflation and the balance of payments deficit both rose. Labour's warnings about the dangers of the consumer-led boom of the 1980s were proving to be well founded. But newspaper headlines often focused on Labour's internal personality-led feuding, and Kinnock's personal poll ratings stubbornly refused to improve.

Then, towards the end of 1990, the Conservative Party, which had seen Margaret Thatcher turn from its greatest asset to its greatest liability, dumped her, electing the chancellor of the exchequer, John Major, as her successor. Major hastened to ditch the unpopular poll tax. Labour's climb in the opinion polls halted and even started to go into reverse. When, in January the next year, Major sent in British troops to help the Americans drive Saddam Hussein's invading army out of Kuwait, Kinnock supported him. 'I reflected,' wrote Major later, accurately, 'how frustrating the conflict must have been for [Kinnock]. Before I became Prime Minister Labour were well ahead in the opinion polls, but my election had turned them round. How, when he must have wished to sink his political teeth into a new Prime Minister, he was forced to support him.'[49] It was even more frustrating that the public blamed Thatcher and former chancellor Nigel Lawson for Britain's economic woes – and did not blame Major at all.

Kinnock had now become the longest-serving opposition leader of the twentieth century, and it was taking its toll on him. The strain of imposing iron discipline on both his naturally ebullient character and his naturally fissile party was showing, and the party remained fractious. The Blair mythology has it that Kinnock was angry with his shadow chancellor, John Smith, but the truth is that his frustration embraced the whole cabinet, including Tony Blair. In fact, it was Blair, more than anyone else, who regularly told friends in 1991 that he expected Labour to lose the election.[50] Many people believed that Mandelson, Blair and Brown were preparing for a future without Kinnock, in which they would rule. Nonetheless, Labour's 1991 conference was a triumph for Neil Kinnock, and with a slender lead in the opinion polls, it was still possible for him and those around him to believe that he would attend the next conference as prime minister.

On 11 March 1992, John Major announced that the general election would be held on 9 April. Labour entered the campaign with a fragile three-point lead. Somehow, between March 24 and April 9, that turned into an eight-point Conservative lead, enough for an overall Conservative majority of 21. Right up until the last moment Labour thought it might just triumph. On polling night John Smith approached his Scottish Liberal colleagues and told them to book overnight flights so they could arrive in Heathrow early in the morning to discuss a Lib–Lab coalition. Unlike Blair's later 'big tent' deal with Paddy Ashdown in 1997, this was simply a pragmatic move. Smith calculated that if there was a 'hung' Parliament, the two opposition parties could oust Major, using a move that Wilson had pioneered in the first 1974 government. By 3 a.m. on election night, Menzies Campbell, who would have gone into government under the deal, was asked to cancel his flight from Aberdeen airport.[51]

There is, even today, no more sensitive question you can ask in the Labour Party than: why did Labour lose in 1992? Your answer, in Blairite circles, defines you as a friend or an enemy. Good Blairites insist it was all John Smith's fault. His tax pledges frightened Middle England. But Bob Worcester says: 'Smith's tax pledges had already been discounted by the electorate – everyone knew what he was going to do for six months before the election. The polls say you can raise tax for health and education.'[52] Worcester's polling provides some compelling evidence for this. Two years before the election, Labour had pledged to raise the top rate of tax to 50 per cent and remove the national-insurance ceiling to pay for pensions and child-benefit increases. If redistributory tax promises are fatal, how was it that Labour continued to lead in the polls?

The reason Smith has to bear the blame in Blairite mythology is that the other explanation for Labour's defeat would mean blaming it on the Blairites and the image-makers. Labour went into the election with a communications operation still in turmoil in the aftermath of the noisy departures of Peter Mandelson and Colin Byrne. Its campaign manager was Jack Cunningham, whom Roy Hattersley had unsuccessfully begged

Kinnock to replace, and he was working with Robin Cook. 'Cook and Cunningham were at each other's throats throughout the election,' says Bryan Gould. Colin Byrne, who was brought back to help with the campaign, talks of the 'lack of discipline' in the way it was run.

Labour also went back to its bad old 1983 habits, when it had a huge and unwieldy campaign committee. Gone was the tight, six-strong group which had run its 1987 campaign; the committee had swelled to about twenty people. The 1987 campaign co-ordinator Bryan Gould, who was invited to join it at a very late stage, says:

> It was very much polling-driven. The major item of business each morning was a session with Philip Gould, when he brought his polling data, which was mostly focus groups – very little quantitative research. They would change the election priorities each day in response to what Philip Gould told them. Some members could not make some of the meetings because of other commitments, so you never knew who was going to be there. I was shocked by it.

Worcester, however, has no doubt that the deciding factor was the huge rally Labour organised in Sheffield, just eight days before polling day. On the eve of the rally, three polls came out, showing, respectively, a seven-point lead, a six-point lead and a four-point lead for Labour. That was the day Labour peaked. It was all downhill from then on. The pollsters' predictions of a Labour victory were confounded. Polls are snapshots of opinion at a point in time, and that point is when the fieldwork is done, not when they are published. The polls were a matter of hours behind the swing of public opinion. After the election, an enquiry into polling errors by the Market Research Society concluded: 'After the final interviews there was a … swing to the Tories. It seems likely that this was the cause of a significant part of the final error … . We estimate that late swing … probably accounted for between a fifth and a third of the total error.'

Bob Worcester told us:

> I spoke just after the election to the 21 Club, the 21 Conservative MPs with the most marginal constituencies. Every single one of them said that without the Sheffield rally they would not be in Parliament. Labour candidates out canvassing that night, just after the rally went out on the news, had people saying, I'm sorry, I can't vote for you any longer. Statistically and anecdotally, Sheffield was the turning point.

Sheffield was, quite simply, a massive and unforgivable miscalculation by the image-makers who went on to run New Labour. Together with an ineptly run campaign, it probably cost Labour the 1992 election.

'Our aim,' one of the event's planners wrote in an unsigned internal memorandum

> will be to make it a TV spectacular. It will be full of music, movement of people, light effects and an audio visual presentation on a giant screen. The overall theme will be a gathering of forces nationwide in support of Labour ...
>
> The entire shadow cabinet will be present ... Neil Kinnock will arrive by helicopter and the event will climax with his speech from the podium, surrounded by the shadow cabinet. Budget planning for the event allows for the employment of our own outside broadcast TV crew so that the very best pictures can be obtained, using a special remote-controlled camera that will move across the ceiling of the hall ...
>
> The closing sequence will be timed to coincide with the opening titles of the main BBC News and the reporter's piece to camera ...
>
> The out-of-vision MC will welcome contingents of about fifty party members ... starting with Scotland, led by a pipe band; Wales, preceded by a brass band ... . Regional groups will be provided by us with US convention style banners identifying their regions as well as carrying the main campaign slogans ...
>
> Neil Kinnock's arrival will be announced and we will see him on the big screen arrive by helicopter on a field adjacent to the arena. While he is travelling by car to the arena, the first of the celebrity endorsements will be shown on the big screen. Neil Kinnock will then make an entrance into the arena ... Neil Kinnock will be announced and will walk the length of the arena, accompanied by the shadow cabinet ...
>
> The closing sequence will be a special arrangement of the Red Flag for two voices, followed by 'Jerusalem' sung by Alison Moyet ...
>
> As the main BBC News comes on air, we will set off the indoor pyrotechnics, light shows and confetti guns ...[53]

It would have been a disaster even if it had all gone according to plan. On the day, earlier speakers overran, Kinnock appeared ten minutes late, and at that point the 10,000 keyed-up people in the hall erupted with excitement. Neil Kinnock's repeated cry of 'All right!' went down a treat in the hall, but came across dreadfully on television. The problem was not Kinnock's performance: it was the gaudy triumphalism of the whole affair. And in any case, if the spin doctors had not kept the lid so firmly closed on the real Neil Kinnock, the dam inside him might not have burst on that Sheffield stage.

The election lost, Kinnock departed with haste but dignity. His papers were rapidly swept up, and, at Charles Clarke's insistence, went to Churchill College, Cambridge, which already housed the papers of Clarke's distinguished father as well as those of Margaret Thatcher. Left-leaning archive centres, such as the Labour Movement Library in Manchester, were furious. But perhaps it was a sign of the times.

The lesson of Labour's 1992 defeat was that Clarke and Kinnock got it wrong five years earlier. They concentrated on pushing through their policy changes, while leaving the image-makers to get to work. And the image-makers let them down. But this was not the lesson Blair drew from the debacle. Blair's agenda was yet more policy changes – more far-reaching than Kinnock would ever have contemplated.

CHAPTER EIGHT

CHAFING UNDER JOHN SMITH'S
LEADERSHIP

Neil Kinnock believes to this day that if only Bryan Gould had followed his advice, then Gould, and not Blair, would have become Labour leader in 1994 and prime minister in 1997. 'The reason he only got 12 per cent of the votes when he stood against John Smith for leader is because 88 per cent of them wanted him for deputy leader. And who knows what would have happened if he'd concentrated on winning the deputy leadership.'[1]

Gould rejected the advice and decided to stand for leader. It was not just that he felt that some of Smith's policies would be wrong for the party; he also felt that if he stood for the deputy leadership he would simply be clearing the way for Smith. 'I thought, if I only stood for deputy leader, people would think they could safely vote for me as deputy with a clean conscience, and vote for John Smith as leader for the sake of their careers,' he says. He also remembers Kinnock's advice slightly differently. 'Neil telephoned me at home on the Sunday after the 1992 election defeat to confirm that he was going and he said: "Stick around to pick up the pieces." I thought he was telling me to keep my powder dry and wait for next time.'[2] Gould's decision to stand for leader probably cost him the deputy leadership. The interesting point is that Kinnock wanted Gould to be deputy leader. He wanted to position Gould, not Brown or Blair, as the leader after Smith.

The day after the election, Blair was telling journalists that Labour had not changed enough, simultaneously pointing out to fellow MPs that the party's share of the vote had advanced only 3 per cent since 1987. That day he was also the only member of the shadow cabinet to telephone Neil Kinnock and commiserate – another example of the careful approach to personal relationships that has served him so well.

But in the days that followed, Blair and Brown were firmly focused on their own futures. Their first thought was whether one of them had any chance of becoming leader straightaway. Blair wanted Brown to stand for leader. This sounds generous until you remember that neither of them stood a realistic chance of defeating John Smith. A Brown candidature would have been a gesture, little more, even though, years later, the Blairites claimed that at the time they thought Brown had a realistic chance of winning. It is revealing that Blair wanted Brown to make that gesture. He quickly rejected the idea of standing himself.

Today, Blair's friends say that Brown did seriously consider the idea. But Brown had promised John Smith he would not oppose him, and he has always denied the suggestion that he contemplated breaking that pledge; there is no evidence to suggest he is being untruthful. The Blair camp's line may be explained by their desire to excuse Blair's behaviour two years later. 'Gordon had his chance in 1992 and he ducked it,' they say.[3]

Blair's next proposal was that Brown should stand for deputy leader. Brown took this idea to John Smith, who told him: 'Having two Scots with constituencies 75 miles apart makes no sense.' Brown would have to make do with the key job of shadow chancellor, which Smith had promised him.[4] This should have swayed Blair, who was later to use the argument that the party needed an English leader in order to advance his own claim over Brown's. But it did not: Blair wanted Brown to defy Smith and stand anyway. When Brown refused, Blair thought briefly about standing for deputy leader himself, but Smith was not keen on that idea either.

John Smith knew exactly whom he wanted as his deputy. He wanted Margaret Beckett. She was English and a woman, both of which would help when it came to an election. And she was on the left of the party. It would be a sign that Labour was finally moving on after the disastrously divisive 1980s. Blair looked at the arithmetic and recognised he could not beat Beckett if she had Smith's support.

Having abandoned the idea of making their own bid for one of the two top jobs, it would have been logical for the modernisers, if they meant what they said, to have mounted a campaign to get Gould elected instead of Smith. He was the key Kinnock supporter in the shadow cabinet, and he alone was putting the modernisers' view in the campaign. It was Gould who was saying that Smith was complacent and therefore would not make the huge policy changes in the party that the modernisers considered essential if Labour was to win the next election.

In fact, Bryan Gould did have the enthusiastic support of the less ambitious modernisers like John Carr and Margaret Hodge. Carr explains:

John Smith was part of the old Northern Labour mafia, so many of the Blairites were aligned to Gould. Margaret Hodge is the exemplar – there is no more Blairite person than Margaret. Blair himself certainly felt that the swift election of Smith would mean the end of the modernising project. The core of the modernisers' message was that Labour had to change massively.[5]

Yet Mandelson, Brown and Blair refused to support the candidate who was the leading exponent of their own views. Partly, no doubt, this was because of Gould's view on the European exchange rate mechanism (ERM) – he was, broadly, against it. But the main reason was that Blair and Brown both wanted the crown for themselves – if not now, then in due course – and Mandelson wanted it for one of his two friends. Gould was younger than Smith, and in better health; the fifty-four-year-old Smith had had a serious heart attack a few years earlier, and some observers (though not Smith himself) feared his tenure might prove to be short.

Blair must also have calculated that Smith would be an easier target if and when the time came to make a direct challenge for the leadership. It would be very hard to undermine Gould when he was likely to say and do the things the modernisers wanted of the leader, and he could not be portrayed as part of Labour's past. Mandelson, as we have seen, had long ago abandoned his enthusiastic advocacy of Gould in favour of his two younger protégés, and was briefing journalists that Gould was in decline and Brown and Blair in the ascendant.

An ambitious politician, when the time comes to vote for a new leader, votes for the person who is going to win and will have the spoils of victory to hand out. Thus Blair voted for Smith in 1992 in the same cynical spirit in which he voted for Kinnock in 1983.

Today, Blairite mythology has it that, back then in 1992, Kinnock's mantle was already falling on Tony Blair. But the truth was that during the weekend after the election, while Kinnock was trying to ensure that Bryan Gould positioned himself to inherit the leadership one day, Blair and Brown were working out how to ensure that they, not Gould, triumphed. They met up several times that weekend, along with Mandelson and Nick Brown, the Newcastle East MP.[6]

Bryan Gould's adviser Nigel Stanley, who ran Gould's campaign for leader, came up with the phrase 'One more heave' as a contemptuous way of caricaturing Smith's approach. The phrase appeared in a five-point memorandum written by Stanley for Gould's campaign in which he identified Smith's supposed weaknesses – a document which could have been written by Peter Mandelson or Tony Blair. But Mandelson was busy undermining the only candidate who stood for the things in which Mandelson and Blair themselves believed.

Today, most Labour insiders believe that either Blair or Mandelson invented the phrase; Anthony Seldon, Blair's recent biographer, thinks it was Blair. Stanley, now head of communications at the Trades Union Congress, often does not bother to correct this suggestion. But if you are lucky enough to catch the band in which Stanley plays bass guitar at one of its occasional London pub gigs, you will be reminded exactly whose phrase it was: the band is called One More Heave.

There is an interesting footnote to the 1992 campaign which is worth recording. Kinnock's departure from the leadership led to a decision by Charles Clarke, his closest adviser, to quit his job. He left the Westminster hothouse and did not return until he secured a nomination for the Tory marginal seat of Norwich South in 1996. He went into the world of political lobbying – but not in the conventional, money-making sense that attracts many an ex-politician or adviser. He became an anti-lobbying lobbyist. In an interview he gave to one of the authors for the *Guardian* in 1993, Clarke talks about how many lobbyists 'con clients'.

He said: 'Lobbying is a gigantic con trick trading on the mystique of Parliament … . Thousands of pounds are spent by firms getting information which they could easily get themselves for half the cost.' He set up his own company, Quality Public Affairs, in a tiny office above the Fabian Society's headquarters, and his clients included charities, trade unions and a small number of public companies.[7] It prospered: by the time he wound it up, at least one client was paying £1,000 a day for his advice.

But what Clarke never mentioned in the interview is that his career could have taken another direction – he had received an extraordinary offer that many people would not have turned down. He was headhunted by the security services and offered a job working for MI6. They approached the departing leader, Neil Kinnock, for a detailed reference.[8] Clarke had all the attributes of a good spy. He was intelligent, well-travelled, discreet, inscrutable, and brilliant at arranging clandestine political meetings. Kinnock tried to persuade his old adviser to take the job, pointing out the opportunities for promotion and his suitability for secret service work. But Clarke would have none of it; he was set on creating his new lobbying company. He must have known that such a drastic change of direction would have meant giving up a political career for good. It is still an amazing tale; in the genre of 'if only' it is in the pantheon of the greats. In 2003, instead of saving Blair's bacon over the tuition fees revolt, he could have been advising his leader over going to war with Iraq – and giving evidence to Lord Hutton. It was not to be.

Smith and Margaret Beckett were duly elected leader and deputy leader. It was one of the smoothest elections in Labour's history, with few of the plots, tantrums and dramas of many leadership elections. There was a growing feeling that the solid, reassuring John Smith would be the next prime minister. That feeling hardened into certainty on 16 September 1992. On that day the chancellor of the exchequer, Norman Lamont, raised interest rates, first from 10 to 12 per cent, and then again to 15 per cent, as he struggled to support the pound in an old-fashioned devaluation crisis. Then, soon after 7 p.m., he announced the suspension of Britain's membership of the ERM. By then, almost £10 billion – 40 per cent of the national reserves – had been squandered in a vain attempt to buy sterling out of trouble.

It was, as Roy Hattersley writes, 'the greatest economic fiasco in modern British history', for which 'the real reason was the government's insistence on treating the pound like a status symbol rather than a currency'.[9] The Conservatives' reputation for good economic management was suddenly in tatters, and from that day on, as their rift over Europe turned into an abyss, they never for one moment recovered in the opinion polls or looked like a party capable of winning the next general election. Despite what the Blairites would say later, there was not then, nor is there now, the smallest doubt that Labour under John Smith would have won the 1997 general election handsomely.

Gordon Brown became shadow chancellor, as Smith had promised. Tony Blair's obvious ability and charisma were rewarded with another top post, as shadow home secretary. Smith actually offered him a choice – foreign secretary or home secretary. Blair was attracted to the former because of the opportunities for foreign trips and the chance of meeting world leaders. It was Brown who persuaded him that shadow home secretary was a more high-profile job – and one which would give him a chance of taking the Tories on and beating them at their own game.

Brown gave Blair some further, equally valuable advice once he had taken up his new post. Blair told Brown he wanted to get rid of Labour's image as being soft on crime, and he thought of using the catchphrase 'Tough on crime'. Brown advised him to add 'and tough on the causes of crime' because it would play better to Labour Party people. (Today, it is generally believed that the whole phrase was Brown's invention, but that is not quite true.) Blair followed the advice, though never seeming to understand the point of the amendment. Thus was born the catchphrase most people associate most closely with Tony Blair, and it was the one thing that did most to make him into a potential Labour leader.[10] Blair launched it on BBC Radio 4's *The World This Weekend* on 10 January 1993. Those few words did more than any other single factor to help him edge ahead of the man who had helped coin it for him.

It was during his time as shadow home secretary that Blair really made his name with the public. He also showed himself to be a sufficiently good debater to take on, on equal terms, two of the cabinet's biggest hitters – first Kenneth Clarke, then Michael Howard.

In the meantime, Smith embarked on the one great reform which was seen as unfinished business left over from the Kinnock era: that of destroying the power of the trade union block vote within the Labour Party by instituting a system of one man, one vote, or OMOV as it came to be known. So you would have thought Brown and Blair had little to complain about, but complain they did, especially Blair, even though he had voted for Smith and turned down the chance to vote for someone whose views were closer to his.

Unlike Brown and Blair, their friend Peter Mandelson might well have felt he had something to complain about. He had been Kinnock's close friend and confidant, but he was not to enjoy this status under the new leader. Smith did not want him around. Perhaps it was this more than anything else that made Blair less than totally loyal to Smith.

Why did Smith exclude Mandelson? Several explanations have been put forward, and they are all mistaken. It has been whispered that Smith was uneasy because Mandelson was gay, but Smith's wife Elizabeth had several gay friends with whom her husband was completely at ease. It has also been suggested, more credibly, that Smith thought he could not trust Mandelson. He did, but that was not the reason either. A top politician has to work with lots of people he does not trust. And it has been said that Smith thought Mandelson was without ability, but he did not think that, though he realised that Mandelson's reputation as a master of media relations relied upon his being known to be an intimate of the leader. For him, Mandelson's great skill was that, like his famous grandfather, he understood the nuts and bolts of the Labour Party and knew which levers to pull.

The real problem was a simple, human one, and it had to do with that quality of seductiveness which Bryan Gould noticed in Peter Mandelson. Friendships between senior politicians can prove difficult, and Smith did not make many close friendships in politics. The very few exceptions were very old, close friends like Donald Dewar: Smith and Dewar had been undergraduates together at Glasgow University. His reluctance to forge new close political relationships increased when he became leader, because, he said, you never knew when you were going to have to fire someone.

That did not mean that Smith was dour or distant with his colleagues. On the contrary, he famously held court on the Thursday-night Glasgow sleeper train with fellow Scots – both Labour and Liberal Democrat colleagues – discussing the latest Westminster gossip over several glasses of malt whisky or beer. Their occasionally noisy revels meant that few went to bed before the train reached Carlisle at four in the morning.

But Smith had seen the way Mandelson wriggled his way into Neil Kinnock's life, eating with the Kinnocks as part of the family, often twice or three times a week, becoming an intimate, a favourite with the Kinnock children. That was also the relationship Mandelson was to establish with Tony Blair. But Smith recognised Mandelson's need to be loved, and it made him uncomfortable. With Smith, that relationship was not on offer. And Smith sensed that Mandelson would accept nothing less from his leader. Mandelson, he believed, sought power through intimacy. Smith felt Mandelson was looking for something from him and his family that they could not give.

Furthermore, he did not need a Mandelson in the way that Kinnock before him and Blair after him needed one: he was less nervous about the media and about his party. He did not even have his own senior spokesman. The funding Kinnock had secured for his office staff did not transfer to Smith, and Smith had other priorities for the small amount of money available. So he asked the head of campaigns and communications at Labour Party headquarters, David Hill, to double as the leader's spokesman. Hill was for many years Roy Hattersley's adviser, and Smith felt he could trust him.

Hill's partner, Hilary Coffman, had been Kinnock's assistant press officer, and she was the only member of Kinnock's staff to stay with Smith, in an enhanced role. Smith did a great deal of the media relations work himself: every national newspaper editor and political editor had Smith's own home telephone number.

Nonetheless, he knew that Mandelson was a significant factor in Labour Party politics, and he made sure he knew what Mandelson and others were doing. No doubt he had regular reports about the secret cabal of modernisers who met every six weeks or so in Islington. Blair himself was at pretty well every meeting, along with Mandelson, Margaret Hodge and John Carr. So was Jack Dromey, a national official of the Transport and General Workers' Union and the husband of Labour

MP Harriet Harman. Another regular attendee was Sally Morgan, national women's officer for the Labour Party. The venue for these meetings was either Blair's house or that of Margaret Hodge. Hodge was formerly the ideologically rigid Bennite leader of the People's Republic of Islington – otherwise known as Islington borough council. Today her ideology has lost none of its rigidity, but it is now Blairite instead.

There were two notable absentees. Gordon Brown, though always invited, never turned up in person; he generally sent a member of his office staff in his place. Once he sent Derek Draper, who worked for Mandelson, but he was told not to do so a second time. Sally Morgan, fearful that Labour Party headquarters would find out that she was attending, and believing Draper to be indiscreet, said she would stop coming if he came again.

Carr's wife, Glenys Thornton, who had by now put her Bennite views firmly behind her, was general secretary of the Fabian Society and therefore felt it was inappropriate to take part in factional activity. All the same, she supported the modernisers in spirit, and Fabian literature at the time was notable for the large amount of coverage Tony Blair seemed to get. She is now Baroness Thornton.

This little cabal was crucial to what was to happen two years later, when Smith died. Though Gordon Brown was theoretically a part of the group, to the members of the cabal it was Blair, not Brown, who was the standard-bearer of modernisation. To them, it became more and more clear as the months passed that the crown, whenever it became vacant, should go to Tony Blair. That is why they were able to start plotting literally within minutes of the news of John Smith's death. It was from these meetings that Blair derived his ideas and the confidence that enabled him to make clear, discreetly but unmistakeably, his view that his leader was lazy and complacent.

The trade union leader Richard Rosser, then a member of Labour's national executive, remembers talking to Blair during a coffee break at an executive meeting. 'He started to say that we needed to go far further down the road of change than John Smith was leading us. Then he pulled back, as though he felt he shouldn't be saying it.'[11] This is vintage Blair. Blair never says anything by accident, but always likes to give the impression of being diffident and loyal. He could say it, and then seem to unsay it.

Outside Westminster, other forces were working to ensure that Blair and not Brown became the heir apparent. Blair's famous father-in-law, actor Tony Booth, was an active member of Arts for Labour, and Booth and his playwright friend Ron Rose, who also knew Cherie well, were in the habit of making themselves available to constituency Labour parties for performances. A couple of years before the 1992 election, Booth said to Rose: 'Tony's going to be Labour leader and prime minister one day.' They rather liked the idea. So they agreed to go wherever there was a by-election, give their show, and then tell the candidate: 'Tony Blair sent us.' They reckoned that a small group of newly elected MPs who felt that they owed Blair something might prove useful in future.

After the 1992 election, Blair's growing strength was being felt by those who feared it as much as by those who welcomed it. Denis MacShane, then working in Switzerland as the head of communications for a trade union international, remembers entertaining leftwing shadow cabinet member Michael Meacher when he came to Geneva. MacShane predicted that the next English (as opposed to Scottish or Welsh) Labour prime minister would be Tony Blair. Meacher, he says, 'exploded with anger' and said: 'That man is nothing. Nothing. Nothing.' MacShane disagreed. 'You watch some people on television and they jump out at you,' he says. 'Clinton and Schröder were like that, and so is Blair.'[12] MacShane became minister for Europe, but, like Meacher, is now on the backbenches.

Over the twenty-two months of John Smith's leadership, with Bryan Gould growing disenchanted and starting to think of a career outside politics, and Gordon Brown becoming semi-detached from the compulsive Islington group, Blair was increasingly becoming the one man upon whom the modernisers' hopes rested. The key battleground was to be the trade unions. The need to destroy union power in the Labour Party was for them an article of faith, and it was the article Blair was keenest on.

In 1992 the Labour Party national executive, on the advice of its general secretary, Larry Whitty, set up a working party to sort out the party's relationship with the unions: the Union Links Review Group. For Whitty, who had come to the job from the GMB trade union, the relationship with the unions would always be special, but he knew there would have to be fundamental changes. Bryan Gould was the nearest thing to a modernisers' representative on the working party. But Gould resigned from the executive after a dispute over the party's support for the principle of monetary union, and a replacement had to be found. Whitty had noticed – you could not be on the executive without noticing – that Tony Blair was muttering darkly about the working party's slow and cautious progress. 'Tony Blair and Gordon Brown were sniping from the sidelines,' says Whitty, 'so when Bryan Gould came off, I suggested to John Smith that Tony Blair should go on instead. From then on there was never any consensus. The meetings became very difficult. Some of the trade union representatives on the working group were upset that Blair was trying to write the unions out of all influence in the Labour Party.'[13]

Given the modernisers' constant denigration of Smith's complacency, both during his leadership and after his death, it is ironic that the greatest legacy from his short time at the head of his party was the ending of the trade union block vote. Unlike either Kinnock or Blair, he staked his leadership on achieving it and would undoubtedly have resigned the leadership had the party conference denied it to him. Smith had said in his acceptance speech: 'We must base our internal democracy on the principle of one member one vote, and not on the basis of block votes.' Six months later, he said: 'One trade union general secretary casting millions of votes will not happen in the future.'[14] His intentions were quite clear.

There were three areas where the trade union block vote was vital. Nationally, unions cast their block votes on motions at the Labour Party conference, and in the elections of Labour's leader and deputy leader. Locally, union branches used it when constituency Labour parties came to select their parliamentary candidates. Without this system Tony Blair would not have become MP for Sedgefield in 1983, for it was what enabled a regional union mogul like Joe Mills to make a few telephone calls and deliver a parliamentary nomination. Neil Kinnock had tried to end the system, but was defeated. The best Kinnock had been able to deliver was a complicated electoral college for parliamentary candidates in which a maximum of 40 per cent of the votes were held by the unions.

John Smith wanted to do what needed to be done through agreement with the unions. This was partly to ensure a smooth passage for his proposal at Labour's conference, and partly because, like all Labour leaders before him, but unlike Blair who followed him, he saw unions and unionism as the rock upon which the Labour Party was founded.

In the first two areas he succeeded. He went to the conference with a deal already done on the voting arrangements at the Labour conference, and on the election of Labour's leader and deputy leader, which massively cut back the unions' influence. The problem, from a modernisers' standpoint, was that he had compromised with the unions, which had not been publicly put in their place. So the modernisers decided to make sure no deal could be done on the third area, the selection of MPs. During the summer of 1993, trade union votes piled up against Smith, as union conferences voted to instruct their delegations to the party conference to oppose one member one vote. Smith told his private staff that they could be out of a job after October, since if he lost he did not feel he could carry on as leader. There is not the slightest doubt in the minds of anyone who knew him that he meant it.[15]

But he and the union chiefs he was negotiating with hoped to avoid a confrontation. 'We thought we'd done a deal,' says John Edmonds, leader of the GMB and one of the two or three key union leaders. 'We'd done a deal on the two really difficult issues. We thought, if we can settle those two matters, why can't we settle the third? The issue of selecting local candidates ought to have been the easiest of the three.'

The shape of the deal as it emerged was as follows. Those union members who paid the political levy to the Labour Party could have a vote. But no block votes would be allowed. Unions would have to register those of their members who paid the political levy, and these members would be entitled to an individual vote when it came to selecting their local Labour parliamentary candidate, just like other Labour Party members. The unions bought it. Smith, at first, bought it. The problem, says Edmonds, was that two members of Smith's shadow cabinet, Gordon Brown and Tony Blair, were determined to scupper the deal; and that they had sent Peter Mandelson to the press desk at the conference to say so. 'Mandelson was briefing that the modernisers thought it ridiculous to do a deal with the unions over reform,' says Edmonds. 'The leader should tell the unions what was to happen. He was saying that the row was over the block vote, though by then it was not about that at all. The block vote was dead.'

Nonetheless, Edmonds thought a deal could be done. 'I knew John Smith was not keen on having a battle. We'd settled the big things. It wasn't a hard thing to settle.' But then Edmonds was approached by Murray Elder, another experienced Labour Party hand who ran Smith's private office. 'He told me Smith had a lot of respect for Mandelson's judgement,' says Edmonds. 'Then I realised that something was changing. The media bought it, Mandelson won, Blair and Brown told him that a battle with the unions was necessary, and John had to fight. The party leadership decided that trade unionists should have no votes. They had managed to get him in a position where if he did a deal with us it would affect his credibility.'[16]

The deal was dead. Union members who paid the political levy were not to have a say in the choice of Labour parliamentary candidates. That was the policy which Smith now had to force through the conference. If he lost the vote, he intended to return the next day with the same motion, and a sentence added expressing confidence in the leader. If he was again defeated, he would have to resign. His friend John Edmonds told him privately that, if this happened, the GMB could then abstain on the motion, his mandate from his own conference to oppose OMOV notwithstanding, because he had no mandate to get rid of the party leader.[17] But even the GMB's abstention would not guarantee victory.

Smith very nearly lost the vote. Without a last-minute deal with one large union, MSF (a crucial decision pushed through by Labour MP and former MSF president Doug Hoyle which earned him a peerage in 1997), and without a storming performance from the platform by John Prescott, one of the members of his shadow cabinet who was closest to the unions, Smith would have lost. He won by a majority of 0.2 per cent and was able to tear up the resignation speech he had written over lunch.

Blair and the modernisers had forced Smith into a confrontation with his trade union friends – one that Smith privately thought was avoidable – over what was really the thinnest of issues: whether union members who paid the political levy to the Labour Party could cast individual votes to help select their local Labour parliamentary candidate. They had managed this by presenting the issue as being the block vote, which in reality it was not. They had ensured that, for the next few months, media coverage of the Labour Party would once again be focused on internal wrangling rather than policy. They never forgave Smith, and they continued to grumble about his efforts to do deals with union leaders like John Edmonds, a potent hate figure for them ever since Blair had tried to get his friend Tom Burlison elected as GMB leader, only to see him lose to Edmonds.

Smith, who was determined that this should be the last round of internecine party warfare, salvaged one thing from the wreckage: he announced that there would be no further constitutional changes; Labour could now concentrate on policy. For Blair and Mandelson, this was a profoundly depressing pronouncement. But there was nothing they could do about it while John Smith lived. Even more galling was Smith's evident determination to heal the wounds in the Labour Party, to make peace with people with whom Blair, Mandelson, Brown and their friends had more or less sworn eternal enmity.

Making Margaret Beckett his deputy leader had been just the tip of the iceberg. Smith took an early opportunity to make a fellow Scot, Gavin Strang, the agriculture spokesman. To the modernisers, Strang was a dangerous and unreconstructed relic of Labour's leftwing past who had, among other sins, resigned from the frontbench because of his opposition to the Falklands war in 1982. But the fifty-year-old Strang also had a

PhD in agricultural science, and he had been number two at the agriculture ministry when Labour was last in government. More than that, he had been the driving force behind the bill that abolished tied cottages, a tradition which had caused dreadful hardship among the poor in the countryside. So, in the view of the farm-workers' trade union, he was easily the most liked and trusted person in Parliament. He might well help the party win a rural seat or two, come the election.

Smith also brought leftwingers Clare Short and Tony Banks back onto his frontbench. He gave David Blunkett, who had been Bryan Gould's campaign manager and was still in those days seen as a leftwinger, a much bigger promotion than he was expecting, making him shadow health secretary. Those he did not promote, he nonetheless treated with friendship and respect. While Kinnock had refused to speak to dissidents like Tony Benn and Ken Livingstone, Smith went out of his way to be friendly towards them.

This had always been Smith's way. Years before, he had been invited onto a television programme with Livingstone because the producer thought they would make good television by attacking each other. Smith's solution was to have dinner with Livingstone and sort out a way to avoid the collision. No wonder Livingstone predicted, just before Smith's election: 'It will be like the liberation of Europe having a personally secure man in charge. I am sure I shall go on disagreeing with him. I shall keep banging on about defence cuts. But it will be a whole different atmosphere.'[18]

Blair and his friends knew that, too; it was exactly what they were afraid of. For them, people like Livingstone were historically the enemy. Charles Clarke, Gordon Brown, Peter Mandelson, John Carr and many other modernisers had grown up in the hothouse of student politics in the early 1970s. As young men, they had cut their political teeth fighting what in those days they would have called 'the Trots' or 'the ultras' (meaning ultra-leftwing). Kinnock, in a slightly earlier generation, had done the same. Tony Blair once asked Kinnock, in that flattering way he has, what was special about Kinnock and the people round him. Kinnock replied that they 'had been student union officers very young, and after that they came and worked for me'.[19] They learned their political skills early.

Kinnock had been president of his own university student union. Many of those around him had done that and more. Charles Clarke had gone on to head the National Union of Students. Gordon Brown was the first student to be elected rector of Edinburgh University. Peter Mandelson had run the British Youth Council. The rising young moderniser Jack Straw, now foreign secretary, was another former NUS president. Others who had graduated from student politics included key members of Kinnock's staff like Neil Stewart and John Reid, who is now health secretary. Fighting the ultras was in their bones.

There was an old student joke about one of that generation of student politicians walking across London Bridge on his twenty-first birthday, singing, 'Twenty-one today, twenty-one today!' – and then meeting Ken Livingstone, throwing him into the river below, watching him drown, and walking on, singing, 'Twenty-two today, twenty-two today!' Politics for that generation was the continuation of student politics by other means.

Blair was different. While Clarke was fighting the International Marxist Group in the NUS, Blair was politely exchanging ideas with IMG members in his Oxford lodgings. While Clarke was striving to get students to adopt realistic policies and tactics, Blair was discreetly cultivating top lawyers and politicians.

Kinnock's soul had been seared by a fierce, old-fashioned, ideological battle on the left, in a long tradition of such battles. Blair did not come from that tradition and had not fought that battle. He came without the old shared hatreds. He had to learn them. But he proved a fast learner. Perhaps that was because he did not start out with leftwing ideals, as Clarke and Kinnock did.

As Labour leader, Smith had a far easier task than Kinnock. In the early days of the Kinnock leadership there was the need for some strict, and sometimes heavy-handed, vote-fixing on the national executive. Part of Smith's legacy from Kinnock was a large national-executive majority, so he did not need the same sort of operation. Smith's laid-back style caused confusion, says his biographer Andy McSmith, among 'some of the less bright committee members, the little-known functionaries sent along by their trade unions, who were not accustomed to having to make up their own minds on questions outside their immediate sphere of competence'. This caused annoyance among advisers like Clarke, a group described by McSmith as 'people who had entered politics to make a career of it, often beginning in the National Union of Students or National Organisation of Labour Students; fast-risers who liked working to a clear chain of command, with a strong leader at the top as a source of quick decision-making'.[20]

The style of Smith's critics, though the point is not often mentioned these days, was learned from the Communist Party, which still controlled NUS elections in Clarke's day and whose support was key to both Clarke and Jack Straw becoming president of the NUS. From the

Communists, they had learned the crucial importance of always getting the line right.

Mostly they kept their resentment within a tight circle, voiced in such places as the cabal meetings in Blair's or Margaret Hodge's Islington homes. It was known about, but it was not destabilising, if only because Smith was in so strong a position that he was impregnable. In public, their opinions were voiced through people like Alastair Campbell, then political editor of the *Daily Mirror*, who wrote of the conflict between 'frantics' and 'long gamers', and journalist Martin Jacques, former editor of the Communist party's *Marxism Today*, which had influenced the modernisers. Jacques wrote in the *Daily Mail* about John Smith's 'breathtaking inactivity and complacency' and urged him to talk to 'entrepreneurs and industrialists, to programmers and advertising consultants, to Essex man and to the *Femail* reader'.[21]

Only one insider went public. Colin Byrne was another former NUS hand. He had been NUS press officer until he moved to the Labour Party to work under Peter Mandelson. He was, and still is, a close friend of Mandelson. When Mandelson gave up his job as head of communications in 1990, Byrne was – as we have seen – passed over in favour of John Underwood; and in early 1992 he had quit, angry that Mandelson had been, as he saw it, forced out. He took up a career in public relations, which some years later saw him become chief executive of Britain's biggest PR consultancy, Weber Shandwick. This success he attributes in part to Mandelson's wise career advice.

He vented his feelings in an explosive letter to the *Guardian* soon after the 1992 general election. He says today that he 'woke up on the Sunday morning after the election to hear the obnoxious John Edmonds on television, saying Neil Kinnock was a lightweight and only John Smith had impressed during the campaign. It was a personal and angry response and I did not consult anyone.'[22] His memory is a little faulty: Edmonds did not rubbish Kinnock. But he did say that when Kinnock resigned, there would be only one name on everyone's lips; and everyone knew he meant Smith.[23]

When they heard what he had done, Blair, Gordon Brown and Byrne's close friend Peter Mandelson were all quickly on the telephone to ask him to withdraw the letter. Mandelson told Byrne it would not help the modernisers, and after Byrne insisted on going ahead, Mandelson refused to speak to him for three months. The letter blamed Smith's tax policies for losing the election and attacked his record on what Byrne called 'the radical reforms Labour ... must go on making if it is not to tread water, sink and die'. He attacked 'the right' – meaning

Smith and his friends and supporters, though in the conventional meaning of the word, they were now, if anything, more leftwing than the modernisers. The charge sheet was long. They had, he said, done nothing about Militant until Neil Kinnock became leader. They had done nothing about 'reforming the party's relationship with the trade unions and its industrial relations policies'. They had not helped Kinnock over Europe, or over the Gulf War. They had 'sat on their hands and let the Kinnocks and the Blairs take the flak'.

Byrne continued:

> Last autumn, after three years as head of Labour's press office, I quit … . Until now I have not publicly commented on why. The truth is simple: I refused to be part of what I believed to be a conspiracy which for over a year had been manoeuvring John Smith into position to walk into the leadership should Labour lose and had orchestrated the ruthless undermining and behind-the-scenes rubbishing of perceived rivals in a future contest … . I have seen the way these people operate and abuse their position and then call it politics. In short, it stinks.[24]

It was, of course, not Smith but Byrne's friend Mandelson who had organised the undermining of Bryan Gould. But by 'perceived rivals' Byrne did not mean Gould; he meant Blair. That is why he wrote of the 'Kinnocks and the Blairs' taking the flak, even though Blair had taken no more flak than most shadow cabinet members. And the use of the name 'Blair' in the letter, without the addition of the name 'Brown', was a key early indicator of the way the modernisers were thinking. Byrne himself says: 'It was always my view that if we were going to make the breakthrough, we probably needed Tony Blair and not Gordon Brown, because [Blair] was closer to Middle England.'[25]

Apart from Byrne, few people voiced the modernisers' frustration publicly. But they voiced it in the corridors and bars of Westminster. No Labour politician, no lobby journalist was unaware that Byrne was saying publicly what Blair and Mandelson were saying privately.

And what of Kinnock? Did he join the campaign against Smith that was supposedly mounted in his name? On the contrary, he maintained a front of absolute loyalty to Smith, and he was not among those who whispered privately against him. What he had to say he said directly to Smith. At a dinner in May 1994, he advised the leader to give a series of policy lectures setting out his strategy for modern socialism. Smith said: 'That's a good idea, we'll get stuck into it after the conference.' Kinnock, frustrated, said that was not soon enough: Smith ought to deliver at least two of the lectures before the conference.[26]

The conversation became academic faster than either man could possibly have imagined. At 8.05 the next morning, 12 May, Smith suffered a massive heart attack in the bathroom of his London flat in the Barbican complex, and he was pronounced dead at St Bartholomew's Hospital at 9.15 a.m.[27]

CHAPTER NINE

THE MAN WHO WOULD BE KING

Glenys Thornton, general secretary of the Fabian Society, telephoned her husband John Carr from her office at 9.30 a.m. on 12 May 1994. Labour leader John Smith had been dead for less than an hour, and most of the world knew nothing about it – the announcement was being delayed as long as possible so that Smith's elderly father could be reached before he heard it on the news. Glenys had the information in confidence from Labour communications chief David Hill. He had heard it from his assistant, Hilary Coffman, who had been in Smith's flat waiting to collect him for a day's canvassing when he suffered his fatal heart attack.

By 10 o'clock Carr, one of Blair's close friends from Hackney politics, was on the telephone to Peter Mandelson. While the world remained unaware of the Labour leader's death, Carr was already discussing the succession, telling Mandelson: 'It's got to be Blair.' 'No,' said Mandelson. 'It's got to be Brown.'

The argument became heated. Whether Mandelson meant what he said, or whether the Brownites are right that he had always planned to ditch their man and was merely dissembling to Carr, we will never know for certain. What we do know is that before the day was over, he had changed his mind: he decided it had to be Blair.

Blair himself was campaigning in Aberdeen that morning with local Labour organiser Norman McCaskill, and when McCaskill told him that the *Evening Standard* that day carried a full-page feature headed 'Why I say Tony Blair should be the next leader', by Sarah Baxter, former political editor of the *New Statesman*, 'He expressed extreme distaste.'[1] The article had in fact been written the previous day, with no idea that there would be a vacancy so soon, and rushed into print when the *Standard* heard the news about Smith's death.

Mandelson expressed similar sentiments, according to Roger Pope, political adviser to chief whip Derek Foster. Taxed by Nigel Griffiths, MP for Edinburgh South, and a strong Brown supporter, about the *Evening Standard* piece and asked who could be possibly be talking to the press to promote Blair before Smith had even been buried, Mandelson condemned the article. 'I can't possibly think who would want to do such a thing,' he told Griffiths.[2]

Whatever Blair's real feelings about the *Standard* piece, he had already reached a firm decision that he would run for the leadership. Carr managed to reach him at about 4 p.m. 'Don't let them talk you into letting Gordon be the candidate,' he said. 'Don't worry,' said Blair. 'They won't.'[3] An earlier Labour leader, Hugh Gaitskell, was once said to have 'a will like a dividing spear'. The description matches Blair exactly.

While John Carr was needlessly stiffening Blair's spine, another politically minded neighbour, Barry Cox, the London Weekend Television executive, was talking to Cherie Booth as she set off to meet her husband at Heathrow Airport. They agreed that her husband must run himself and not give way to Brown, and that they would both try to persuade him of this. Like Carr, they found that Blair needed no persuading.

Back at his Westminster office there was heavyweight political support from the 'Kinnocracy': Charles Clarke, now working as a lobbyist; Kinnock's former parliamentary private secretary Adam Ingram; and John Eatwell, Kinnock's economic adviser, now a Labour peer. From outside the Kinnock circle came offers of help from shadow cabinet members: Mo Mowlam, Jack Straw, Harriet Harman, Chris Smith. A Labour whip, Peter Kilfoyle, gave Blair an encouraging estimate of his support among Labour MPs. From that first day, none of them had the smallest doubt that Blair would run, because Blair himself had none.[4]

The unexpected opportunity presented by Smith's death put the relationship between Tony Blair and Gordon Brown under the spotlight much sooner than either of them had expected. Ostensibly, they were still allies, though, as we have seen, Brown was at most a semi-detached member of the modernising cabal that met regularly in Islington. Within the shadow cabinet, Brown was generally regarded as the more senior of the two, except by those who were members of Blair's inner circle. And that is certainly how Brown saw it.

Each man's view of the other must have been formed during the years they spent sharing an office while junior spokesmen in the 1980s. Those who were familiar with them both say that Brown was extremely untidy, leaving papers strewn across his desk, files half open and telephone numbers scrawled on scraps of paper. Blair, in contrast, while not quite

obsessively tidy, always put documents away in drawers before leaving
for the day and kept his desk neat.

Brown was volatile, prone to moodiness and brooding. After mobile
phones became commonplace, Brown frequently had to replace his
because of his habit of hurling against the wall to switch it off – particularly after a row with one of his colleagues. A friend bought him a specially padded mobile in an effort to reduce the rate of attrition. Blair, on
the other hand, was calmness personified. His anger, when it came, was
cold, controlled and calculating.

Later, the two had separate offices on the same corridor, but by the
time of Smith's death Brown had moved out to 7 Millbank, some fifty
yards down the road, into a suite of offices that befitted a future party
leader, while Blair stayed in the refurbished office at 1 Parliament Street.
The physical separation no doubt allowed both camps to plot with
greater ease and less risk of embarrassing encounters.

As the conversation with John Carr recounted above makes clear,
Blair had no doubt that he should and would be a candidate for the leadership in the event of a vacancy arising. But the extraordinary fact is that
Brown was, it is said, unaware of the extent of his rival's ambitions until
it was far too late. In his eyes, Blair was a colleague he had been happy to
help in the past because what was good for Blair would be good for the
Labour Party – the party Brown confidently expected to be leading when
the time came.

In the immediate wake of John Smith's death, despite his inward resolve,
Blair the charmer initially disguised it behind a façade of indecision –
modest, hesitant, asking advice. He even asked Gordon Brown's advice,
when it was obvious that, whatever the advice was, it was going to be
ignored. He feigned reluctance when Roy Hattersley advised him to
stand.[5]

Entire rainforests have been consumed by the attempts of political
analysts to decipher the communications that took place between Blair
and Gordon Brown over the next few days, culminating in Brown's
announcement that he would stand down in favour of his rival: their
meetings in various North London homes and in the Granita restaurant in
Islington, and the various king-making manoeuvres of Peter Mandelson,
as recorded by the journalists he did or did not brief, and the articles he
did or did not inspire. What actually happened was to cause poisonous
resentment for years, down to arguments not only over policy but even
over who should get particular jobs, triggering the first row within days
of Blair becoming prime minister, as we shall see later.

For what it's worth, we can reveal a previously unknown meeting in Durham City Hall, a short drive from Sedgefield. John Burton arranged for the chief executive to vacate his office and asked a local councillor, Charlie Magee, to collect Brown from Durham station, where Brown broke his journey from Edinburgh to London, and take him in by a back entrance to avoid the press. Blair went in by the front entrance; as a local MP his presence would not signal anything out of the ordinary. After the meeting Brown was collected and taken to the station for the onward journey to London. Burton asked Blair what had transpired. Blair said they would give it a few days and decide who looked the strongest after that. The weaker of the two would then drop out.[6] He did not tell Burton that he knew he was going to run for leader from the moment he heard of Smith's death. He has never told him that.

Whatever happened, a deal was eventually struck (and has largely stood the test of time) that divided up the spoils. Brown was to be given free rein over domestic policy, while Blair could concentrate (as he had always wanted) on foreign policy. The most disputed element was a promise from Blair, regarded as sacrosanct by the Brownites, that Brown would succeed him if he did not contest the leadership now. Brown agreed to this and stood down, but he probably should have known better. It is this element that has since disintegrated, as such pacts are bound to do when ambitious politicians spot a chance of becoming prime minister and begin to enjoy the trappings of power.

Brown has never ceased for a moment to believe he was deprived of the crown by the treachery of Peter Mandelson. Paul Routledge has written biographies of both Mandelson and Brown, and Brown seems to have particularly wanted Routledge to mention the undeniable fact that Brown spent the days after Smith's death in Scotland, mourning an old friend, while Blair was in London, plotting. He also seems to have been particularly keen for Routledge to reproduce a long, self-serving and rather creepy letter Mandelson wrote to Brown four days after Smith's death. The letter is clearly designed to persuade Brown to stand down in favour of Blair, but contains an implied (and surely disingenuous) promise to work for Brown if he insisted on standing.

Brown's supporters also felt that Gordon's absence in Scotland for the Whitsun recess lost him momentum. There is no question that Brown hesitated. His friends were worried that, when compared to Blair, not being married would count against him. The Commons hothouse is a cruel place, where gossip and innuendo against individuals is rife. Certainly at least four prominent Labour people – two of whom later joined Blair's cabinet – wrongly believed Brown was gay.

Those who worked closely with him testify the opposite – his hetero-sexual love life would shame a Mills & Boon novel in its scope and com-plexity. At least two of Brown's girlfriends were whisked off for romantic weekends on the Cote d'Azur in Geoffrey Robinson's luxurious seaside apartment on Hesperides Avenue in Cannes, while others were invited back to his Scottish home in Fife. One friend, George Foulkes, even sug-gested that, if he stood in a leadership election, one of Brown's old flames, a Romanian princess, should be brought back to canvass with him for support, to kill such a rumour.

Some of his strongest supporters at the time were heartbroken when he pulled out of the contest, but they believed that Blair just had an edge. Roger Pope remembered writing a long and frank letter to Brown after Blair had won, saying that he knew Brown must be very downcast. He pointed out that, in the Commons, Blair's charm offensive 'particularly through Anji Hunter' had won over many MPs, while Gordon's researchers had been 'arrogant and overbearing', which had not gone down well. He ended the letter: 'I shall always support you, Gordon, because when the going gets tough you are going to be the one to hack it.'

Brown himself was certainly bitterly disappointed when he had to stand down. One of his supporters, Saul Billingsby, described how, after he had made his statement to television news reporters that he would not stand, he slammed his private office door. Those outside heard something apparently being kicked around his office; a severely dented wastepaper bin was later recovered.

The Blair campaign had, of course, got underway well before Gordon Brown announced his fateful decision. It started with a meeting in Barry Cox's Islington home attended by Blair, Cox, John Carr, Charles Clarke, broadcaster and novelist Melvyn Bragg and the thriller writer Ken Fol-lett. It was held in secrecy; there was a frisson of concern when the assembled conspirators saw television cameras outside. But the cameras were there to film a documentary about the rundown Holly Park Estate opposite and failed to notice the procession of expensive cars turning up at the pleasant terraced house across the road.[7]

Barry Cox took charge of raising money for the Blair campaign. Jack Straw and Mo Mowlam agreed to be its joint chairs. John Carr took charge of organisation and hired offices in Abbey Orchard Street, in an old building newly converted to offices. There was a big open-plan office and a smaller space used for storing leaflets and other campaign material. Key staff in the office, apart from Carr and Cox, included Cherie Booth's half-sister Lauren Booth and Kim Dewdney, researcher to a friendly MEP who had loaned her to the campaign, as well as Tom Happold, who later became the *Guardian*'s online news editor.

The first meeting of the Blair campaign's parliamentary team was held in a small office in 1 Parliament Street. Peter Kilfoyle remembers it well for one startling incident. Both he and Mo Mowlam wanted an absolute assurance that Mandelson was to play no part in the campaign. At the time Mandelson was in the wilderness, to which he had been banished by John Smith, and was thought to be working with Gordon Brown to get him the leadership. So both of them put a straight question to Blair, in front of Barry Cox, the LWT executive, warning him that if Mandelson got involved, they would have no part in the campaign.[8]

Blair lied. He gave them an assurance that Mandelson would not be working for him. What followed was a famous and elaborate cover-up by Blair and Mandelson, which involved Mandelson being given the code name 'Bobby' – a ploy more usually associated with student politics than a campaign for a new leader of a national party. Kilfoyle admits he was fooled for the whole duration: 'It was only when Blair won and paid tribute to "Bobby" at the celebration to mark his victory that I suddenly realised that he was talking about Mandelson.'

Such slick manoeuvring was all very well in the hothouse world of Westminster, but Blair was not always equally at ease on the campaign trail trying to get votes from the rank and file. Peter Kilfoyle recalls a meeting with Labour activists in St Helen's.

> Tony was hugged and smothered with kisses from a lot of working-class women at the local Labour club. He was highly embarrassed and it was then I realised that Tony had quite a lot of difficulty relating to working-class people. He came out saying 'I hope I am not going to have put up with a lot of that.' I said 'Tony, you better get used to it, it's going to happen quite a lot.'

However, none of this really mattered. Despite the frantic efforts that went into the campaign, from the moment Brown withdrew Blair was coasting home. The two remaining candidates, John Prescott and Margaret Beckett, were both seen as electoral liabilities, and after fifteen years of Conservative rule, most Labour MPs and many rank-and-file party members believed that electability was the only thing that mattered. On 21 July 1994 Blair received more than half the votes on the first ballot and was elected as the fifteenth leader of the Labour Party, the heir to Keir Hardie who became the party's first leader in 1906. John Prescott beat Margaret Beckett to become Blair's deputy.

*

It is interesting to look, for a moment, at the events of this crucial period in Blair's career through the eyes of his loyal friend in Sedgefield, John Burton, who is convinced that Blair tells him everything.

Shortly before Smith died, Burton remembers walking in Trimdon with Blair, when Blair said: 'You can make the best speech of your life, but you can't do anything if you're not in power.' And Burton replied: 'You know, you might have to lead this party one day.'

Blair suddenly stopped walking, looked as though the idea had never occurred to him, and said: 'Do you really mean that?' Burton said: 'There's been Callaghan, Foot and Kinnock, all Welsh; Smith, Scottish; we need an English leader.' 'But I'm Scottish,' said Blair. 'You came down to England early, we'll not count that,' replied Burton magnanimously. Burton still believes that he put the idea of leading the party into Blair's head.

Burton had just taken early retirement from teaching, aged only fifty-three, and at the same time Phil Wilson, whom Blair had employed to look after constituency matters, left for London to take up a job Blair had found for him at Labour Party headquarters. Burton told Blair that he would like to take on Wilson's constituency job. Blair did not seem at all keen. 'I don't know about that, John,' he said. 'We're friends. It might not work out.' He wouldn't, he said, want to risk spoiling their friendship. But then, says Burton, 'John Smith died and I think he was glad to have me here watching his back. I've been here ever since.'

Burton believes to this day that, for a good couple of weeks after Smith's death, Blair was considering standing aside for Gordon Brown. Burton has been sadly misled. As for the famous dinner between Blair and Brown at Granita in Islington, Burton does not believe the generally accepted version that it was agreed Blair should run. 'I never heard of the Granita deal, and Tony would have said something,' he says.[9]

Blair's first act as Labour's new leader was to get rid of the general secretary Kinnock had appointed in 1984. Larry Whitty had never been thought of as a leftwinger; Kinnock had brought him in as a man who would, Kinnock believed, be equal to the task of modernising Labour headquarters. But none of this reconciled Blair to Whitty: he thought Whitty was too close to the unions and too leftwing. It did not help that he was close to several union bosses.

It was one of Blair's many complaints against John Smith that Smith had refused to fire Whitty. Two years earlier, when Smith became leader, Blair and Brown had been to see him to insist that the party must have a new general secretary, but Smith thought Whitty was doing a perfectly good job. When Smith heard that Peter Mandelson also wanted Whitty out, it probably confirmed him in this view.

During the 1994 leadership election, Whitty had to remain carefully neutral, but Blair must have noticed that Whitty was not excited by messianic talk of modernisation, and seemed more comfortable in the company of Margaret Beckett than of himself. Blair simply did not want Whitty around.

A week after his election, Blair asked Whitty to come to his room in Parliament Street. At this meeting Blair said he thought Whitty ought to be 'moving on'. He pointed out that Whitty had been in the job for ten years, and even gave a remarkable hostage to fortune by adding that no one ought to be in a job for ten years. He himself, he said, would not be Labour leader for more than ten years. The year 2004 was, of course, Blair's tenth as Labour leader. He might argue that the job changed fundamentally when he became prime minister, in which case he will have been in the job ten years in 2007.

Whitty pointed out diplomatically that getting rid of the general secretary was a decision for the National Executive Committee; the job was not in the leader's gift. Technically this was true, but Whitty also knew that the position of a general secretary who does not have the leader's confidence and support is impossible. Whitty, as he himself says, could probably have fought and won a battle for his job on the NEC: 'But what would I do the next day?'

So Whitty negotiated. What was he being offered in return? Blair dangled the prospect of a research job preparing a policy paper on European social democracy. That did not interest Whitty, and they agreed to leave the question until another time. Later that same day, Whitty discovered to his annoyance that Blair had already offered his job to Tom Sawyer. Sawyer had been the leftwing leader of a public sector trade union, but, like many others, he had undergone a sudden Damascene conversion and was now an enthusiastic Blairite.

That, Whitty felt, freed him to confide in party chairman David Blunkett and the two other senior figures on the national executive. They were all horrified and said they would support Whitty if he chose to fight. Eventually, a deal was done with deputy leader John Prescott acting for Blair. Whitty was given responsibility for building relationships with other European social democratic parties, working under Prescott. Blair also hinted at a peerage for Whitty, which he delivered two years later.[10]

Richard Rosser, then general secretary of a small trade union, the Transport Salaried Staffs Association, and a member of Labour's NEC, would have liked the general secretary's job. When they heard that Whitty was going, several other NEC members suggested that Rosser – quiet and modest but effective and efficient, a lifelong moderate trade unionist who had been utterly loyal to Kinnock and Smith and was to prove equally loyal to Blair – would be the ideal man to replace him. Rosser approached Blair, because he did not want to apply unless he knew the leader would welcome his application. At first, Blair said that the possibility of having Rosser was interesting, but when Rosser persisted, the new leader admitted he had made up his mind that he wanted Tom Sawyer.

'He always had a clear idea about who he wanted in Labour Party jobs,' says Rosser, who on retirement ten years later became Lord Rosser. 'He always knew who was going to get a senior job before it was advertised.' Rosser does not mean this as a criticism – quite the reverse. He was grateful for Blair's openness in telling him what was in his mind, and he did not apply for the job.[11]

Whitty had an interesting four years on the European circuit, working out of John Prescott's office. Under the Labour government he was, for a while, a junior minister in the Department of Agriculture. He can see his departure from Labour HQ from Blair's point of view – Whitty was too close to the unions for Blair and 'he needed to make the change'– but cannot resist adding: 'At least the party was solvent when I was there. It's seldom been solvent since.'

Whitty agreed to resign after the Labour Party's October conference. There, many delegates interpreted his farewell speech (rightly) as a coded warning not to get so carried away with modernisation as to forget what the Labour Party was for.

That conference will be remembered for two things, one symbolic and one fundamental to the nature of the party.

Neil Kinnock and John Smith had both rejected feverish demands from the image-makers, led by the hyperactive Philip Gould, to 'rebrand' the Labour Party as New Labour. But here, at Blair's first Labour Party conference as leader, Gould's ultimate triumph was there on the stage for all to see: a pistachio background (most people thought it was green, but Gould called it pistachio) with the slogan 'New Labour, New Britain' plastered over it.

Tony Blair quickly made it clear that he intended his 'new' party to be new not only in name but also in nature, for it was at the conference that he launched the campaign to get rid of Clause IV of the Labour Party constitution. The clause was drafted in 1917 by Sidney Webb and Arthur

Henderson, neither of them leftwingers, as a simple statement of what the Labour Party was about. Neither Webb nor Henderson believed in nationalising everything, and neither of them was an admirer of Lenin and his Russian Revolution, which was taking place in the month they were at work.

Clause IV stated that the party aimed

> to secure for the workers by hand or by brain the full fruits of their industry and the most equitable distribution thereof that may be possible, on the basis of the common ownership of the means of production, distribution and exchange, and the best obtainable system of popular administration and control of each industry and service.

No Labour leader had ever interpreted that to mean that he had to nationalise everything, and no one was ever likely to do so. In 1959 Hugh Gaitskell had focused attention on Clause IV and tried to get it changed, but his attempts had been rebuffed by the conference. His retired predecessor Clement Attlee remarked at the time: 'The Labour Party's passion for definition should always be resisted. Hugh excited it. He should have sedated it.' Sedating it had been John Smith's plan. A Smith government was never going to go in for wholesale nationalisation, but neither was it going to make an issue out of getting rid of Clause IV.

Blair set up a so-called 'grass roots' campaign to get rid of Clause IV. It was to be run by two of the youngest Blairites – Derek Draper, Mandelson's special adviser, and Tom Happold, who had distinguished himself as Blair's chief envelope-licker during his leadership campaign. Anji Hunter originally planned to hire a swish office suite in Victoria Street, Westminster, for the campaign headquarters, until Draper pointed out to her that perhaps a swish office would rather give the game away. Certainly it hardly fitted with the traditional working-class image of Labour. The initial choice of venue showed that neither Blair nor Anji Hunter had a clue about the true nature of Labour campaigning.

So instead they settled for an empty shopfront in Lambeth Walk, across the river from Westminster. There, behind the iron grilles, the diminutive Happold set about organising the campaign, half the time worrying that he might be mugged on the way home across the concrete desert that made up parts of inner-city Lambeth.

Blair himself was still puzzled about why they really needed such a campaign. Draper recalls that Blair asked him once: 'Why can't the Labour Party organise this?'

'No, Tony, it can't. It is supposed to be neutral about the change.'

Happold also remembers Blair going ballistic when he was told that the Labour Party newspaper was going to run two articles – one for abolition and one against. 'I remember he insisted a phone was brought over and rang up the editor telling him in no uncertain terms that this was not to be the case. Eventually, it turned into seven people supporting the change, and just one arguing the case to retain it.'[12]

The determination to get rid of Clause IV came out of those secret modernisers' meetings in Islington that had been going on throughout the previous two years. In his biography of Blair, John Rentoul records a final council of war in September 1994 attended by just eight people, including Blair, Brown, Mandelson, Labour's pollster Philip Gould, Blair's new press secretary Alastair Campbell, Roger Liddle (who was still a Liberal Democrat at the time) and Michael Wills. The weekend at the Chewton Glen Hotel in Hampshire was paid for by the ubiquitous Colin Fisher of SRU, the shadowy figure who, back in 1983, was paving the way for more focus groups and less quantitative polling, and in 1990 was employing Peter Mandelson on a flexible contract so that he could still make himself available to advise Neil Kinnock.

Outside this elite group, the only person who knew of Blair's plan before the conference was the deputy leader, John Prescott. He was told later than the modernisers, and he went along with it on condition there were no more internal party reforms before the general election. Everyone else was ambushed at the conference.

Blair's speech was distributed to journalists with the last three pages missing. Before delivering it, Blair met behind the stage with a few key union leaders. He told them, according to John Edmonds, that he was about to do something spectacular. Bill Morris of the TGWU asked if the pages held back were about Clause IV. Blair denied it.

Blair privately told Edmonds that John Smith had not needed so spectacular an initiative because of the personal authority he possessed. Blair, lacking that authority, needed to make changes that Smith could have avoided. This was a nicely judged, modest-sounding compliment, because Edmonds was a friend and an admirer of Smith; but it was quite untrue. One of Blair's complaints against Smith was that he was not prepared to tackle Clause IV. 'We were bounced,' says Edmonds.

Edmonds recognised the harsh political reality: Blair had the unions just where he wanted them. He had needed their votes to become leader, and they gave them because they were desperate to be rid of the Tory government and feared that Prescott or Beckett might prove to be votelosers. He needed the unions again in the battle over Clause IV, and Edmonds persuaded the GMB delegation to support Blair on the issue.

Without that support Blair would have gone down to an embarrassing defeat. 'I thought that if he was defeated on Clause IV, once he had made his intentions public, the bubble would burst,' says Edmonds. Blair, as he was often to do in the next three years, raised the spectre of a fifth election defeat. Weakening Blair would mean weakening Labour.

'It's a myth that we did not know what we were getting with Blair,' says Edmonds. 'We knew exactly what we were getting. The only optimistic thought was that the party might be able to put pressure on him.'

What the unions were getting was a man who, as Edmonds puts it, 'feels fear and contempt for the unions'.[13] The story of Blair's three years as opposition leader is the story of how the unions, after waiting eighteen years for a government of what they still considered to be 'their' party, had the cup dashed from their lips at the last moment by a Labour leader determined that they should not taste it. The Conservative Party was Blair's weapon in his war with the unions.

The unions were puzzled at how difficult they found their own meetings with Blair. 'He liked meetings where we chatted around the issues, then he'd say, "We must do this again," but next time you don't start from where you left off, but from the beginning again, as though the previous meeting had not taken place,' says John Edmonds. 'If things are left hanging, nothing happens.' Blair, says Edmonds, is brilliant at dealing with individuals.

> He likes to make us as individuals feel we're his buddies – that's his word – but he can't cope with the idea that when he saw us, he was seeing representatives of the trade unions, not individuals. He's no idea of what unions do or how they work.
>
> The charm lasts until you say no to something. We helped him on Clause IV, on devolution in Scotland, but one day there was bound to be something we couldn't do, and then none of the help you've given before gets you any credit.[14]

There were two sorts of trade unionist whom Blair was able to get on with. One was the far right of the movement, men like Ken Jackson of the engineers' union, who set themselves up around him as a protective phalanx and refused to tolerate any criticism of him. He tended to make use of their power, but not to trust them with important jobs; sometimes they could be an embarrassment. 'Garfield Davies wanted to be a buddy of Blair's but was so loyal that Blair realised it was counter-productive,' says John Edmonds.

The other kind was former Bennites like Tom Sawyer: these were people Blair felt he could use. Messianic apostles of Blairite modernisation tend not to come from among the Old Labour and trade union moderates – people like Larry Whitty – but from the ranks of the former leftwing ideologues, like Chris Mullin. Mullin, who had been the scourge of both Michael Foot and Neil Kinnock because he believed they had betrayed the spirit of socialism as represented by Tony Benn, voted for Blair as leader and has been astonishingly loyal to him. This may have something to do with the intolerance of the Bennites, a characteristic that many of the converts have retained in their new Blairite incarnations. They admired pure faith, and poured scorn on the smallest deviation. They were, in the purest sense, Stalinists. As Nick Cohen wrote,

> Many of [New Labour's] ideologues are refugees from the wreckage of Marxism. Read Geoff Mulgan, the former Militant Tendency member and former adviser in the Downing Street Policy Unit [now the head of a Cabinet Office specialist unit] or Charles Leadbeater, once a communist and now an independent adviser, and you hear a familiar, hectoring tone. 'We know the future,' a brash voice shouts. 'Resistance is futile and moral argument an infantile diversion.'[15]

Cohen was describing a group that was called the Democratic Left in 1999 and is now called the New Politics Network. It is, given the group's antecedents, an odd irony that its members should have been the fiercest advocates of Blair and New Labour, before and after Blair became leader, and the first group for whom Blair as Labour leader addressed a trade union audience. The Democratic Left was a tiny relic, less than a thousand strong, who had influence entirely disproportionate to their numbers because they controlled £3.5 million given by Stalin and Lenin to help nurture communism in Britain.

When, after a long and bitter battle, the Eurocommunists won control of the Communist Party from the old guard in 1991, they wound up the party and renamed their organisation the Democratic Left. They ditched all the old communist policies, becoming instead what they called a 'space where new ideas can germinate'. Their slogan was 'Caring, sharing, daring', which is of course no more than a collection of rhyming feel-good words.

Already the journal they had captured from the hardliners some years before, *Marxism Today*, had been an inspiration to Neil Kinnock, and it was the nursery of many of his and Blair's advisers, including Geoff Mulgan. When *Marxism Today* eventually folded, it was replaced by the influential Blairite think-tank Demos, run by Mulgan. The founders of Demos were John Carr, John Norton (who later married Mo Mowlam) and *Marxism Today*'s editor, Martin Jacques.

Their main complaint about the communist old guard was that over the seventy-one years of the existence of the Communist Party they had accepted money from Moscow. Now the Democratic Left had won control of all that money and the property in which it had been invested. Membership started at less than a thousand and has steadily decreased until it is now thought to have fallen below three hundred; but the organisation still has an income of about £200,000 a year from renting out properties bought with the proceeds of the sale of 16 King Street in London's Covent Garden, which was acquired by Lenin in 1920 for the Communist Party. They also have capital from the sale of the party's various businesses.

Nick Cohen continued:

I doubt if one person in 100,000 has heard of the New Politics Network. The all but unrecognisable remnant of the once militant Communist Party of Great Britain has been rebranded and repackaged like a flagging line of groceries, until every distinctive principle its members once held has been liquidised into a consensual mush. Its active membership could fit into the snug bar of a country pub. Its propaganda is banal and unread. Outside London, it scarcely exists. And yet in Labour circles the network is eyed with envy and fascination. New Labour movers and shakers take breaks from their busy lives to write position papers for a minute readership.

The group campaigned for Blair to be Labour leader, and were delighted with his election. Their secretary, Nina Temple, hailed it on the front page of their publication *New Times* in an open letter to Blair: 'Throughout the election you managed to speak beyond the party to the nation and convey a new mood of opportunity ...' Her article was the first expression – Blair was to leave a decent interval before he joined in – of the modernisers' joy that Labour was not to be led into the next election by that Old Labour fogey John Smith.

Temple asked, knowing quite well the answer:

Will you follow the cautious strategy of your predecessor? Preferring to allow the Tories to expose their own shortcomings, and not risking any initiatives that could rebound in Labour's face? Even if this approach could deliver a general election victory, I do not believe it would build the sense of popular commitment to a Labour, or Labour-led, government that will hold people's support during the difficult decisions that will have to be faced during any real process of national renovation ... Breaking out of Labour's isolation involves creating a generous inclusive political culture ... . These coalitions for renovation need to be cross-

party, and also to connect with wider civil society, involving the unions,
the churches, and women's institutes, among others ...

The phrase 'or Labour-led' is the first public mention of a cherished
Blairite project to unite the Labour and Liberal parties, which, as we shall
see, Blair was determined to do, right up until his 1997 election victory.
The Democratic Left – not a party but a 'space', as Temple calls it, a 'network' that networked relentlessly with top politicians – was to prove an
important behind-the-scenes bulwark for Blair, and to give his vague
aspirations for Labour the appearance of a coherent philosophy. As soon
as he was elected, Geoff Mulgan wrote a panegyric about 'Blair's agenda'
for *New Times*:

> Blair has enthused Labour ... He is asking some of the fundamental
> questions – as with Clause IV – about the party's defining ethos and its
> core principles ... Most of those around him are not in any way defin-
> ably Labourist. Having to deal with trade union leaders when shadow
> employment spokesman was a key experience. He was genuinely
> shocked at the arrogance with which they threw their weight around.
> Blair has little romanticism or nostalgia about the labour movement's
> traditions. He is very different culturally from his predecessors and from
> the rest of the party.

Mulgan stressed how important it was that Blair was English, not Scottish or Welsh: 'Blair is also able to some extent to talk a language of
nation and patriotism in a way which Labour has felt unable to do
because of its Celtic identity.'

Two years later, an editorial in *New Times*, signed by editor Julia Gal-
lagher, said: '[Democratic Left] sees Blair as an enormously important
force to work with. A strategy document which aims to "define a new
leftist project in relation to new Labour" will be launched in the autumn.'
Blair, it said, had produced the year's 'big idea': the 'stakeholder society'.
By then, Conservative MP Alan Howarth had defected to Labour, and
Blair wished to find him a safe Labour seat. *New Times* undertook the
trawl on Howarth's behalf, under the banner headline: 'Give this man a
seat!'

To many people the hallmark of Blair's three years in opposition was
instant rebuttal – the creation of a computerised system that would
enable the party to respond instantly and effectively to anything that was
said about it. The idea came in 1994 from Patricia Hewitt, whose years as
Kinnock's press secretary had given her a clear idea of how necessary it
was in dealing with united media hostility.

The solution had come from the United States. Two years before Blair was elected Labour leader, Bill Clinton was elected US president, and Hewitt talked excitedly about the way the Clinton campaign had employed new technology. Blair sent Hewitt to Washington DC, accompanied by his old friend John Carr, now an independent management consultant and an expert in new technology. They went to the White House and talked at length with Clinton's press chief George Stephanopoulos, as well as the Democratic Party national committee. They saw the office housing Clinton's rapid-rebuttal computers, with software brand-named Excalibur. The principle, as one American politician put it to them, was that 'it's very hard for anyone to badmouth you if you've got your fist down their throat'. 'Never,' said another, 'let a lie go unanswered.'

They were told that during the Republican convention in Houston, where George Bush senior was nominated to run for a second term, the Democrats managed to get an advance copy of his acceptance speech. They hired students to get casual jobs in the hotel where the press were staying and instructed them to obtain the fax numbers of all the political correspondents. As Bush was speaking, they faxed a rebuttal of every point he made to every important political correspondent in the land.

Blair decided he wanted Excalibur for Labour. Ken Follett agreed to pay the £1 million it was going to cost. Carr became consultant to the project and the organising brain behind British use of the software. But then came a disaster, one of Blair's own making. The newly elected Labour leader and his wife were due to dine at Follett's home just after the Labour conference where he had launched his attack on Clause IV. It was supposed to be a private occasion, but when Blair arrived he saw that television cameras were recording his arrival. He was furious and blamed his host. Follett protested that he had not leaked details of the occasion; he had merely given out the full guest list to all the guests, and one of the others must have leaked it. Blair would not be mollified and refused to have anything more to do with Follett. Alastair Campbell was even told to run down Follett when briefing the press. And no Follett: no money for Excalibur.

For a time it looked as though the Excalibur project was doomed; it seems extraordinary that Blair was prepared to sacrifice what he clearly thought was an important electoral weapon on what seem like trivial grounds. There was no chance of the desperately cash-strapped party headquarters finding the money. Eventually, John Carr persuaded Philip Jeffrey, then owner of the *New Statesman*, to fund it, and the installation went ahead. Two years later, in 1996, just before the election, Carr handed it over to Labour Party headquarters in full working order.

The real importance of Excalibur was psychological, says Carr. 'Excalibur was big and new and expensive and Blairite. It had an immediate effect on party morale.' Conservative Party chairman Brian Mawhinney told his policy adviser Danny Finkelstein to find something better, and, after researching the alternatives, Finkelstein reported that there was nothing better – Excalibur it had to be. In the end, says Carr, 'the Tories spent five times as much on theirs and never got it to work properly.'[16]

Quite why Blair and his entourage felt the continuing need to run down John Smith, even after his death, is unclear. Perhaps it was because if it seemed that Smith could have won comfortably in 1997, then little Blair did as opposition leader could be justified. The first posthumous criticism came during the subsequent by-election in Smith's Monklands East constituency. The election was called quickly by Labour to make sure that the core Labour vote would turn out before Scotland's schools closed for the summer holidays at the beginning of July. As a result, it took place before Blair became leader but after Gordon Brown had decided not to stand.

It also coincided with a big scandal over sleaze, which was being worked up by the Tories and the press. Allegations of corruption were made against the ruling Labour group on the local council. The national press had already seized on it because it was in John Smith's seat. It suited John Major to play it up to distract attention from the long-running 'homes for votes' gerrymandering scandal involving Dame Shirley Porter, the former leader of the Tories' flagship Westminster council.

Labour chose Helen Liddell as their candidate, because she was thought to be tough and plain-speaking and able to cope with any controversy thrown her way. Tom Clarke was the neighbouring MP in Monklands West and a shadow cabinet member who had worked closely with John Smith. He also had an agreed line on the corruption scandal: call for an independent inquiry and don't get involved in the details.

At least that was the line until Blair – by then the frontrunner for the leadership – came up to speak at Airdrie. Then, in a U-turn that could have only come from London, and which Tom Clarke suspects came from 'Bobby' Mandelson, Liddell started suggesting that there might be more to the corruption scandal and, in a monumental gaffe, said too much money was being spent in Coatbridge at the expense of Airdrie – driving a wedge between Labour voters in the same constituency.

Clarke, who knew nothing of this, was caught off guard by a TV interviewer in London – and got the blame for not toeing the new line. Worse, when he returned to his campaign office in Coatbridge the next day, the entire Labour by-election team had walked out in disgust. The result was that Liddell scraped home – with a majority of just over 1,600 in what had been John Smith's former Labour stronghold.

Clarke lost his seat in the shadow cabinet, but was vindicated a year later when an independent inquiry cleared the council leadership. Blair called him in and said he could no longer have the shadow international development portfolio – but would he like to do disability instead? So Clarke took on rising Tory star William Hague; he proudly remembers coming within thirteen votes of forcing the government to set up a disability rights commission.[17]

While Smith was leader, no doubt he was fair game for the whispering campaign conducted in the corridors of Westminster and described in the previous chapter. But continuing it after his death was deeply distressing to Smith's friends, and even more so to his family, who felt they could not reply – it would only make them look foolish. 'I thought, this man is dead, how can a dead man still be a live issue?' says someone who was close to Smith. 'Why did they need to do that? It seemed that for Tony Blair to flourish as a leader, he needed to deny the legacy of John Smith. To be a Tony Blair supporter you had to deny John Smith.'

For Smith's family, the wound did not start to heal until ten years later, when the public tributes to Smith on the tenth anniversary of his death reassured them that his reputation was still high in many quarters.

Blair and his entourage enthusiastically cultivated the myth that Smith was on course to lose the 1997 election, until by good fortune he died and Tony Blair was able to bring in from the cold the indispensable Peter Mandelson.

Philip Gould's book *The Unfinished Revolution: How the Modernisers Saved the Labour Party* was the most overt weapon in this battle to show that Labour was saved by the vision of Blair and the genius of Mandelson. Gould claimed that Smith was heading for election defeat. He said that the lead in the polls Smith had when he died in 1994 could have disappeared before the general election, just as the mid-term Labour lead had disappeared before the 1992 election. But, in fact, the polling evidence shows that the two periods were completely different in nature.

Before the general election in April 1992, the polls had been volatile for five years, with the Labour and Conservative parties taking turns to have narrow leads. After the 1992 election it was a very different story. Within three months the Tory lead in the polls was wiped out, and it never reappeared. Labour's lead steadily increased: to 4 per cent in July 1992, and then, after Britain's withdrawal from the ERM, to 10 per cent in October and 13 per cent in November; by December 1993 it was 18 per cent, and by January 1994 20 per cent. Smith was the most popular and respected Labour leader since Attlee, whom he resembled in many ways. He steadily scored better than John Major in the polls on all counts, including the crucial 'capable leader' criterion.

After Blair's election, there was a honeymoon period, as is usual with a new leader, and Labour's lead briefly reached an unbelievable 39 per cent for a few days in December 1994. Then it settled to round about its 1997 election level of 13 per cent. Bob Worcester of MORI says the polling evidence suggests Smith would have won the 1997 election with a majority that was smaller than Blair's but still very comfortable – probably near to a hundred.

So what was 'modernisation' all about, if it was not about electoral success? Dennis Potter, writing in 1993 about the BBC, wrote: '... each age, even each decade, has its little cant word coiled up inside real discourse like a tiny grub in the middle of an apple. Each age, even each decade, is overly impressed for a little while by half-way bright youngish men on the make who adeptly manipulate the current terminology ...'. Potter said that 'the little cant word' of the 1990s was modernisation.[18]

Having found the little cant word, the Blairites gave it the Humpty Dumpty treatment: 'When I use a word, it means just what I choose it to mean – neither more nor less.' If they decided that modernisation meant privatisation, or grammar schools, or the Millennium Dome, or slavish adherence to whatever theory the latest management guru has come up with, then, if anyone questioned these things, they could say with a sneer: 'You're against modernisation, then?' And as the Blairites said this, they sounded uncannily like the Bennites of the early 1980s, saying: 'You're against democracy, then?'

One thing that clearly needed modernising, in New Labour eyes, was the membership of the parliamentary party. And so, while Blair was publicly replacing Labour's socialist egalitarianism with family-friendly and business-oriented values that would not offend Middle England, an exercise in physically removing Old Labour from the scene was underway in private. Blair was ruthlessly reshaping his party in the House of Commons by shedding as many of the Old Labour MPs as he could decently drop, without either they or the wider public realising the scale of the operation.

Just as the trade unions were being replaced as the mainstays of party funding by big business and wealthy entrepreneurs, so the old guard on the backbenches were being replaced by less dogmatic young Blairite, and Brownite, candidates.

A number of Old Labour people disappeared at this same. Doug Hoyle, the former party chairman and a critic of Mandelson – the man who had helped save John Smith from being forced to resign at Labour's 1993 conference – became Lord Hoyle, vacating his seat in Warrington North for Helen Jones. Former shipyard worker John Evans, who had served as a junior whip under Callaghan, quit St Helen's North to make way for David Watt and became Lord Evans. Geoffrey Lofthouse got a knighthood to make way for a New Labour journalist, Yvette Cooper, in Pontefract; Cooper subsequently became a Brown ally. In Scotland, Norman Hogg stood down in Cumbernauld in favour of Rosemary McKenna, a member of the Blairite New Politics Network. Stuart Randall stood down in Hull West to make way for a favoured Blairite modernising trade unionist, Alan Johnson. He was later gazetted as Lord Randall of St Budeaux.

Mandelson asked the *Daily Telegraph*: 'Isn't it good to get all these bright young Blairites into the House?'

Another veteran MP Blair was anxious to see move up to the Lords was John Gilbert, the Labour MP for Dudley East, a former junior minister in the Wilson and Callaghan governments. Blair wanted him to quit his seat so that Charlie Falconer, Blair's former housemate and fellow lawyer, could get into Parliament. Gilbert, though, had his price: he not only negotiated a peerage but also the promise of a job in his favourite department, the Ministry of Defence. Blair kept his word and made him minister for defence procurement. Sources in both Labour and the Liberal Democrats have a simple explanation for Gilbert's success: 'He talked posh, went to Oxbridge and Blair was impressed.' Unfortunately, Dudley East were not impressed with the posh-sounding Charlie Falconer. They refused to endorse him as their candidate because he sent his children to private school, and Blair eventually had to give him a peerage as well in order to get him into the government.

At the same time as he was purging the backbenches of Old Labour figures, Blair was effectively turning the working machinery of the Labour Party inside and outside the Commons into a decorative ornament. All the bodies still met, but the decisions were always made elsewhere, among Blair's courtiers. Power was centralised but the institutions still remained.

Three examples of this stand out. Labour had an internal policy-making body, chaired by Gordon Brown, which was meant to take decisions on how the party handled issues. The members included Peter Mandelson as well as other key figures like the party chairman, Doug Hoyle, and Derek Foster, the chief whip. Mandelson himself never turned up to meetings. But it soon became clear that many of the decisions taken at the forum were being ignored. Mandelson was announcing decisions that had never been discussed.

This tendency became so marked that a delegation, including Doug Hoyle and Derek Foster, went to see Blair to complain. They pointed out this discrepancy and accused Mandelson of usurping the process. Blair tried to calm them down.

'What do you want me to do?' he asked the delegation and then answered the question himself rhetorically. 'Take him out and hang him from the yard arm?'

'Yes, we could sell a lot of tickets for that,' came a muttered reply. In fact, Blair had no intention of doing anything about it; he had personally sanctioned Mandelson to go ahead.

A similar situation developed with a high-powered committee set up under another Labour sympathiser, journalist Geoffrey Goodman, which included a former head of the civil service, Lord Bancroft, and trade union leaders like Fred Jarvis, the former general secretary of the National Union Teachers. It was supposed to provide the leadership with advice on the transition to government, but its reports began to disappear into a void. Blair and Mandelson had instead called in management consultants and asked the shadow cabinet to play 'game scenarios' on what it would be like to be in power.

The most dramatic change of all concerned party donations. John Smith had asked Derek Foster to set up a careful vetting procedure of potential Labour donors from the business community. The Labour leader was worried that as the party became more popular it might attract dubious donors, and he wanted it to avoid becoming besmirched – the Conservative Party had already experienced a lot of problems with donors such as Asil Nadir, who fled Britain to escape prosecution when his Polly Peck business collapsed.

Foster asked Blair if he still wanted to receive the reports. There was no reply. The reason was that Blair was already making other arrangements. He had decided to appoint his tennis partner, record promoter Michael Levy, as the party's chief fund-raiser. Levy, a key figure in Labour Friends of Israel, knew a lot about arm-twisting people to persuade them to give to causes. He had soon replaced the traditional Labour fund-raisers in Millbank with a team of staff drawn from his Jewish charities. The results were spectacular and Labour started getting donations on a scale that rivalled the Tories. The roll call of honours and peerages in Blair's first list as prime minister reflected this. Levy himself was ennobled. Eleven other individuals have been ennobled after donating more than £5,000 (at that time the only public statistics to be released) to the party between 1996 and 1999. Between them, their donations ran into millions of pounds, which completely transformed the party's finances.

Big donors include the publisher Lord Hamlyn, who later left £1 million to the party in a bequest, and businessman Lord Sainsbury, who made donations in 1996 and 1997 before receiving his peerage and later became science minister. Another businessman, Lord Bernstein of Cragwell, donated money in 1997 and 1999. Northern Foods chairman Christopher Haskins donated money every year between 1996 and 1999 and chaired the better regulation task force at the cabinet office. He was given a peerage in 1998.

Among the ennobled artists who made substantial donations during this period were novelist Melvyn Bragg, film-maker David Puttnam, and crime writer Ruth Rendell. The media moguls included former Guardian Media Group chairman Bob Gavron. The lawyer Peter Goldsmith, who was to become attorney general during the Iraq war, also gave a substantial sum. Oxfam chairman Joel Joffe was another big donor, as was the late Michael Montague, though he had also donated large amounts during the days of John Smith.

It would be wrong to infer that all these supporters got their peerages because of their donations to the party – they do have honourable records in public life. But one cannot help remembering the famous quip that Lord Burlison, Blair's helpful GMB regional organiser from 1983 who was also ennobled in 1997, is said to have made to friends: 'I don't know how I got here; I appear to be the only one who isn't a millionaire.'

There was just one more piece that needed to be put in place to complete Blair's transformation of the Labour Party into New Labour. Just before he became prime minister, in 1996, the leaders of the Confederation of British Industry, the employers' organisation, asked for a meeting with him, to be kept secret from everyone – including the TUC.

Blair agreed, and a meeting was set up with CBI chairman Colin Marshall and director general Adair Turner. Marshall and Turner told Blair they were concerned about the rights granted to workers and their unions by the European social chapter, which Labour was committed to signing. The CBI had successfully prevented the Major government from signing up to the social chapter by persuading Michael Howard to threaten to resign as employment secretary if it went ahead.

Blair told them he had to sign the social chapter because it was a Labour Party commitment which he could not safely dishonour. When he was shadow employment secretary, the reason he had given for ending the closed shop was that it would be inconsistent with the social chapter. But he would, he promised them, block any other pro-worker and pro-union proposals in the social chapter, on maternity benefits, or health and safety, or anything else, if the CBI disapproved of them. In effect, he extended to them a virtual veto on new measures in the social chapter. Marshall and Turner went away very pleased with their day's work, as well they might have been.

TUC leaders were told nothing of this meeting, and that is why they continued to besiege the Blair government with requests which Blair had already given a solemn promise to the employers to turn down.

CHAPTER TEN

DIVIDING THE SPOILS

When John Major announced on 17 March 1997 that he was calling a general election, Tony Blair should have been highly confident of victory. The Tories had been mired for months in a series of scandals over sleaze that refused to go away. Within twenty-four hours, New Labour's wooing of Rupert Murdoch paid handsome dividends with a ringing endorsement from the *Sun* – a stark contrast to the brutally unfair denigration of Neil Kinnock in 1992.

Part of the Blair mythology is that this turnaround was achieved by brilliant public relations. The truth is that Murdoch, the CBI and the City knew that they had nothing to fear from a Blair government. The secret pledges made after Blair became leader convinced them that he would not harm their interests. And any lingering doubts about Labour taking a pro-Europe stance were removed with a deeply Eurosceptic article by Blair in that day's *Sun*, pledging to 'fight any bid to foist on Britain the high costs which are hampering business on the continent'.[1] This was a message aimed more at Murdoch and the CBI than *Sun* readers. In those circles, 'high costs which are hampering business' is well understood to be code for laws that assist trade unions and extend the rights of employees.

But the main issue that dominated the beginning of the election campaign was sleaze. Major's decision to call the election meant Parliament would rise on 21 March. That just happened to be four days before one of the most controversial reports ever to come from a parliamentary watchdog was due to be sent to the Commons standards and privileges committee: the findings by Sir Gordon Downey, the parliamentary commissioner for standards, into the notorious 'cash for questions' affair.

The scandal had poisoned the atmosphere in the Commons ever since 18 October 1994, when the *Guardian* broke the story under the headline

'Tory MPs were paid to plant questions says Harrods chief'. The kernel of the tale was that two backbench MPs, both ministers in Major's government – Tim Smith, MP for Beaconsfield, and Neil Hamilton, MP for Tatton – had been paid up to £50,000 by Harrods owner, Mohamed al Fayed, to ask questions in Parliament in the 1980s.

At the time of publication, Tony Blair himself had been extraordinarily reluctant to take up the story. On the eve of publication an arrangement had been made for a Liberal Democrat MP, Alex Carlile, to raise the story on a point of order in the Commons at 11 p.m. One of the journalists responsible was one of the authors of this book, David Hencke. Mindful of his own inability to contain his excitement about the impending disclosure, he took refuge in a friendly Labour MP's room rather than be seen around the parliamentary press gallery – that way he could avoid rival journalists who might pump him for his exclusive story. But no sooner had he popped in to see Alan Williams, an avuncular and senior member of the Commons public accounts committee, than he blurted out the extraordinary story he was supposed to have kept secret from his lobby colleagues.

Williams, being a shrewd operator, immediately contacted the opposition chief whip, Derek Foster, who came over, listened to the tale, and said: 'I am going to contact Blair.' He went off for a meeting. Half an hour later he came back: 'I don't think Blair is keen on us raising this. He will see how the story runs.' Williams, surprised, questioned this, and it emerged that Blair had immediately consulted Alastair Campbell, whose view was based on the messenger rather than the substance of the message. When he learned that it was a *Guardian* story, Campbell's advice was: 'Don't believe anything you read in the *Guardian*; you don't want to go on that.' Foster had other ideas. He took away the typed transcript and contacted one of Blair's old friends, frontbench spokesman Stuart Bell. Bell was up for it and the deal was that Labour would jump in behind Carlile.

Eleven o'clock came and went and it soon became clear that the Liberal Democrats were not going to raise the point of order. So Bell went out on his own, reading the transcript of the *Guardian*'s front-page story into the Commons records, thus guaranteeing parliamentary privilege for any newspaper or broadcast outlet that wanted to follow it up.

But three years later, with a general election to be fought, Blair's position was different – partly, no doubt, because Hamilton's own libel case against the *Guardian* had collapsed in 1996. He used his last appearance at prime minister's questions to attack Major for the non-publication of Downey's findings. 'Justice demands this report be published. If you fail to have this report published, when everyone knows you could, it will leave a stain on the character of your government.'

But Major felt he could ignore Blair and fight the election in the knowledge that the report would be safely locked away until Parliament returned. How wrong he was. What Major did not know is that the confidential transcripts of evidence taken by Sir Gordon had been given to all parties in the dispute. These included highly damaging admissions by Tim Smith that he had in fact taken the cash.

The *Guardian* was in possession of these transcripts but was officially constrained from revealing them until the inquiry published its report. What should it do? The editor, Alan Rusbridger, faced a breach of privilege charge if he broke the rules. 'They can lock you up in the clock tower beneath Big Ben,' he was told.

However, since Parliament was not in session, Rusbridger technically could not be in breach of it. It seemed highly unlikely that the Conservatives would return to office and pursue him, and equally unlikely that a New Labour government would wish to do so. And so, alongside a leader proclaiming 'We believe in elections fought in the light, not in the dark', the *Guardian* printed the details of Tim Smith's admission and four other pages of evidence implicating Hamilton, Michael Brown, the MP for Cleethorpes, and Sir Andrew Bowden, MP for Brighton Kemptown.

Smith initially held out but then felt obliged to quit. After he resigned, the former vice-chairman of the Beaconsfield Conservative Club, Caroline Strafford, said: 'Four days of sleaze in the newspapers was too much for the constituency.'[2]

The damage was done. It must have been incredibly sweet for Blair to see the man who humiliatingly defeated him as a novice candidate in 1982 stand down from one of the safest Tory seats in the country.

The sleaze factor was to continue to surface throughout the campaign – helped by Neil Hamilton's determination to tough it out in Tatton, and the high-profile intervention of 'the man in the white suit', ex-BBC war correspondent Martin Bell, as his main challenger. Bell was to cause one of the biggest upsets in electoral history on the night by defeating Hamilton, overturning a seemingly impregnable 16,000 Tory majority.

The rest of the campaign was, on Labour's part, deliberately low-key. Blair avoided the challenge of a televised debate with Major, quite content for all three parties to become bogged down in dogmatic, legalistic squabbles over how it should be conducted. Blair's advisers did not want a debate because they felt it would dominate the election campaign. Instead, Blair acquitted himself creditably in interviews with David Dimbleby.

At the time, the UK press and many politicians thought Blair was appearing cautious and right-leaning to avoid any last-minute 'red scares' from the Tories. Much of the Labour Party felt he was being, perhaps unnecessarily but understandably, careful to give no ammunition to the rightwing press. In retrospect, we can see that what he was actually doing was signalling that his agenda was a million miles from Labour's traditional agenda, and that is how many European papers viewed his performance. Their comments seem remarkably prescient and would not be out of place seven years later.

Le Figaro, France's main right-of-centre daily paper, commented:

> To judge by the reverence shown by the Labour Party for the 'Conservative revolution', the great victor of the May 1 poll will be neither Tony Blair nor John Major: it will be Margaret Thatcher ... . The electorate is beginning to wonder why it should choose a Labour copy when, with the Conservatives, they have an original. Suddenly Tony Blair seems just too slick, his smile too mechanical, his preaching too calculated. .... Why pick Tony Blair if he has no other goal than seizing power?

El País, Spain's liberal daily, likened Lady Thatcher to a heavenly body: 'Both contenders do nothing but take the ex-Iron Lady as their point of reference: Major, just in case, marks a certain prudent distance so as not to be burnt by the sun of his predecessor; Blair, so as to come nearer to the star which today illuminates British reality.'

The *Frankfurter Allgemeine Zeitung*, Germany's leading newspaper, was more blunt about Blair and Major. 'Both men are the same. Instead of distancing themselves from one another, Labour and the Tories want to be as similar as possible. The Labour Party looks like a virgin who has spent the last eighteen years waiting for an offer of marriage.'

Il Sole-24 Ore, Italy's main financial paper, identified Blair's insincerity and lack of political depth. It commented: 'Our impression is that Blair's party right now is like a huge soufflé, which looks great and is beckoning', subsequently adding that the New Labour soufflé 'is without substance'. *La Repubblica*, another influential Italian daily, was equally dismissive. Regarding Blair, the paper commented: 'When he's on stage he becomes decisive and impassioned. He's an excellent actor. Now, he's interpreting the role of New Labour, which he embodies in body and soul.'

Until the last few days of the campaign, Blair emphasised the cardinal policies of New Labour: controlling the unions, more privatisation, and a detachment from European socialism. On privatisation, he went out of his way, in addressing the City of London on 7 April, to emphasise to the banks and venture capitalists that there was 'no overriding reason' for preferring the public provision of services. He told them Labour was not in the business of 'pressing the rewind button' to reverse the economic reforms of the 1980s: 'What counts is what works.'

John Monks, general secretary of the TUC, went on BBC Radio 4's *World at One* to defend Blair. He claimed Blair was signalling that Labour was not opposed to privatisation; he did not expect Labour to implement such a policy in power. 'I wouldn't expect a Labour government to go down the direction that the Conservatives have been down – which is to clear out every potentially lucrative bit of the public sector,' he told the programme. Whether Monks really believed what he was saying, or whether – being a clever and experienced operator – he was saying what he wanted to happen in the hope of helping it to happen, is uncertain. Either way, he knows different now, after Blair and Brown have part privatised the National Air Traffic Service and sold off the research arm of the Ministry of Defence.

Ken Clarke, the Tory chancellor, called Labour a 'collection of unprincipled scoundrels making up policy as they go along. These people have spent their entire parliamentary lives fighting privatisation in principle. Overnight, we are asked to believe the Labour movement is now in favour.'

For good measure, Blair told the City how he would handle Europe.

> It is misguided to rub our hands with glee when the French and the Germans get into difficulties. If we are to grow, we need them to flourish. They have to make a big adjustment to a more competitive world – slashing subsidies to lame ducks, opening up protected markets to competition, changing the balance between pay-as-you-go and funded pension schemes, and most of all moving from protecting jobs to promoting employability.

Similarly, Blair made it clear to diplomats in a speech in Manchester on 21 April that he had no plans to work with his socialist allies in France and Germany. Promising that a Labour government would make a 'fresh start' in Europe, he set out his five key priorities for the forthcoming EU summit in Amsterdam, saying that he would expect the declaration agreed at the end to cover all of them. The priorities were: completing the single market and removing remaining barriers to trade in aviation, telecommunications and financial services by June 1988; enlarging the EU to the east; reforming the Common Agricultural Policy; tackling unemployment and promoting flexible labour markets; and making foreign policy co-operation real. Much of this was on the existing Tory agenda.

At the end of his speech, Blair strayed from his prepared text to emphasise a fundamental patriotism: 'I am a British patriot and I am proud of
being a British patriot. I love my country. I will always put the interests
of my country first.'3

Only towards the end of the campaign did Blair offer any statement
of political philosophy. At Southampton on 16 April, he laid out his
views on the family and the need for honesty and integrity in government. He said:

> This election is about more than personalities, policies and programmes;
> it is about the basic values we want for this country.
>   The only way to build a nation is to build a decent, strong society
> that underpins it. That is what this election should be about; it should be
> about that passion and conviction for a decent society. We must judge
> this society by the position of the weak as much as the strong.

Blair said he regarded the family and the way children were brought up
in the home as the bedrock upon which many Labour policies, particularly on education and law and order, were founded.

> There is nothing more important than the way we bring up our children.
> It is in the family that we first learn right from wrong. So our social
> policy will revolve around the family. The family will have priority in
> our legislation. We are the family party as well as the national party. The
> health of the family and the strength of the nation ultimately reflect the
> quality of honest, decent, truthful government; government which has a
> moral dimension and which always makes sure that justice has a high
> place at the cabinet table.

On 29 April, in a speech in Bristol, he invoked the legacy of John
Smith. He recalled that the night before his death in May 1994, Smith
had said: 'All we ask is the chance to serve.' Blair, he said, wanted to see

> a nation in which people want to get on, to prosper and do well and
> where they want their children to do better than they did – the great
> British dream I would like see back in this country where each genera-
> tion does better than the last. The country I believe in is where people
> get on by merit, not privilege, where we believe it does not matter
> where you come from, it is what you are that counts, a country where
> there is no discrimination on the basis of sex or race or sexuality.

Gordon Brown was given the task of chairing the campaign strategy
committee, and Peter Mandelson managed the campaign. That was a
problem in itself, for the two were still hardly on speaking terms. According to Mandelson's close friend Colin Byrne, brought back once again to
advise, it was all Brown's fault. 'Peter tried to do business as usual, but

Gordon would scowl and make it all a bit awkward.' The twelve-strong campaign committee also included Derry Irvine, and Byrne wondered why he was there and what he had to contribute: 'A trait of Tony's I could always have done without is the tribal mentality, wanting to lean on people from the past. Some of his loyalties are misplaced and Derry is one of them.'

The only suggestion of scandal on the Labour side concerned Peter Mandelson, and was quite undeserved. A rumour started that he was having an affair with the Tory Party's leading campaigner, Howell James – presumably based on nothing more than the fact that James, who is gay, had enjoyed a long-term friendship with Mandelson and had been once been on holiday with him.

The rumour was false, but it did give rise to an interesting exchange. A Labour candidate for one of the key swing seats in the south was out-raged when he heard the story and broached the subject with Blair: 'What the hell's going on, here we are in the middle of a crucial election campaign and two opposing campaign organisers are fucking each other?' he asked. But Blair, who may or may not have known the story was false, appeared relaxed. He is said to have told him: 'It might be quite useful, you never know what we might learn about our opponents through pillow talk.'[4]

Despite Blair's hopes of obtaining useful information from the Tory camp, the only embarrassing leak of the campaign went in the other direction. A so-called Labour 'war book' outlining the perceived strengths and weaknesses of the parties was leaked to the Tories. A gleeful *Daily Telegraph* seized on the tale, saying the party had 'plans for scare campaigns on health, education, crime and VAT in the run-up to polling day'.[5] In fact, Labour's main scare tactic turned out to be capitalising on a story that the Tories would privatise the old age pension; the 'war book' itself portrayed Major's strength as being the general perception that he was 'decent and honest'. There is no suggestion that the leak had any-thing to do with Mandelson – it appeared that the Tory Party had received the document before the campaign started.

Blair won by a majority of 179 – far more than he had anticipated.

No wonder there was a stunned silence in the small private jet taking Blair and his close associates to London on the day of the election victo-ry. Tony and Cherie Blair, Anji Hunter, Alastair Campbell – the closest of the inner circle – sipped mineral water and whispered occasionally to each other. Only John Burton from Sedgefield looked like someone who was celebrating, stretching out his legs, patting his ample stomach, sending the steward for a double whisky, and contentedly lighting his big Sherlock Holmes pipe. 'I hate you,' Anji Hunter whispered to Burton as they left the plane. 'I had to sneak into the toilet to have a quick cigarette.' Burton was not, and never has been, bound by the new puritanism.[6]

Then came the division of the spoils. Few prime ministers have used their power of patronage so lightly, or with so naked a determination to reward loyalists and punish dissidents.

The Blair game plan at this juncture was not only to change the Labour Party but to bring the Liberal Democrats into government and even attract the best of the moderate Tories. What was to wreck this vision was the scale of Labour's victory. Because Blair won 419 seats in 1997, a majority of 179 when he had only expected a majority of 50, this part of the project foundered.

Some of the signs were noticeable during the election campaign. A big role was given to Alan Howarth, the Tory MP for Stratford-on-Avon who had defected to Labour and was now contesting the safe Labour seat of Newport East. He was put in charge of a 'switchers unit', aimed at attracting disillusioned Tories, and given a high-profile appearance with both Blair and Brown at an election press conference.[7] Howarth was effectively taking on Blair's dream, first attempted at the Beaconsfield by-election fifteen years before, to get committed Tories to vote for him in droves.

Blair's campaign to bring the Liberal Democrats into an alliance with a future Labour government had a long gestation, going back to the period before he became party leader. His first tentative approach had been made in secret, many years earlier when John Smith was Labour leader – though it was kept from Smith, who would have been furious had he known. Blair and Mandelson arranged to see Charles Kennedy, then the president of the Liberal Democrats. The meeting took place at Derry Irvine's London home in Hampstead. The aim was to sound out the young Kennedy about his party leader, Paddy Ashdown. They wanted to know his views on a 'centre left coalition' between the two parties and whether he thought Ashdown would be sympathetic. The answer to the latter question was yes. This resulted in Blair's first meeting with Ashdown, on 14 July 1993 at the London home of the lawyer Anthony Lester and his wife, Katya. It was the beginning of a long friendship between the Blairs and the Ashdowns. Jane Ashdown is an extremely energetic, intelligent woman. Menzies Campbell, the current deputy leader, says: 'Jane is the sort of women who can be baking drop scones and discussing the merits of CND at one and the same time.' She immediately took to Cherie and the two women became firm friends; they still keep in touch today.

Ashdown's diary records a revealing comment from shadow home secretary Blair at that first meeting. 'The history of the Labour Party is littered with nice people who get beaten. I don't intend to be one,' he told Ashdown. Otherwise Blair was very cautious, but he left Ashdown with the distinct impression that he was in favour of realignment between Labour and the Liberal Democrats.

Serious discussions did not begin until 4 September 1994, after Blair had been elected leader. Over dinner at his Islington home, Blair confided to his close confidante Anji Hunter that he had talked over the idea of working together with the Liberals and wanted to be committed to a programme of co-operation. Intriguingly, he had not consulted anyone else, not even his chief of staff Jonathan Powell, at this stage. Real progress did not begin until May 1995, but what followed over the next two years was a tortuous, sometimes tense and complex negotiation which Blair managed to keep secret from most of the rest of his party and which Ashdown revealed only to a select group within his smaller organisation.

When, in October 1996, the two parties publicly announced that they were setting up a joint working party to explore the questions of proportional representation, devolution and Lords reform, most Labour MPs believed that this was partly, as one put it, 'a tease' to keep the Liberal Democrats sweet before the election. It was nothing of the sort. It was a ruthless, calculated attempt by Blair to realign politics in secret. Ashdown was a very willing partner; one of the Liberal Democrats close to him told us: 'In the end Ashdown and Blair almost agreed on everything; there is not a lot politically between them.' The meetings were held at Derry Irvine's Hampstead home, where the participants quaffed superb wine and were overwhelmed by Irvine's remarkable collection of British art (some of the paintings are being put up for sale at the time of writing), ranging from Lucian Freud female nudes to Stanley Spencer's memorable religious scenes relocated to Cookham. Paddy Ashdown noted in his diaries: 'I found that eating my dinner confronted by moist images of female pudenda did little for my appetite.'

On Labour's side, only Robin Cook, Donald Dewar (then chief whip), Gordon Brown and Peter Mandelson were kept properly informed. The Liberal Democrat team in the know were Bob Maclennan, Archy Kirkwood, Menzies Campbell, Richard Holme – later to be joined by party treasurer Tim Razzall. Roy Jenkins acted as a mentor figure to Blair. Charles Kennedy went out of the loop.

The discussions, which intensified as the election approached in 1997, ranged from how and when to implement proportional representation for European elections, for the devolved governments which were planned

for Scotland and Wales, and for the Westminster Parliament, to co-operation over areas of policy and co-ordination in the Commons in making
challenges to the Major government. The twists and turns have been well
documented, but probably the most extraordinary deal – played down in
Ashdown's diaries – was dubbed the 'big thing' or the 'full Monty'. The
Liberal Democrats were to join the new Labour government – even if it
had a majority of up to fifty seats.

There is no question that right up to the day after the election Blair
wanted this to happen. Parallel to the secret meetings at Derry Irvine's
home, Blair and Ashdown were also having talks at another forum, a
secretive Westminster dining club. Known as the Other Club, it had been
set up by Winston Churchill after he was blackballed from another establishment club in the 1930s. This club meets regularly and is an opportunity for senior politicians from the three main parties and other leading
luminaries to share views and discuss issues entirely privately. Ashdown,
Blair and Gordon Brown were members from 1991. Other members
include Prince Charles, Derry Irvine, Chris Patten, William Hague,
Michael Howard, Charles Kennedy, Menzies Campbell and John Profu-
mo. The present chairman is Nicholas Soames, restoring the link with
Churchill, for Soames is Churchill's grandson.

The most extraordinary decision taken by Blair was to reserve two
cabinet seats for the Liberal Democrats in advance of the 1997 election
campaign. The details were worked out by two 'mechanics' – the name
given to Peter Mandelson and Richard Holme, nominated by Blair and
Ashdown respectively to sort out problematic issues every time their
broad-brush commitments ran into a snag. Ashdown did not want to
commit his party to joining a Labour government until a more detailed
deal had been thrashed out. Once this had been done, it was left to him
to inform the lucky members of his party who were to get a job and for
Blair to make sure his own shadow cabinet was kept in the dark.

Menzies Campbell – already part of the negotiating team – was the
first to learn that he would join a Blair government, as defence secretary.
He is said to have immediately queried how Labour's shadow defence
secretary, David Clark, would take the news. He was told not to worry,
as Clark was never going to get the defence portfolio. Within Labour's
inner circle he was known as 'the sponge' – he was meant to sit there
soaking up all the criticism that Labour could expect from the Tories for
being weak on defence. But Blair never considered him sufficiently capable to undertake the real job. Clark himself knew Blair's views about his
ability and was at the time expecting to become agriculture minister
instead.[8]

Alan Beith was to be the second Liberal Democrat member of the cabinet, working under Gordon Brown as chief secretary to the treasury. There were a number of problems here – not least that Beith was outside the inner circle of negotiators and was one of the old school of stand-alone Liberals who had won and held his Berwick-upon-Tweed seat by appealing both to disenchanted Tories and to the minority Labour mining vote. Beith's conversations with Labour members were usually confined to small talk on the late-night express train from King's Cross to Edinburgh. His stop, Berwick, was three stops further than Darlington (the seat of rising backbench star Alan Milburn), two stops past Durham (Blair, Derek Foster and Hilary Armstrong), and one stop away from Newcastle (Nick Brown and another backbench rising star, Stephen Byers).

Ashdown decided to broach the subject with Beith at a private meeting. He made sure that, in explaining to the surprised Beith the details of the deal, he added breathlessly: 'And you, Alan, as part of this are to become chief secretary to the treasury.' Beith, taken aback, agreed. Alistair Darling, then shadow chief secretary to the treasury, would have been even more surprised. It was just as well that Darling travelled home on Thursday in lively company on the west coast sleeper train, rather than going up the east coast mainline with Beith. Luckily, Charles Kennedy also remained ignorant of the deal, since he had taken to flying home to Inverness instead.

As for Gordon Brown, he would have been furious if he had known about all this, so Blair never consulted him. The question of how Brown was to square Liberal Democrat spending priorities with Labour's decision to stick to Tory spending plans, with Beith as his chief secretary, was a minefield left unexplored. Those close to Brown say that Blair was obviously hoping to charm Gordon after Labour's victory. But one said: 'Gordon would never have stood for it; there would have been an enormous row.'

The main opponent of the deal within Ashdown's party was the Liberals' Scottish leader, Jim Wallace – ironically the one person who did go into government with Labour, after Scottish devolution. Already angered by Blair's indecision over giving the Scottish Parliament tax-raising powers, he was furious when Ashdown told him about the deal with Blair. A senior Liberal Democrat, asked to join them in Ashdown's room in the Commons, found both men speechless and quivering with rage. Finally, Wallace shouted at Ashdown: 'What's in it for me?' when he realised his two colleagues were going to be in Labour's cabinet and he had been frozen out.

This deal stuck firm until the Sunday before the election. At that point, through an agreement to share private polling, it became clear that both parties were doing well but Labour had a commanding lead. Ashdown had a few qualms, because it looked like his party was going to gain more seats than he expected, while Blair's advisers suddenly realised that they could win by a bigger margin than fifty.

But even though the plans for key Liberal Democrats to join the cabinet were not implemented, Blair retained a lingering desire to head a coalition. Some Liberal Democrats suspect that, inwardly, he was nervous at the prospect of taking power by himself after eighteen years of Tory rule. He wanted a few experienced hands to guide him – and the Ashdown–Roy Jenkins axis was one way of achieving this.

Certainly Blair was still hesitating a day after the landslide. After David Clark had been to see him at Downing Street on the Saturday to be offered, to his surprise, the post of chancellor of the duchy of Lancaster, he told friends about his puzzlement over the fact that Blair's full cabinet list had two blank spaces – defence secretary and chief secretary to the treasury. Little did he realise this was because two Liberal Democrat names had been erased.

The abandonment of the plans to include the Liberal Democrats certainly complicated things, but even so, Blair's first cabinet list is a remarkable document, full of blank spaces, crossings-out and handwritten additions, illustrating the turmoil surrounding the changes.

The top offices of state went to those who had shadowed them. Gordon Brown became chancellor of the exchequer, Derry Irvine became lord chancellor, John Prescott became deputy prime minister in charge of a superministry embracing environment, transport and the regions. Robin Cook got the Foreign Office. Jack Straw became home secretary. David Blunkett got education.

After the top posts were handed out, the new prime minister's priority was to appoint Ann Taylor as president of the council and leader of the Commons. Taylor had to be put in place quickly so that she could prepare Blair's totally inexperienced team to attend the swearing-in ceremony in front of the queen; she was one of the very few ministers who had served in government before.[9]

Next, Blair had to take the decision to move Donald Dewar from chief whip to Scottish secretary, replacing George Robertson, who was not keen to stay on. Blair needed an experienced negotiator and safe pair of hands like Dewar's to handle the huge constitutional change planned for Scotland with the establishment of the Scottish Parliament. Where could he put Robertson? At this stage, it appears that he still had his heart set on bringing in Menzies Campbell, but he also knew Robertson was really keen on the defence post. A telephone conversation with Ashdown on Friday finally killed off the coalition, so Robertson got his dream job; it was later to lead him to the general secretaryship of NATO.

Blair also decided to move Chris Smith from his health portfolio to national heritage. It seems likely that this had been arranged so that Alistair Darling could be slipped across to health if Beith joined the government. As it was, with no coalition on the horizon, health remained vacant and it stayed vacant until the Saturday after the Thursday election. For the situation had become so traumatic that Blair could not complete his cabinet by the end of play on Friday. On Saturday he still had four vacancies: agriculture, chancellor of the duchy of Lancaster, health and transport. He also had seven elected shadow cabinet people to whom he had given nothing – Jack Cunningham, David Clark, Frank Dobson, Gavin Strang, Michael Meacher, Derek Foster and Tom Clarke.

Cunningham had been shadowing national heritage. He was offered both the Cabinet Office and the transport job. But he wanted his own department and did not want to be anywhere near either Prescott or Mandelson, and he knew that Mandelson had already been given the minister without portfolio post in the Cabinet Office. So Cunningham got agriculture.

Clark, who had been half-expecting to get agriculture, got a job in the Cabinet Office: the chancellor of the duchy of Lancaster. Surprised, he told Blair: 'I don't really know a lot about the Cabinet Office.'

'It's all right: you'll be working with Derek Foster [the current shadow spokesman] – he'll be your minister of state.'

'I am in the cabinet, aren't I?'

'Yes, you are in the cabinet; Derek is not.'

In the event, as we shall see, Foster was to remain in the government for just twenty-four hours and was therefore unable to offer much help to Clark.

Then there was Frank Dobson. Blair was not a fan of Dobson. If anybody appeared to be unreconstructed Old Labour, it was Dobson. Working-class, grey-bearded, middle-aged and slightly overweight, he was not one of Mandelson's 'beautiful people' who could be wheeled out to look good on TV. He also told crude, politically incorrect dirty jokes, which would certainly have offended Cherie. His repertoire of dirty jokes became so notorious that the US government prepared memos for the administration warning them about his propensity to shock polite company when he visited the United States.[10]

This one-dimensional view of Dobson is unfair. He may be very direct, but he is also a cultured, sensitive, thoughtful character, who faithfully represents working-class values, champions the underprivileged in the third world, particularly in Bangladesh, and loves going to art exhibitions. Nevertheless, Blair did not really want him in his cabinet. He once saw Dobson's stout figure in the Members' Lobby and remarked to a colleague in a sneering tone, 'God, we are going to have that in a Labour cabinet.' But Dobson made it to the cabinet table as health secretary in preference to Meacher – once described to one of the authors by a Blairite MP as a man 'Blair totally detested' because of his one-time role as 'Benn's vicar on earth'.

Michael Meacher had been an elected member of the shadow cabinet continuously since 1983, an MP since 1970, and at fifty-eight was one of the few remaining links with the last Labour government, in which he had been a parliamentary undersecretary. He got an apologetic call from the prime minister: 'I'm afraid the most I can offer you is minister of the environment.' Meacher did not know if this would carry a cabinet place. It would not: he was to be a minister of state and his boss was to be John Prescott. But Blair tried to sweeten the pill by saying he would make Meacher a privy councillor. Meacher said this did not help and asked instead for an area of policy in which he was interested to be placed in his remit. He heard Blair ask someone else in the room, 'That's OK, isn't it?' before agreeing, and guessed that Peter Mandelson was there to oversee the making of the government.[11]

Gavin Strang was a problem for Blair. In the last shadow cabinet elections he had come top among the male candidates (everyone had to vote for a certain number of women, so three women came ahead of him), ahead of Blair's closest colleagues – Gordon Brown, Robin Cook and Jack Straw. He had shadowed agriculture effectively and had been a junior minister at agriculture in the last Labour government, when he had been responsible for the legislation that brought to an end tied cottages for farmworkers. He had an agricultural background and knew a lot about the subject. But Blair did not want him around. Strang was considered terribly Old Labour – he was one of those who had been brought in from the cold by John Smith, and he possessed awkward leftwing views.

On the morning of the Saturday after the election, Strang still hoped he might get the one job in politics he wanted: minister of agriculture. That hope vanished when the agriculture portfolio went to Cunningham. Blair sent for Strang and said he realised he would rather have agriculture, but transport was all Blair could offer him. And transport was not to be an independent ministry: Strang would be a minister of state in John

Prescott's department. The position did, however, give Strang a seat in the cabinet. He became the last person to be included; so late was his appointment on Saturday that he was the only member not to get any training from Ann Taylor on how to approach the queen for the swearing-in ceremony.

The story of what happened to Derek Foster's promised seat in the cabinet is an instructive one. When Blair became leader, Foster was opposition chief whip; he had been Kinnock's parliamentary private secretary from 1983 to 1985, then his chief whip and, since 1992, John Smith's chief whip. He had also won every internal Labour parliamentary election for the job – making him impossible to budge by way of a direct electoral challenge.

A grey-haired, softly spoken, wiry working-class Northerner, Foster is not the sort of man who stood out among the middle-aged male mass that made up the bulk of the Parliamentary Labour Party in the mid-1990s. He is also Parliament's sole representative of the Salvation Army and a teetotaller – but to stick those labels on him would give far too simplistic a picture of the man. He ran a classic Jaguar, built his own bungalow himself and frequented pubs with his friends – even if he didn't drink alcohol. His constituency, Bishop Auckland, is next door to that of Blair, and various boundary changes meant that they had a shared working-class electorate.

None of Foster's attributes would endear him to the metropolitan, boozy world of the lobby journalists, nor would he be a guest around the sharp-tongued, sophisticated North London dinner tables frequented by the Blairs and their court. As a result, both groups woefully underrated him, though Blair had been very happy to go along to the chief whip's private dinners with trade unionists, council leaders and businesspeople sympathetic to Labour when he was a rising star in the shadow cabinet.[12] But, unlike Blair, Foster believed in the thoughtful brand of socialism that comes from the grass roots, and his religious beliefs arose from the experience of working with the underprivileged. It was no accident that one of his closest constituency friends at the time was the 'Red Bishop' of Durham, the Reverend David Jenkins.

Blair's first significant move against Foster came a year after he took over the leadership. On the surface it looked more like an offer of promotion than a cunning scheme to remove a man who is, in private, one of Peter Mandelson's fiercest critics. Roger Pope, Foster's political adviser, recalls getting a call from Foster asking him to return urgently from Brussels: 'Derek rang to say he had received this personal call from Tony Blair

– asking whether he would consider standing down from the job if he guaranteed him a place in the cabinet. What should he do?'

The request would hurt Foster financially in the short term, since the opposition chief whip and the leader were the only two posts funded by the taxpayer. Blair told him the main reason for the change was that he wanted a 'speaking' rather than a 'non-speaking' chief whip – one who would take a high public profile rather than be a behind-the-scenes fixer. He had earmarked Donald Dewar for the job. The real reason appears to be that Blair needed a chief whip who would be willing to play a part in his discussions with the Liberal Democrats – which Foster would have opposed on principle. Dewar was expected to be more co-operative.

Foster decided to consult Gordon Brown – he was closer to Brown than Blair. 'Take it. You got a better deal than me. I haven't got a guarantee that Blair will have me in his cabinet,' replied Brown somewhat disingenuously. 'But how shall I know Blair will keep his word?' asked Foster. 'Why don't you insist that Alastair Campbell is present and makes a statement about the deal to the lobby? Or you could always take Anne [Foster's wife] along as a witness,' suggested Brown.[13]

Foster asked Campbell to attend, duly stood down, and Campbell briefed the lobby. The lobby hardly believed a word of it.

Foster went on to shadow the Cabinet Office, but in early 1997 he started reading in the papers that Blair wanted him to stand down in Bishop Auckland, take a peerage and become chief whip in the Lords. The suspicion at the time, according to Roger Pope, is that Mandelson, intending to unsettle Foster by getting Blair to renege on his original deal, had placed the stories in the press. Foster decided to challenge Blair directly: 'I keep reading that you want me to go,' he told him. Blair replied: 'I don't know where this is coming from but it is not from me – our deal still stands.'

So Foster told his general management committee that there was no truth in the stories – he had got a reassurance from the leader himself. He was unanimously endorsed to stand in May 1997. Two weeks into the campaign, he received a telephone call from Blair: 'Derek, I have been thinking – I would like you to stand down and become my chief whip in the Lords.'

'But, Tony, I am sorry, I have given my word to my constituency that I am standing again and I can't break it in the middle of the campaign.'

'OK, if you really can't, it has to be. But don't worry, our deal will still stand.'[14]

The day after the election Blair did offer Foster a job in government but not in the cabinet. He became a junior minister to David Clark in the

Cabinet Office. The other junior minister in the department was Mandelson – the chief suspect behind Foster's downfall. Foster reluctantly accepted, but thought better of it and resigned twenty-four hours later – having been in government for just a day. Gordon Brown later berated Blair for his treatment of Foster, claiming it was in breach of the famous deal concluded at the Granita restaurant in London. Blair promised some other big job for Foster and asked his new chief whip, Nick Brown, to find one. Brown made eight attempts to find something suitable – including a botched effort to force Betty Boothroyd to accept Foster as deputy speaker – but in the end Foster was left out in the cold. Blair admitted to Nick Brown: 'Yes, I did offer him a job in the cabinet. But unfortunately it isn't always possible.' Exit Derek Foster, stage left. He is now a peer.

Tom Clarke's treatment by Blair was even more shameful than that of Derek Foster. A quietly spoken Scot with an intimate knowledge of Clydeside's labyrinthine internal politics and a passion for cinema, Clarke has won an accolade rare in the vicious, competitive, back-biting world of Labour politics: most people describe him as 'a genuinely nice person'.

With hindsight, Clarke believes now that Blair double-crossed him by not giving him a seat in the cabinet. He dates Blair's change of mind from the extraordinarily mishandled by-election campaign in 1994 to choose a successor to John Smith, which cost Clarke his seat in the shadow cabinet. He was given the disability brief before being re-elected into the shadow cabinet in 1995, after which he expected Blair give him another frontbench job. But when Blair saw him he said: 'I want you to continue doing your good job in disability.' And then, in an extraordinary aside, Blair added: 'Next year if you still want international development, it will be vacant. You will get it, Tom. It will be yours.'[15] What Clarke did not know and Blair did not tell him was that Joan Lestor, then shadowing international development, was dying.

The following year, Clarke got an even bigger vote in the shadow cabinet elections. He did not see Blair immediately but was confident that, with Joan Lestor now gone, the leader would keep his word. Returning that afternoon to his offices in Millbank, Clarke was surprised to see a throng of journalists outside the building. He stopped and asked what was going on. One reporter, not realising the significance of the news to Clarke, explained: 'It's all about Clare Short – she's been demoted to international development.'

Clarke went into his office, where his shocked staff were waiting for him. Apparently, that morning Clare Short had walked out of a TV interview about a London tube strike and Blair had removed her as transport spokesperson on the spot. Clarke immediately got on to Blair's office – but was put through to Jonathan Powell, who tried to placate him. Clarke insisted on seeing Blair. 'I am very unhappy,' he told him. Blair replied: 'I still want you to do disability, but don't worry, Tom, you will be in my cabinet.'

Clarke: 'But I must question you, Tony. You have promised cabinet posts to at least twenty-six people and there are only twenty-one places. I did not go to Fettes, but I know that this does not work.'

Blair: 'Yes, but you will get in before four or five others.'

In the course of the conversation Blair assured him no fewer than five times that he would get a cabinet job.[16]

Two days later, Blair dropped Clarke's deputy, Robin Corbett, from the shadow team, saying he had to let him go because he was too old and he needed his job for younger people. Clarke should have seen what was coming. But on the day after Labour's election victory, he confidently expected the call to come from Downing Street, still relying on Blair's promise in opposition, repeated five times, that he would be in the cabinet. Initially he was relaxed, as the news bulletins reported that Blair had only made his top appointments. On Saturday morning he received a call from Nick Brown, the new chief whip. Delighted that his friend was calling from his new office at 12 Downing Street, he was then devastated to learn he was not in the cabinet.

Nick Brown was shocked when Clarke related the sorry story of Blair's repeated promises and told him: 'But I am to tell you that Tony says you can have any minister of state job you want.' The two talked and concluded ruefully, in Clarke's words: 'We have now established the true nature of the prime minister of Great Britain.'[17]

After talking it over with an adviser, Clarke chose to be film minister in Chris Smith's Ministry of National Heritage – so that at least he could pursue his passion. But it was only when he met Smith the following Monday that he realised Blair had not even told Smith that he wanted Clarke to have the job; Smith had gone away from his interview with Blair believing he could allocate the portfolios of his ministers himself.[18]

At the next level down there was even more grief, with eight people to be told they were not going to be in government, all of whom had been led to believe they would be. Blair made such a hash of telling the first two disappointed people that Nick Brown had to handle the rest. This included dropping Joan Ruddock, MP for Deptford and former chair of the Campaign for Nuclear Disarmament, who refused to accept Nick Brown's call telling her that Blair's decision was final. She insisted on contacting Blair herself and thus secured responsibility for women's issues in the Department of Social Security.

Among others dropped were two of Blair's old colleagues from the North East, who had helped him on the way to power. Giles Radice, the MP for Durham North who had recommended Blair to union boss Joe Mills for the safe Sedgefield seat, was seen as too old, and Stuart Bell, the MP for Middlesbrough who had introduced Blair to GMB boss Tom Burlison, was also left out.

In his book *Tony Really Loves Me*, Bell recalls a weekend of waiting. He contacted the Department of Trade and Industry, where he found officials standing by to meet him as the new minister of state. He even discussed driving down to London to 'hit the ground running' in his new job. But by Monday, he had realised it was all over. He got a phone call from Nick Brown. He recalls: 'He announced with the utmost regret and genuine sadness that I was not in the government. He could offer no explanation. He explained the prime minister had not rung personally because it would simply have lifted my expectations, only to see them shattered.'

Bell's longstanding Anglican faith served him well: the Archbishop of York intervened to secure him a job as church commissioner in the House of Commons – a post he still holds today.

Old scores had been settled, old friends ruthlessly dropped.

But Blair was still not wholly content with his ministerial appointments, which included people who were clearly not fully signed up to New Labour. So it was not long after the election before the skids began to be manoeuvred into place beneath two of Blair's least-favoured ministers, Michael Meacher and Gavin Strang, neither of whom are in the government today.

The briefing against Strang started very early. Strang thought it would make his job safer: Blair, he believed, would not want to fire him if it looked as though he had been forced into doing so by the press. Strang seems to have been slower than most of his colleagues to realise that when lobby correspondents wrote about the decline of a ministerial career, they had normally been given a direct steer from Downing Street. But he must have started to guess the truth after three months in the job, when Bernard Ingham, Margaret Thatcher's former press secretary, appeared on television pointing out that Downing Street was already briefing journalists against one minister – Gavin Strang.

He survived for fifteen months and was devastated when Blair sacked him. On the eve of his sacking, he told David Clark, who knew that he himself was on the way out: 'You might think you are going, David, but I shall be staying on in government.' Even when Blair sent for him, Strang seems to have allowed himself to hope that this was not the end of his ministerial career, but his chance to get his cherished place at agriculture. Instead, Blair told him he wanted his job for someone else. Blair added, rather oddly, that he was sorry about all the unpleasant press speculation. It was not clear whether he was referring to the speculation over the past fifteen months that Strang would go in the next reshuffle, or the speculation during the previous three months that he was about to be replaced. But why was the prime minister apologising for press coverage, unless he had inspired it?

Strang had only had one serious disagreement with Blair as transport minister, but it would have been a fatal one, given New Labour's plans for the future. Strang had made it clear privately that he opposed the privatisation of air traffic control, and he had managed to water down the proposal so it only said there would be consultation on the subject.

Meacher was more fortunate. He proved more enduring, defying the perennial lobby hack's tale that he was for the chop until well into Blair's second term of office.

CHAPTER ELEVEN

THE BLAIR COURT TAKES CHARGE

The Labour Party had waited eighteen years to form a government. Now it had done so, Blair was to prove very quickly that he intended it to follow much the same policies as the Conservative governments it replaced. Gordon Brown had already committed Labour to sticking to the Tories' spending plans for its first two years; and Tony Blair would soon show that the cloak of financial prudence was not the only garment it had stolen from its Conservative predecessors. With the government's very first actions, on the Millennium Dome and on trade unions, he signalled his intentions so clearly that they should not have been misunderstood.

When Tony Blair walked into Downing Street with that huge 179-seat majority, he told the nation in blunt terms what was to be his watchword: 'I say to the people of this country – we ran for office as New Labour, we will govern as New Labour.'

His triumphal entrance had been arranged in advance by Tim Allan, deputy to new press secretary Alastair Campbell, who orchestrated the flag-waving supporters on the pavement outside Number 10 – all of them Labour supporters issued with plastic Union Jacks rather than Labour Party banners, which had been banned by Downing Street officials. In fact, according to Jonathan Haslam, the outgoing Downing Street press chief, packing the street with party supporters was not an idea invented by New Labour. John Major had made sure that his own Tory supporters were there in 1992 – but they were a little more discreet and less noisy than the ecstatic Labour crowd ushering in a historic victory.

The priorities of the new administration were clear from the very first words Campbell uttered to Haslam: 'We need to get out a press release announcing our victory. How shall we spin it?' Haslam replied, 'But you don't need any spin or angle; it just speaks for itself. Just tell it as it is.'

Campbell's words highlighted what was to prove a fatal flaw in the first Blair administration. It was a flaw enshrined in a special order in council that gave two political appointees, Campbell and Jonathan Powell, executive powers over civil servants, and was reflected in the big jump in the number of special advisers under David Miliband, the head of the Number 10 policy unit. No decision was likely to be released by Downing Street as straightforward fact, and all decisions by other ministries were likely to be monitored by two rival courts – Downing Street and the Treasury.

All this was accompanied by an informal American style of government – with a prime minister who preferred to dress in open-necked shirts and jeans whenever possible. Blair spent that first evening with Nick Brown, his new chief whip. The pair were still friends on day one of the new government, despite the rift over the leadership (Nick Brown had wanted Gordon Brown to be leader). This did not please Cherie Blair, who had told Peter Mandelson at a private dinner in Church House a few months earlier: 'Nick Brown is going to be chief whip over my dead body.'[2]

The two men went to see Brown's offices at 12 Downing Street. As they entered the building – Brown in a suit and Blair dressed in a pair of ice-blue jeans and a white open-necked shirt – an official stopped Blair: 'Excuse me, sir, can I ask who ...' He suddenly broke off, realising that he was challenging the new prime minister, who was not yet instantly recognised when he had 'dressed down'.

Blair's combined passions for informal decision-making, good publicity and distancing himself from Old Labour were what led to the first, dreadfully mistaken, decision of his premiership. It was a decision, we can now show, that had effectively already been made months before he set foot in Downing Street, though few of the ministers who joined him around the cabinet table, ready after eighteen years to start taking decisions instead of criticising the decisions of others, knew this. They thought they were in charge.

The story of the Millennium Dome is one of hubris – a vision, a political fantasy, based on a badly conceived proposal that failed to work. The newly elected Blair seemed to believe he had the Midas touch, that he could transform a derelict toxic waste site into an embodiment of Cool Britannia that would stay in the minds of the next generation for their whole lives. Instead, it became an expensive albatross around the government's neck, a butt of comedians' jokes and a byword for waste and extravagance.

The idea of marking the millennium by building a dome-shaped exhibition space on a derelict site near Greenwich predates New Labour. It was originally the brainchild of Tory deputy prime minister Michael Heseltine and Simon Jenkins, formerly editor of *The Times*. Both were members of the Millennium Commission, a bi-partisan quango set up by the Tories and charged with lining up suitable celebrations for the arrival of year 2000. Even they disagreed over what should go in the Dome, Heseltine believing it should be a showcase for British trade and technology and Jenkins wanting it to be a new palace of fun, like the 1951 Festival of Britain.

But before even the site was cleared it became apparent that the mechanism established to create the Dome was flawed. The commissioners could not themselves put up ideas for the Greenwich site – like any other proposal in the rest of Britain, the idea had to come from the community. So when architect Richard Rogers came up with the idea of an eye-catching big tent on the site, the commission either had to accept or reject the idea before they knew what would be inside it. The commission – using National Lottery money – had the cash, but other people were responsible for the contents.

The plans were already behind schedule when in January 1997, five months before Labour was elected, the Millennium Commission decided to back the Dome and spend £200 million to develop a business case, begin preliminary work and assign the first major contracts.

Michael Heseltine blames the delay on what he calls the 'disreputable and dishonourable conduct of Jack Cunningham', then shadow heritage secretary. 'While the commission was meant to be bi-partisan and non-political with a Labour and Tory member on the board, Jack Cunningham was effectively blocking any progress,' says Heseltine.

This seemed to be confirmed as Labour's view by a comment reported five months later by Ewan Macaskill of the *Guardian* that Lewis Moonie, Jack Cunningham's deputy, had described the project as 'a crock of shit'.[3] In a pre-election interview, one member of the cabinet, Clare Short, described the Dome as 'a silly, temporary building' to a Catholic aid agency magazine.[4] Unfortunately for Short, the interview was published four months after the election, by which time the new Labour government had decided to support the project.

Nonetheless, before the 1997 general election, when the Tories knew that their chances of getting re-elected were virtually non-existent, Heseltine decided to try and secure the Dome's long-term future by getting personal approval for it from Blair. He went to see him privately to get a guarantee that Labour would not dump the project when it won the election.

Later on, when the project had manifestly failed, it suited Blair for it to be thought that he was never very keen. So John Rentoul, his early biographer, was encouraged to write that Blair's response was sceptical. Rentoul claims, with an excess of generosity, that Blair 'gave the nod to the idea of bi-partisan support when he was not concentrating'.[5] Rentoul adds that Blair told Heseltine, when he agreed to the latter's proposal, that Heseltine 'must understand that I am perfectly prepared to walk away from this whole thing'. The political journalist Andrew Rawnsley, presumably also relying on sources close to Blair, maintains that the opposition leader was in 'a terrible pother' about it.[6]

This is all nonsense, according to Heseltine. He has no recollection of Blair expressing any doubts at their meeting and emphatically states that Blair did not introduce such a strong caveat, or indeed any serious caveat at all. He says: 'This exchange is something I do not recognise. I went away knowing that we had the guarantees we had sought to go ahead.' Recollections from senior officials at the Millennium Commission appear to confirm Heseltine's version. They remember that before Virginia Bottomley, then national heritage secretary, issued a statement to Parliament on 20 January, the full statement was read through to Alastair Campbell, Blair's press secretary, for Blair's approval.

The statement could not have been clearer:

> The government has discussed the Millennium Commission's plans in detail with the opposition, who are represented on the commission. The opposition remain enthusiastic about the proposed exhibition at Greenwich. They will want, if elected, to review all aspects of the project *delivery* [our italics], to ensure it is cost-effective and properly implemented, so that it will come within the existing budget.

The key fact, conveniently muddled in Rentoul's account, is that Blair had approved the expenditure of £200 million of lottery money for the project before he was elected prime minister. Effectively this was the first big government decision taken by the Labour leader, and it was taken five months before he entered office, without consulting the shadow cabinet.

Blair's only doubt was how the project was going to be managed. The National Audit Office, in an official report on the Dome published on 9 November 2000, confirms this by using the same word that had been used in Bottomley's statement: 'The then official opposition agreed to these arrangements but reserved the right to review every aspect of the *delivery* [our italics] of the project when elected to government.'

But officials also add that during meetings, the late Michael Montague,

Labour's millionaire donor on the commission, would have been well aware that the figure could well rise above £200 million and that discussion had begun about extending the life of the Millennium Commission beyond the end of 2000 – so it could attract more Lottery cash to prevent other initiatives being swamped by extra demands from the Dome.

Blair had another opportunity to scrap the project days after he was elected, but he chose not to do so. Chris Smith had been a successful shadow health spokesman and had hoped to get the health portfolio in government. Blair gave this instead to Frank Dobson, offering Chris Smith the post of national heritage secretary in his new cabinet. Chris Smith made three requests before taking the new post. The first was that the title of the job and the department be changed, and the second that he could introduce a bill to reform the National Lottery. The third was: 'Do we have to go ahead with the Dome?'

Blair quickly agreed to the first two – later creating the new department of culture, media and sport and giving Smith a relatively free hand in drawing up plans to reform the Lottery. But he refused to promise to scrap the Dome; instead its future would be reviewed. Chris Smith accepted the compromise.

Before the future delivery of the Dome was even discussed, Downing Street effectively provoked a row with the directors of Camelot, the company that runs the National Lottery and the cash cow for the Dome. Company results showed that the directors of Camelot were due to share a £2.35 million bonus from previous years – just at a point when profits were falling and ticket sales starting to decline. The disclosure was characterised in the press as a typical 'fat cat' tale – and Chris Smith issued a statement mildly rebuking the company. Then, spurred on by phone messages from Alastair Campbell, he turned up the volume, accusing the directors of 'profiteering' and demanding they hand the money over to charity.[7]

The issue exploded in Smith's face when it turned out that the deal was legally fireproof and the directors threatened to quit. Downing Street had failed to think the issue through. Whitehall came to the rescue in the shape of Hayden Phillips, permanent secretary at the department of national heritage – an unctuous but wily operator, skilled at smoothing over difficult situations. He crafted a face-saving formula which enabled the directors to keep the cash and the company and instead to hand over interest from unclaimed prizes to 'good causes'.

When Chris Smith had turned for advice to Downing Street, Alastair Campbell was nowhere to be seen. Instead, an extraordinary story appeared in the press. It suggested that Mandelson had put pressure on

Smith to back down, to save Blair from calls from worried businesspeople believing Labour had started to revert to 'tooth and claw' socialism only days into government. The story was self-serving nonsense. Mandelson had nothing to do with it – it was Campbell covering his back (and Blair's).[8]

The result of this affair was that any alternative plan Chris Smith might have for the Dome was seriously weakened when two reports commissioned on its future came before the cabinet. One was a paper for the new home and social affairs cabinet subcommittee, prepared by civil servants at Smith's new ministry, the other was by the staff of the Millennium Commission.

The Millennium Commission report was completed first and discussed by the cabinet on 4 June. After examining the business plan of the operator, Millennium Central (later the New Millennium Experience Company), it concluded that the scheme was high-risk and would cost £758 million to build, requiring a subsidy of £399 million from Lottery funds – double the initial estimate. The commission report decided to err on the cautious side, because of the uncertainty of ticket sales, and put aside £449 million. This turned out to be completely inadequate. It also assumed that the Dome would be pulled down and the land sold for £15 million to developers.

But the most damning finding was that there were no plans for what was to go inside the Dome. It was an empty vessel. As the National Audit Office reported later with its usual restrained language: 'They were concerned that the plan lacked detail on commercial, operational and pricing strategies and that there was no substantive information in the plan on the key driver for the company's business – the content of the Dome.'[9] Deloitte and Touche Consulting Group, called in to vet the potential visitor sales figures, did not have a clue how many people would turn up. They concluded that the plan for 12 million to visit the Dome 'was dependent on the creation of a significant "wow" factor'. They had 'to assume that the contents would be of such a high standard that it could satisfy the build-up of press and public expectation'.[10]

So by 10 June, when the cabinet subcommittee met to consider the civil servants' report, Chris Smith was already armed with a deeply disturbing report from the commission. He knew the Dome could be built on time, but he also knew there was nothing to put in it. The civil servants' report recommended that the plans should be scaled down – with a new emphasis on education rather than some grand super-attraction, because nobody had decided what the Dome was for. If this did not work, the report suggested it should be scrapped. This scaled-down proposal was never discussed seriously. Officials at the Millennium Commission were never asked to look at it.

Within the government there was virtually no support for the Dome. It only had two champions. One was Blair's loyal lieutenant Peter Mandelson, minister without portfolio at the Cabinet Office, who waxed lyrical about the scheme as New Labour's equivalent of the Festival of Britain (the proud achievement of his grandfather Herbert Morrison). But Mandelson did not attend cabinet meetings. Jack Straw, the home secretary, who supported the Dome because he, too, remembered the Festival of Britain, was its chief advocate in the cabinet.

The paper from Smith's own civil servants concurred with the Millennium Commission's views. It also contained a key fact that was never made public. The cost of scrapping the Dome was not, at that point, the £200 million which Blair later claimed would have been lost if the project had been cancelled. It was only £50 to £60 million. The commission had not yet irrevocably committed all the cash. Officials say that, in fact, only £28 million of contracts had been assigned; the rest would have been given as compensation to English Partnerships – another quango – for acquiring the site. This was still a large and embarrassing sum of money, but it was nowhere near the figure given by Blair.

No final decision was taken for another ten days. On 20 June the cabinet had to decide what to do. In Downing Street a group of ministers and officials including Blair, Chris Smith, Gordon Brown, Peter Mandelson and John Prescott held a pre-meeting with press secretary Alastair Campbell and chief of staff Jonathan Powell. Here a sceptical Gordon Brown suddenly produced 'five tests' for the Dome before it could go ahead – a precursor of his famous five tests for whether Britain joined the euro. Remarkably, these five tests then emerged in the press a day later in a *Times* article by Dominic Kennedy and Daniel McGrory.[11] But they were no longer Gordon Brown's tests: they were spun as Blair's own idea.

The article reported that the commission and the New Millennium Experience Company had been 'baffled by the five new demands sprung upon them by Tony Blair'. These included a demand that the exhibition would be permanent – at a stroke putting up the cost by £15 million, as the site could not then be sold. Other demands were that no new public money should go into the project; that the targets of £175 million business sponsorship and £136 million ticket sales must be reached; that the Dome's content must be more exciting and relate to the whole nation; and, finally, that a new management structure be set up to 'provide ideas and a creative force'. Given that there was still nothing to go into the

Dome, nor even any suggestions as to what might go in it, these conditions caused total confusion for the builders and organisers.

At the pre-cabinet meeting, it was clear that enthusiasm for the dome had grown. John Prescott started reminiscing about how much he had enjoyed his childhood visit to the Festival of Britain, remembering the Skylon with particular affection. Peter Mandelson recalled touchingly how his grandfather had been behind the successful venture. Blair himself remained largely silent.

At the cabinet meeting that followed, Blair had to depart early to attend a service at St Margaret's Church in Westminster, leaving John Prescott in the chair. So, after Blair had made his case for the Dome, Prescott tried to get the cabinet's approval. But he only got the support of Jack Straw and was left facing the wrath of cash-strapped health secretary Frank Dobson and education secretary David Blunkett, antagonism from Clare Short, and scepticism from Gordon Brown. So all that came from the meeting was an instruction to Chris Smith to produce a further paper for the following week's cabinet on how the scheme could proceed without extra Treasury cash. Crucially, no vote was taken. If it had been, the Dome would have been halted. Prescott had either been told, or knew instinctively, that his boss did not want the project killed off.

That afternoon, Blair took matters into his own hands. He decided to go down to the Greenwich site himself to see what was going on and face the media in a photo call. He travelled by car with Prescott, Mandelson and Smith. On the way down he said to them: 'If the millennium passes and we have nothing big and substantive to show for it, what kind of country are we?' At the photo call he told the media: 'In the year 2000 all the eyes of the world will be on Britain. This is our chance to make a statement of faith in our capacity in Britain to do things bigger and better than anyone else.'

Blair had taken the decision to go ahead with the Dome despite almost every factor being against it. It was clearly a huge risk; the National Lottery would have had £350 million to spend on other millennium celebrations if he had dropped the idea. But of course he couldn't, because he believed in his commitment six months before to Michael Heseltine – the commitment which he later tried to pretend was so much less categorical than Heseltine thought it was. The two reports commissioned by Chris Smith effectively warned ministers about the potential dangers and gave them a possible (relatively) cheap exit from the whole project. Instead, Blair adopted an increasingly high-profile role in personally promoting the dome – with the result that its later failure completely overshadowed most of the much more successful millennium projects outside the capital.

Chris Smith himself still downplayed Blair's passion for the scheme. In a press release on 26 June he said: 'The Millennium Experience at Greenwich will be the focus of much celebration and activity. But it is important to put it in context, it represents only a quarter of the commission's overall commitment of more than £1.6 billion.'[12] Blair, though, forged ahead regardless. He appointed Peter Mandelson to take charge of the project. The promotion of Herbert Morrison's grandson to oversee its construction reflected Mandelson's passion for the scheme but was also intended to assuage his vanity at not being appointed straight to the cabinet. Mandelson as minister without portfolio had little to keep himself occupied. He needed a high-profile job. John Lloyd wrote in the *New Statesman* that Mandelson got the job because of 'his swathe of connections and acquaintances in the worlds of media and showbiz; his appetite for work and organisation; his flair for histrionics and the grand gesture' and because the 'high-wire nerviness' of the project appealed to the 'impresario side of the man'.[13]

It therefore fell to Peter Mandelson to decide what should actually go inside the Dome. A New Age-style acrobatic show provided the focus of the entertainment, but most of the space inside the Dome was divided into a series of zones, whose commercial sponsors were able to mix exhibits with promotion of their products – a kind of microcosm of a privatised Britain. This arrangement offered Mandelson regular opportunities to mingle with captains of industry like Bob Ayling, the head of British Airways, and Labour luvvies like architect Richard Rogers.

Chris Smith was relieved to see responsibility for the Dome move away from himself and his department. This was wrongly interpreted as a snub to the minister who had misread Blair's mind. In fact, the reason was to prevent a potentially serious conflict of interest. Smith had inherited the job of chairing the Millennium Commission. If he had been the minister responsible for the Dome, he would have found himself responsible for monitoring the expenditure that the Millennium Commission under his chairmanship had authorised – hardly an independent audit. Given the problems that later arose, when Mike O'Connor, the chief executive of the Millennium Commission, twice challenged the government by refusing to approve extra cash without a ministerial direction, this turned out to be a rather farsighted move. It saved Chris Smith from being involved in a rather embarrassing scandal later on – and from criticism by the powerful Commons public accounts committee and the National Audit Office.

If only Peter Mandelson had exercised the same circumspection in his dealings with sponsors; and if only Tony Blair had been a bit more cautious about promoting the project.

Mandelson's relations with some of the big donors could have got the government into a lot of trouble. Tesco's, for example, gave £12 million to the Dome, just at the time when John Prescott dropped a plan for a new tax on supermarket car parks. Similarly, the close relations between British Airways and the government – Prescott had a say over lucrative transatlantic slots at Heathrow – would always make bad reading if any deal coincided with a donation.

Blair's enthusiasm for promoting the project reached hyperbolic proportions over the next few months. At a launch at the Royal Festival Hall on 24 February 1998 to set out the Dome's attractions, he declared:

> It will be the most exciting day out in the world. There will be a lasting legacy. The Dome will last a decade, it will become a national landmark. This is Britain's opportunity to greet the world with a celebration so bold, so beautiful, so inspiring it embodies at once the spirit of confidence and adventure in Britain and the spirit of future in the world.

Unusually, he even put his eldest son, Euan, into the spotlight by backing the point made by Simon Jenkins that the Dome would have to pass 'the Euan test' – to become so exciting that the average thirteen-year-old boy would want to go. He attacked the 'snipers and cynics' who criticised the project, contrasting their attitude with his own visionary, innovative courage: 'It's easy to say don't do something, to say it won't be done on time, that it costs too much, that no one will visit it. It takes little courage to say no to a new idea.'[14]

Michael Heseltine has some sympathy for Blair's dilemma at this point: 'Basically he is caught between a rock and a hard place. Like Concorde, you need to sell the idea or you will never get the results. He has to act as a super salesman and sell the Dome to attract the twelve million people to come in the first place, or it will fail.'

Nothing, it seems, had prepared Blair for the disastrous launch of the Dome, nearly two years later, on New Year's Eve 1999. As the reports in 1997 had predicted, the dome itself was completed virtually on time and only marginally above budget. The problem was the content – just as the experts had warned.

Before the big night, Blair applied pressure on his cabinet colleagues to make sure they would attend. This was one of the rare occasions when he failed to impose his will on them. Some of them may have quietly decided that they did not want to be too publicly associated with what they knew – and anyone knew who had read all the relevant papers – was likely to be an expensive fiasco. As Melissa Kite reported in *The Times* on Christmas Eve, Gordon Brown, Geoff Hoon, Alan Milburn and David Blunkett all pleaded prior engagements. Derry Irvine, the Lord Chancellor and Blair's old legal boss, decided to give a New Year's Eve reception in the House of Lords. Irvine later compromised and agreed to hold a grand champagne reception at the House of Lords earlier in the evening for the Millennium Commission award-winners and invited senior officials from the commission to come; they would then have to jump on the tube from Westminster to Greenwich to attend the midnight bash at the Dome. Mandelson made sure that he attended both parties.

Blair's insistence that key guests should travel to the event by special tube trains also generated some doubt. Robin Cook insisted on going 'off message' by using his ministerial car. Michael Heseltine made sure he avoided the London Underground by arriving with the queen on the royal barge. On the night, almost everything that could go wrong went wrong. Numerous VIPs, including senior businesspeople and newspaper editors, were left waiting outside in the cold for hours after the special trains laid on from Stratford to Greenwich broke down. The actual celebrations took place at a time when the rest of London was enjoying a fantastic firework display. But what the great and good saw in the Dome, when they eventually got there, was a mixture of twenty-first-century kitsch and a traditional rendering of 'Auld Lang Syne', as well as prayers from the Archbishop of Canterbury.

The only two things that didn't happen that night were the dreaded 'millennium bug', which never materialised, and a feared IRA attack – which had led MI5 to advise that the entire royal family and cabinet must not be in the Dome at the same time. But the subsequent howls of derision from the press, encouraged by newspaper editors who had been left shivering in the cold at Stratford, wrecked any chance of the project being a success – not that there had been any realistic chance of that in the first place. Jennie Page, the highly paid head of the New Millennium Experience Company which organised the event, got the sack.

The low visitor numbers over the following weeks created a highly embarrassing situation: the Dome, it emerged, was technically bust – its £50 million reserve was quickly used up – and another £76 million had to be found to keep it afloat. Chris Smith twice had to issue a ministerial direction – first for £29 million and then for another £47 million – to stave off bankruptcy. He also issued a warning letter to the Dome's owners, the New Millennium Experience Company, about the state of their finances. His permanent secretary, Robin Young, had to apologise to the Commons public accounts committee for not telling Parliament that the Dome was broke.

Business sponsors got special indemnities to prevent them having to meet the losses. The number of people coming to the Dome slumped from a predicted 12 million to 5.5 million (even including a million free tickets), rising again later to 6.5 million due to a last-minute rush before it closed at the end of 2000. And a number of the key figures who promoted the Dome – including Jennie Page and Bob Ayling – never made it onto any New Year's honours lists.

Eventually, the government was forced to take desperate measures. It called in David James, who was famed for his ability to rescue companies that were in deep trouble, so much so that he was known as the City's 'Red Adair' (after the Texan troubleshooter who had extinguished the Kuwaiti oil wells set ablaze by Saddam Hussein's retreating army). James has had a colourful career. He once freed a dozen engineers held by Libyan revolutionary guards in Tripoli and helped MI6 trace Saddam Hussein's secret 'super gun'. Recently married for the first time at the age of sixty-six, the multi-millionaire, now advising the Tories on waste, has been known to fly to Sydney and back to see a Test Match, and takes three weeks off every year to pit his wits against the bookies for serious cash at Ascot, Cheltenham and Goodwood.

By this time, Blair's interest in the Dome had waned, and Alastair Campbell made sure that the prime minister's name was kept out of the picture. Only David James and Lord Falconer – Blair's former flatmate Charlie Falconer, who succeeded Mandelson as minister for the Dome – were expected to make any public pronouncements. Lord Falconer, following instructions from Campbell, did his best to say as little as possible.

But Blair couldn't resist one last intervention. It ended in fresh tears and brought the government close to yet another major Dome scandal. Two weeks before the Dome was due to close in December 2000, when Blair heard that the first deal to sell it to a Japanese company, Nomura, had collapsed, he personally rang David James to urge him to postpone the closure. Four years later, James told BBC Radio 4's *Today* programme: 'There was a very determined effort made, led by Tony Blair ... when he said, "Look, the figures have improved greatly, the numbers of people coming through are at an all-time high for the whole year. Why don't we ... give it a few more months?"'[15]

The government had an obvious interest in keeping the Dome open as long as possible: it made it more valuable to potential bidders, who would be less eager to acquire a deserted and derelict site. But no additional money was available from the National Lottery to fund such an extension, which is why James turned down Blair's suggestion.

Blair was, presumably, concerned because a second bidder, Legacy plc, led by City property developer Robert Bourne, was now offering to buy the dome and develop a hi-tech business park, Knowledge City, there. Bourne was no ordinary developer – he was a Tory member turned Labour donor who had contributed £100,000 to the Labour Party (including £33,000 given after he made his bid for the Dome), and was close enough to Mandelson, the former Dome minister, to organise a birthday party for him.

Bourne had also given £2,000 to the Islington South Labour Party, the constituency party of Chris Smith, secretary of state for culture, media and sport. The donation meant that Chris Smith would have to rule himself out of any involvement with the bid. Legacy was 80 per cent owned by Treasury Holdings, run by two controversial Irish property developers, John Ronan and Richard Barrett, who had been branded 'deliberate liars' by the Irish Parliament. Mr Barrett once wrote to a rival property developer: 'Certain opponents of ours have underestimated our ability to cause legal chaos to their detriment.'

Ronan and Barrett were also prolific political donors. They had given money, through Castlemarket Holdings, their joint venture-capital company, to a Fianna Fail senator who had a consultative role in a Dublin shopping centre redevelopment. They also gave money to the Progressive Democrats; Fianna Fail; Ruari Quinn, the Irish Labour Party leader; and the Irish minister for foreign affairs, David Andrews.

The Cabinet Office had given Legacy 'preferred bidder' status. But other parties were more cautious. Sir Robert McAlpine, the global construction company who were to handle the construction if Legacy's bid succeeded, pulled out. And John Prescott was clearly jittery, because he publicly called on Legacy to bring in more partners – which would dilute Treasury Holdings' grip on the company. The scheme collapsed at the last minute – or rather the government ran away from the deal – when serious questions led Jack Straw, once one of the Dome's biggest cheerleaders, to advise ministers to pull out. Whitehall sources say Straw's action saved the prime minister considerable embarrassment.

Even today the fate of the Dome is not totally secure, despite various business proposals to develop the site – although, thanks to good management by David James and good stewardship by the Millennium Commission, the company responsible has been able to return £25 million of its bloated budget to the National Lottery in 2004. David James, however, never received the honour that he had apparently expected his efforts would earn for him.

Michael Heseltine, probably the Dome's greatest supporter, admits that mistakes were made and now says:

> When the next celebrations are planned in fifty years' time [2051], and there will be celebrations then, they will need to be in hands of one organisation – run by an entrepreneur – who can take all the decisions and have control over the project. The system of using the Millennium Commission to oversee projects which were dependent on other people delivering did not work.

Sir John Bourn, the head of the National Audit Office, drew an unfavourable comparison between the Dome and the much more successful 1951 Festival of Britain – for which a special dedicated government department was set to take control of events. He concluded that Herbert Morrison was able to do a much better job than his grandson, Peter Mandelson.

In short, the Millennium Dome had turned out to be a tawdry failure and a financial nightmare. There were lessons Blair could have learnt from the episode: that spin and salesmanship are no substitute for substance; that Labour was considerably less competent at management than it imagined itself to be; that his fondness for thrusting himself into the limelight could have unexpected repercussions; and that when the Whitehall machine advised caution, it might be prudent to listen. He chose to ignore them all.

The way in which the decision to go ahead with the Dome was taken was also an ominous indication of Blair's approach to the tradition of cabinet government. If the cabinet had taken the decision, the project would have been scrapped. If the minister responsible for it at that time, Chris Smith, had taken the decision, it would have been a totally different project. It went ahead in what proved to be a disastrous fashion because the decision was taken by the prime minister and his new, all-powerful court without taking heed of the views of either the cabinet or the minister responsible.

The Blair court is a loose, fluid group which takes momentous decisions over coffee in the 'den' and does not trouble with such bureaucratic, Old Labour formalities as taking minutes. Most, but not all, of its members are senior officials in the vastly inflated Downing Street staff; a few are elected politicians.

Jonathan Powell is Blair's chief of staff and a key member of the court, especially when foreign affairs are discussed. He started his career in television, working for the BBC and Granada, before becoming a career diplomat. Blair recruited him in 1995, when Powell was First Secretary at the British embassy in Washington. Powell's political instincts are a million miles away from those of traditional Labour members, though when he first approached the Blairs, he was actually interested in becoming, like his future boss, a Labour MP.[16] It is a curious coincidence – though it now seems less curious than it initially appeared – that he is the brother of Sir Charles Powell, Margaret Thatcher's former chief of staff.

Powell had been responsible for Blair's only speech on foreign affairs during the general election campaign, which bore little resemblance to the party's manifesto. There was no mention of controlling the arms trade and little about third-world poverty. Robin Cook, shadow foreign secretary, was appalled by it and only just succeeded in persuading Blair, minutes before delivering the speech, to remove a sentence by Powell which read: 'I am proud of the British Empire.'[17]

At the beginning, Peter Mandelson, minister without portfolio, was the chief politician in the court. But the key member was almost a mirror image of Mandelson: Blair's press secretary, Alastair Campbell, around whom a powerful mystique has grown up. Though superficially very different from Mandelson – he is aggressively heterosexual and sometimes almost laughably macho – Campbell shares several of his key characteristics, in particular a deep personal insecurity which means that he needs a strong, charismatic leader to follow and idolise.

You often find such people in politics, though they seldom rise to the top, because to do so they need a leader who responds to adoration. John Smith did not; while Neil Kinnock did, but with sensible reservations. It is only under a leader like Tony Blair that uncompromising acolytes like Campbell and Mandelson can find seats at the top table.

Blair was the third leader Campbell had followed and idolised. The first, when he worked on the *Daily Mirror*, was its larger-than-life proprietor, Robert Maxwell. His devotion to Maxwell was so great that on the day of Maxwell's death, he started a nasty brawl in the House of Commons with Michael White, the *Guardian*'s political editor, who had insulted his hero's memory with a jokey remark – a White trademark.

With Maxwell dead, Neil Kinnock became Campbell's hero for a while. 'On his desk in the office ... carefully placed in a position of honour,' write his biographers Peter Oborne and Simon Walters, 'was a

photograph of Neil Kinnock. He would often admire it ostentatiously.'
When Kinnock was defeated in 1992 Campbell lapsed into deep depression. He told one of the present authors, David Hencke, that he could not
see Labour ever winning an election.

He had been appalled at the way some of his journalist colleagues
tried to destroy Kinnock, and he did his loyal best to build him up. Kinnock and his wife Glenys responded to his devotion and loyalty, but they
worried about his obviously troubled behaviour. They seem to have
thought Campbell's problem was alcohol. They were probably mistaken.
Campbell was certainly a heavy drinker, as many national-newspaper
journalists were in those days, but he was probably not an alcoholic.

It was during his Kinnock-worshipping years, in 1986, that he suffered a serious nervous breakdown. He puts it down to drink, but every
observer of his behaviour during his last year in Downing Street in 2003
agrees that he came very close to another breakdown, and by then he had
been teetotal for seventeen years.

Neil and Glenys Kinnock, who are instinctively kind people, played a
key role in helping Campbell regain health. Oborne and Walters write:

> It is impossible to exaggerate the closeness of the friendship that devel-
> oped between Alastair Campbell and Neil Kinnock … . Campbell would
> do anything for the Kinnocks. He was a mixture of adviser, minder,
> speech-writer, family friend and manservant. Along with [his partner]
> Fiona Millar, he would babysit the children, pick up the shopping, draft
> a press release, give a view on the handling of a sensitive problem. The
> two families went on holiday together.[18]

The closeness persists to this day; when the authors spoke to Kinnock in
2004, Campbell and Millar were due to spend the following weekend
with the Kinnocks in Brussels.

The passage above could just as easily be a description of Campbell's (or indeed Mandelson's) relationship with Blair. Blair, only half in
jest, has said that the first word uttered by his youngest child, Leo, was
'Alastair'.

'The morning I heard about John Smith's death,' says Alastair Campbell, 'I was in the back of a BBC car taking me from Television Centre,
where I'd been reviewing the papers, to Westminster [where he worked
as political editor of the *Daily Mirror*]. I knew two things at once. First,
Tony Blair would be leader. Second, I would end up working for him,
though we had never discussed it.'[19]

Neil and Glenys Kinnock thought this was a rotten idea, and so did
Fiona Millar. When Blair offered Campbell the job of press secretary they

all urged him – begged him, really – to turn it down. Kinnock had already turned down Campbell's offer to be his own press secretary back in 1992. He was sure the job would destroy Campbell. He knew, as well as anyone alive, the ultimate frailty of Campbell's character and feared the job would tear his friend apart, perhaps bringing on another nervous breakdown. He was right.

In 1994 Kinnock was so determined to save Campbell from this fate that he even offered him an alternative attraction. Now a European commissioner, he asked Campbell to come to Brussels with him as his *chef de cabinet*. Hearing of this, Tony Blair turned up in person at Campbell and Fiona Millar's holiday home in Avignon to press his offer of a job. If what Campbell has said to his recent audiences is to be believed, Blair's trip was unnecessary, but it is a measure of how determined he was to secure Campbell's services.[20]

After the 1997 election, Fiona Millar took on the job of looking after the prime minister's wife – arranging her diary, deciding who she should see and what she should wear, that sort of thing. She gave up her trade of journalism for this task – and perhaps also to be there for Campbell if he needed her. Today, Neil Kinnock puts it carefully but unmistakeably: 'Fiona has more distance than Alastair and she is more political.'[21]

Peter Mandelson was against the appointment of Campbell; unsurprisingly, he saw Campbell as a potential rival in the Blair court. It could hardly have escaped his notice that Campbell's method of ingratiating himself with the leader was just like his own. He pressed the case for appointing the political correspondent of the *Sunday Times*, Andy Grice, instead, but Blair wanted Campbell.[22]

Yet Mandelson knew that Blair would still depend on him. 'Tony needed Peter for the missing bit of his brain that did not understand the Labour Party,' says someone who knows both of them well. The same source confirms what Michael Meacher surmised, that Mandelson sat with Blair throughout most of the process of cabinet-making: 'Choosing cabinet ministers and junior ministers, knowing who must be in, who can be left out, is meat and drink to Peter.'

Today, Campbell tells the audiences at his roadshow that what attracted him to Blair when they first met were Blair's 'smile and his badly fitting suit'.[23] The first is Blair's trademark. The second is probably an invention; no one else has ever spoken of Blair being badly dressed. Campbell, like many clever but insecure people, was smitten with Blair from the first moment he met him, in 1983. Blair attracts what might almost be called the natural courtier. They gravitate towards him. They sacrifice themselves for him; they defer to him even when their own private opinions conflict with his. Campbell is – in a muddled, unread sort of way – far more leftwing than Blair, but defers completely to Blair's opinions.

And when a lightning conductor is required – when someone is required to stand up in public and take the incoming fire that would otherwise hit their leader – Campbell and Mandelson will fight for the job. They will happily lay down their own reputations for that of their leader. And both of them, as we shall see, have been required to do so in the years since 1997.

Anji Hunter, Blair's long-time adviser and confidante, and Cherie Booth, both clever, attractive and slightly insecure women, have some of the same characteristics. They, too, compete for Blair's ear. They, too, have little in common with him politically. When she moved in to 10 Downing Street, Cherie Booth was still considerably to the left of her husband politically, while Anji Hunter, though she is not much interested in political ideas, is the authentic voice of middle-class England. While Cherie tried to give her husband some socialist backbone, Anji would remind him of the 'real people' she mixed with around her home in Haywards Heath, Sussex, whose aspirations she felt Blair ought to be representing.

Sally Morgan, who became Blair's political secretary, is less of a courtier and more a traditional party official. She had worked for Labour Party headquarters most of her life, and her contribution during Blair's leadership of the opposition was to ensure the selection of safely Blairite candidates in safe seats.[24]

Morgan's deputy, John Cruddas, was an unexpected character to find in the Blair court, though he was only on the fringes of it. He had good trade union contacts and had worked closely with Larry Whitty, whom he admired, during Whitty's time as Labour Party general secretary. He says Blair's determination to get rid of Whitty was really a compliment: 'Blair thought highly of him – that's why he wanted him out. He thought Larry would shave some of the excesses off the modernising agenda.' Cruddas was almost the only pro-trade union voice in the Downing Street court; and he left Downing Street after three years, convinced there was nothing more he could achieve there.[25] He is now the Labour MP for Dagenham and an occasional rebel, not trusted in Blairite circles.

While Cruddas remained in Downing Street, it was his job to keep in touch with the trade unions and vice versa, and he faced an uphill task in getting union concerns heard. He had been in Congress House, the TUC headquarters, on the night of the 1997 election, and recalls union leaders' growing apprehension as they saw the scale of the election victory. They knew that the stronger Blair was in Parliament, the less chance they had of getting a pro-union government. 'Many of them thought: we ought to jump before we're pushed,' he says. 'They thought: this means the full Blairite agenda, including ditching the unions and linking up with the Liberals.'

They didn't jump. Instead, John Monks, the general secretary of the TUC, and Cruddas formed a partnership to lobby for the trade unions. Cruddas says: 'Tony Blair is unlike any previous Labour leader in that he does not think a Labour government ought to enhance collective bargaining. Every previous Labour leader has believed that trade unionism is basically a good thing and union membership ought to be encouraged.'

Cruddas regularly found himself summoned into the 'den' by Blair to fight it out with Geoff Norris from the Downing Street policy unit, whose job was to keep in touch with employers and the CBI. Dotted around the room might be any combination of Charlie Falconer, Sally Morgan, Jonathan Powell and Ian McCartney (then minister of state at the Department of Trade and Industry). Of these, only McCartney had any sympathy with the trade unions. Sometimes Cherie Booth would join the group, and Cruddas found her to be his best ally: 'She was always sympathetic and technically very competent.' Cruddas would put the union view, Norris the employers' view, and Blair would arbitrate between them.

'It was a cold climate for pro-union ideas in Downing Street after the 1997 election,' says Cruddas. 'There was a lot of empty Third Way rhetoric, the cult of newness. It wasn't a labour-movement place at all. I was tolerated because they knew they had to work through some sort of package.' Blair, he says, thought that 'trade unions were endearing in an old-fashioned way, part of the legacy he had to work through'.[26]

It is hardly surprising that trade unionists started to feel – as John Monks famously put it – like 'embarrassing elderly relatives at a family gathering'. Looking back over Labour's first term, Monks did not feel it had been a total washout, though it was disappointing. 'We did get a few things,' he says. 'Trade union recognition turned out better than I thought it would, largely because Ian McCartney fought for us.' Nevertheless, the prevailing atmosphere in government was the one in which Peter Mandelson could say, when trade unions were mentioned at a meeting of Labour donors: 'Ah, trade unions – the enemy within.' And then pause before adding: 'As some would have it.'

If John Monks felt that, with Cruddas' help, he had at least persuaded Blair to compromise on some union issues at home, he could feel no such satisfaction when he looked back at the wider European scene after taking up a new job in 2003 as general secretary of the ETUC, the European Trades Union Congress, which represents European trade unions in Brussels. When Labour came into office in 1997, the European Commission was trying to introduce a directive on information and consultation, designed to stop employees hearing on the television (or, in some notorious cases, by text message) that their factory had been shut and they were out of a job. The directive would require employers to inform and consult trade union representatives when closures were contemplated. Soon after Blair became prime minister, ETUC was startled to find that the directive had a strong and determined enemy in the new British government. 'Britain went to war to block the directive' is how John Monks puts it.

The story of that war has never been told. Blocking the directive was going to be hard, because four countries were required to veto it and there were only three which opposed it, including Britain. So the Blair government set itself to recruit a fourth – Germany. But trade unions in Germany already had these rights to consultation, so German employers saw no need to block the European directive. In fact, they were rather in favour of it, because they did not see why other employers should not have to operate under the same constraints as themselves.

So Blair and Adair Turner of the CBI turned their attention to the German employers' organisation. Peter Mandelson was sent on a secret mission to Germany as Blair's emissary. He explained to Chancellor Kohl's office how important the British government considered it was to block the directive. Kohl took some persuading, but in the end he and the German employers' organisation agreed to change their stance – as a favour to the Blair government. Afterwards, the then general secretary of the ETUC found out and protested to Blair, but to no effect.

John Monks heard about Mandelson's mission from his ETUC contacts. So, when a TUC delegation visited Downing Street, they told Blair they thought it incredible that a Labour government should place itself in this position. Blair's reply was that he could not do something on labour law once a year on behalf of the TUC. He must keep the business community on side. He went on to say that he did not want the British people to think he was dictated to by the TUC, and that Britain was not ready for a German-style system.

Soon afterwards, the Christian Democrat Kohl was voted out of office, and a new Social Democratic chancellor, Gerhard Schröder, succeeded him. Schröder was sympathetic to the directive but said he could not change his government's stance before the next German election, in

2001. After the election, if he won, he would be able to do something about it. But until then the directive was dead.

In 2001 Schröder was re-elected, and he privately told both Blair and the ETUC that he would no longer block the directive. So it went through, though Britain managed to get it watered down. The British representative at the ETUC, now Peter Hain, abstained rather than be defeated. 'The British government led the opposition in the corridors of Brussels throughout,' says John Monks.

It also led opposition to the proposed directive on agency workers, which would give these workers the same rights as permanent workers. It was fast becoming standard practice for some employers to use agency staff as a way of avoiding employment legislation. If an employee was classified as an agency worker, he or she could be fired at a moment's notice, with no explanation. Agency workers have very few rights. 'The British government blocked that ferociously,' says John Monks. 'We would have it without the [intervention of the] British government.' Patricia Hewitt was regularly sent to Brussels to argue against it.

Later, there was the working time directive, which Blair has so far managed to block. The directive said that normally no one should work more than forty-eight hours a week, and that if they did it should be part of a collective agreement. European social democrats, and even Christian Democrats, were amazed at how determined Britain was to block this. An Irish diplomat told the Irish cabinet that he had never seen a diplomatic effort like the British campaign to veto the directive. A Dutch ETUC official was shocked to be told by a brisk young Blair aide, despatched to Brussels to reinforce the British position: 'We don't do collective bargaining.'[27]

One member of the court who felt far more at home than John Cruddas was Andrew Adonis, education adviser in the Number 10 policy unit.

Blair had told the electorate that his three priorities were 'education, education and education'. So it was hardly surprising that he wanted to control education policy. But the extent to which he and Adonis have sidelined and humiliated his education secretaries is unprecedented.

In December 1996, several months before the election, Blair saw an article in the *Observer* headlined: 'Let Blair be his own education chief'. It began: 'Tony Blair should take two posts in the next Labour government: prime minister and education secretary.' That way, it continued, Blair would 'make the plight of the nation's youth a prime Whitehall concern'. If he did not want to take the actual title, Blair could at least control the substance of policy. He could find a cipher who would implement his policy: 'Enter David Blunkett.' Blunkett was Labour's education spokesman.

Blair hastily arranged to meet the clever young journalist and academic who wrote the piece – Andrew Adonis – and offered him a job in government without any reference to the hapless Blunkett. It was Adonis, not Blunkett, who controlled education policy throughout Blair's first term as prime minister.

In his mid-thirties at the time, Adonis is the product of a private fee-charging school and Oxford University, where he gained a first-class degree in modern history at Keble and a doctorate at Christ Church; he was subsequently an Oxford fellow for three years. He now lived, naturally, in Islington. A Liberal Democrat councillor during his time in Oxford, he had never thought of joining the Labour Party, though he did consider defecting to the Conservatives. He became the public-policy correspondent of the *Financial Times* in 1991, moving to the *Observer* in 1996. He shared with Blair a contempt for what he saw as the Old Labour ideologies standing in the way of improving Britain's education system.

Blunkett had an early indication of the way the wind was blowing. Most Labour activists, as well as the teaching unions and probably most teachers, desperately wanted to see the back of Chris Woodhead, the combative head of Ofsted, the education standards watchdog. It would have been a quick and easy way for the government to make it clear to teachers that the new government, unlike the old one, valued them properly. But before the election, Blair announced that Woodhead would keep his job under Labour. Blunkett was not consulted; he was not even told in advance. 'I hope you don't think it was my idea,' he told Roy Hattersley. 'I didn't even know it was going to happen.'

Early in the life of the New Labour government, Woodhead confided to someone with whom he then worked closely his contempt for the intellectual qualities of all the education ministers. 'There was an evident tension between Blunkett and Woodhead,' we have been told. 'It was always genteelly disguised, but it was obvious when serious discussions were going on about the direction of policy.' Woodhead did not need to be polite to Blunkett – he had more powerful friends; Andrew Adonis, for one.

Woodhead was allowed to deride his political masters in public in a way that was virtually unprecedented for a civil servant. When Blunkett praised the 2000 A-level results, furiously rebutting the Conservatives who sneered that A-levels were getting too easy, Woodhead blithely contradicted the education secretary, taking the Conservative line: that the only reason A-level results were good was indeed because A-levels were getting easier, and it was time the government put some rigour back into them.

When the minister for lifelong learning, Malcolm Wicks, started a competition to find Britain's oldest learner (the winner was aged 107), the headlines were grabbed by Woodhead making fun of the whole idea. Wicks had to nail a ghastly smile to his face and say he really didn't mind. When ministers talked of mass higher education, Woodhead poured scorn on the idea. When ministers insisted that British university degrees were academically rigorous, Woodhead told the press airily that many of them were 'vacuous'.

There was one glorious moment when Blunkett thought he might be rid of his tormentor. The *Observer* alleged that Woodhead might have had an affair with a pupil while he was a teacher. (Woodhead admitted to an affair, but only after the girl had left school.) A spokesman for Blunkett told the paper that the chief inspector's days could be numbered. But the following day, Blunkett himself was quoted as supporting Woodhead. The two statements were almost certainly separated by an awkward interview with Andrew Adonis.

In the early days of the government, Blunkett was overheard complaining bitterly to one of his advisers: 'Someone's got to decide who's running this thing.' After a while, he seems to have realised that someone had already decided, and the decision had not gone his way. Blunkett had a stark choice: knuckle under or resign. He knuckled under. By the time the next election was on the horizon, he was saying publicly that he thought he had done everything he could do at education – after the election it would be time for a change. He told journalists, off the record, that Jack Straw was making a terrible mess of the Home Office brief. No one was surprised when Blunkett became home secretary after the 2001 election.

If you had wanted to predict the course of the government's education policy, you would only have needed to study Adonis's copious published work. He co-authored a book called *A Class Act* in which he argued for a selective secondary school system, with grammar schools for the brainiest children and less prestigious schools for the rest. In his *Observer* article he wrote: 'The sterile leftwing debate about abolishing successful schools – whether state or private – is over.' By 'successful' schools he meant selective grammar schools, and by 'abolishing' them he meant removing their right to select their pupils. At that time, Blunkett was promising to end selection. He soon modified his pledge: there would be no more selective schools, but in areas where the eleven-plus survived it would remain. Parents, however, would get the chance to vote it out.

Blunkett was not permitted to keep even this modest pledge. Although he established a ballot system which would allow parents to get rid of selection locally, it was so fiendishly complicated, and so weighted in favour of keeping selective schools, that the cost of mounting a campaign – in time, money and expertise – was beyond the reach of any voluntary group. The electoral roll was devised so that it included, where possible, parents whose children went to the grammar schools or were likely to do so; and excluded, where possible, the parents of children who went to the comprehensives, or were likely to do so. Unsurprisingly, there was not one single successful ballot to abolish selection. All the 166 grammar schools that had the right to select their pupils in 1997 retain it.

The Conservatives had allowed schools to apply for grant-maintained status and opt out of local authority control. Schools that did so were funded more generously than their neighbours and could apply for permission to select all or part of their intake on the basis of ability. Blunkett was permitted only to change the name: they became foundation schools.

The Conservatives invented city technology colleges – privately owned schools, with a small proportion of private capital, which were funded more lavishly than the rest. Labour kept the fifteen CTCs already in existence and created new schools on the same model, called city academies.

When Blair made a speech roundly condemning comprehensive schools, Blunkett was privately furious, partly because he was not told beforehand: he read about it in the newspapers while on government business in Canada and could not protest. But when Alastair Campbell announced the end of the 'bog-standard comprehensive', Blunkett took issue with him publicly. As so often under Blair, you could kick the monkey, but woe betide you if you contradicted the organ grinder.

Poor Alastair Campbell: he did not even believe in what he was saying. He and his partner Fiona Millar are passionate supporters of comprehensive education, which they have chosen for their own children. They dislike Blair's education policies intensely and believed that the Blairs' decisions about schooling for their own children sent out the wrong message to the public. Today, on his roadshow, Campbell even admits that he found Labour education policy difficult to swallow. Yet he advocated Blair's policy so vigorously that Blunkett was allowed to reprove him publicly. It is rather like a medieval court, where the king can do no wrong and all criticism has to be directed at his bad advisers.

By the time of Labour's 2000 conference, Blunkett was forced to concede that he had lost the battle on selection. He met with anti-selection campaigners and explained rather limply that the government had decided not to make an issue of selection lest it 'derail' the rest of their policy. The truth was that, while Blunkett did not believe in selection, Blair and Adonis did. Afterwards, a Labour MP told Adonis that condemning comprehensives, which are attended by some 90 per cent of the nation's eleven to sixteen-year-olds, was unhelpful. 'That's not what the focus groups say,' was Adonis's reply.

It was Adonis who forced through the idea of paying teachers by performance; Blunkett's role was to take the flak from the teachers and their unions. It was Adonis who wanted to encourage private fee-charging schools, and in 2000 Blunkett's schools minister Estelle Morris, a fierce opponent of such schools when in opposition, gave the strongest speech in favour of fee-charging schools that any senior Labour figure had ever made.

Adonis and Blair believe that there is nothing the public sector can do which the private sector cannot do better. This article of faith led them into the morass of Education Action Zones. These zones are now pretty well forgotten – they were formally abandoned immediately after the 2001 general election – but in 1997 they were Blair's Big Idea for education.

The plan was to set up zones of up to twenty schools and appeal for companies to support their improvement. Each zone would be run by a local partnership, which could include local authorities, educational organisations, local businesses and other institutions. Blunkett was presented with this half-baked idea and told to make it work.

He couldn't do it. He offered up to £250,000 of government money for each zone, as long as it was matched by the same amount from the private sector. Later, he increased the government contribution to £750,000, but left the amount to be raised from industry at £250,000. The private sector was still not coughing up. So Blunkett tried telling them that it did not have to be hard cash. 'Benefits in kind' would do fine, thank you. A couple of unwanted and outdated computers, the time of an executive who was too tired to be of any use but too senior to fire – anything that might give a fig leaf of commercial respectability would do.

Not one of the bids had a credible private-sector funding proposal. They were lyrical about the good things extra cash would do for their schools. But when it came to private-sector money, you could almost hear the embarrassed coughing and shuffling of feet that went on in the local-authority offices where the bids were drawn up. Cumbria had no business offers: 'However, it is anticipated that a great deal of support will be provided in kind.' In Sandwell: 'At this stage, it has not been possible to identify the partnership match funding.' Blackburn found an ingenious way around the problem: business people would sit on the committee that ran the zone, and Blackburn would value their time at £80,000 a year.

The government's flagship borough for Education Action Zones was Newham, whose bid had BT down for £250,000 and construction giants Mowlem and Laing for £20,000 each. But in truth BT had promised nothing at all. Mowlem and Laing, when asked, admitted they were not giving any money – but both companies have training facilities in Newham. Their contribution would consist of welcoming teenagers into these centres and asking them whether they fancied a career in the construction industry, which was experiencing a recruitment crisis.

Only in one policy area did Blunkett appear to defeat Adonis. Adonis wanted the most prestigious universities to be allowed to charge 'top-up' fees. Blunkett and his higher education minister, Baroness (Tessa) Blackstone, were passionately opposed to this, believing it would create a two-tier system – ivy-covered universities for the rich, concrete former polytechnics for the poor. So this proposal had to await Blair's second term. Blunkett, nothing if not a realist, wryly told those vice-chancellors who wanted top-up fees: 'I won't be education secretary for ever.'

The case of Adonis and Blunkett is an extreme example of the Blair habit of taking power away from ministers, who are responsible to Parliament, and giving it to unelected officials of whom the public knows nothing. It is a style of government that transcends the civil servant's boring insistence on correct procedures, minutes and all the rest of the paraphernalia of democratic rule.

Andrew Adonis, immortalised by the education writer Ted Wragg as 'Tony Zoffis', came to exemplify the Blair style of government, effectively running education policy from his office at 10 Downing Street with Blair's support under four education secretaries: David Blunkett, Estelle Morris, Charles Clarke and Ruth Kelly. It was the Blair style as much as anything else which came under fire in the run-up to the June 2005 general election, and Blair responded by saying that he was, after all, listening, and there would be a less top-down style of government.

So, after the election, Mr Adonis no longer ran education policy from

Downing Street. Instead, he was made Lord Adonis and given an office in the Department for Education and Skills, nominally under Ruth Kelly. Ms Kelly, like her predecessors, was forced to nail a smile to her face and say how pleased she was.

It was the strongest indication, according to BBC political editor Andrew Marr, that Blair had defied his critics. 'In his third term you see the prime minister saying: "Well I don't care what the critics are saying – I'm going to have around me in key jobs people I personally trust and feel close to," and that will have a reaction in other parts of the Labour movement, no doubt about it,' Marr said.

In the first Queen's Speech after the 1997 election, having watched their opponents floundering in the mire of sleaze allegations, Labour had smugly promised to govern with the 'highest standards of honesty and propriety in public life'. Their message was simple: 'We are the good guys.'

Blair's most infamous breach of this pledge came to light only a few months later, with the Bernie Ecclestone affair. The decision to exempt Formula One from a new ban on tobacco advertising after the Labour Party had accepted £1 million from its previously Tory-donating boss caused enormous embarrassment to Blair. The controversy ended with an Alastair Campbell-scripted televised apology by the prime minister; the donation was returned to Ecclestone after Blair naïvely asked Lord Neill, chairman of the committee of standards in public life, what he should do. He got the obvious reply.

But an equally serious breach of Labour's supposedly high standards went pretty well unnoticed: for this was not one big story, but a whole raft of small stories up and down the country that only added up to a picture of the sleazy use of patronage when you put them all together. It involved the appointment of people to the country's health trusts – the bodies responsible for overseeing the National Health Service. Unlike the Ecclestone affair, which involved one man's donation to the Labour Party, this scandal involved the payment of a large portion of taxpayers' money to hundreds of Labour Party people, and more specifically New Labour supporters, who were appointed to public bodies, some regardless of merit. The hotspot for complaints was in Blair's own backyard, around Sedgefield and County Durham. Some of the appointments involved the very people who had campaigned fourteen years earlier to select Blair as their parliamentary candidate.

There is now a system in place to ensure that all such appointments are made on merit. But this was not achieved through Labour's commitment to the 'highest standards of honesty and propriety'. It was achieved despite the government's best efforts to prevent it happening. It was a victory for the determination of unsung people in Whitehall to make sure that the government of the day does not abuse its authority.

Dame Rennie Fritchie is one of a small band of commissioners who occupy what she calls 'the no-woman's land' between appointed civil servants and politicians. She is an independent-minded and impeccably fair official, whom people cross at their peril, and who will not stand any nonsense, least of all, as we shall see, from a beleaguered secretary of state. What she definitely is not is part of any man's club. She is not someone who tries to avoid embarrassing the powerful by 'having a quiet word in the ear of the right person'; she always plays by the book.

Her official title is the commissioner for public appointments. The commissioner is independent of the government and her role is to monitor, report and advise on over 11,000 ministerial appointments to public bodies in England, Scotland and Wales. The story begins in her office in 1999. A Conservative MP, Graham Brady, who represents Altrincham and Sale West, went to see her to raise allegations that Labour was packing NHS trusts with its own appointees.

On 11 April he went public with the allegations, telling the *Sunday Telegraph* that 189 Labour councillors had been appointed as chairmen or non-executive directors of health trusts since the 1997 general election, compared to 25 Liberal Democrats, 11 Conservatives and 3 Independents. Given that salaries of up to £19,000 were being paid to each appointee, this was not small beer. Mr Brady did not mince his words:

> Tony Blair promised the people of Britain the highest standards in public life but here we see pork-barrelling on a grand scale. It is scandalous that nearly £1.4 million of taxpayers' money a year is going into the pockets of Labour councillors. There must be a full, independent inquiry to find out what is going on in our health service.[28]

But it was relatively easy to brush aside Brady's allegations, for the previous summer Sir Len Peach, Dame Rennie's predecessor, had given Frank Dobson, the health secretary, a clean bill of health. He said there was no evidence that ministers were influencing appointments.

There the story might have rested – just another party political spat over cronyism – if Brady had not gone a bit too far. After seeing Dame Rennie, he announced she was planning to hold an inquiry, when, in fact, she had decided that there was not enough evidence to do so. Dame Rennie was not amused and was preparing to rebuke the MP when events took an extraordinary turn. The phones in her office began to ring. The publicity given to Brady's announcement of her non-existent inquiry had encouraged to people to contact her with complaints about health trust appointments. None of these complaints had emanated from the Tory MP; they came from disillusioned people on the ground. And the complaints were not from all over the country; they kept coming from two Labour-dominated health regions – the Northern and York-shire region and the North West region.

Dame Rennie cancelled her phone call to berate Brady and instead went ahead with her own inquiry. She also took the brave step of tack-ling Labour head-on by concentrating her investigations in the North and in Yorkshire and Humberside, including Blair's own constituency of Sedgefield.

In July the *Guardian* was passed confidential documents suggesting that the procedures in Durham health authority had not been followed correctly. Zalida Mansour, chair of the authority, had circulated a short list of candidates for the North and South Durham health trusts following the normal recruitment procedure. Then, at the last moment, Paul Trip-pett, bar steward at the Trimdon Labour Club and one of the 'famous five' credited with getting Blair the seat, was parachuted into the job of chairman of the South Durham health trust. At the same time, Kevin Earley, former leader of Derwentside council and a close ally of Hilary Armstrong, the MP for North West Durham and a junior minister, was appointed to chair North Durham health trust. Two other close support-ers of Blair also got jobs. Rita Taylor, Blair's constituency party secretary, became a member of Durham health authority, and Charlie Magee – the county councillor for the district in which Blair had his constituency home and the man who in 1994 had been entrusted with the task of escorting Gordon Brown to his secret pre-leadership talks at Durham City Hall – became a member of South Durham health trust.

Just before the *Guardian* was due to run the story, Downing Street got extremely agitated. Instead of calling back in response to a query from one of the present authors, David Hencke, Alastair Campbell rang the editor, Alan Rusbridger, to tell him the story was not true and to insist that Blair had nothing to do with it. The story was published neverthe-less, but it showed just how sensitive Downing Street had become over the issue.[29] Minor appointments to health authorities would normally be well outside Campbell's sphere of interest.

Dame Rennie says the resulting article was remarkably useful in her subsequent inquiries. She does not put the blame directly on Frank Dobson, the health secretary, but says: 'What is more likely is that Dobson wanted more local people to serve on authorities, particularly councillors. This got interpreted by the NHS to mean more Labour people at local level.'

Dobson himself does acknowledge that there was some political intention, aimed at breaking a Tory stranglehold on the authorities, since the previous two administrations – those of Thatcher and Major – had made no secret of systematically packing the trusts with their own supporters. He says that in the case of Zalida Mansour, Blair instructed him to replace the outgoing Northern and Yorkshire regional chairman with a Labour appointee. Mansour was chosen as the best of several candidates. But in the case of the other appointments highlighted in the *Guardian* article, there had been no attempt to follow prescribed procedures.

Dame Rennie Fritchie's inquiries revealed some damaging anecdotes that illustrated how far things had gone wrong. For example: 'I was told that on one health board every member thought they must become a member of the Labour Party.' In another case, she was told of a candidate turning up at the interview with, in addition to a curriculum vitae, a photograph of the candidate with a senior government minister. There is no evidence that Dobson or his minister of state, Alan Milburn, were aware of such things. Milburn went out of his way to tell David Hencke that special measures were put in place to ensure that he had only a say on appointments in London and the South East, specifically to avoid charges that he might have influenced appointments in his own backyard. This followed the appointment of the wife of the chief executive of his own health authority, Darlington, to a local health trust.

What Milburn did not mention was that under Labour's new rules, local MPs could nominate and comment on those who made the local short list. Effectively, this meant sponsoring people to sit on their local health trust. It meant that any local MP, including Blair, Milburn and Armstrong, had the right to intervene at the short-listing stage. And there is no question that two people – one close to Armstrong and another close to Blair – had suddenly been added at this stage after failing to get onto the original list.

But if Milburn seemed squeaky-clean during the investigation, his subsequent behaviour, when Dame Rennie was about to produce her report, shows the darker side of New Labour. By then, Blair had promoted Milburn to secretary of state for health. Dame Rennie had been punctilious in keeping the Department of Health informed about the inquiry: she had briefed officials when it was set up, given them a progress report and presented her findings and conclusions.

But she was not born yesterday. Before she went to the final meeting with officials, she made sure that the report had been sent to the printers so it could not be changed. She also refused a request for an advance copy from government officials: 'I wanted to make sure that this report was not spun. I was aware that giving a copy to the department even two or three days before publication would be enough for a selective version to be given to the press.' During the final meeting with officials at the Department of Health, civil servants were seen furiously scribbling away to note down her every comment. They did not like the direction in which she seemed to be heading. But she warned them: 'You can say what you like about the report, but you cannot contradict the findings. If you do, I think you should know I have drawers full of evidence to back me up.'

The officials passed the bad news on to Milburn. Fearing fresh allegations of cronyism, he decided he must see the report in advance. He rang up Dame Rennie directly. She refused to hand it over. Milburn was beside himself. He started swearing down the phone and demanded that she give him the report.

Dame Rennie remembers being surprised at this, but she remained dignified in her response. She told him: 'I can see that you are upset, minister. But I do not have to put up with this.' With that, she put the phone down on the secretary of state. Milburn did not ring back. His officials told him that Dame Rennie was independent of the government, and therefore he couldn't talk to her the way he sometimes talked to civil servants.

The findings of the inquiry were damning. In the Northern and Yorkshire regions, 80 per cent of the Labour Party activists who applied to serve on health trusts in 1998 were nominated. That compared with 66 per cent of the Tory applicants and 54 per cent of non-politically active applicants.[30] The report was critical of MPs' involvement. Allowing MPs to nominate people and comment on people short-listed had politicised the process, the report said.

> They [the MPs] believe they are being asked to sponsor candidates, and there is evidence that candidates, too, hold that belief. Some can turn up unprepared at interview expecting to collect a job. Some MPs ring up regional offices requiring to know why their candidate has not been selected.

It went on:

> There is some evidence to suggest that candidates nominated by MPs are treated more favourably than others because panels can feel under pressure to pass them ... many of those [candidates] who are on the borderline are given the benefit of the doubt and placed on regional registers. This calls into question the principles of selection on merit and openness and transparency. It can also swell the number of candidates.

But Milburn was able to take revenge. After the report was published, the government issued a short press release and put forward a solution that had not even been suggested by Dame Rennie. Milburn said he was considering delegating to health authorities the responsibility for board-member appointments to NHS trusts. Later, he proposed the setting-up of a NHS appointments commission, which would be outside the future scrutiny of Dame Rennie. Ministers also declined to meet her to discuss her findings – effectively blackballing her for having the temerity to put the phone down on Milburn.

But Parliament came to her rescue. Tony Wright, the Blairite but independent-minded chair of the Commons public administration committee, called her in to make a statement. By July, the committee had issued a strongly worded report including comments on Milburn's behaviour that were relatively blunt, if qualified by the usual parliamentary language.

> When the minister gave evidence to us no minister had yet contacted
> Dame Rennie to discuss her findings. There had only been a press
> release on the day of publication containing a proposal on future
> appointments that was not among Dame Rennie's recommendations and
> had never been discussed with her. This has now been followed by a
> written answer to a parliamentary question in the House of Lords con-
> taining a further response. We recommend that the secretary of state
> should hold discussions with the commissioner on her report and recom-
> mendations and the government's response.[31]

A year after the report was published, the government finally conceded that the system was open to cronyism, but it did so reluctantly and with bad grace, and without having to retract any of the appointments that had been made.

Milburn simply stopped ministers from having any involvement in NHS appointments. He set up an NHS appointments commission, but he backed down and agreed to an arrangement that would still allow Dame Rennie to keep an eye on its work. It remains in place today.

This was not, perhaps, a major national scandal, but the story is indicative of the way that New Labour thinks and acts. Had it not been for the integrity and determination of a tough-minded individual, the government would probably have succeeded in burying the whole issue. It is good to know, as we write, that ministers and Whitehall are once again feeling the wrath of Dame Rennie, this time over the influence they exercise over appointments to quangos.

CHAPTER TWELVE

THE ROAD TO FOOT AND MOUTH

If the last chapter gives the impression that there was nothing at all radical about Tony Blair's first government, that is not quite true; almost, but not quite.

The radical measures were taken right at the start. As expected, the government signed up to the social chapter and withdrew the ban on trade unions at the GCHQ spy headquarters. Unexpectedly, Gordon Brown's first act as chancellor was to hand future decisions on interest rates over to the Bank of England. At once, one of the recurring themes of the Blair government emerged: the speaker of the Commons, Betty Boothroyd, complained that the press had been told before Parliament knew anything about it.

In his first Budget, Brown abolished tax relief on the investment income of company pension schemes and introduced his windfall tax, a one-off charge on people who had made a great deal of money out of privatisation. Brown wanted to make the latter group pay for his schemes to get young people back to work. He devoted a lot of effort to making the tax legally watertight, and the key to this was the head of Cherie Booth's old chambers, Michael Beloff QC, who had worked on the scheme for a discounted fee while Labour was still in opposition.[1]

Blair, meanwhile, went to Europe and lectured his counterparts on the 'Third Way'. 'Modernise or die,' he told them, which irritated France's Lionel Jospin, who thought social democracy had not yet had its day. Before he left, he made time to entertain Margaret Thatcher in Downing Street, ensuring that her visit was carefully leaked in such a way as to ensure maximum publicity.[2]

Back from his travels, he was told that the *News of the World* was about to publish details of Foreign Secretary Robin Cook's longstanding affair with his assistant, which Blair, like most senior politicians, had known about for some time. The dramatic scene that followed has often been described in the press: Cook and his wife Margaret were travelling to the airport en route to a holiday when they were interrupted by a telephone call from Alastair Campbell, who insisted that Cook must choose, right away, between his wife and his mistress. The result was that Cook ended his marriage in the VIP lounge at Heathrow's Terminal 4.

Plans for welfare reform were thrown into disarray after Blair, probably without realising it, appointed to draw them up a politician with whose views he was in fundamental disagreement. Frank Field, who has spent much of his life studying welfare, was bound to come up with plans which required the better-paid to make increased contributions to their pensions and tax rises to fund higher pensions for those who were worse off. Under John Smith, Field might have been a sensible appointment. Under Blair, he was a disaster, especially since he assumed, reasonably enough, that since the prime minister had appointed him, the prime minister must agree with his well-known opinions. His appointment was trumpeted by one of those glib, meaningless phrases from a management textbook that Blair often falls back on: Field, he said, was to 'think the unthinkable'. It could have been worse: Field might have been told to 'think outside the box'.

Field and his nominal boss, Harriet Harman, found that their widening divisions became the subject of press speculation, and they both received a brusque dressing-down from Alastair Campbell about leaks. They blamed Campbell, of course, but Campbell, as usual, was only doing the prime minister's bidding, and at this early stage in his administration, Blair personally bolstered his press spokesman's authority. Asked if Campbell was allowed to issue instructions to ministers, he said: 'He acts with my authority absolutely.' Soon afterwards, Field and Harman were both dispatched to the backbenches.

For ever after that, his ministers knew the score, and Blair was seldom obliged to remind them that what Campbell said came directly from Blair. That enabled Blair to distance himself from several brutal things he wanted to be done, but did not want to be seen doing.

That is why, when Andrew Rawnsley's 'senior source inside Downing Street' talked of Gordon Brown's 'psychological flaws', we can safely assume Blair was well aware that the wounding jibe was being fed to a journalist. That incident, like the Field–Harman debacle, occurred in the second year of the government. The trigger was the publication of Paul Routledge's biography of Brown, in which the leadership election of 1994 was revisited, with Brown's dignified period of mourning after John Smith's death being contrasted with Blair's instant scrabbling for the prize. Everyone knew Routledge was close to Brown, and, as we have seen, Brown asked specifically that some letters he had received from the Blair camp should be included in Routledge's book.

In addition to the slur on Brown, Blair also revenged himself on Routledge by scuppering his next job. Routledge was political editor of the *Independent on Sunday*, and his editor, Rosie Boycott, was moving to edit the *Daily Express*. She asked Routledge to come with her and be political editor of her new paper. Then she abruptly withdrew the offer. The job eventually went to a Blair admirer. She has never denied that political pressure was applied to the *Express*. The best-informed explanation of the affair comes to the present authors from Peter Wilby, who edited the *Independent on Sunday* before Boycott and later became editor of the *New Statesman*. Boycott, he says, did not understand the finer political nuances of New Labour. When she took over from Wilby at the *Independent on Sunday*, she said to him over a drink: 'Don't worry, the politics of the paper won't change – I'm very close to Tony Blair.' Wilby, an Old Labour type who has no time for Blair, almost choked on his beer. He says Boycott would have told Blair in 1998 that she had appointed a good Labour man (Routledge is a lifelong Labour Party member), expecting to be congratulated. Blair's outraged reaction would have come as a nasty shock, and Boycott would have been left in no doubt that her paper's relationship with Downing Street was at stake.[3]

In Blair's first cabinet reshuffle in July 1998, Brown's friends suffered and Blair's prospered. It was probably Blair's way of reminding his one-time friend where the real power lay. Peter Mandelson joined the cabinet for the first time, while Gavin Strang and David Clark were fired along with Harriet Harman and Frank Field.

Roger Pope recalls the feelings at the time: at a dinner at Langhams he remembers Nick Brown gloomily speculating, 'They [Blair's people] will take two out this time, two out the next and then they will go for Gordon.'

The reshuffle also saw the first sign of David Blunkett's frustration at not really being in charge at education and his ambition to rise higher. With Andrew Adonis dictating much of his policy and Gordon Brown, through his loyal press aide Charlie Whelan, stealing all the best lines in his education announcements, Blunkett felt he was going nowhere. So he demanded an 'economic meeting' with Blair, basically so he could bring himself to the prime minister's attention.

But he had no agenda. Half an hour before the meeting was due, cabinet office officials rang up asking for one: 'The prime minister wants to know what you want to discuss.' So officials made one up, literally on the back of an envelope – and Blunkett got his thirty minutes.[4] When it came to the reshuffle, Blunkett made a bid to replace Straw as home secretary. Blair initially agreed – provided Jack Straw was willing to vacate the Home Office. Straw appeared to be keen; he wanted the environment portfolio instead. But during Straw's talk with Blair, it became clear that John Prescott's superministry would retain overall control; Straw would still be in the cabinet but as a glorified minister of transport – a replacement for Gavin Strang. He refused to budge and Blunkett had to wait.[5]

Nick Brown was sacked as chief whip and moved to agriculture. The decision marked a major turning point in the relationship between Gordon Brown and Blair – and the end of any real friendship between Blair and Nick Brown. An angry meeting of disappointed Gordon Brownites behind closed doors is recalled by Roger Pope, Derek Foster's former political adviser who was still helping him out. Nick Brown is reported to have told them: 'We are going to be destroyed. They have got two of us this time, they will get another two next time and soon there won't be anybody left.' It turned out to be untrue – but it was here that all the rumour and speculation that Blair ultimately wanted to sack Gordon Brown began.

The reshuffle also saw the final demise of the film minister, Tom Clarke, who was sacked. Clarke was said to have left in tears, but that isn't true. He left in style. He was already involved in a bitter dispute with Julian Eccles, a special adviser at the Department of Culture, over his plans to change the British film industry. He was furious that Downing Street wanted to alter his recommendations and that Eccles appeared to be going along with this. When Blair sacked Clarke, they had an angry exchange. So cross was Clarke that he almost forgot he was entertaining two film stars, Hugh Grant and Elizabeth Hurley, that night in the Commons. Realising that the loss of his post destroyed the aim of the meeting, he said to an aide, 'I'd better ring them up and tell them what's happened.' He duly did so and got back an unequivocal message: 'Don't worry, we are still coming. It makes no difference.' So that night, envious MPs saw the sacked minister having drinks on the House of Commons terrace with the two famous actors. It was an A-list celebrity date that Blair and Cherie would have killed for, if their passion for wining and dining celebrities at Chequers is any indication.

By this stage, Blair was deeply involved in Northern Ireland, that graveyard of political reputations. In opposition, this was one area of policy he had effectively taken out of the hands of his spokesman (in this case, Kevin MacNamara) and had changed Labour's policy in a way that made it more acceptable to the unionists – and less acceptable to the republicans. Soon after he became prime minister, he gave the unionists something like a pledge: 'None of us in this hall today, even the youngest, is likely to see Northern Ireland as anything but a part of the United Kingdom.'[6] For a man whose wife was both a cradle Catholic and a socialist with strong Irish roots, this was a remarkable statement; it would have seemed even more remarkable had Blair's own Roman Catholicism not been a closely guarded secret. Blair's wooing of the unionists was effectively balanced by his choice for Northern Ireland secretary, Mo Mowlam, who was liked and trusted by the republicans. A ceasefire and new talks were brought about. The Good Friday agreement of 1998 looked at the time like the historic breakthrough that had eluded all previous prime ministers. Blair worked very hard to get the agreement, and then to make it stick. It earned him a rare tribute from Tony Benn, who had been in the cabinet thirty years before, when troops were first sent to Northern Ireland. Benn offered his

> sincere congratulations to the prime minister on the time, effort, patience and imagination that he and my right honourable friend the secretary of state [Mo Mowlam] have shown and for which there is absolutely no precedent from any previous prime minister.[7]

But soon after Benn had paid this tribute, the unionists rejected a joint proposal from Blair and Irish Prime Minister Bertie Ahern. Blair reverted to the traditional political habit of scapegoating by moving Mo Mowlam out of the job; he turned to his old friend, Peter Mandelson, to replace her.

Mandelson had already been forced to resign from one cabinet job because of a mini-scandal over a loan he had accepted from millionaire MP and treasury minister Geoffrey Robinson to help him buy his home. Robinson had resigned, too; unlike Mandelson, he has never been brought back. Mandelson had compounded his offence by lying on his mortgage application, but he was far from being the only cabinet member to benefit from Robinson's generosity. The Blair family's first summer holiday as residents of Downing Street was in Geoffrey Robinson's Italian villa in San Gimignano.

Moreover, Blair, as we now know, received a gift from Derry Irvine to help buy his family's constituency home in Sedgefield. True, this had been many years earlier, but eyebrows might have been raised had people known that he had appointed as lord chancellor a man whose money assisted him to buy a house.[8]

It now fell to Mandelson to work with the power-sharing executive that had been set up under the Good Friday agreement. But it was not to be for long. Mandelson's second resignation came over an allegation that he had intervened in 1998 with the immigration minister, Mike O'Brien, over the passport application made by multi-millionaire businessman Srichand Hinduja. At the time of the alleged conversation, Mandelson had been responsible for the Millennium Dome, which contained the Faith zone that Hinduja and his brother had sponsored to the tune of £1 million.

Mandelson was bundled out of the cabinet for a second time with what appeared to be unseemly haste. This meant that, afterwards, he was able to argue that no one had actually produced any evidence of his alleged conversation with O'Brien. An inquiry was set up under Sir Anthony Hammond, who delivered a report that was inconclusive – he was unable either to prove or to disprove that the conversation with O'Brien had taken place. Mandelson then produced some new documents which he claimed would establish his innocence, and Hammond was asked to go back and review the evidence once more. He found circumstantial evidence that Mandelson could have talked to O'Brien about the Hinduja passport application. A handwritten note from Mark Langdale, Mandelson's private secretary when he was minister in charge of the Dome in 1998, says: 'Perfectly legitimate for you to raise [underlined] issue with O'Brien. Agreed you cannot be seen [underlined] to push this much further.' Another memo lists the telephone number of O'Brien's private secretary with a large arrow pointing to it, suggesting that there had been an enquiry from the minister's private office.

Hammond therefore concluded for the second time, much to Mandelson's chagrin: 'Although the new material does not provide any support for the existence of a telephone conversation between them, it does not persuade me that I can revise my original judgement about the likelihood that such a telephone call took place.' In other words, his original view that there *could* have been a telephone call still stood. In the first draft of his second report, Hammond also criticised Mandelson for breaking Whitehall rules by removing documents that should have been left in his office. But this criticism was removed in the final draft.

On the basis of Hammond's findings, Mandelson rung up lobby journalists to announce that he had been cleared of any wrongdoing. (In July 2004 he did so again when he was appointed by Blair as a European commissioner, just in case they had forgotten.) O'Brien was not powerful enough to counter these briefings, except in a quote to the *Guardian*.[9]

Even so, it is puzzling that Blair moved so precipitously to eject his old friend and chief supporter. When asked why, Colin Byrne, Mandelson's closest friend, says resentfully, 'You'd better ask Alastair

Campbell.' Mandelson himself blames his downfall on Alastair Campbell, and Campbell recently accepted responsibility in the course of a curious television interview with Mandelson, which seemed like a carefully rehearsed verbal minuet. Blair's name was not mentioned.

Another answer might be that there was a mildly embarrassing skeleton in Blair's own closet relating to the Hinduja brothers. Early on in his premiership, he had unwisely accepted an invitation to one of their parties, to which Cherie turned up in a sumptuous Indian sari provided by her hosts. Anji Hunter pressed her boss to go – she thought it would make a good photo opportunity – and Peter Mandelson told him it would help to get money out of the Hindujas for the Dome.

The foreign secretary, Robin Cook, begged Blair not to go to the party. The fact that the Indian government was investigating the Hindujas for corruption over the Bofors arms deal was in the news at the time, and Cook thought ministers should have nothing to do with them. Told that Blair had already accepted the invitation, he said: 'Find an excuse. Break a leg rather than go.' He warned Blair that he would be showered with gifts and photographed receiving them. In the event it was not quite as bad as that, but the photographs of Cherie in the gifted sari were to prove deeply embarrassing.

The Hinduja episode was just one instance, and a minor one, of Robin Cook's inability to get his voice heard in Downing Street, despite the fact that he had been a fully paid-up member of the Kinnocracy. Past services did not buy Cook a place in the Blair court. Even more than most prime ministers, Blair likes to run foreign policy himself, and he felt especially able to do so because his chief of staff was the experienced diplomat Jonathan Powell. When Cook announced on his appointment in 1997 that he would run an 'ethical foreign policy', Powell said to his colleagues at Number 10: 'What a load of crap!' When Cook blocked contracts to supply Indonesia with £1 million worth of arms, he was rebuked by Downing Street, for Blair likes to keep the arms companies on his side.

In 1998 Cook advised that the American missile strike on the al-Shifa pharmaceuticals factory in Sudan was probably illegal; he was ignored. It turned out, after the factory had been razed to the ground, that there was no trace of the nerve gas production alleged by Washington: all the factory made was veterinary antibiotics. Blair's recovery statement looks now like a dress rehearsal for his later statements after the Iraq war. Perhaps the gas had not been there, he said, but the bombing still gave 'a very clear signal' to terrorists.

It was Blair, not Cook, who made the running in the campaign against ethnic cleansing in Kosovo. Blair pressed on President Bill Clinton the need first for a bombing campaign, and then for ground troops. It put a tremendous strain on his relationship with Clinton, who in one telephone call told him to stop the 'domestic grandstanding' that was threatening to tear NATO apart.[10]

Eventually, after the 2001 election, Cook was removed from the Foreign Office in favour of Jack Straw, a much more biddable incumbent, and made leader of the House. This allowed David Blunkett finally to realise his ambition of taking over the Home Office.

Tony Blair's most flamboyant piece of domestic grandstanding took place over a domestic issue, the last great crisis for the government before it faced the electorate again: the foot and mouth epidemic that swept Britain in the months leading up to the 2001 general election.

The epidemic seemed to come out of nowhere, and reached such proportions that Blair was forced to postpone the long-planned date for the general election by a month. The account in Andrew Rawnsley's *Servants of the People* paints a picture of panic-stricken farmers, incompetent vets, civil servants and politicians causing the epidemic to spread. It suggests that the whole scene was then transformed when Blair and Alastair Campbell took charge.

In Rawnsley's version, Blair and Campell take off from Carlisle airport like Batman and Robin coming to rid the country of the evil scourge that threatens the nation (and, more importantly, Blair's Commons majority in the forthcoming election). They bring in the top scientists, call up the troops, and hey presto, within a couple of months the vicious disease is nothing but a sad memory. Real life, as most comic-book aficionados know, is a bit more complicated than that. This story is worth recounting in detail: not only because it was indeed a major crisis for the government, but also for what it reveals about Blair himself.

The first important point is that the crisis might have been avoided. Gavin Strang, who shadowed agriculture for Labour in opposition but was not given the agriculture portfolio in government, and who has a PhD in agricultural science, had intended to ban the feeding of swill to farm animals and had John Smith's support for this. However, Nick Brown, agriculture minister when the epidemic blew up, subscribed to the belief that if swill is properly treated before it is given to animals it is perfectly safe. Swill was the principal cause of the outbreak.

Moreover, the Ministry of Agriculture had some grounds for its confidence that it could handle the situation. Some six months before the foot and mouth outbreak, the Ministry of Agriculture had experienced a sort of trial run when it saw off an outbreak of highly infectious swine fever which could have wrecked pig exports. By taking over a disused basement near Westminster's MI5 headquarters and working round the clock during their summer break, civil servants and vets from the Ministry of Agriculture managed to contain it. Known as 'Pig Command', the operation was a total success and therefore was given little publicity. Nick Brown, the agriculture minister, said afterwards that the swift action had stopped it becoming a major 'silly season' story during August, traditionally a slow month for news. 'By stamping on the problem at once we seem to have stopped it, touch wood, from spreading and turning it into a crisis', said a relieved Brown on 1 September.

Not so in spring 2001, when the first cases of foot and mouth disease broke out. Unlike swine fever, foot and mouth attracted sufficient publicity to interest the prime minister. The story of how he took personal control, undermining his officials and ministers and doing nothing but damage to their efforts to control the disease, is one of the most revealing episodes of his premiership. No one who knew the story could have been surprised at the way the Iraq war was handled later. Unfortunately, almost no one knew the story at the time. It is told in full here for the first time.

Foot and mouth disease is not dangerous to humans – only cloven-hoofed animals. But it has a three-week incubation period, it is difficult initially to diagnose and it affects cattle, sheep and pigs differently. It is most difficult to control in sheep because the symptoms are less obvious. The disease is not normally fatal, but animals never fully recover from its effects and its extremely high infectiousness means that it will quickly become widespread if not controlled. The only two means of control available are prophylactic treatment with a vaccine, which has to be universally administered if it is to be effective, or the slaughter and safe disposal of all stock which have been in contact with infected animals – the policy which Britain had always adopted in the past.

When a vet from a meat hygiene service reported a suspect case on 19 February 2001, found in pigs at an Essex abattoir, it was not immediately clear what was happening. By late evening, when Nick Brown was informed, the vets still did not know whether it was foot and mouth or swine vesicular disease. The next day, the Ministry of Agriculture decided to inform the press that a 'highly suspicious but not confirmed case' of foot and mouth disease had been reported in Brentwood, Essex, and they halted the issue of export certificates for animals and meat products. During the afternoon, Nick Brown's trip to a conference in Cambridge was interrupted by the news that the Institute of Animal Health was 99 per cent certain it was foot and mouth. An exclusion zone was declared.

The press did not rush to highlight the story. The following day, the Guardian reported in a news-in-brief column: 'A five-mile animal exclusion zone has been put round an abattoir near Brentwood, Essex, and two farms – one in Buckinghamshire and another on the Isle of Wight.' On 21 February Nick Brown was advised that the case was now formally confirmed, and the ministerial team rushed back from Cambridge to London. By the next day, the situation was beginning to deteriorate. The National Farmers Union was briefed, a third case was confirmed and then a suspect fourth case was discovered in Northumberland. The Guardian reported in a bigger story the following morning:

> A 'highly suspicious' new case believed to be foot and mouth disease was found last night in pigs at a farm in Northumberland. It could be the source of the original outbreak of the virus, which has thrown the British farming industry into fresh crisis …
>
> Tony Blair, on a visit to Canada and the US, said the outbreak was 'the very last thing that farmers need' in the aftermath of BSE. 'This is a very, very tough time for them,' Mr Blair said in Ottawa. 'We have to contain the outbreak. We've taken the action necessary to do so, and we will look into the consequences for individual farmers, of how we help them, at a later time …'

The necessary action was to prove pretty drastic. Later that day, as the Northumberland case was confirmed, Nick Brown rang Blair in the United States to tell him that he wanted to impose a national ban on livestock movements. Blair agreed.

The discovery that the disease probably started in Northumberland much earlier than had previously been suspected was the most worrying thing. It meant that during the previous three weeks, while the disease was incubating, animals had been dispersed all over the country. But worse news was to come. The discovery that sheep as well as pigs and cattle had been infected was a serious blow. When Jim Scudamore, the ministry's chief vet, reported that the disease had occurred in Devon – about as far south of Northumberland and west of Essex as it is possible to get – it was clear that it could now break out anywhere. The chances of it spreading nationwide made the large-scale culling and disposal of slaughtered animals inevitable.

The Guardian's report on February 28 – nine days into the outbreak – was now on page one.

Six new foot and mouth outbreaks were confirmed yesterday, affecting four counties previously free of the disease, as disruption to normal life in Britain worsened. All race meetings were abandoned for a week and the rugby union international between Wales and Ireland on Saturday was cancelled. Emergency orders were rushed through Parliament to give councils the power to ban the use of footpaths and public rights of way.

... as the air of crisis deepened, Tony Blair chaired a meeting of ministers from most Whitehall departments. In a webcast from No. 10, Mr Blair admitted the gravity of the situation: 'The funeral pyres of farm animals are the worst nightmare for the livestock farmers. And it is not just financial loss, massive as that is; the heartbreak also comes from all the hard work and planning, often over many years.'

Such plans and expertise as the Ministry of Agriculture possessed were based on the previous outbreak, thirty years earlier. But however well it had been prepared, the enormous growth in the long-distance transport of animals – for which the British government's over-zealous application of EU directives on abattoirs was partly responsible – would have made this new outbreak extremely difficult to control. Blair initially left the handling of the crisis to Nick Brown – until the prime minister and his advisers realised that the local elections and then a possible general election would have to be postponed. At that point the government became consumed with panic for political reasons. Andrew Rawnsley puts it well:

Tony Blair was haunted by many fears that something would happen to deprive New Labour of the second term. What had never occurred to him, nor anybody else, was that his best laid plans could be imperilled by a livestock disease which had not been heard of in mainland Britain for more than three decades.[11]

The scale of the problem is illustrated by a *Guardian* report from March 16, which followed a statement from Nick Brown that it might be necessary to kill all animals within a three-kilometre radius of an outbreak. The announcement was made after discussions at Downing Street, though Downing Street later denied any responsibility for the initial decision.

A massive slaughter scheme that could kill up to a million healthy animals in the next month was announced yesterday by Nick Brown, the agriculture minister, in an attempt to prevent the foot and mouth outbreak dragging on for months.

Although he is acting on advice from Jim Scudamore, the government's chief veterinary officer, the dramatic clearing of all farm animals from large areas of countryside is also Tony Blair's last chance of running for election on May 3 without the campaign being overshadowed by foot and mouth. The decision to move into a new gear was taken in the last few days as it became clear existing measures were not working fast enough and that the outbreak had reached epidemic proportions as it moved uncontrolled from farm to farm.

It was this announcement that sent Blair into overdrive. He had a private meeting with Sir Ben Gill, president of the National Farmers Union, in the cabinet office. Gill told him that the picture was worse than the Ministry of Agriculture had suggested and complained about the amount of red tape involved – including the issue of sorting out whether to bring in the army to help. This had been delayed by bureaucratic procedures which infuriated the NFU. 'Everything has to be signed in triplicate,' Sir Ben told the prime minister. According to Gill, Blair was livid and immediately summoned Sir Jonathan Powell, his trusted chief of staff.

On 21 March Powell was sent over to the Ministry of Agriculture to find out why the disease was getting out of control. Powell produced a damning report questioning the ministry's competence and the ability of its vets to cope. In making this assessment, Powell ignored the fact that the department had been under-resourced for two years and had sought, but failed to obtain, funding from Number 10 or the Treasury for more vets. And it conveniently ignored the fact that it would be weeks before anybody knew how far the disease had spread, because of the incubation period. The report was never shown to Nick Brown.

The following day, Blair took action. He changed his diary, delaying a visit to Sweden so that he could visit some of the worst-affected areas in Cumbria, where farmers had been begging him to come and witness the devastation of their industry for the past two weeks. Blair's cavalcade pulled up outside the Auctioneer pub in Carlisle. The setting was symbolically perfect: a farmer's drinking-house decorated with watercolours of lambs, next to a deserted cattle market. It was five miles from the burning livestock pyres and the stench of thousands of carcasses lying, hooves up, in farmyards. The prime minister met for forty-five minutes with a dozen representatives from farming, tourism, the local council, the army and vets before leaving for a European Union meeting in Stockholm. Outside the pub, around forty protesters gathered, shouting: 'The only good Blair is a dead one.'

As the *Guardian* reported the next day: 'Tony Blair ran flinching from his Jaguar and into a Cumbrian pub last night as farmers in tears shouted: "You're a coward, you don't give a shite about the North."' Blair's final humiliation came when he arrived at Stockholm airport that evening to be greeted with not a red carpet but a fumigation team to make sure his arrival would not spread the disease to the pristine Nordic peninsula.

With the prime minister's intervention came a switch from fighting the disease with facts to a reliance on spin and central control. Jim Scudamore was sidelined and replaced with Professor Sir David King, the government's chief scientist, who was dispatched to the Ministry of Agriculture. In a scene that would not have looked out of place in a *Yes, Minister* script, he asked Nick Brown to send all his officials out of the room. Brown's special adviser remained with him. King glared at the adviser, who meekly said: 'Am I to go too?' 'Yes,' came the reply. Once they were alone, he told Nick Brown that his civil servants and veterinary team – the same people who had run the successful Pig Command operation six months previously – were inadequate and incompetent.

King was sent to front the operation because, according to Alastair Campbell, he is 'a good media performer'– even though, as a chemist, he has no professional knowledge of infectious diseases. Scudamore, who does have experience in this field, apparently does not come across as well on TV. The Cabinet Office set up its own briefing room (COBR) to provide daily co-ordination and take overall control of the emergency.

The army was finally brought in, and the media were given the impression that they were running the show; it was the defence secretary, Geoff Hoon, not the minister nominally in charge of the foot and mouth crisis, Nick Brown, who chaired the COBR meetings – meetings that Brown did not even attend. Tony Blair, who according to one senior civil servant 'behaves like an eleven-year-old schoolboy whenever he comes into contact with a military uniform', made sure that when he was photographed it was always with army officers or scientists in full protective clothing. The image of an energetic can-do premier taking decisive control of a military operation was complete, right down to bringing in General Sir Michael Jackson, the hero of the Kosovo liberation, to oversee the cull.

Another key player brought in by Downing Street was a controversial figure. Professor Roy Anderson, head of the Department of Infectious Disease Epidemiology at Imperial College Faculty of Medicine, University of London, was enlisted by Downing Street to assist Professor Sir David King. His appointment was another example of Downing Street taking over from the Ministry of Agriculture. The ministry had already appointed its own epidemiologist, Professor John Wilesmith of the Veterinary Laboratories Agency, a veteran of BSE, to model the consequences. At his disposal was a 'decision-support system' called EpiMAN, which can help predict the course of an epidemic and then develop a strategy to control it, using a tool called Interspread to map its movement across the country. But this system was never used, owing to the intervention of Professor Anderson.

Anderson was a curious choice. He was previously head of the Wellcome Trust Centre for Epidemiology of Infectious Disease at Oxford University, and his main field of interest was nothing to do with foot and mouth – he was an expert on human diseases such as AIDS, CJD, malaria and tuberculosis. He had also taken a close interest in measles, mumps and rubella vaccination. But he prepared his own computer analysis at Imperial College, which he constantly updated each day, with the result that it became increasingly accurate – enough to tell Blair that it was safe to hold a general election on June 7, and for King to say that this decision was based on unimpeachable independent advice.

As soon as it was put in charge of the crisis COBR decided on a 24-hour slaughter, 48-hour burial policy – something that proved unsustainable, at least initially. But Blair had a solution to cover this: he cancelled the daily briefings to specialist journalists by the Ministry of Agriculture and replaced them with daily briefings to the lobby – attended by political journalists who have little or no specialist knowledge. This is one of the oldest tricks in the book. If a politician does not want to field difficult, well-informed questions, he makes sure he does not have to face specialist correspondents. It is a cynical misuse of the lobby system.

Paul Brown, environment correspondent of the *Guardian*, remembered the ploy well:

> From Monday March 26 2001, Nick Brown's daily press conference was cancelled. Downing Street briefed lobby correspondents. Farming and environment correspondents who had previously been covering the outbreak and knew all the details and could spot a deception a mile off were totally excluded from briefing and MAFF was instructed not to speak to journalists and refer everyone to Downing Street.
>
> The information reaching journalists became inaccurate. On April 3 I wrote a story saying that the daily updates of dead animals and animals buried on the MAFF website had been removed. The website was being redesigned, at this crucial moment – to make it clearer, was the official explanation. There had been a growing discrepancy between the Downing Street briefings showing that the outbreak was under control and the MAFF website showing it was getting worse.
>
> The main problem was that the number of animals slaughtered was increasing but the numbers being buried by the army were not catching up. In other words, there were thousands of animals lying in the fields rotting.

Blair's response to media criticism was to confront them with the media-friendly King. Paul Brown continues:

On April 4, Professor, now Sir David, King, the government's chief
scientific advisor, was wheeled out by Downing Street after mass journalistic complaints about lack of information. It was the first scientific
briefing in ten days. Previously, under Nick Brown, there had been one
every day by the forthright Jim Scudamore, the chief vet. In contrast to
Scudamore, David King said the worst was over and the outbreak was
under control.

King 'revealed that by 7 June the epidemic would be fading fast and at
worst there would be fewer than five new outbreaks a day'. On 12 April
he gave another upbeat assessment, clearing the way for the general election. There is no reason to believe that King was wrong, although in fact
there were still at least five cases a day being recorded by 7 June.

In retrospect, says Paul Brown,

> The whole episode was a clear example of Downing Street taking over,
> masking the facts and then wheeling out people to give an optimistic
> picture of the crisis to deflect criticism and change the mood in order to
> facilitate the calling of a general election. Brown and Scudamore never
> recovered ground lost with Downing Street, basically because they were
> honest about the gravity of the situation.[12]

But Downing Street still had one more extraordinary media trick up
its sleeve. Towards the end of April, the tabloid press picked up the story
of Phoenix, a Devon calf that had apparently been overlooked by the
slaughtermen and, it was claimed, had lived without food or water for
five days, hidden by the dead body of its mother. The fact that a calf left
unfed for five days would have surely died from starvation was seemingly
overlooked by the tabloids – a more likely explanation is that the children of the farmer rescued it and hid it in their house. Whatever the case,
it gave the *Mirror* an opportunity to launch a 'Phoenix must be saved'
campaign.

By this time, Ministry of Agriculture vets were already arguing with
Anderson for a relaxation in the policy of culling healthy herds within
three kilometres of an outbreak. Up until now they had been overruled
by Downing Street, but that was before the discovery of Phoenix, whose
plight obviously moved Blair and Campbell as much as it had the *Daily
Mirror*. On 25 April Downing Street decided to discuss a relaxation of
policy with Nick Brown.

A large and long meeting concluded that the policy should be relaxed
and that this would be announced the next day by Nick Brown. After the
meeting at the Ministry of Agriculture, Nick Brown went for a pint with
Sir Ben Gill of the NFU at the nearby Marquis of Granby. As they were

enjoying their drinks, *News at Ten* was making the dramatic announcement that Tony Blair had 'intervened' to save Phoenix from the slaughterhouse. Brown woke up the next day to hear this news via BBC Radio 4's *Farming Today*.

Until Phoenix hit the headlines, Blair had been the foremost advocate of a rigorous implementation of the culling policy. Later, Alastair Campbell was to tell an inquiry that he did not 'recall the precise timing of particular information and its relation to the finalising of policy decisions'.[13]

An equally glaring though less conspicuous case of government by fear of the tabloids was the extraordinary treatment that Blair meted out in the middle of the crisis to one of his most loyal ministers, Baroness Hayman. She was Nick Brown's minister of state and had been extraordinarily hard-working through both the swine fever and the foot and mouth outbreaks. So loyal was she that she even ate a bacon sandwich at a celebratory pork-roast party mounted by East Anglian farmers to mark the eradication of swine fever – her hosts had not realised she was Jewish when they invited her.

That Easter, at the height of the epidemic, she had arranged with her husband to take a break in the Caribbean to celebrate their twenty-fifth wedding anniversary with her family. Nick Brown gave her permission to go and promised to undertake all her duties. When Blair heard of this, he refused to allow her out of the country. He told her that he could not risk a tabloid tale of a minister holidaying in the Caribbean while the outbreak continued. She was heartbroken and her nineteen-year-old son, Jake, was even more angry that his parents could not go.

Blair decided he could resolve this unpleasantness by sweet-talking the son. He got Jake's private phone number and rang him up. One of his flatmates took the call. 'It's Tony Blair, he wants to talk to you,' said the flatmate in amazement. 'Tell him to fuck off, I am not talking to him,' came the reply. There was much private gratification in the Ministry of Agriculture when the story was relayed. Baroness Hayman never recovered from Blair's treatment of her and later left the government.

At the height of the foot and mouth crisis, Jonathan Powell became extremely anxious when a number of aristocratic landowners who bred pedigree animals pleaded directly with Downing Street for a switch from the policy of slaughter to one of vaccination. Some offered to vaccinate privately, which was illegal, because animals vaccinated against the disease can still carry and transmit it. The most senior complainant was Prince Charles himself. An extraordinary four-page letter obtained by the authors and reprinted as an appendix shows how passionate and deferential the heir to the throne still was in his dealings with Tony Blair.

Always susceptible to lobbying by the affluent, Blair was inclined to agree. But this flew in the face of the views of the National Farmers Union, as well as another powerful group with a vested interest in the supply of fresh meat: the supermarkets and the food industry. That did not stop Downing Street suggesting that Nick Brown – who was privately opposed to the change of policy – should write a memo proposing the switch.

When Brown refused to do so, Blair decided he would continue to explore vaccination. He arranged a private meeting with Sir Ben Gill at Chequers – with only David North, his private secretary, present. He told Gill he had decided to proceed with vaccination because it would stop the slaughtering of animals. But Gill disagreed – pointing out that if there was no market for vaccinated animals, they would still get slaughtered in the end. Blair, under pressure, began to back down but then alluded to the fact that there was royal opposition to the continued cull, saying, 'You do realise you will no longer be on his Christmas card list?' 'That's all right,' replied Gill, 'I was never on it in the first place.'[14]

Blair, however, continued to canvass the idea of a change of policy at a Chequers summit attended by much of the food industry. The final blow came when the Tesco representative told Blair that they would not sell meat from vaccinated animals because their customers would regard it as inferior.

A more expensive incident involved the compensation to be paid to farmers for dead animals – the Livestock Welfare (Disposal) Scheme. Both Gordon Brown and Nick Brown were determined that payments made to farmers whose stock had been slaughtered should be strictly limited to the market value of the animals affected. Not only would this save money, it would also avoid offering temptation to unscrupulous farmers, who might take the opportunity to abuse the system and gain extra cash subsidies from the exchequer. But the National Farmers Union wanted as much cash for their members as possible.

A wrangle ensued at a Downing Street meeting chaired by the prime minister. Suddenly Blair said to the assembled company: 'Just give them the money' – effectively undercutting his chancellor (who was not present) and his agriculture minister. Gill recalls that Blair listened carefully to both sides before coming down firmly in principle against the Treasury and backing the farmers' case.

That was what actually happened at the meeting – but it was not what was recorded in the minutes. Private secretary David North told an inquiry later: 'The prime minister had left before the end of the meeting and the minister of agriculture and his officials had brokered the final terms of the scheme.'[15] The only possible basis for this claim, says Sir Ben Gill, is that the final, tiny details, down to the last penny payment for each animal, were sorted out with the Ministry of Agriculture twenty-four hours later.

But the most disgraceful decision of all was only taken after foot and mouth had been stamped out. Blair decided there should be an inquiry. It was not to be an independent public inquiry, like the one demanded by environment minister Michael Meacher, who was slapped down for suggesting it. Instead it would be held in private with no transcripts and chaired by a man already sympathetic to the prime minister's views. Dr Iain Anderson CBE had been chairman and chief executive of a world-wide range of Unilever subsidiary companies involved in agribusiness, speciality chemicals and food. He had worked for Unilever for thirty-three years and was already known to Downing Street as an adviser on millennium compliance issues. According to Sir Richard Packer, the former permanent secretary at the Ministry of Agriculture, 'He was about the most sympathetic person to the PM's views that he could decently get away with.' In *The Times* on 19 February 2002 countryside editor Valerie Elliott reported the setting-up of the inquiry very succinctly.

> Tony Blair is to give a personal account of the government's handling of the foot and mouth epidemic – but the public will never know what he says. He has agreed to be interviewed by Iain Anderson, the head of the government's 'lessons learnt' inquiry, but there will be no recording or transcript of his words. Instead, in civil service style, his version of events is to be 'minuted'.
>
> Details of the policy emerged in the High Court yesterday during a judicial review hearing challenging the government's decision not to hold a full public inquiry.
>
> A spokesman for the inquiry confirmed the rule and said that it would apply to all other ministers and senior officials who were questioned.
>
> He denied that the condition had been imposed by Mr Blair or anyone from Downing Street. He said: 'We are not taking a full transcript of what we are doing. The minute of each interview will provide the salient points.'
>
> Last night Peter Ainsworth, the shadow rural affairs spokesman, said: 'To have this special protection accorded to ministers and officials pulls the rug from under the credibility of the Anderson Inquiry.'

The inquiry saw only a limited number of witnesses. Professor Sir David King, who took over the presentation of the culling policy, did apparently give evidence. His views were accepted readily by Iain Anderson, and

King did not attract any criticism for his limited knowledge of the issues. But Jim Scudamore, the much-maligned chief vet, faced a prolonged grilling and criticism in the inquiry's findings. Blair received a polite hearing – and was allowed to escape any serious challenge. The 'minutes' of the inquiry show that Blair was able to say that decisions on foot and mouth had nothing to do with the general election – even though it was patently obvious the election date had been put back as a result of the crisis. He was not questioned in any detail on why Nick Brown was never included on the Cabinet Office emergency team.

There were also some extraordinary undercurrents that were never reported at all. Nick Brown discovered that Jeremy Heywood, then the principal private secretary at Number 10, had lunched with Alun Evans, secretary to the inquiry, during the hearings. Evans is a former director of communications for the department of transport. He had also previously held posts in Downing Street.

The discovery that Evans and Heywood had been in contact with each other led Nick Brown to believe that Blair was making a crude attempt to manipulate the inquiry into blaming his agriculture minister for the foot and mouth crisis. So serious were Brown's concerns that the Treasury solicitor was, at one point, providing legal advice to both Brown and Downing Street, and the correspondence is said to include a warning from Brown that he would sue for defamation if his suspicions were confirmed by the inquiry's report.

In an extraordinary submission, Brown said he wanted the report to lose its parliamentary privilege so that he could sue the authors if they tried to make him a scapegoat. As it turned out, Brown's fears were proved groundless. The final report did not single him out for blame, and the prospect of a confrontation between the government and one of its own ministers (Brown was in the department of work and pensions at that time) faded away.

It should be added that Alun Evans has been very careful to deny that he had been party to any impropriety. In evidence to the Commons public administration committee on the running of the Anderson Inquiry, he told Kelvin Hopkins, Labour MP for Luton North:

> I met a number of departments in my work because obviously we were dealing with more than one department, we were dealing with DEFRA, and we were dealing with the cabinet office, the MoD, and a number of other devolved administrations. I do not think I ever had lunch with anybody during that time. I certainly would not have discussed the type of findings we might be bringing forward in the inquiry, although there was a lot of contact on a day-to-day basis.[16]

Evans confirms that he did meet Heywood at the time and that they did have
one lunch – the two were old friends – but he very firmly rejects any suggestion that they ever discussed the inquiry or that anything improper occurred.

There was one further repercussion from the foot and mouth scandal.
Two senior civil servants at the Ministry of Agriculture who had direct
dealings with Blair were transferred from their posts. This may well have
been the second time that Blair intervened in the ministry's staffing
arrangements. Before foot and mouth broke out, he seems to have been
instrumental in pushing the former permanent secretary, Sir Richard
Packer, into early retirement by leaking to the *Financial Times* the story
that Packer was leaving his job. Packer is convinced that Campbell
briefed the paper that he and Sir Terry Burns (now Lord Burns), the permanent secretary to the Treasury, were to be sacked.

Sir Richard raised the matter directly with Lord Butler, the cabinet
secretary, and was told the report was untrue. But, just as in the cases of
the unfortunate cabinet ministers reassured by Blair that press reports of
their imminent demise were unfounded, the stories turned out to be
deadly accurate.

Blair told Nick Brown he wanted Sir Brian Bender, the permanent
secretary at the Cabinet Office, to replace Packer. Blair told Brown that
he could appoint Bender right away or have an internal or external
appointment panel. What he could not have was Packer staying in his
job, nor could he have either of the two other experienced civil servants
in that department. The job was eventually allocated through an external
appointment panel, which chose Bender, but Packer points out that if it
was known Blair wanted somebody in particular for a job, 'it would take
a brave panel not to take this into consideration'. Packer adds: 'The
appointment of a permanent secretary to a ministry should be nothing to
do with the prime minister.'

Blair's actions during and after the foot and mouth crisis show what a
consummate, ruthless politician is concealed behind that toothy grin. He
puts presentation before facts. He is prepared to ride roughshod over
individuals. He cares nothing for maintaining correct boundaries between
the government and the civil service. He is by nature a centrist rather
than a devolutionist. Truth is always the first and last casualty. And he is
not beyond seeking revenge as much as a year later, when an issue has
faded from the public gaze.

In one sense, the short, sharp shock of handling foot and mouth was
almost a dress rehearsal for the much bigger project that dominated his

second term: the war on Iraq. Certainly, the informal way in which he runs the government – which came under fire from Lord Butler, the former cabinet secretary, after his inquiry into the handling of intelligence before that conflict – was used extensively in the war on foot and mouth, according to the sources who have talked to the authors.

CHAPTER THIRTEEN

THE RICH AND THE ROYAL

Even the most cursory study of the Blairs suggests that they are fascinated by the rich, the powerful and the famous and that they have used their position to widen their acquaintance with them. Their pursuit of such people is not very sophisticated; indeed they often seem to view them with the kind of awe and uncritical admiration characteristic of *Hello!* magazine.

Nobody would suggest – not even Alastair Campbell – that the prime minister and his wife would be crude enough to invite *Hello!* to Chequers or Number 10. But all the evidence suggests that neither Blair nor Cherie can get enough of hobnobbing with celebrities in private. The guest lists for their parties in Downing Street and their weekends at Chequers frequently feature performers of one kind or another – pop singers, soap stars and TV presenters – people who would seem, on the face of it, to have little to contribute to discussions of government policy and not much to offer by way of insights into the lives of the Blairs' fellow citizens.

Royals are, of course, a very special kind of celebrity, and, while she was alive, the top of the royal A-list was undoubtedly Diana, Princess of Wales. It was through the Blairs' relationship with Diana – particularly that of Cherie – that a close bond was first created with the royals. The connection was later to prove extraordinarily potent at the time of Diana's death, when the royal family faced its biggest crisis since the abdication of Edward VIII in 1936.

Blair's only meeting with the royal family before becoming Labour leader was when he was invited to meet Prince Charles in the early 1990s. At the time, he had begun to make his name as a very photogenic shadow employment secretary, and, along with a number of other up-

and-coming New Labour MPs, he attended a dinner given by Cathy Ashton – now Lady Ashton – the socialite and well-connected partner of journalist and commentator Peter Kellner, at which the Prince of Wales was a fellow guest.

A more significant link between the Blairs and the prince was established two years before Blair became prime minister, and the man who forged it was a long-time friend of Peter Mandelson. Tom Shebbeare – now Sir Tom and director of charities to the Prince of Wales – was then chief executive of the Prince's Trust, a charity set up by Prince Charles in 1976. The Trust funds various programmes, worth over £50 million a year, that help deprived young people to gain qualifications. Shebbeare is an amiable, unpretentious character with a great sense of humour and a shock of grey hair, recently more neatly cropped after his latest promotion. He is of the same generation as the Blairs and Peter Mandelson.

His links with Mandelson go back some twenty years, to the period when Mandelson was chairman and Shebbeare was secretary of the British Youth Council. This body, like the National Union of Students, was a training ground for budding politicians. Funded mainly by the government, it was an umbrella group for a variety of youth organisations, from the Girl Guides to the Young Communist League. It came to prominence in 1977, when it sent a delegation to the controversial World Youth Festival in Cuba – an event that also involved the young Charles Clarke, then a heavily bearded, leftwing student politician with both political and facial affinities with the Cuban leader, Fidel Castro. Other participants included Paul Boateng, now a cabinet minister, and Trevor Phillips, now director of the Commission for Racial Equality.

Through Mandelson – by now MP for Hartlepool – it was suggested that Tony Blair should meet Prince Charles for a private dinner at St James's Palace, arranged by Shebbeare, so they could get to know each other better. The venue, a small intimate dining room in Apartment 30B, seats no more than ten people at a pinch, and looks out onto Colour Court – the inner courtyard in the heart of the palace. This was the start of a series of regular meetings between Blair (and, on one occasion, Cherie) and the prince.

The two men seemed to have a lot in common. Blair was a fresh-faced Labour leader hoping to be elected to govern on an agenda different from traditional socialism. Prince Charles was Great Britain's heir apparent and appeared to share some of New Labour's values. The potential for a meeting of minds seemed enormous. Both were said to be interested in developing new approaches to traditional roles – Blair as leader of a 'modernised' Labour Party, and the prince as the future head of a modern, scaled-down monarchy. Indeed, royal sources suggest that Blair went out of his way to flatter the prince's interest in Labour's Third Way philosophy by all but suggesting that he himself could lay some claim to the idea. At the very least, Blair was careful never to contradict the prince's mistaken idea that he had contributed to the concept.

This particular dinner was key to laying a firm foundation for what was to become a very close relationship between the prince and the prime minister. It also gave Peter Mandelson the opportunity to try to establish a closer connection with the prince – using his perceived position as the gatekeeper to the mind of the future prime minister.

By this point, Mandelson was already moving in exalted rightwing circles – he numbered among his friends the socialite Carla Powell, wife of Lady Thatcher's close adviser Sir Charles Powell. Carla and Charles Powell gave a dinner party to celebrate Mandelson's forty-third birthday to which Tony and Cherie turned up for drinks; the guest list included a number of other prominent New Labour figures, including John and Jane Birt, Gavyn Davies and Sue Nye, and a rather uncomfortable Alastair Campbell and Fiona Millar.[1]

On this occasion, in October 1996, Sir Charles is reported to have addressed Tony Blair as 'prime minister', even though he was still leader of the opposition. Sir Charles has also said, no doubt only half in jest, 'Many Tories have gathered around my dining table in the past but on this occasion there are only two – Blair and myself.'[2] Peter Mandelson regularly told friends about the 'joys of Carla' and how he 'flirted madly with her'. It was through Lady Powell that Blair first met Camilla Parker Bowles, giving him another link to the royal circle.

Blair's meetings with the prince also led to the Blairs forming a close relationship with the prince's estranged wife, Diana. According to royal sources, 'Diana threw herself at Blair', making it clear that she believed she had much to learn from the putative prime minister, and she is said to have enjoyed discussing political issues with his wife. There were many meetings between the Blairs and Diana, particularly in the early days of Blair's premiership. Cherie would have lunch with the princess and the two women got on very well. Cherie was a formidably intelligent woman, while Diana had an inquiring mind. Diana was fascinated by Cherie's personality, single-mindedness and determination. Cherie was impressed by Diana's campaigning zeal – which included her controversial (at least for a royal) public stand over landmines.

Diana had been applauded for this by the Clinton administration. Dispatches between the US embassies in Angola, London and Washington in January 1997 made much of the embarrassment she had caused to Prime

Minister Major and Foreign Secretary Malcolm Rifkind during a visit to Angola, when she had publicly backed the British Red Cross's campaign for a ban on all landmines – which far exceeded the commitment made by the Tory government. To add to Major's woes, the British ambassador in Angola, Roger Hart, told the Americans that the trip had been approved by the queen, as part of a plan to get Diana to promote new public causes. The cables also revealed that Diana had refused 'to be seen wining and dining with the social elite'. She agreed to attend a dinner given by the Angolan president's first lady, Ana Paula dos Santos, so long as it was 'small [twenty-six guests ate from a buffet of catered Chinese food], short [it ended at 8.10 p.m.] and there be no press or speeches'. Hart was reduced to slipping in local directors of Shell, BP and De Beers, who were desperate to meet the glamorous royal, among the twenty-six guests.[3]

All this would have appealed to Cherie. Royal aides insist that their friendship was a real meeting of minds – the 'Queen of Hearts' and the consort of a republican-minded prime minister. A more cynical analysis might suggest that they got on so well because they both came from dysfunctional families.

The increasingly close relationship between Cherie and Diana went a step too far very soon after Blair won the election. He and Cherie decided to invite Diana and the two young princes, William and Harry, to Chequers. Unfortunately, they did so without telling Prince Charles. Cherie hoped that William and Harry might become friends with their own children, Euan, Nicholas and Kathryn. Alastair Campbell and Fiona Millar frequently came over to Chequers for the weekend and their children would enjoy a game of football in the grounds with the Blairs' offspring. The intention was to bring about a repeat performance, but this time with the royal progeny.

It was not a success. Prince Charles found out, and he subsequently made it very clear to the prime minister that to invite the two boys without him was a serious breach of protocol. The princes did not get on with the younger generation of Blairs, and Prince William is reported to have told his mother that he found 'the children very badly behaved'. This appears to have followed an incident when thirteen-year-old Euan sloped off to the bike sheds at the back of Chequers for a quiet smoke – which seems to have attracted considerable royal opprobrium. No doubt there was maternal opprobrium too: Euan's mother enforces a strict smoking ban on visitors inside Chequers and even tries to stop people lighting up in the grounds. The visit was never repeated.

Apart from this blip, relations between the prince and the prime minister were quickly consolidated. The cement was the Prince's Trust and the implementation of a New Labour policy that was really the work of Chancellor Gordon Brown and his advisers. Called 'Labour's New Deal', it involved using the money raised by a windfall tax on the excess profits of the utilities privatised by the Tories to provide training programmes for the young and long-term unemployed. This policy was embraced by the Prince's Trust because it exactly fitted Prince Charles and Tom Shebbeare's own agenda to help regenerate deprived areas and give new entrepreneurial opportunities to the poorly educated and dispossessed. The Prince's Trust had just celebrated its twentieth anniversary and it embraced the New Deal in a big way. Blair was thrilled; he had got a popular policy endorsed by Royalty. The Prince's Trust became one of the scheme's biggest promoters. That was reason enough (if any were needed) to ignore the jibes from the Tories and any protests from business.

Diana also got in on the act: she infuriated Prince Charles by ringing to tell him in what has been described to us as her most maddeningly sugary voice how important the 'New Deal' policy would be for his causes – and how he should get 'close to the PM' – something Charles would have been quite capable of working out for himself.

Then, in the early hours of 31 August 1997, Diana was killed in a car crash in a Paris underpass with her new lover, Dodi Al Fayed. Blair and Cherie were spending the weekend at Myrobella, their constituency home in Sedgefield, and had gone to bed exhausted, desperate for a decent night's sleep. After two hours they were awakened by a call from Downing Street, informing them that the British embassy in Paris had received reports of a serious car crash in which Dodi had been killed and Diana severely injured. Blair immediately woke his wife to tell her the news. By 3.30 a.m. they had heard that Diana had died in hospital. Alastair Campbell, who had also been disturbed by phones constantly ringing through the night, called Blair later.

According to Andrew Rawnsley's account, the two men quickly agreed, in an expletive-ridden conversation (at least on Campbell's part), that they were dealing with an enormous story.[4] What had also emerged by the morning was that the queen had not grasped the significance of the news. Blair's speech the next morning outside St Mary Magdalene church in Trimdon was made in the knowledge that the royal family planned to say nothing about Diana's death in front of British or American TV cameras. The speech – including a tabloid touch famously attributed to Alastair Campbell: the use of the phrase 'the People's Princess' – changed the whole tone of Tony Blair's premiership.

Using his acting ability and communications skills to the full, Blair captured the sense of shock that had gripped the nation.

> I feel, like everyone else in this country today, utterly devastated. Our thoughts and prayers are with Princess Diana's family – in particular, her two sons, her two boys – our hearts go out to them. We are today a nation in a state of shock, in mourning, in grief that is so painful for us.

He went on to praise her as a wonderful and warm human being, saying:

> People everywhere, not just here in Britain, kept faith with Princess Diana. They liked her, they loved her, they regarded her as one of the people – the People's Princess – and that is how she will stay, how she will remain in our hearts and memories forever.

Under any other circumstances, such words would have seemed totally over the top, but it turned out that Blair and Campbell had judged the mood of the public perfectly. The week that followed saw the front of Kensington Palace and almost the entire length of the Mall carpeted with tributes of flowers. People wept openly in the streets – the famous stiff upper lip of the English had been dumped in favour of raw Latin emotion. By the time of Diana's funeral, the mood had intensified until it seemed that something close to hysteria had gripped the entire nation.

In the immediate aftermath of Diana's death, the royal family appeared distant, outdated, outmoded and completely out of touch. They were also divided. As a result, Downing Street was able to seize the initiative. If Diana's death was the culmination of an *annus horribilis* for the royals, as the Queen later described it, it became the culmination of an *annus mirabilis* for Tony Blair. Swept into power by a landslide, he was now – with the help of his aides – able to orchestrate a makeover for the royal family, just as he had for the Labour Party.

Royal aides say this was the one moment when the monarchy was genuinely in jeopardy. In the course of numerous meetings between representatives of Downing Street and Buckingham Palace, it soon became clear that the old guard of royal aides under the Earl of Airlee, the Lord Chamberlain, did not know how to cope with this outpouring of emotion for someone they had detested in life and who now seemed to have triumphed over them in death.

Buckingham Palace was at war with Kensington Palace and the Spencer family; St James's Palace was at war with both Buckingham and Kensington Palaces; and Downing Street was in danger of finding itself at odds with all three. In these circumstances, Tony Blair's secret weapon was Anji Hunter, who was to become the vital intermediary between the Palaces and Number 10. Hunter, along with Blair's 'funeral expert',

Hilary Coffman, who had organised John Smith's official departure from this world, tried to smooth over bad relations. Prince Charles and Blair also received advice from Peter Mandelson, always 'anxious to help'. Sir Robin Butler, the cabinet secretary (now Lord Butler), who was, unlike Alastair Campbell, a staunch monarchist, also played a key role in trying to persuade the queen to make a more sympathetic response to the out-pouring of public grief.

The Prince of Wales took advice from both Downing Street and his own advisers and followed his instincts by flying to France to escort Diana's body on its journey back to London. The aim, which was to some extent achieved, was to distance Prince Charles from his fellow royals, who remained aloof at Balmoral.

Hunter's meetings at Buckingham Palace, combined with Blair's per-suasive powers, applied to the monarch in the course of a telephone con-versation, finally persuaded the royal family to emerge from their seclusion and do a walkabout among the crowds outside Buckingham Palace. The queen (who doesn't 'do live', as an aide put it) agreed to speak from a prepared script on the *Six O'Clock News*.

The funeral itself was overshadowed by the sharp comments about the royals made from the pulpit by Diana's brother, Earl Spencer. In an emotional but dignified address, he told the congregation:

> Diana was the very essence of compassion, of duty, of style, of beauty. All over the world she was a symbol of selfless humanity. All over the world, a standard-bearer for the rights of the truly downtrodden, a very British girl who transcended nationality. Someone with a natural nobili-ty who was classless and who proved in the last year that she needed no royal title to continue to generate her particular brand of magic.

He attacked both the press and the royals for their treatment of his sister: 'It is a point to remember that of all the ironies about Diana, perhaps the greatest was this – a girl given the name of the ancient goddess of hunt-ing was, in the end, the most hunted person of the modern age.' He appealed for better treatment for the new generation – sticking the knife into 'the Firm' with a vengeance.

> She would want us today to pledge ourselves to protecting her beloved boys, William and Harry, from a similar fate and I do this here, Diana, on your behalf. We will not allow them to suffer the anguish that used regularly to drive you to tearful despair.
>
> And beyond that, on behalf of your mother and sisters, I pledge that we, your blood family, will do all we can to continue the imaginative way in which you were steering these two exceptional young men so

that their souls are not simply immersed by duty and tradition but can sing openly as you planned.

The damage to the monarchy had been immense, while Blair's reputation reached such dizzy heights that it seemed he could all but walk on water. International reactions were illustrated by an extraordinary dispatch from the US ambassador to Britain, Admiral William Crowe, to Madeleine Albright, the US secretary of state under Bill Clinton.[5] Written a fortnight after the funeral, it says of the royal family:

> The firm whose aloofness and lack of emotion were criticised by Diana in life, had a rough ride last week. They might have been mourning Diana and comforting her sons. But they were not seen to be doing so. Their gestures to public sentiment appeared reluctant and extracted under duress ... . For the moment the Royal Family seems locked in an unequal struggle with Diana's memory. It will be difficult to change the public perceptions of the Queen and Prince Charles. In middle to old age, they are what they are, with a strong sense of duty but styles that lack empathy.

Of Blair, the ambassador wrote:

> Once again TB showed his uncanny ability to correctly read the nation's mood. If the public are disillusioned with the tawdry excesses and rigidity of the Windsors, they still revere royalty and British tradition. Tony Blair has once again taken the public pulse and steered a conservative course that nonetheless brings the nation a step closer to the modernist ideal.
>
> At the same time his leadership in guiding the nation – the people, the monarchy and its ancient institutions – through a traumatic and potential divisive period can only enhance his political standing at home and abroad.

And he added:

> Behind the scenes Blair worked effectively to mediate between the views of the Royal Family and the Spencers to ensure that the public got the opportunity to express its grief through a unique and well-planned public funeral. Blair was also seen as directly counselling the Royal Family to take the people's criticism seriously and take a more visible note as the nation struggled to express its grief.

The ambassador concluded that Blair's handling of Diana's funeral 'bodes well for Britain performing equally brilliantly in its role as president of the European Union and for the G8 summit next year in Birmingham'.

Blair's aides had one last task to perform on behalf of Prince Charles. They were still not convinced that the public really believed he felt any guilt or grief over the loss of Diana, and they were right. He would never recover popular support unless the public's perception changed. An opportunity arose when Charles had to make his first public speech after the funeral in Manchester a couple of weeks later, on 19 September. He was very reluctant to acknowledge any guilt. His view, according to one royal source, was that 'nothing that had happened had anything to do with him' and he wanted to stick to that. But Peter Mandelson and Alastair Campbell felt that he should say something or else the press would have a field day. And they had the backing of Blair to press their case. So, between them, they scripted his speech.

Tom Shebbeare remembers the day well.

> Prince Charles had a packed schedule the day he flew to Manchester. I remember him getting off the plane and carefully adjusting his tie, deep in thought, before he met the media. He first went to the Manchester United ground at Old Trafford and met David Beckham. He then went on to a local school where he made the speech which acknowledged Diana's role.

The prince used the occasion to praise his children's courage in coping with Diana's death. He told his audience:

> I am unbelievably proud of my children. They have been quite remarkable and I think have handled an extraordinary difficult time, as I am sure you can all imagine, with quite enormous courage and the greatest possible dignity.
>
> They are coping extraordinarily well but obviously Diana's death has been an enormous loss as far as they are concerned *and I will always feel that loss.*
>
> But if I may say so, the children have been hugely comforted by the vast number of really touching letters of condolence – I think something in the region of 250,000 that have been received from all over the world, and in particular, of course, from this country. The letters have meant a huge amount to us and wonderful and heartfelt expressions of sympathy have made such a difference.

The italics are ours – but they are the only public expression of sorrow at Diana's death that has ever been made by her former husband. This incident marked the high tide of Downing Street's influence over the royal family. Not only had Blair's aides helped to script the prime minister's own response to Diana's death; they had now put words into the mouth of the heir to the throne. Campbell had even 'rebranded' the prince's dead wife as the People's Princess. Relations were never going to get any better than this.

As it turned out, they were going to get rapidly worse. So far, Blair had managed to introduce his reform programme without particularly angering the prince. Prince Charles did not approve of the Scottish Parliament, Welsh devolution or the plans to abolish hereditary peers in the Lords, but he let these things pass, since the government had a landslide majority. Blair, for his part, had apparently gone so far as to temper party policy on fox hunting, a sport that was greatly enjoyed by Prince Charles, Camilla and Prince William. According to aides, he personally assured the prince that 'hunting will be banned slowly' – a private pledge that he was to keep, despite the fact that Labour was publicly committed to introducing a complete ban. The delay was achieved by means of long and tortuous proceedings over the issue that took up the first two parliamentary sessions and the subsequent setting up of an inquiry by Lord Burns into the ill-fated policy of a so-called 'middle way', which would have allowed hunting to continue in some areas.

But the real row between the future king and the prime minister exploded over quite a different matter: genetically modified food. The prince has always had strong views on interfering with nature and was an early opponent of GM foods. Guests (including Mandelson and Blair) arriving at his private home in Highgrove are greeted by an extraordinary sign, rather like those that leftwing local authorities used to place on their boundaries to tell visitors that they were entering 'a nuclear-free zone'. Positioned outside the Orchard Room, the venue for many a seminar, the sign reads: 'This is a GM free zone.'[6]

So it was predicable that the prince and the prime minister would soon clash over this issue. The catalyst was a decision by the prince to write an article for the *Daily Mail* on the evils of GM foods – or 'Frankenstein foods', as the *Mail* had christened them. Blair was pretty angry when the article turned up in the press cuttings at Number 10. Not only had the prince attacked one of his pet causes – Blair has always been an enthusiastic supporter of new technologies – but he had chosen (unwittingly according to aides) to place the article in the *Daily Mail*, the 'enemy within' which led the 'forces of conservatism'. If Prince Charles had intended to enrage the prime minister, he could not have chosen a better subject or a better medium.

The article, published with an accompanying front-page story by Richard Kay, the *Mail*'s royal correspondent, on 1 June 1999, caused a storm. The prince fiercely denounced the GM crops and food that Blair was on the record as supporting and indeed actively promoting. The *Mail* gleefully reported:

The Prince ridicules as 'emotional blackmail' one of the government's main arguments in its attempts to persuade Britain to accept GM food in that it can prevent global hunger. His article, his most controversial yet on the issue, is certain to set him on a collision course with Tony Blair.

Only four days ago, the prime minister accused the media of whipping up 'hysteria' over the issue and he has stressed that he is happy for his family to eat GM food. Charles, on the other hand, refuses to eat or serve it to his guests.

Charles's own words were equally provocative. He warned:

Since bees and the wind don't obey any sort of rules – voluntary or statutory – we shall soon have an unprecedented and unethical situation in which one farmer's crops will contaminate another's against his will … . Instinctively we are nervous about tampering with nature when we can't be sure we know enough about all the consequences.

He went on to describe the damage to caterpillars of the monarch butterfly caused by the growing of GM maize in America, asking: 'If GM plants can do this to butterflies, what damage might they cause to other species?' He also questioned whether growing GM food would relieve world hunger in the poorest countries in Africa and Latin America – directly challenging Blair's own position on the issue. 'Is there any serious academic research to substantiate such a sweeping statement?' he asked. And he concluded with a direct challenge to the whole philosophy of the government: 'Are we going to allow the industrialisation of life itself, redesigning the natural world just for the sake of convenience and embarking on an Orwellian future?'

In an accompanying editorial, the *Daily Mail* announced that 'Britain's future King has done us all a service'. It added:

Mr Blair may have a huge majority, but he should remember that in a democracy a government that ignores the feelings of most of its people does so at its peril.

His insouciance about GM foods – and that of his minister Dr [Jack] Cunningham – smacks of New Labour arrogance at its worst.

In response, Downing Street issued a statement that ignored the issues that most concerned Prince Charles, simply saying:

His interest in this area is well known, as are his views. The government has been in the forefront of calls for a sensible, rational debate on GM foods rather than the scare-mongering we have seen in some of the media. Prince Charles's article should be seen in that context.

The next day, with the story at the head of news bulletins, it was clear that the prince had hit a raw nerve. However, Downing Street wanted to play down the controversy. Blair was offered a column in the *Daily Mail* but declined, obviously fearing it would further fan the flames.

The issue at stake was Blair's support of Britain's role as a world leader in science, and GM research in particular. Blair had appointed as his minister for science Lord Sainsbury – a man whose family firm has a strong financial interest in fostering new developments in biotechnology. Not only did the Prince of Wales oppose GM crops, he was also highly critical of stem-cell research as well. Almost a year later, he used a BBC Reith Lecture, recorded at Highgrove, to condemn the 'potentially disastrous consequences' of both GM foods and cloning. He said opposition to growing GM food was wrongly dismissed as 'a sign of weakness or even a wish to halt progress. On the contrary, I believe it to be a sign of strength and of wisdom.' With regard to both GM food and cloning, he added:

> If literally nothing is held sacred any more, because it is considered synonymous with superstition – or in some other way irrational – what is there to prevent treating our entire world as some great laboratory of life, with potentially disastrous long-term consequences?

Prince Charles's views were little different from those of Friends of the Earth, who had long been campaigning against GM foods. Like them, he believed that the giant American firm Monsanto, a company linked to Bill Clinton, was involved in a plot to force GM food down British people's throats and would do anything to bully and cajole the government to license the growing of GM crops in Britain. Monsanto, in his view, was just one of the big American corporations hell-bent on globalisation and driving traditional British firms out of business.

Eventually, three years later, an exasperated Lord Sainsbury was provoked into retaliating. In an interview with *Saga* magazine, he attacked Prince Charles for publicly promoting his personal views. 'It is at least debatable that these issues were political and therefore the Royal Family should not get involved,' said the unelected peer, businessman and friend of Tony Blair.

Relations with the royals were also soured by less serious issues. Prince Charles had been irritated by the informal style that Blair adopted in correspondence between Downing Street and St James's Palace. An American-style informality was a trademark of New Labour's modernising agenda; everybody in Downing Street addressed each other by Christian names and every letter from the prime minister was signed: 'Yours, Tony'.

When Blair corresponded with the Palace he signed himself in the same matey fashion, and he addressed the Prince of Wales not as 'Your Royal Highness, the Prince of Wales' but as 'Dear Prince Charles'. The prince pointedly replied by writing 'Dear Prime Minister' rather than 'Dear Tony'.

All this might have remained an irritation rather than a running sore if there had not been a ham-fisted meeting between the prince and Jack Straw, then home secretary. Straw, who is quite casual even on the most formal public occasions, went to meet the prince at St James's Palace and began the conversation in a rather curious way. 'I am not really sure how I should address you,' he told the prince. 'Do you like being called "Your Royal Highness", or shall I call you "Charles" or "The Prince of Wales"? How would you like to be addressed?' 'Well, how about calling me 'Sir'. That will do fine,' came the frosty reply.

The prince blamed Straw's remarks on Blair's lax and informal style, something that sharply differentiated his premiership from those of John Major and Margaret Thatcher. Both of Blair's predecessors had been punctilious in following centuries of custom and practice in acknowledging the status of the royals. In a letter to the prime minister, the prince demanded that Whitehall issue a special memo to all ministers telling them to address him as 'Sir' in future and outlining basic lessons in royal protocol that should be followed in future correspondence.

The next blow to the relationship came with the highly embarrassing disclosure in the *Guardian* on 22 December 1998 that Peter Mandelson, had lied about the way in which he had financed the purchase of his £475,000 Notting Hill home in London. The infamous 'Mandy home-loan scandal' brought about Mandelson's first resignation from the cabinet within forty-eight hours of the story hitting the streets.

Mandelson had received an undisclosed £373,000 loan from a fellow minister, Geoffrey Robinson, which he had used to buy a town house in one of London's most desirable areas. The disclosure was particularly damaging since Mandelson was secretary of state at the Department of Trade and Industry and the department's inspectors were investigating Robinson over his links with Robert Maxwell, the dead disgraced tycoon. Mandelson had not told his permanent secretary or the cabinet secretary, Sir Richard Wilson, about the loan. To make matters worse, the *Daily Mail* followed up the *Guardian*'s story with the disclosure that Mandelson had lied on his mortgage application form when he borrowed money from the Britannia building society to supplement the loan from Robinson.

The prince was aghast at the first revelation; when he realised that the minister had also lied in his mortgage application, he was even more shocked. The result was a decision to cut Mandelson out of any future social engagements. The prince resolved to write to Mandelson a personal note making it clear that he was *persona non grata* so far as St James's Palace was concerned. But his aides persuaded him at least to delay the letter, fearing that it would be leaked, given that the *Guardian* and the *Mail* had already been able to get so much information on the story in the first place.

Prince Charles's decision was a huge blow to Mandelson, once dubbed a 'star-fucker' by press magnate Rupert Murdoch because of his obsession with getting to know wealthy celebrities. This was the man who had gone to great lengths to get an invitation to the prince's fiftieth birthday party and boasted that he was the only cabinet minister to attend. In fact, his invitation had come from Camilla Parker Bowles, not from Prince Charles, and it was part of a thank-you gesture to Peter Brown – a partner in the lobbying company Brown Lloyd James. Brown was a friend of Mandelson who had helped the prince and Camilla to achieve very favourable media coverage in New York.

Mandelson had also managed to spend a weekend at Sandringham, the Queen's Norfolk estate, with Charles and Camilla. His eagerness to ingratiate himself with the royals had made him the butt of jokes at the Downing Street leaving party for Tim Allan, Alastair Campbell's deputy, who said he was privileged to be 'a friend of Peter's … when I am not, as far as I am aware, a member of the royal family'.[7]

The prince eventually sent his letter to Mandelson once the story had disappeared from the headlines, confident that the Palace could rely upon a crestfallen Mandelson to keep its contents to himself. Their confidence was clearly justified, since Mandelson apparently told neither of his biographers about the letter.

The irony of Mandelson's passionate determination to gain an entrée to royal circles is that Prince Charles did have a good relationship with two other ministers who did not go around bragging about it. Both were from working-class backgrounds and probably had far more conversations with the prince than Mandelson ever did. They were Nick Brown – both as agriculture minister and minister for work – and John Prescott, the deputy prime minister.

The prince was keen to talk about farming and GM foods with Nick Brown – even if the two did not see eye to eye on the latter issue. He kept in close contact with Brown during the foot and mouth crisis and they had indepth conversations about the slaughter of animals. He also had long discussions about the New Deal for young workers with Brown when he was at the Department of Social Security.

The biggest initiative on which Brown and the prince collaborated was an attempt to get a better deal for small British farmers by promoting regional specialities and organic food. Two events were held – including a dinner at Kew Gardens, which was owned by MAFF – where the two discussed the issue while wining and dining on organic British fare. Nick Brown later used his annual New Year's party for the media to promote organic and regional products, including cheeses and organic beef, beer, gin and vodka.

But Prince Charles also made some more personal gestures. When he found out that Nick Brown's mother was seriously ill, he arranged for a box of Duchy of Cornwall organic vegetables to be sent to her home. And he went out of his way to offer kindness and friendship after Brown was profoundly embarrassed by the *News of the World*'s disclosure that he was gay – something he had not told his mother. The contrast between the prince's sympathy and support for a man whose private life had been exposed by the media (Prince Charles had endured horrendous coverage of his private life with Diana) and his disgust at Mandelson's dishonesty over the home-loan affair could not have been greater. For the next two days he solicitously inquired how the agriculture minister was bearing up under the pressure – offering tea and sympathy.

As for John Prescott, he paid the prince the extraordinary compliment of adopting some of his guidelines for developing new communities after being taken down to see Poundbury, the Prince's model 'retro' community village in Dorset. Prescott spoke at two conferences – one at St James's Palace in 1998, discussing sustainability, and another at the Prince's Foundation in London in November 2003. At the latter event, Prescott went out of his way to endorse the contribution of Prince Charles in proposing new guidelines for urban development that would shape Labour's plans to build 200,000 new homes in the South East. He took the opportunity to praise Poundbury – which had been attacked by critics as 'twee' and resembling the pictures on a Quality Street chocolate box.

Prescott delivered a paean of praise to the prince in his speech to the audience:

> I believe the Prince of Wales and I share these goals in common. I am
> very pleased to share the platform with you today. You have done so
> much to make people aware of the built environment and demand a
> better quality of design for the future.

While the relationship with Prescott still remains strong – if on a purely professional basis – the prince lost a useful connection to Tony Blair when Mandelson was excommunicated, and he would soon lose another.

As we have seen, Anji Hunter had served as a very effective intermediary with the royals during the crisis over Diana's death. She was now asked to repeat the role. The relationship between Camilla Parker Bowles and the prince had been troubling Blair and Cherie. For a start, Cherie did not get on with Camilla, who in her eyes was not a patch on Diana. Camilla was certainly not on the same wavelength as Cherie and her views were diametrically opposed to those of Diana. If she had any private political leanings, they were conservative with a small C. She believed, as an aide put it rather neatly, in Britain being best.

Why the Blairs should be bothered about the status of the relationship, beyond the constitutional niceties relating to Camilla's position as the acknowledged mistress of the future king of England, is not clear. It may be that Cherie's Catholicism was a factor; however, both she and her husband felt that if Charles was serious about Camilla, he should 'do the decent thing' and marry her, rather than continuing to lead the life of a middle-aged playboy. There was, as one aide put it, 'a feeling that Charles ought to grow up'. So Anji was despatched to St James's Palace to sound out the prince's aides on his future intentions. She was also meant to convey a private warning to the prince that it was 'make your mind up' time.

Anji Hunter is not as clumsy as Jack Straw, but the moment she raised the issue the aides made it clear that the prince would have nothing to do with it. After a rather short discussion, the aides said that the matter was closed and it was never raised again. The incident showed the Blairs that while in 1997 they might have been able to dictate terms to the entire royal family, their views carried little weight three years later.

Relationships were to deteriorate even further during Blair's second term of office, when Downing Street got involved in an extraordinary row over protocol at the Queen Mother's funeral. The problem was that Blair badly wanted to have a prominent role in the funeral, but official protocol did not allot him one.

The ensuing spat between Blair and Sir Michael Willcocks, the parliamentary official known as Black Rod, is probably best recounted in Sir Michael's own words.

> I received the news of the Queen Mother's death in the late afternoon of Saturday 30th March and quickly established with Buckingham Palace that I could give the order to 'execute' the plan for lying-in-state immediately. The first Palace co-ordination meeting was set for 11.00am on Monday 1st April and I therefore called my initial meeting for all the Palace of Westminster staff on Sunday afternoon 31st March.

It was on my way to that meeting from my house in Oxfordshire that I received the first of many telephone calls from the staff at No. 10 Downing Street.

The substance of this call was to query the role of the Prime Minister in the coming ceremonials. Phrases such as 'doesn't the PM greet the Queen?, 'doesn't he meet the coffin? and finally 'well, what is his role?' were used.

However, on that first occasion, it was what I would have expected of such a call. I answered all such questions by pointing out firmly, there being no latitude in the planning, that the PM had no such roles but would merely lead the tributes of the House of Commons and if possible be present with the House in Westminster Hall for the arrival of the coffin on Friday 5th April.

Sir Michael went on to explain that the lying-in-state was a parliamentary as opposed to a government occasion and there was no official role for the prime minister. But Downing Street were obviously not prepared to accept this. The memo continues:

After this initial contact, and throughout the next five days, my staff and myself were telephoned, at times it seemed constantly, by staff at No. 10 repeating these questions on the role of the PM, but also exerting rather more pressure along the lines of: 'don't you think the PM ought to be at the North Door? [of Westminster Hall] ...'; 'he must have more of a role surely ...'; 'Don't you think that he ought to be given a role?' etc.

Although, because of the demands of the circumstances, we could not keep a complete telephone log, the records that we do have show at least a dozen or so of such calls and a personal visit by a member of No. 10's staff, all of which followed the pattern above. The feeling we all had was one of sustained pressure from that quarter and, although it is true that at that stage, I was never asked to change the arrangements, the clear impression was one of being made to feel that we should.

This was reinforced by being told that if there were to be any varia-tion 'we could always get back to Ms Claire Sumner at No. 10.' [Claire Sumner was an official – though not a senior one – in Blair's office.]

Downing Street was still not satisfied, wrote Sir Michael, and that is why he devised a procedure that allowed all MPs and peers to file past the coffin led by the prime minister and the leader of the opposition.

At one stage on the telephone I had to take a No. 10 official through the entire ceremonial for the arrival of the coffin, minute by minute, and person by person.

It was largely because of this experience that I proposed that the two Houses of Parliament should, once the Royal Family had taken its leave,

file past each side of the coffin to exit via the North Door led by the PM
and the Leader of the House of Lords respectively.

There were also the practical considerations of how to get the
number of Peers and MPs out of the Hall in a dignified fashion. I was
thus able to give the PM a role and show him the plan for the ceremonial, which was subsequently collected by No. 10.

But Blair was still not satisfied, and on the day he decided, perhaps
remembering his prominent role around Diana's death, to create his own
special role – literally minutes before the queen and the royal family were
due to arrive. Black Rod's memo continues:

> Shortly before the arrival of HM the Queen at the North Door, and
> when the reception party of the triumvirate and the Archbishop of Can-
> terbury and myself were lined up to greet her, I received an urgent mes-
> sage from No. 10, via the Co-ordinating Officer for the Police
> Protection Officers, saying that the PM intended to walk to the Palace
> from Downing Street and wished to know if he could enter via the
> North Door.
>
> I had a fairly public discussion on the merits of such a walk, with
> among others the Lord Chancellor, and sent back a message to say that I
> didn't advise it.
>
> By return I received a more insistent request that in any case the PM
> be allowed to enter through the North Door. I said that I didn't think it
> was a good idea so close to HM the Queen's arrival but also that 'he is
> the PM so of course he can if he wants to.'
>
> In the event, he arrived by car and not via the North Door.

Blair's extraordinary course of action resembles a desperate bid by an
ageing matinée idol to make a comeback. It was not the behaviour of a
confident prime minister who knows when he should be centre stage and
when he should stand in the wings. It almost suggests that – like his
friend Peter Mandelson – he just can't bear not to be in the limelight,
even for one day.

Certainly it did not play well with the public – or, one can safely
assume, the royal family – when three newspapers subsequently reported
the gist of what had happened. Downing Street vehemently denied that
there was any truth in the story. Campbell, at Blair's request, unsuccessfully pressed the papers to apologise and, when they refused, referred the
matter to the Press Complaints Commission. It was at this point that Sir
Michael Willcocks wrote down his own record of the events that we
have printed above, determined that Downing Street's denials should not
go unchallenged. In the event, Guy Black, then director of the PCC,
went to see Campbell and told him that Blair had no case. Blair called in

Sir Richard Wilson, the cabinet secretary, to see if he could still pursue a complaint. Sir Richard advised him to withdraw the complaint. Blair did so.

The final area of disagreement between the Blair court and an increasingly isolated Prince of Wales concerned foreign policy – culminating in Blair's decision to go to war in Iraq.

Prince Charles was already strongly opposed to the government's policies on globalisation and GM food. He became even more agitated when Blair wanted to seal a new relationship with China by organising a state visit to Britain. The prince was bitterly opposed to this on human-rights grounds. Not only did he feel it would be shameful when the massacre in Tiananmen Square was still a recent memory, he was also deeply offended by the way the Chinese Communist leadership had treated the Dalai Lama and his followers in Tibet. But both Jack Straw and Blair brushed aside his protests. The visit went ahead; but although Prince Charles attended the formal function at Buckingham Palace, he pointedly declined an invitation when the Chinese organised a reciprocal banquet in London.

The prince was equally critical of Tony Blair's relationship with George and Laura Bush. When the Bushes, in turn, were invited to pay a state visit, the queen was happy to do her duty and entertain them at Buckingham Palace. However, the prince saw George Bush as a flag-waver for GM foods, globalisation, global warming and everything else that was wrong in the world.

He was also pro-Palestine rather than pro-Israel, and he thought it was wrong to intervene in Iraq without the support of the United Nations. The prince was strongly influenced by the royal family's close links with the Saudi Arabian monarchy and he was also more aware than most, through his links with other Muslim leaders, that the unilateral action in Iraq had caused deep offence across the Muslim world. His views were remarkably similar to those of the anti-war protest movement. But the prince has never publicly spoken about his views on these subjects. It was left to Tristram Hunt, the historian and former adviser to Peter Mandelson and Lord Sainsbury, to explain them in an article in *Prospect* magazine in the summer of 2004.

> Perhaps most damaging of all for Downing Street relations, Prince Charles is said to have harboured deep reservations over war in Iraq and its effect on Anglo-Islamic relations. Because of their reverence for king-ship, religiosity, and sense of tradition, Charles has always held dear a romanticised ideal of Islamic societies. A classic 'orientalist', he spoke

lovingly at King Hussein of Jordan's memorial service of the monarch's 'wonderful combination of the virtues of the Bedouin Arab and, if I may say so, the English gentleman'. He also retains a dynastic affection for the House of Saud, as revealed in his diplomatic efforts to free the wrongly imprisoned British workers, and he was quick to visit Iran after last year's earthquake in Bam.

While his patronage of Islamic art and architecture is extensive, the prince's engagement with Israel and America is noticeably sparser. Like many of his future subjects, he is unconvinced by their Middle East strategy and instinctively hostile to the rampant modernity of the US.[8]

The prince's opinions were, by now, becoming less and less important to Downing Street. He had become accustomed to firing off handwritten missives – known as 'black spider memos' – from St James's Palace. But Blair decided first to ignore and later to isolate him. The prince continued to send his memos but found that he was getting a much cooler reception. Prince Charles, as one aide said, 'had been put back in his box'.

What started out as a promising and vibrant relationship between the prime minister and the heir to the throne has declined into a distinctly cool acquaintanceship. No doubt, in Blair's case, the novelty of a close relationship with the monarchy has worn off. Today, there is no meeting of minds between an embattled prime minister and an isolated prince.

Tom Shebbeare says the prince is unlikely to regret this:

You must remember that for the prince the issues he keenly supports – such as opposition to GM food and building a new community in Poundbury – are over a sixty-year timescale, affecting a whole generation. He sees things over the long term – something that is outside the timescale of the prime minister of the day.

While the Blairs may have taken the royals off their celebrity guest list, this did not mean that their passion for a wealthy and well-connected lifestyle had been put on hold. On the contrary, it was blossoming.

The Blairs' main centre for entertaining is the prime-ministerial residence of Chequers, a very grand Tudor house with handsome grounds and a beautiful art collection, nestling amid the Chiltern Hills in Buckinghamshire. It was donated to the nation in 1917 by Lord Lee of Fareham as a country gentleman's estate and is run as a private charity for the use of the prime minister of the day. Its accounts are confidential. It enables the Blairs, like their predecessors, to enjoy the prestige and privacy that has traditionally been afforded to the political ruling class.

The list of guests invited to Chequers since Blair became prime minister gives many clues to the kind of people favoured by the Blair court.

Unlike John Major and his family, the Blairs spend little of their leisure time at their constituency home, choosing to regularly entertain people at Chequers instead. Unlike many previous prime ministers, however, they seldom use the house as a venue for cabinet get-together. Frank Dobson once suggested to Blair that he could hold 'team-building' dinners for the whole cabinet there, but Blair did not even think this was worthy of a reply.

As Peter Oborne noted in the *Spectator*:

> Most weekends the Blairs pile into their people carrier and head north-west for Chequers. Fundamentally, it is a family retreat, and all guests note with pleasure the agreeable signs that it is a family home: goalposts on the lawn, bicycles lying about, a playpen in the hall – that sort of thing.[9]

Some of the visitors would be on any prime minister's guest list. World leaders like Clinton, Putin and Chirac must of course be invited to stay when they come to Britain, and the occasional use of the mansion for conferences and foreign-policy seminars is quite normal. But the rest of the guest list reads like a curious mixture of Cool and Uncool Britannia, leavened with a sprinkling of selected newspaper editors, business leaders, relatives, and, of course, the members of the Blair court. Most dinners at Chequers comprise an eclectic mix of all these categories.

Cherie is the main person responsible for deciding who is 'in' and who is 'out'; Alastair Campbell and Fiona Millar also had some influence over who should be invited (and, more importantly, who should be blacklisted). The couple's penchant for meeting pop stars, authors and film directors shows up time and again. Some, like Cilla Black, are remarkably Uncool Britannia – it appears that Cilla got on the list because of Cherie's admiration for a 'Scouser who done good', as another guest, Clare Short, saw it. Other guests have included ageing pop guitarists like Jim Capaldi from Traffic; singers Billy Bragg and David Bowie; film directors like Michael Winner and David Puttnam; and even some of Tony's boyhood heroes, like former motor-racing champion Jackie Stewart. Mick Hucknall, the Simply Red singer, with his latest glamorous girlfriend in tow, has been a regular at Chequers. Joan Collins has also been entertained there – though her United Kingdom Independence Party membership would probably preclude further visits. The occasional Spice Girl has been invited, as have newsreaders such as Anna Ford.

The inner circle of the Blair court has usually been represented by people like the author Robert Harris, novelist Melvyn Bragg, and chief of staff Jonathan Powell. The first two would often return the compliment to the Blairs: the Braggs invited them, along with Bill and Hillary Clinton, to their summer party at Turville, another Chilterns beauty spot nearby.

The politicians fall into two groups and are not exclusively Labour. Blair's mentor, Roy Jenkins – or 'the great Pooh-Bah', as Paddy Ashdown used to refer to him – was a guest. Lord Ashcroft, the businessman, Tory fund-raiser and former senior party treasurer of the Conservative Party, was a more recent visitor. Trade union leaders are notable by their absence, though Roger Lyons, the former general secretary of the MSF union, and his wife, Kitty, managed to secure an invitation. A cabinet minister and his or her partner would always be there – and they would stay overnight. Early on, Derry Irvine was a regular guest. Others have included Peter Mandelson, Robin Cook and Clare Short. Frank Dobson, Nick Brown and David Clark were never invited.

Newspaper editors are clearly divided between those who are in and those who are out. Those who are never invited to dinner include Paul Dacre of the *Mail*, the *Daily Telegraph*'s former editor Charles Moore, the *Mirror*'s former editor Piers Morgan and the *Sun*'s former editor David Yelland. (The latter two were invited to tea instead. Tea is normally reserved for lesser mortals than editors, usually political correspondents and leader writers, such as the *Guardian*'s Michael White and Martin Kettle.) Those who have been on the guest list include the *Sunday Telegraph*'s Dominic Lawson (Cherie is patron of a charity run by his wife) and Andrew Marr, when he was editor of the *Independent* and again more recently as political editor of the BBC. Alan Rusbridger, the editor of the *Guardian*, twice a guest at the Blairs' Islington home before 1997, has also been invited once. But he is not eager to go; he says he is happier when the Blairs don't make vain attempts to try and exercise influence over the *Guardian*.

A typical dinner party was held in the summer of 1998, a year after Blair came to power. Guests were greeted at the door by the housekeeper and served drinks by Royal Navy staff. After aperitifs, they were guided into the long wood-panelled dining room for dinner.

Among the sixteen seated at the table were the lawyer and novelist Sir John Mortimer and his wife, Penny (Cherie had enthused about Mortimer, whose creations include the barrister Horace Rumpole, at a book launch); the pollster and guru of the focus group, Philip Gould, and his wife, Gail Rebuck, the wealthy and powerful publisher; Elisabeth Smith, John Smith's widow, and one of her daughters, the Channel 4 reporter and news presenter Sarah Smith; Gerry Robinson, one of Blair's business supporters and a big Labour donor; and Cherie's mother, Gale. The statutory cabinet minister was Robin Cook and his new wife, Gaynor. Not surprisingly, Cook kept an uncharacteristically low profile, having recently hit the headlines, courtesy of Alastair Campbell, over his split with his first wife, Margaret.

The Blairs always like to ask their guests how well New Labour is doing. They expect to be praised – criticism is definitely not welcome. On this occasion, they got a bit of shock when Penny Mortimer, a socialist supporter of hunting, asked why Blair had decided to ban fur farming. 'What damage has this ever done? We are supposed to have the best-run fur farms in the world,' she said. 'I didn't know my government was doing this,' murmured Blair, rather abashed.

Some of the discussion became intrusive and embarrassing. Philip Gould decided to ask Penny Mortimer why she had brainwashed her distinguished husband, Sir John, into supporting fox hunting when the polls told everybody that it was very unpopular. After she pointed out that Sir John was quite able to make up his own mind, the conversation turned rather too personal.

'How long have you been with John – it is quite a long time, isn't it?'

'Well, quite a while.'

'He's getting very old, isn't he?' said Gould.

Penny Mortimer replied, 'Well, he's seventy-five and he's a bit dicky in the leg department, but I can assure you that his brain is firing on all cylinders.'

'Why do you stay with him – is it love or duty?'

'Both,' replied Penny. She later wished she had said: 'We have great sex – which is something I don't think you know about.'

To the discomfort of both the Blairs, this part of the conversation appeared later in the *Daily Telegraph*.[10]

After dinner, the guests went out on the terrace as the weather was warm. Penny Mortimer, a chain-smoker, said: 'Oh, Cherie, you don't mind if I smoke out here do you?' Cherie replied: 'Well, I'll allow you just one if you have to, but it's a filthy habit.' A rare Chequers rebellion then broke out: Penny was joined by Sarah Smith, another ardent smoker, and the two of them didn't smoke just the one – they stayed outside puffing away at one cigarette after another for some time, in brazen defiance of their hostess.

Cherie eventually stomped off to start the highlight of the evening: the official tour of the building. Former guests say that Cherie has put quite a lot of work into researching this and obviously enjoys doing it.

One guest we spoke to says: 'Her tours of Chequers are well researched, witty, erudite, really good.' But on this particular evening, the rebellious smokers only caught up with the tour when it came to the last room in the house, where Cherie was showing off a gold ring said to have been owned by Elizabeth I. The locket ring opens to show two portraits: one of Elizabeth herself, and the other of her mother, Anne Boleyn, who was executed on the orders of King Henry VIII in 1536. It was said to have been taken off the queen's finger when she died and taken to Scotland to prove she was dead.

Cherie told the party, with just the slightest hint of name-dropping: 'It's a big ring. I was speaking to Princess Diana about it when she came here and we thought it was probably a thumb ring – it was too big to be on her finger.' This was slightly too much for the rebellious smokers to take. Penny Mortimer called out from the back that there had been a theory that Elizabeth I was a man. For the second time that evening, Cherie was not amused. 'Oh, male-chauvinist nonsense!' she retorted.

Before the end of the evening, Philip Gould returned to hold centre stage on the importance of his focus groups. The guests, by now a little inebriated, couldn't help leading him on.

'Can anyone join a focus group?' asked one.

'Yes, anyone.'

'Can we?' another asked.

'Yes, of course you can.'

'Do you serve a good lunch?' enquired Sir John.

'Oh, I am sure we could lay one on for you,' replied Gould.

'What about wine?'

At this point, Gould began to realise that this was not just an innocent inquiry – he was being gently sent up – and he quickly dropped the subject.

The guests then went home, except for the Cooks, who, like most ministers and their partners, stayed overnight. It was the end of a typical evening of entertaining for the Blairs.

Practically every summer since Blair took over the leadership, his family have enjoyed at least one holiday amid the kind of luxury and privacy afforded only to the very wealthy – usually at a fraction of the cost others would have to pay. From the Tuscan palace owned by the former minister Geoffrey Robinson to the exclusive Barbados villa of the veteran pop singer Sir Cliff Richard, the Blair family have been able to take their pick of the most exclusive retreats in the world.

Blair's choice of holiday destinations is strikingly different from those of his Labour predecessors. Harold Wilson, for example, was happy with a small cottage on the Isles of Scilly; Blair's tastes seem to have more in common with those of some of his Tory predecessors, like Margaret Thatcher – or with the celebrity lifestyle of some of his Chequers guests.

The Blairs' appetite for unbridled luxury was first whetted by one of Gordon Brown's friends, Geoffrey Robinson, who later had to resign over the Mandelson home-loan affair. Robinson, now sixty-six, is a political enigma. A grey-haired, softly spoken industrialist, you would not give him a second glance if you spotted him among the mass of middle-aged MPs that make up the Parliamentary Labour Party. Yet he has had an incredibly flamboyant life. He married an Italian opera singer, Marie-Elena Giorgio, and was later left a small fortune by Madame Bourgeois, a Belgian heiress. His business dealings with the corrupt Labour tycoon Robert Maxwell were so complex that – mostly through absent-mindedness – he regularly fell foul of the parliamentary standards committee by forgetting what he owned. But he was incredibly generous to the left: he bankrolled the leftwing weekly, the *New Statesman*, and proved a lifesaver by funding Gordon Brown's research when Labour was in opposition. Through a blind trust, he financed work that Brown previously had to pay for out of his own bank account.

But it was his generosity to his fellow MPs that really made him so well loved. Peter Kilfoyle recalls going out for a meal during a summer holiday with his wife and five children in a restaurant in San Gimignano, near Robinson's Tuscan villa. When he offered to settle the bill, the proprietor said 'No, *signor*: it is already paid.'

'But I haven't paid it,' protested Kilfoyle.

'I know, *signor*,' said the owner. 'Signor Robinson, he pay. He tell me you coming and he pay the bill.'

Kilfoyle, for once lost for words, accepted Robinson's hospitality and left the restaurant – still perplexed at how Robinson could even have known he was in the area.[11]

The Blairs seem to have accepted Robinson's hospitality without question. Their first visit to his splendid villa in 1996 not only included the children but also Cherie's mother, Gale, who baby-sat so the couple could go out. Blair even managed to fit in a game of tennis with Rory Bremner, the TV impressionist, who was no doubt observing the future PM's every gesture so that it could be honed to perfection later on *Bremner, Bird and Fortune.*

The Robinson villa is more like a palace, with marble floors, a huge terrace, a courtyard complete with fountain, and a forty-five-foot swimming pool set in nine acres of gardens. Called 'Il Mucchio' (literally, The

Pile), it stands on top of a hill hidden by a cypress grove. The early-nine-teenth-century, creamy-white, three-storey mansion was commissioned by its original owners, the Pompedoni counts. At the bottom of the hill is a fourteenth-century monastery, which has been restored by Robinson and includes a reconsecrated private chapel. Robinson also owns a further 140 acres of land, which is let out to farmers to grow sunflowers and wheat.

The Blairs had their meals prepared by Robinson's personal chef and dined under giant sunshades on the terrace overlooking olive groves and fields of sunflowers. They were immensely grateful for the hospitality – until two years later, when Robinson started to be criticised in the press and their friendship began to cool. By that time, Blair was already known on the international circuit and did not need wealthy Labour Party members to entertain him. He had grander ideas.

In the summer of 1998, the Blair family were guests of Prince Giro-lamo Strozzi at a fifty-room, fifteenth-century villa. In 1999, amid con-siderable controversy, the Blairs stayed at the Villa Gombo, owned by Vannino Chiti, a former Tuscan president and said to be a friend of the family. The twenty-two-room villa, near to a private sandy beach, boast-ed ten double bedrooms, seven bathrooms, a team of chefs to prepare the Blairs' meals and a 60,000-acre park. Alastair Campbell and Fiona Millar and their family joined the party for a week. A row broke out when an adjoining public beach was closed and restrictions were introduced which even prevented local wine producers from going about their busi-ness. State cash had been used to renovate the villa to high standards, which made the Blairs very unpopular with the local communist leader, Roberto Pucci.

In 2001 and 2002 the Blairs settled for the Ariège region in France, staying first at Sir David Keane's twelfth-century château at Saint Martin d'Oydes, and the following year renting a manor house, Le Château du Moulin, at Le Vernet. It was not quite as grand as the Italian sojourns, and nor was the company. In 2001, in a rather kind gesture, the Blairs invited the former cabinet minister Chris Smith and his partner, Dorian, over for a lazy Sunday lunch.

The gesture was all the more surprising because Blair had sacked Smith from his post at the Department of Culture the previous June. The two had ended up swapping cross words on the telephone, with Smith warning him: 'I think when you have consulted a lot of people in the arts world, you will find you are making a mistake.' Blair was left with a guilty conscience, because Smith had still been on the cabinet list until Blair's closest advisers, including Campbell, Jonathan Powell and Anji

Hunter, intervened. They had argued for fresh cabinet talent, which meant promotion for Tessa Jowell, a passionate Blairite, who became culture secretary. Blair took Smith for a long walk to look at the local medieval church and admitted that his prediction had been right – there had been a lot of critical comments from the arts world after Smith was removed. But he was not about to change his mind.

During the last two years the Blairs have gone in for even grander venues. Cherie's friendship with Sir Cliff Richard (Cherie appears to have rather suspect taste in pop music; her other musical heroine is Cilla Black) provided an exotic new holiday home. Sir Cliff's holiday retreat in Barbados is perched on cliffs overlooking the Caribbean; the secluded, modern, six-bedroom mansion is part of the exclusive Sugar Hill estate.

In 2004 the Blairs were the guests of Silvio Berlusconi, the billionaire newspaper and broadcasting proprietor and Italian prime minister, at the Villa Certosa on a 100-acre Sardinian estate that boasts a private jetty, a wild-boar reserve, numerous swimming pools and an open-air theatre. Perhaps this was when their friend Carole Caplin heard all the details of Signor Berlusconi's facelift, which, as we will see, she later recounted on her company's website.

Berlusconi must surely be the least likely person ever to have shared a jacuzzi with a leader of the Labour Party. Not long before the Blairs' visit to Sardinia, he had been denounced by the austere and normally conservative *Economist* magazine as unfit to be the leader of a modern nation. The manner in which he has abused his power as a media mogul to advance his political and business ambitions has been so frequently discussed that there is no need to repeat the allegations here. The Blairs' infatuation with power and wealth must have soared to extraordinary heights for them to even consider it appropriate for their family to accept hospitality from such a person.

CHAPTER FOURTEEN

THE COURT AT NUMBER 10

The account of life inside the beleaguered walls of 10 Downing Street in Peter Oborne and Simon Walters' rollicking biography of Alastair Campbell make it sound like something out of a *Girls' Own* comic book.[1] It could be summarised like this.

> Cherie used to be Best Friends with Fiona. She told Fiona everything, and Fiona told her what to say and what to wear. But then Cherie met Carole and she and Carole became best friends. So Carole started telling Cherie what to wear and what to do. Fiona was jolly miffed, and she jolly well told Cherie exactly what she thought about it. 'You keep lying to me,' she said. But Cherie thought Carole was more fun, and she carried on being best friends with Carole, so Fiona jolly well stormed off.
>
> Meanwhile, Cherie thought that Anji fancied Tony and that she used to go out with him and wanted to get off with him again. Anji just curled her lip and laughed. Cherie angrily told Tony to send Anji away, but for ages he wouldn't. He went on taking Anji to his den for private little chats. One day Cherie and Anji met in the corridor and started pushing each other. Cherie said it was Anji's fault but Anji said it was Cherie.
>
> But when Sally came along, Cherie told Tony he ought to talk to her instead of talking to Anji. Cherie knew Sally wasn't going to steal Tony. Tony tried to get Cherie to let him go on having his private chats with Anji, but in the end he agreed to start chatting to Sally instead. So Anji jolly well stormed out too.
>
> Tony often doesn't know what to do about it all. He phones his best friend Peter who comes along and calms them all down. 'It's called Being Pete,' he says soothingly, and everyone feels better.

Oborne and Walters describe oestrogen-fuelled disputes and jealousies in the midst of great decisions about war and peace. It would be funny if they were not describing the most powerful household in the land.

But is the Oborne and Walters portrait accurate? Yes, with some quali-fications. All the principal characters have been given ample opportunity to deny the account, not least by the present authors, and have declined to do so. The normal way the Blair court deals with unfavourable coverage is to seize on the smallest error to discredit it. Fiona Millar considered talking to the present authors on this particular subject, and after much soul-searching she wrote to say that she would have to put up with the inaccuracies in the Oborne-Walters account. She did not, of course, speci-fy what those inaccuracies were.

Alastair Campbell declined to be interviewed by the authors, but when he is asked questions about the Oborne-Walters biography at the road-show he has been taking around the country, he refers people to the review written by his friend, and Blair's journalistic cheerleader, David Aaronovitch. In a thousand words of psychobabble in the *Guardian*, Aaronovitch claimed to deduce from the book that Oborne and Walters are at heart a pair of closet queens who really want a night of passion with Alastair Campbell. Campbell says: 'Aaronovitch shows they are homoerotic about me.' But this is not very likely.

There is, however, a flaw in the Oborne-Walters account. They have fallen into the same trap as most authors who try to penetrate the closed, inward-looking world of Blair's Downing Street. Every time something dishonest, or bullying, or even eccentric is uncovered, one of the courtiers is found to be at the bottom of it. Blair is always guiltless, while the courtiers acquire a dreadful public image. So, according to the conven-tional analysis, Mandelson is devious, Campbell is thuggish, Cherie is a bit dippy – but Blair, at the centre of it, is simply, in his own words, 'a pretty straight guy'.

No one has listened carefully enough to the truest thing Alastair Campbell ever said: 'Everything I do, I do because the prime minister wants me to.' Blair's old friends Peter Mandelson and Alastair Campbell, and even the wife he is said to still be in love with – all of their reputa-tions have been ruthlessly thrown to the wolves when necessary, in order to protect the reputation of the prime minister.

The Blair court makes enormous efforts to prevent biographers and journalists from interviewing Cherie Booth (as she is still known profes-sionally) or anyone who knows her. Nearly all our interviewees have become edgy and nervous when we mentioned her name, for they know how sensitive a subject it is. It has always been maintained that this is because Blair is fiercely protective of his wife. The truth, as we have grad-ually been able to unravel it, is more complicated and multi-layered – and more cynical.

After Blair posed for photographers at the front door of Downing Street with Cherie, Euan, Nicky and Kathryn on the day New Labour won its historic victory in 1997, the pictures that appeared in the press were symbolic of a bitter dispute that was to fester between the Blairs and the tabloids over the next seven years of his government. The Blairs, just like any other celebrity couple, get enormous attention from the media. The tabloids in particular were keen to run any stories or gossip that they could garner about the family, including the children. The inherent conflict between Downing Street's insatiable appetite for favourable coverage on the one hand, and the tabloid editors' hunger for stories of scandal and double standards on the other, was always going to lead to trouble.

The conflict even divided Tony and Cherie. She had what Lord Wakeham, the former chairman of the Press Complaints Commission, the self-regulating watchdog for media standards, called 'a commendable mother's instinct to protect her children' from the prying eyes of the tabloids. Her husband was naturally ambitious for their children and wished to give them the best possible start in life. So the Blairs' three children were given regular access to all the celebrities a prime minister can command – from backstage visits to the theatre and cinema to meet Kate Winslet to meetings with Euan's football heroes – but Blair did not want there to be any media coverage of this. The fact that the children only met these people because their dad was famous seemed to escape Blair's attention – he wanted them to enjoy the anonymity any ordinary cinema-goer or football supporter would expect.

Both Blairs are fiercely ambitious for their children. This is perfectly normal in upwardly mobile professionals. If they lived next door to you, you would class them – without condemnation – as pushy parents. Roy Hattersley recalled for us a lunch with *Daily Mail* executives when Blair was opposition leader. One of the journalists asked why the Blairs should not simply send their children to the local comprehensive. 'Your children will go to university wherever they go to school,' he pointed out. Blair said he wasn't so sure: 'It didn't work for Harold Wilson.' The journalist observed that Wilson's children had done all right: one was a head teacher, the other an Open University lecturer. Blair retorted contemptuously: 'I hope my kids do better than that.'

But Blair also had another dilemma. He was desperate to woo television and the rightwing tabloids. This led him to make compromises over his wish to keep his children out of the public gaze. As John Rentoul relates, Blair faced just such a problem early on, when he was standing for the leadership in 1994. During an interview with Michael Brunson, ITN's political editor, Cherie had made, on camera, some remarks about looking forward to moving to Downing Street. Blair needed no spin doctor to tell him that this was going to look bad. So, out of Cherie's hearing, he did a deal with Brunson. If Brunson would agree not to broadcast Cherie's remarks, he would let Brunson film him playing football with Nicky and Euan, and Euan playing the family piano.

Much has been written about Blair's obsession with wooing Rupert Murdoch and his determination that the *Sun* should support New Labour. Blair was prepared to go to great lengths to make his party acceptable to the Australian media mogul. But he also had another obsession that dominated the early days of his leadership and premiership – the *Daily Mail*. Just as Blair craved votes from the posh houses in Beaconsfield and Sedgefield more than those from the council houses, he would have loved to secure the support of this essential organ of Middle England. As it happened, before the election, Sir David English, then the editor-in-chief of the *Daily Mail*, also had a craving that needed satisfaction: he was desperate for a peerage.

John Major would have dearly loved to oblige – but every time English's name got near the top of the list, the *Mail* erupted into a frenzy over Major's stance in dealing with his Eurosceptic rebels. So it was out of the question. But in the run-up to the 1997 election, there was an alternative prime minister in the wings. It was therefore no surprise that a series of discreet lunches took place in the Blairs' Islington home between the paper's proprietor, the elderly Lord Rothermere, David English and the Blairs. The *Mail* executives certainly had more lunches in Islington than the Blairs' near neighbour, Alan Rusbridger, editor of the *Guardian*. Blair calculated that the *Guardian* would be on Labour's side anyway.

So Blair was keen to get the *Mail*'s support for New Labour, while English was anxious to please. English even took advice from Lord Wakeham – a former Tory cabinet minister as well as chairman of the Press Complaints Commission – on what would be the best way to woo Blair. In the end both sides got a result. Rothermere and English decided that the London *Evening Standard* would back Blair but the *Mail* would stay with the Tories. The decision was helpful – some of the biggest swings to Labour in 1997 took place in London, costing Tory stars like Michael Portillo their seats. English was ultimately awarded a life peerage but died from a stroke four days before it was due to be announced. In a statement to the BBC on 10 June 1998, Blair said: 'I counted David English as a friend. He was a truly outstanding journalist. He never lost his love and enthusiasm for his chosen profession and never lost his eye for a good story.' Blair's spokesman said that Buckingham Palace had given its permission for Number 10 to announce that English was to be made a life peer ahead of the public announcement of the birthday honours on Saturday.

In government, Blair initially had a good relationship with the *Mail*. He took advice from some of its journalists; *Mail* executives and staff were regular visitors to Downing Street. They even advised him on where he went wrong when he made a mess of a speech to the Women's Institute in June 2000 – he was slow-handclapped and heckled for claiming to have much improved the National Health Service. But things rapidly started to go wrong. Cherie, who, like almost everyone on the left, has never been a fan of the *Daily Mail* and the Associated Newspapers group, was determined to put an end to any affectionate relationship between her husband and the voice of Middle England.

On 24 January 1999 the *Mail on Sunday* published a contentious article headlined: 'Parents' Fury over Blairs in School Place Row'. The story reported complaints from local parents that the Blairs had received preferential treatment in getting their daughter, Kathryn, into the Sacred Heart High School in Hammersmith – a well-regarded Catholic state school. It highlighted a typical panic among middle-classes Londoners desperate to get their children into good schools, the sort of row in which accusations that 'other people' are getting privileged treatment will frequently fly around. The mistake the article made was to suggest that the complaints were exclusively focused on the treatment given to Kathryn Blair – a point the Blairs were easily able to refute. A complaint was filed to the PCC in both the Blairs' names.

The paper would have been on stronger ground if it had said that there were a series of complaints about other parents – and that it had been able to check the school's admission policy. The *Mail on Sunday* offered to publish a correction to avoid a PCC judgement against it. But it slowly became clear in negotiations between Guy Black, director of the PCC, and Alastair Campbell that Downing Street was not interested in a correction. Black, who became increasingly frustrated at the failure to reach a deal, suddenly became aware it was Cherie that was driving things on. Guy Black said: 'It looked to me that Alastair himself was having difficulty handling Cherie. He made it very clear to me that he must have a win against Associated Newspapers. He told me it was absolutely essential that they had one on them.'[2]

Cherie won the case and the *Mail on Sunday* was duly castigated. But this was followed by another incident that finally destroyed any relationship between the *Mail* and the prime minister. Paul Dacre, the current editor of the *Daily Mail*, is not as at ease socially as was his predecessor, Sir David English. He often appears cold and reserved, and he does not like to be exposed to the glare of publicity. So when he, the new Viscount Rothermere and their respective spouses came to dinner with Blair and Cherie at Downing Street in the autumn of 2000, relations were not likely to be particularly friendly. It was certainly nothing like a group of close friends having a social get-together. So it came as a pleasant surprise when Cherie produced the Blairs' new baby, Leo, for everyone to admire. But what happened next shocked the voices of Middle England. Cherie undid her top and began breast-feeding Leo. Blair, according to *Mail* sources, looked embarrassed. Dacre and Viscount Rothermere took Cherie's action to be a deliberate act of political hostility – aimed at showing the 'forces of conservatism' that liberal values were firmly in control in the most powerful building in the land. Whether this was true or not, the *Mail*'s owners and executives left in a state of shock.

Of course, this story tells us far more about Dacre and Rothermere than about Cherie. But it tells us something about her too. This was not the same Cherie who had entered Downing Street in 1997 determined to make whatever compromises were needed. Back then, she had learned to avoid being too honest. In 1994, a woman journalist asked her what she liked cooking her husband for dinner – and thoroughly deserved the sharp response she got (the journalist obtained her revenge by describing Cherie as 'charmless'). But by 1997, Cherie, under Fiona Millar's tutelage, had schooled herself to put up with that kind of treatment. She had even handed over control of her diary, her clothes and her social life to Millar, who saw it as her job to make sure that her charge did not embarrass the prime minister.

Millar's power over Cherie's life, in those early Downing Street days, was absolute. Millar, a former journalist and an attractive, sophisticated and elegant woman, used an iron hand to control who had access to Cherie and who was denied it. Old friends who tried to get in touch had to run the gauntlet of Millar's interrogation and were only allowed access if Millar approved. One old friend, who had dined with the Blairs many times, had attended their wedding, and had cause to be grateful to Cherie for drawing on her legal expertise to assist when his employer wanted to fire him, telephoned her several times after 1997. He would find himself being cross-examined by Fiona, who would promise to pass his message to Cherie; he never knew whether she did so or not. Eventually, he called up and said to Millar: 'You know I'm an old friend of Cherie's?' Millar replied: 'You're an old friend, not a new friend.' Cherie never returned the call. Once, he bumped into Cherie at a reception. After a few minutes of friendly conversation, Millar loomed into view and, with a baleful glance at him, whisked Cherie away. He has never spoken to her since. He asked us not to give his name, as he hopes the old friendship will be resumed when Blair is no longer prime minister.

Another old friend, a barrister who went to their wedding and was often invited to dinner in their Hackney home, says: 'Right up to the time Tony became prime minister, whenever I met Cherie in the Temple we would stop and talk. After that, instead of coming to talk, she would wave and walk. It was an acknowledgement, not a recognition.' He thinks it was 'a certain self-importance about being the wife of the prime minister', but it is more likely that Cherie had had it drummed into her that her personal contacts needed to be vetted by Millar. The friend in question wonders: 'What will happen when it all comes to an end?' Tony, typically, is more careful not to give the wrong impression, and when the same friend wrote to congratulate him on becoming prime minister, he received the trademark Blair letter, handwritten in fountain pen.

Millar's hegemony even extended to Cherie's family. Her half-sister, actress turned journalist Lauren Booth, and her father Tony Booth were identified early on as potential problems. Tony Booth's efforts to win party support for Blair in the early years, when he would perform at Labour by-election campaigns and say Blair had sent him, did not save him.

Both Tony and Lauren Booth held awkward leftwing views which they refused to keep to themselves, and they were regarded as indiscreet. Lauren was never in any doubt that she was frozen out after 1997. Today, she is very careful how she speaks of it, but we know that she was hurt at the time, particularly since she had avoided writing about the Blairs or speaking about them. She was also sure that Millar had not only shut her out, but had also briefed reliable journalists to rubbish her. It certainly looked a little like it. Former *Daily Mirror* editor Roy Greenslade, who knows and admires Blair, wrote in the *Guardian*:

> Am I alone in wondering whether Lauren Booth, self-proclaimed 'sister of Cherie Blair', is overdoing her slender connection to the PM's wife? Worse, she affects to protest that it is the press chasing her for that reason, rather than the other way around.
>
> For the record, Lauren is Cherie's half-sister and they have known each other for only a couple of years. They do not spend much time together.
>
> I met her very briefly a couple of months ago, and she convinced me that she was sincere in her attempt to make the transformation from model to journalist.
>
> But her tiresome self-promotion – the latest being a 'flamboyant' fashion shoot in Monday's *Express* in which she flaunted her tiger tattoo – is getting rather tacky ...

The information that the two women 'do not spend much time together' reeks of the usual 'sources close to Downing Street'.

Recognising the lie of the land, after 1997 Lauren backed away from the sister she had only recently discovered. For Blair, she felt personal affection, always remembering how kind and helpful he had been in dealing with her father Tony after he was badly burned in a fire. She seems to have rationalised the situation by deciding that the Blairs had taken a professional and not a personal decision, and that, professionally, the Blairs had decided that anyone who was not for them was against them. Of course, like everyone else, she blamed Campbell and Millar, not Blair. There was a reconciliation much later. Lauren is said to have thought this signified that Campbell and Millar eventually came to see her as a professional journalist. But it may have had more to do with the fact that Cherie was finally kicking her way out of the prison Millar had built around her.

Tony Booth has never quite been banished, but, according to someone who knows the Blairs well, 'Tony Blair takes a deep inhalation of breath every time he knows Tony Booth is to visit. It's because Tony Booth strolls in wherever he goes and wants to tell the world how to do things.' Tony and Lauren Booth have now removed themselves from the scene. Tony went to live in Ireland and Lauren in France; they seldom, if ever, meet the Blairs and loyally avoid talking to journalists about them. Tony Booth's parting shot was to tell the press that government's pension policy was driving him out – 'The treatment of the old is beneath contempt.' Lauren, who owes some, but not all, of her success in journalism to her relationship with the Blairs, continued to write a well-paid column for the *Daily Mail* but gave up her *New Statesman* column. In France she goes by her husband's surname and uses a different Christian name as well.

The limits of Campbell's power became clear the year Blair became Labour leader. That year, 1994, Euan began his final year at primary school, and the Blairs had to decide on a secondary school for him. Blair realised that sending his children to a fee-charging school like the one he had attended would be political suicide in the Labour Party of 1994. Since then, he has striven to change Labour into a party where no one would turn a hair at such behaviour; judging by the recent statements of his education ministers about fee-charging schools, he may well have succeeded.

Campbell and Millar are staunch advocates of comprehensive, non-selective education, and their children go to the local comprehensive school. The Blairs, and Tony especially, are not. Blair discussed this problem on a train journey with his shadow cabinet colleague Harriet Harman, who recommended the school attended by her own son, the London Oratory in west London. The Blairs lived in North London. At the London

Oratory, applicants are interviewed, together with both their parents. In theory it is a non-selective school; the interview is simply to check that the boy and his parents are practising Catholics. But a call to their parish priest could easily establish that – in reality the interview has a much deeper purpose, as the school prospectus makes clear.

'The interview,' it says, 'is an important and decisive part of the admission procedure, and its function is to assess catholicity, practice and commitment and whether the aims, attitudes, values and expectations of the parents and the boy are in harmony with those of the school.' Furthermore, it assesses 'commitment to the ethos of The London Oratory School, to the Church and to Catholic education'. The interview can also, of course, be used to assess the social status of the parents. There is no evidence that the school does so in practice; but no one honestly expected it to turn down the boy whose mother was a high-flying barrister and whose father was likely to be the next prime minister, and it did not. Applicants fill in a questionnaire about their religious devotion, and their parish priest is asked to comment on it. The school also looks at the boy's primary-school record, to check that he has consistently achieved A or B grades for effort in all subjects.

So to call the London Oratory an all-ability school is to play with words. It was just the sort of school to which Labour policy at that time was opposed. Euan was followed to the school by Nicky, and in 2004 the school sixth form – which, unlike the rest of the school, admits girls – welcomed Kathryn.

Campbell and Millar were furious. But their reaction is almost a paradigm of the behaviour of the Blair court. They blame Harriet Harman, and they have never forgiven her. Even this year, on his roadshows, Campbell, asked if he disliked any cabinet ministers, named Harman vengefully, adding: 'That education stuff was very difficult for me.'[3] The instinct of the medieval court, that the king can do no wrong and any mistake must be the fault of bad advisers, is strong, even among the advisers.

At the time, Campbell could not have predicted that before long, Labour's education policy would be to give many more schools the sort of power that the London Oratory wielded ten years before.

Clearly, while Blair could defy Campbell (and later Millar) when he chose to, Cherie was not expected to do so. And for three years, she didn't. The day she breast-fed baby Leo in front of Paul Dacre and Viscount Rothermere in 2000 helps us to date the beginning of her rebellion. By then, the Blair children, as children do, had turned into teenagers, and were not unlike any other teenage children – except that their father was prime minister and was also pushier than the average parent. A pushy parent, insistent on academic success, can be a mixed blessing. Some children react against the pressure, and others find it oppressive. Euan seems to fall into the first category, as evidenced by his insistence on smoking at Chequers in defiance of a maternal edict. Which is why, just a few weeks before Cherie shocked Dacre and Rothermere to the core with a glimpse of her breast, Press Complaints Commission chairman John Wakeham once again had to tiptoe into the family life of the Blairs.

The embarrassment caused by sixteen-year-old Euan Blair being found drunk and incapable in Leicester Square in July 2000 required some firm advice from Wakeham to Alastair Campbell: that while the prime minister might not like the unfavourable publicity, it would be better if his statement showed some parental disapproval; the first draft showed none. Euan had disguised his name and given a false address to hide his identity. The statement from Number 10 finally read: 'Euan is very sorry for the inconvenience he caused to the police, the state he was in, and for the false statement that he made. He is in no doubt of the seriousness of it and the view that his parents take of it.'

The Blairs ran into another furore later that month over baby Leo's christening by Father Caden at the Roman Catholic church in Sedgefield. Blair and Cherie wanted a ban on any photographs of the family as they went to and from the church. The parliamentary press lobby were told on 25 July: 'The prime minister and Mrs Blair consider this to be an entirely private family occasion and are requesting the media to respect this by not sending photographers and reporters to cover the event.' But pictures were taken regardless. The PCC pointed out that they could not ban the press from taking photographs on a public road. Privately, Blair had been advised that he could have had a closed service in Downing Street, Chequers or any private chapel of his choice, but he refused to countenance this. The Blairs reacted by threatening to ban a photo call before they went on their summer holiday, but relented at the last moment.

The PCC promised to consider new guidelines. But Cherie had had enough. She was not interested in new guidelines; she wanted tougher action. In an extraordinary letter to John Wakeham, she demanded a new privacy law and an end to self-regulation. Wakeham was told in no uncertain terms that she expected the commission to act on her behalf and ban newspapers from publishing information on the Blairs' children. She dismissed suggestions that her family, like everybody else, should accept the process set out in the existing code of practice. That procedure – according to three senior people who have seen the letter –

was for 'little people', implying that no such rules should apply to important figures like the prime minister. Cherie's demand was rejected.

But Cherie was not finished yet. In March 2003 Guy Black, the new director of the PCC, was summoned to Downing Street. He has decided to tell the authors about the incident because an inaccurate account was given to the *Sunday Times*, apparently by Downing Street. This included the extraordinary and mistaken suggestion that Black had been summoned by Blair to discuss a proposal that Black's partner, Mark Bolland, who had left his job as the Prince of Wales's adviser, was to be appointed as a new image consultant to the prime minister.

Black remembers arriving at the door and being asked to go up to the prime minister's private flat. Arriving there, he first had to clamber over a lot of toys on the floor – Carole Caplin was playing with Leo. In the room were Blair and Cherie and Fiona Millar. He remembers: 'Cherie looked like a volcano that was about to erupt.' But it was Tony Blair who began the conversation. He said he wanted the advice and help of the PCC in overcoming a very difficult situation which was putting pressure on his children. He wanted to stop all the publicity about them. 'I would like to have a similar agreement which has been reached between the press and the royal family over the coverage of William and Harry.' Effectively, this meant a special press ban covering the prime minister's family – it would not apply to any other member of the cabinet. The Blairs would be treated like royalty.

Black replied:

> I am afraid we cannot do this, prime minister; your children are not going to be public figures in their own right. William and Harry are heirs to the throne. We are certainly willing to take up any complaint about the breach of their privacy – but we cannot give an undertaking to do that.

Blair frowned. Cherie looked furious. Then the prime minister was interrupted – Vladimir Putin, the Russian leader, was on the telephone. Blair rushed off to take the call. Meanwhile, Cherie exploded.

> I must complain to you about the *Daily Mail* – it is a disgraceful paper. They have just suggested that I bought a cheap of bottle wine for Tony's birthday. This is a complete lie – it was a very expensive bottle. What are you going to do about it?

Black replied: 'Well, again, if you have a complaint you should take it up with the editor of the paper and if you are still unhappy you can take it up with us.' Since then, Cherie has inundated the *Daily Mail*'s lawyers with complaints about their coverage of herself and her husband.

Blair's attitude to media coverage of his children is understandable. But by using them when he wanted 'good publicity', he put himself in a difficult position when stories appeared which he did not like. His children appeared in the annual Christmas card and on the steps of Downing Street for photo calls, and the Millennium Dome was supposed to pass the 'Euan test'. This ambivalent attitude annoyed other members of the cabinet who also had young children. Those who complained privately included Harriet Harman and her husband Jack Dromey, now the deputy general secretary of the Transport and General Workers Union; and also Jack Straw and his wife, Alice Perkins, a senior civil servant in the Cabinet Office.

It is interesting to contrast the Blairs' attitude with a decision taken at an earlier date by Jack Straw and Alice Perkins, who sent their two children to have tea with John Wakeham. The idea, according to Wakeham, was to give their children a feeling of what life was like in the real world when you had a famous father and how your actions could get you into trouble with the press. The avuncular Wakeham tried to explain to Will and Charlotte, over tea and cakes, that there are advantages and disadvantages. 'It is not a good idea if your father is home secretary to break the law and take drugs,' he pointed out. Charlotte took the advice seriously. Will was more sceptical – until he was caught buying cannabis in a *Daily Mirror* honey trap and cautioned by the police for possession. Jack Straw thought his children had to accept the reality of the media, but the Blairs did not.

What seems to have happened is that around 2000, after her fourth and last child was born, Cherie got sick of being kicked around by the press and pushed around by her husband's advisers. She is a highly intelligent woman and, by general consent, academically far brighter than her husband. She holds political views that, as has become increasingly clear, are not shared by her husband's government. Her successful career at the Bar owes nothing to his fame. In fact, being the prime minister's wife has probably held her up: otherwise she would be a High Court judge by now, according to lawyers we have spoken to.

She does not deliver the standard bread-and-butter speeches expected of a prime minister's consort. But in the last three years, she has, on carefully chosen platforms and in long, erudite lectures, set out her own beliefs on matters she considers important. She has been circumspect: the platforms will always be unsensational academic ones, or the *Tablet*, an intellectual Catholic weekly. And she avoids using phrases that could be turned into soundbites.

The day before President George Bush was due to visit Britain in November 2003, at a seminar at Georgetown University, she condemned his administration for removing the US from the treaty establishing an international criminal court.[4] Foreign Office officials were dismayed, but knew they could not stop her. Three months later she was damning the Americans' use of the death penalty in an article in the *Tablet*.[5] The implications for British–American relations were unstated but obvious. A recurring theme is that British courts imprison too many people and especially too many women, and she is not shy of returning to this subject when Home Secretary David Blunkett advocates more imprisonment.

She delivered a lecture on human rights to a Reform Synagogues seminar in February 2004. Democracy, she said, was useless without equality, because 'human dignity, freedom and equality are denied to those who have no food, clothing or shelter'. She argued that human rights violations come, not just from terrorism and bad government, but from 'the unfettered pursuit of material gain at the expense of the less fortunate, the defenceless, and the environment'. The lecture is long, learned, closely argued – and devastating, for it is a restatement, in modern and forceful terms, of what the Labour Party used to stand for, before Tony Blair came along.[6]

Her law firm, Matrix Chambers, went public on its conviction that invading Iraq would be contrary to international law. Of course, the name of Cherie Booth QC was not to the fore in this document, but no one doubted for a moment that that was her view – and those who know her tell us that she was appalled at the decision to attack Iraq. In public, she has confined herself to explaining why it matters, from a human rights standpoint, that Saddam Hussein should have a fair trial.

Today, sadly, Cherie seems to have been brought back into line. Her longstanding commitment to the work of Human Rights Watch resulted in her offering to speak for the organisation in February 2004 at a specially arranged seminar on the importance of businesses sticking to human rights norms. But Human Rights Watch had made some trenchant criticisms of the conduct of the Iraq war, and Cherie was told by Downing Street to cancel her seminar. She did, and as we write there are no plans for her to speak for the organisation again. Perhaps she felt she had to listen this time; certainly the preceding year had been a horrific one from her point of view.

Cherie first met Carole Caplin at a fitness class in 1992, and by 2003 she was paying Caplin £3,500 a month for assistance with dress, fitness and 'lifestyle'. It sounds like a lot of money, but judging by the inside accounts we have been given, Caplin was earning every penny. What previous accounts have missed is that Carole was just as close to the prime minister as she was to his wife.

'She was at the Blairs' beck and call,' says someone who knew Carole well. 'I remember her saying she'd just spent seven hours clearing Tony's wardrobe, deciding what to keep, what to throw away, what to give to charity.' She even had her own nickname for him. Carole does not smoke or drink, but she loves chocolate – she has been described to us as a chocoholic – and she called the prime minister 'Toblerone'. It seemed to amuse him.

When Cherie was away, Carole would often go to the Downing Street flat to keep Tony company. 'Cherie's away, I'm babysitting this weekend,' she would say, or: 'He's lonely, I'm going to the flat for a couple of hours.' During the run-up to the Iraq war she went to Chequers and found Tony very tense. 'I gave him a reiki massage. He's really stressed but that'll get him through till Thursday,' she told a friend.

Carole was steadily supplanting Fiona Millar in Cherie's life; Millar and Campbell were doing everything they could think of to loosen her grip and bring Cherie back under their control, but nothing seemed to work.

Cherie was in the throes of wholesale rebellion. Relationships in Downing Street had become fraught. Caplin referred to Millar as 'the bitch from hell' and believed Millar and Campbell were behind all the derogatory newspaper comment about her relationship with Cherie. Millar and Campbell, for their part, were urging the Blairs to banish Caplin from court.

Meanwhile, Cherie herself was unsuccessfully lobbying her husband to banish his own adviser, Anji Hunter. Hunter came from a wealthy family and shared the languid conservatism of the leisured classes, all of which offended the socialist in Cherie. By 2001, Cherie was also feeling resentful towards a woman who saw much more of her husband than she did, and who had known him much longer. To Cherie, Hunter was 'that bloody woman', but Blair refused to get rid of her. Cherie and Fiona Millar, growing apart because of Carole Caplin, were drawn into an alliance against Anji Hunter. They were joined by Blair's political secretary, Sally Morgan.

In 2001 Hunter landed a £250,000-a-year job as director of government relations at BP on the strength of her Downing Street experience; she was also about to leave her Blair lookalike husband for Adam Boulton, the political editor of Sky News. Yet, despite his wife's disapproval, Blair tried desperately to stop Hunter leaving, offering her more status, more money – anything if only she would give him a few more months.

She relented. Cherie was furious and had a terrible row with her husband in the den. Hunter eventually did leave, a few months later, pointing out that BP would not wait for her for ever.[7]

That was how things stood in November 2002, when the tabloids started closing in on Carole Caplin. As they saw trouble looming, Caplin and her boyfriend Peter Foster, a man with a reputation for sharp-dealing who was soon to be thrown out of the country, hired Ian Monk as their PR consultant. A former *Daily Mail*, *Daily Express* and *Sun* journalist, Monk had a client list that included Nick Leeson (the rogue trader who brought down Barings Bank) and Richard Desmond. At the time of writing, having left the consultancy he used to work for and branched out on his own as Ian Monk Associates, he has recently taken Wayne Rooney onto his books. He claims: 'I can pick up the phone to any editor and he'll take my call.'[8]

Caplin told Monk: 'I need someone to protect the reputation of my business because I will get slagged off over my relationship with Peter. And I want to keep Cherie out of it. The press will use my relationship with Peter to damage Cherie.' Sure enough, that weekend the *Mail on Sunday* ran a story about Cherie's purchase of two flats in Bristol, one for Euan to live in when he went to Bristol University that autumn, the other as an investment. The paper acknowledged the rebuttal from Downing Street – that Foster had not negotiated the deals or been Cherie's financial adviser. By Thursday, however, the *Daily Mail* was able to prove that Foster *had* negotiated the purchase of the flats for Cherie.

From that moment on, Alastair Campbell and Fiona Millar worked ceaselessly to ensure that all the blame for what was obviously going to be a highly embarrassing revelation was attached to Cherie, and that none of it stuck to Blair or his office. Newspapers from the *Sunday Telegraph* to the *News of the World* adhered to the Campbell line – that he and Millar had constantly warned Cherie about Carole Caplin and had been ignored. The *News of the World* said: 'Skilled aides Alastair Campbell and Fiona Millar urged the prime minister's wife to keep Carole at arm's length. Instead, she ignored their advice.'[9]

It also emerged that Cherie had been in touch with Peter Foster's solicitors over the Australian government's efforts to extradite him. The solicitors concerned were obliged to issue a statement saying she had done nothing improper. It seems that all she did was to check that the proceedings were being conducted properly – a service any trained lawyer might undertake for a friend.

Oborne and Walters claim that Blair was uncomfortable at seeing his wife trashed in public; but if so, why did he not put a stop to it? The claim that this happened because Campbell was out of control is non-sense. He took his instructions from one person and one person only: the prime minister. This is Teflon Tony at his best. Carole Caplin and the debacle of the flats were Cherie's fault; Carole Caplin and her dodgy boyfriend were Cherie's fault; the vindictive trashing of Cherie in the press was Campbell's fault. Nothing was ever Tony's fault.

The atmosphere inside Downing Street grew poisonous. Campbell was late at a dinner party, and Cherie asked where he had been. 'Getting you out of more trouble,' said Campbell. A crestfallen Cherie said: 'I'm sorry, it's all my fault again.' She talked later to Millar, who refused help or sympathy: 'Because you never listen to me and you don't tell me the truth.'

But Blair was troubled enough to send for his comfort blanket. One telephone call was enough to get Peter Mandelson to hotfoot it over from the United States, and he hardly left Downing Street for the next four days. Mandelson gave the Blairs all the sympathy and understanding that had been denied to him on his enforced cabinet resignations. Blair did recognise the irony. 'It's just like what happened to you last year,' he told Mandelson. This is why, in July 2004, Blair was determined to give Mandelson a third big job, as Britain's European Commissioner.

Mandelson thought Cherie had done nothing fundamentally wrong and advised that she should make a full statement. Campbell and Millar counselled against this. They wanted her to disappear, to withdraw from public life and make no official statements at all. But Blair decided that Mandelson was right, and once he had given his decision, Campbell, as always, obeyed it. So Campbell, Millar, Mandelson, Sally Morgan and Charlie Falconer all gathered around Campbell's computer to write the statement. Later that day, Cherie was made to put out a further statement: 'Having heard how some are reporting her statement, Mrs Blair wants to make it clear that she, and she alone, is responsible for any misunderstanding between the No. 10 press office and the media.'[10]

Six days later, she was required to do it all over again, in more grovelling terms than before. 'I should not have allowed a situation to develop where Tony's spokesman said [Peter Foster] played no part in the negotiations [over the Bristol flats purchase] and I take full responsibility for that.'

British newspapers followed the Downing Street line, and Cherie Booth must have had some of the most unpleasant days of her life. Australian newspapers reported that Carole Caplin was as close to Blair himself as to his wife, and chose his wardrobe 'right down to his underpants', which our sources can confirm; but the British press concentrated its fire on Cherie, just as Campbell had briefed them to do.

In May 2003 Monk handed a strategy paper to his client, Carole Caplin. He said that if she had performed the same sort of service for a US president, she would be appearing on all the networks as a lifestyle guru. He wanted to rebrand her as 'fashion and style adviser to Cherie and Tony Blair'. He told her: 'When we can present you as that, it will stop the innuendo and give you authority as a fashion and style expert.' She took the paper to Chequers and was back in Monk's office the next week. The Blairs had said: not until Tony has left office. Monk tried to persuade Carole to ignore them. He said the Blairs were using her, making her the butt of press derision and innuendo. She said she did not want to trade on the Blairs, and Monk replied: 'But they are trading on you. You are taking all that shit for the prime minister. They are using you.'

The Blairs themselves may have made a bad PR decision. They needed either to dump Carole or to legitimise her. Since Cherie is loyal to friends who remain loyal to her (as opposed to those she feels have betrayed her, like Fiona Millar), they were not going to dump her. A professional PR would probably have advised them therefore to legitimise her. Caplin told Monk how fond she was of the Blairs, but how much she hated the courtiers, like Campbell and Millar. 'Tony hates them too,' she told him, more than once, 'but he's been convinced that he needs them.' He was also utterly fed up with Gordon Brown, saying: 'Why doesn't he get a life?' Cherie, she said, had told her that Tony would retire as prime minister when his wife turned fifty; her fiftieth birthday was in September 2004.

Monk was introduced to Cherie and was struck by her social awkwardness. He put her in touch with another of his clients, the dress designer Lindka Chierach. Caplin took Cherie to see Chierach, and took charge, as she always does with Cherie: 'No, no, she can't wear that, her hips are too big.' Chierach dressed Cherie for her trip to Washington in July 2003, and was amazed that Carole spent weeks ringing up and haggling over the prices. She seemed to think the prime minister's wife ought to get the clothes for free. Chierach sold the clothes to Cherie for about a quarter of their normal price.

In December 2002 Carole miscarried her and Peter Foster's baby, something that she and Cherie put down to the stress of what had become known in the British press as 'Cheriegate'. She paid for Foster's flight back to Australia and, as far as we know, has not been in touch with him since May 2004. But she is still in regular touch with Cherie and a frequent visitor to Downing Street, even though the privilege of an official pass has been withdrawn.

*

Clearly, Caplin had forged a strong bond with the Blair family, a bond that was reinforced by the fact that, by this stage, she had become the employer of Cherie's only full sister, Lyndsey. After Cherie qualified as a barrister in the 1970s, Lyndsey Booth, two years younger than Cherie, qualified as a solicitor and went to do her articles at Russell Jones and Walker in London's Gray's Inn Road. Russell Jones and Walker is one of the two or three top trade union law firms in the country, and the firm used by the Trade Unions Congress. Lyndsey introduced Cherie and Tony (then still practising at the Bar) to the partners at the firm who handled employment cases.

Fraser Whitehead, the partner at Russell Jones and Walker who principally advises trade unions, was one of those who got to know the Blairs through Lyndsey. He started sending work to both of the Blairs, and occasionally still briefs Cherie Booth on cases for the TUC, in the course of which she has successfully challenged the policies of her husband's government. He has less occasion to brief her now that she specialises in human rights, but this serves as a reminder that, however many newspapers and government spin doctors describe her as dippy, she remains one of the most impressive lawyers of her generation. 'She's an imaginative and creative barrister who cuts through detail very quickly,' says Whitehead.

Lyndsey worked as a solicitor until four years ago, when she retrained as a homoeopathist. Carole Caplin gave her a job as resident homoeopathist in her company, LifeSmart, which operates out of Camden Town in north London. Though Lyndsey shared leftwing politics with her sister, she did not share her sister's deeply ingrained Catholicism. In her days at Russell Jones and Walker, she was already immersed in homeopathy and 'New Age' religion. It was in fact Lyndsey, quite as much as Carole, who was responsible for interesting the Blairs in New Age ideas and persuading them to take part in the rituals that have attracted so much derision in the press – though the press has been sold the line that these are practices that Cherie enjoys and that her husband goes along with to indulge her.

Tony and Cherie Blair have become more religious as they have grown older. The *Tablet* is delivered weekly to Downing Street. Cherie is comfortable in the company of *Tablet* people and on friendly terms with both John Wilkins, who retired as editor this year, and his successor Catherine Pepinster. Her husband has always been fascinated by religion. He may not have read the textbooks of the labour movement, but he has read the Bible and the Koran many times and is an eager student of the work of the Catholic theologian Hans Kung.

The Blairs were introduced to spiritualism by Carole Caplin's spiritualist mother, Sylvia. And on holiday in Mexico in 2001, according to the journalist Nick Cohen:

> The Blairs visited a 'temazcal', a steam bath enclosed in a brick pyramid. It was dusk and they had stripped down to their swimming costumes. Inside, they met Nancy Aguilar, a new age therapist. She told them that the pyramid was a Mayan womb in which they would be reborn. The Blairs saw the shapes of animals in the steam and experienced 'inner feelings and visions'. They smeared each other with melon, papaya and mud from the jungle, and then let out a primal scream of purifying agony …

Cohen continues:

> Cherie wears a 'magic pendant' known as the Bio-Electric Shield, which is filled with 'a matrix of specially cut quartz crystals' that surround the wearer with 'a cocoon of energy' and ward off evil forces … Then there have been inflatable Flowron trousers, auricular therapy and acupuncture pins in the ear …

Catholics may purse their lips in disapproval, but Cohen has no sympathy for them. 'If you can believe that wine and a wafer are the body and blood of Christ you can believe anything,' he writes.[11] You do not have to subscribe to Cohen's uncompromising atheism to accept his point that it makes no sense to describe one way of worshipping as respectable and condemn another as superstition. It takes a religious person to experiment with religions.

Beside her interest in New Age ideas, Carole Caplin's views are almost boringly conventional. She advises cutting down on salt, taking a month off alcohol, drinking still and not sparkling water – that sort of thing. She is part of a modern fad for lifestyle coaches and is typical of the breed: clever, self-confident, well dressed, armed with a certainty for every human situation. The articles she writes for her company's website give a reasonable indication of her thinking. One of them praises Italian prime minister Silvio Berlusconi (who invited the Blairs to stay on his Sardinian estate in September 2004) for having had a facelift.

> It looks to me like Silvio's surgeons did a fine job. Not only that, he's also made the effort to lose a stone and a half on a strict exercise and diet regime, which can only be good for his health and mental alertness. Yet any sagging male public figure in Britain who took a few weeks off for a facelift and physical overhaul would never, ever, live down the howls of derision. Forget worrying about bags under the eyes, baggy jowls, double chins and creased foreheads? When it comes to faces, the only attribute we British require of our older men, it seems, continues to be stiff upper lips.

Another article advocates music therapy. A third denies that she took the wife of the Russian premier, Mrs Lyudmila Putin, shopping to choose clothes for her London visit. Mrs Putin's clothes would have been chosen well in advance, she says: 'Spouses of world leaders don't just grab something off a rack on their way to meet the queen.' Anyway, for her clients, 'personal styling almost always comes towards the end, rather than at the beginning, of the transformation process'. In another piece, which looks as though it may have benefited from Cherie Booth's input, she rather startlingly calls for higher pay for midwives.

After Fiona Millar's departure from Downing Street in 2003, she started writing a column in the *Guardian* on health, which offered an opportunity to settle some old scores. In one of her first articles she called for a holistic approach to teenagers, adding, to the titters of those in the know, '... at the risk of sounding like a potty lifestyle guru'.

Millar and Campbell have now left the Blair court, in circumstances to be described in the next chapter, and the Blairs have an uneasy truce with the media. A recent private family problem was kept out of the newspapers after the PCC intervened on their behalf. And the same problem has led to an agreement that will one day be seen as a milestone in the development of the global media. News International proprietor Rupert Murdoch has imposed a worldwide ban on any of his newspapers reporting the matter. Two of Murdoch's foreign titles planned to run detailed articles on the Blairs' family problems. The *Australian* pulled their story after News Corporation's executive chairman, Les Hinton, made a personal call to the deputy editor telling him the tale was off limits. And the *New York Daily Post* withdrew their piece after similar pressure was brought to bear.

As far as is known, no politician has ever achieved such a deal before. Back in 1936, when the British press agreed not to mention the affair being conducted by the Prince of Wales with the divorced American Wallis Simpson, their restraint was mocked when the American papers went to town on it. Today, thanks to the power and reach of the international press barons, political leaders who do business with them can obtain global protection. The deal is thought to have been brokered by Alastair Campbell, who, though he is no longer Blair's press spokesman, still keeps a desk in the Cabinet Office and is believed to be the ambassador of the court of King Tony to the court of King Rupert – and to have sold his own memoirs to Murdoch for £1 million.

The Blairs were not the only members of the Blair court to demand special deals on press treatment from the PCC. In 1998 Peter Mandelson made a similar demand to Guy Black. He was furious that Andrew Pierce, the *Times* assistant editor and diarist, and Amanda Platell, then editor of the *Sunday Express*, were pursuing stories about his partner, Reinaldo da Silva, and he wanted the commission to intervene. In a call that echoed many others to lobby journalists he disliked, he rang up Guy Black to complain.

> I demand that you put a stop to these people pursuing me and my private life. I expect the commission to ban them publishing anything. I am warning you that unless you do this you should be aware that Tony Blair may well bring in new laws on privacy as part of the human rights legislation. We are in a very good position to do this now that the legislation is passing through Parliament.

Black refused, pointing out again that the commission could only act after receiving a complaint about something that had actually been published. Mandelson's threat proved an empty one. He did not get Blair to introduce any legislation to protect himself or his partner from the press. What intrigued the PCC was that Mandelson was prepared to invoke Tony Blair's name in order to try to get his own way in a purely personal matter.[12] We cannot be sure whether Blair knew about this.

CHAPTER FIFTEEN

AMERICA AND IRAQ

The Iraq war was Tony Blair's project. It was not a war into which he was led by his loyalty to George Bush and the US alliance, nor did the advice of the British Foreign Office and his two foreign secretaries play any part in his decision. On this issue, foreign policy was once again taken firmly into the control of the Blair court.

The foreign secretary in Blair's first government, Robin Cook, was never part of the Blair court. Cook was, nonetheless, assured during the 2001 general election that his job was safe. According to our sources, the decision to get rid of him was taken on the afternoon of polling day, 7 June 2001, in Sedgefield, by Blair, Anji Hunter and Alastair Campbell. They wanted to generate a sense of excitement about the new government and felt that in order to do so they would need to change one of the incumbents of the big three jobs: the Treasury, the Home Office or the Foreign Office. Moving Gordon Brown from the Exchequer was out of the question. But both Robin Cook and Home Secretary Jack Straw could be removed without serious political consequences. Straw was shifted to the Foreign Office and Cook was demoted to leader of the House, apparently for 'presentational' reasons.

John Kampfner claims that there were also gentle hints coming from the new US administration under George Bush, elected the previous year, that Cook was not much loved in Washington.[1] Cook's friends say this seems unlikely, as Cook got on well with the Americans, especially Secretary of State Colin Powell, but then Powell himself was not on the best of terms with his president or the neo-conservatives who dominated the administration. On the other hand, Blair may have been anticipating, rather than responding to, neo-conservative sensibilities. One of the mainsprings of the close relationship between Blair and Bush is that both are Christians. Cook is not a religious man. Jack Straw, who got the job, is. And though the 9/11 attacks on New York and Washington were still in the future, Cook's traditional Labour sense of internationalism, which meant putting faith in the United Nations, was already a potential obstacle. One of Bush's main foreign-policy advisers, leading neo-con John Bolton, by now installed with Colin Powell in the State Department, had famously said in 1994: 'There is no such thing as the United Nations. There is only the international community, which can only be led by the only remaining superpower, which is the US.'[2]

Whatever was going on in Blair's head, Cook knew nothing of it until he arrived at 10 Downing Street the day after the election. His first hint that something was amiss was when, in the outer office, Anji Hunter failed to meet his eyes or offer her habitual hug. Straw also had no hint of what was to come; he arrived bearing his strategy for transport, which he thought was going to be his next job.

Straw never had much influence as foreign secretary either – probably even less than Cook, for he is a less forceful politician. All decisions were made by the relevant members of the court: Blair's foreign-affairs adviser Sir David Manning, Jonathan Powell, Alastair Campbell and Anji Hunter. Whenever Straw put anything to his US counterpart Colin Powell, vice-president Dick Cheney would telephone the British embassy to ask: 'What is Blair's view?' Straw's Foreign Office hotline rang only twice during the whole of the Iraq crisis.

Shortly after Straw moved to the Foreign Office, a far more crucial figure joined the court to complete the team that was later to take Britain to war in Iraq. John Scarlett had spent his career in the intelligence services. He had risen to be MI6's station chief in Moscow, expelled when his cover was blown after he was accused of running a spy in the Russian defence ministry. In June, when the post of chairman of the Joint Intelligence Committee (JIC) became vacant, the Foreign Office pressed for it to be filled by one of their own officials, following a long-established precedent. But Blair insisted on the job going to Scarlett, who was a friend of his new foreign-affairs adviser Sir David Manning – and quickly became a 'mate' of Alastair Campbell.[3] The JIC was to be crucial in providing and presenting the evidence upon which Britain went to war in Iraq. On 11 September 2001, Scarlett and Manning had been in their jobs for just a week.

Contrary to widespread opinion, Blair is not simply George Bush's poodle; but it is true that he believes the Anglo-American alliance is, and always should be, the cornerstone of British foreign policy. He is not at heart the good European he needed to appear to be in those long-forgotten days when John Smith led the Labour Party, before the giant of Old

Labour had been entirely slain: he is a deeply committed Atlanticist. The Americans nurtured him from an early stage, identifying him as a key future leader. That is why the younger Blair had the very unusual distinction of going on two paid trips under the American international visitor programme, one in 1986, the other in 1992.

But the left is wrong to suppose he has no influence in Washington. In truth, he has considerable influence, with the Bush White House at least as much as the Clinton White House. It only looks as though he has no influence because, since Bush came to power, Blair has made little attempt to further the causes one would expect to be important to a British prime minister – especially a Labour one. Until his third term, he did not use his influence to try to get President Bush to sign up to the Kyoto agreement. He used it instead to nudge the United States into war and to strengthen the hand of the Washington warmongers.

Recent studies by John Kampfner and Peter Riddell, as well as the testimony of Britain's former ambassador in Washington, Sir Christopher Meyer, show that Blair pressed Clinton into greater intervention in Bosnia and became frustrated with simply policing a no-fly zone over southern Iraq.[4] In Bush, he found a president he could do business with. People wonder at the fact that, after losing his friend Clinton, he so quickly made friends with Bush. In fact, Blair has more in common with Bush than he had with Clinton.

It also seems that Bush needs Blair more than Clinton ever did. Jef McAllister, former Washington correspondent and now London correspondent of *Time* magazine, says the Blair team always had an edge on the Bush team. The Blair team was far smaller, far quicker, far more flexible, and well able to have an important voice in the pace of events. Often, he says, journalists who knew both leaders believed that Blair was articulating Bush's thoughts for him.[5]

During the the 2000 presidential election, Downing Street at first assumed Al Gore was going to win and took little notice of the Bush campaign. But not everyone was so certain; without waiting for instructions from London, Sir Christopher Meyer asked the British embassy's political secretary, Matthew Rycroft (who now works at Number 10 as a foreign-policy adviser), to trail Bush on the stump. Rycroft reported that Bush was brighter than he had been painted and stood a good chance of winning, partly because he responded well to the public. According to Meyer, the Bush we see at press conferences is not the real Bush. Bush loathes the White House press lobby, just as Blair dislikes the parliamentary press lobby. But in private, he said, Bush was effective, articulate, affable and confident.

Meyer also reported that the neo-conservatives were not a cohesive force. There was the interventionist wing under Paul Wolfowitz, which thought it was America's mission to bring the benefits of democracy and capitalism to the Middle East. And there was the school of thought of which Donald Rumsfeld was the key advocate, which saw the role of US foreign policy as cleansing the world of America's enemies. Of course, for many practical purposes the two approaches merge. When Meyer told Downing Streeet all this, Jonathan Powell took little notice – because he and Blair were still convinced of a Gore victory.

But the moment Bush won, Blair decided that he wanted to get as close to him as he had been to Clinton, and he worked hard to do so on his first visit in January 2001. Members of the Blair court who accompanied him included Cherie and Fiona Millar, both of whom had been horrified by the arrival of a Republican from the extreme religious right at the White House. Deep inside Cherie and Fiona, even today, there is an Old Labour core. Cherie, who was, and is, a close friend of Hillary Clinton, felt nothing but dread at the possibility that she might be expected to have the same sort of relationship with the Bush White House. She and Millar urged Blair to keep some distance between himself and Bush. Not for the first time, they misjudged their man.

Meyer took Cherie and Fiona Millar aside to say that it was essential for Blair to get close to the US president and they should not advise otherwise. Both women backed down. But Meyer's intervention was probably unnecessary: there was never any likelihood that Blair would follow their advice.

Blair got closer, faster, to Bush than anyone, even Meyer, supposed possible. There were, no doubt, several reasons for this; but for both leaders, Christianity is a mainspring of their lives and beliefs. As we saw in the previous chapter, Blair has become more and more religious as he grows older, and though he and Bush come from opposite ends of the Christian spectrum, they both believe that Christianity is fundamentally superior to other religions. The difference was that this was an unalloyed electoral advantage for an American politician, but a possible vote-loser for a British one. Clare Short, then international development secretary, recalled for us a discussion with Blair about religious belief guiding people's actions. She was taken aback when Blair said to her: 'Won't people think we are strange, discussing things like this?'

The question was: how was Blair going to use the influence he had so rapidly achieved? And looking at how he used it – and how he did not use it – provides one of the best guides to his own core beliefs and priorities. One thing that he did achieve, in those early days of their relationship, was to persuade Bush to try to make an ally of Russian president Vladimir Putin and to give his blessing to the daily carnage Putin was inflicting on Chechnya.[6]

Blair achieved no concessions over the Kyoto discussions, the comprehensive and legally binding environmental treaty signed by 178 nations – but not by the world's biggest polluter, the United States. He did not stop Bush from torpedoing talks aimed at stopping countries from developing biological weapons. Nor did he prevent Bush from obstructing international efforts to restrict the illegal trade in small arms and light weapons, fatally damaged because the US administration said it could conflict with US citizens' constitutional right to bear arms. Bush, unrestrained by Blair, removed the United States from the treaty establishing an international criminal court, a matter about which, as we have seen, the human rights lawyer Cherie Booth QC felt so strongly that she was later willing to risk embarrassing her husband's government on the eve of a meeting with the president. There is no evidence that Blair made much, or any, effort to influence Bush over any of these matters.

Nor was he any more assertive when British economic interests were directly threatened. He did not use his clout to try to save the British steel industry, though he claimed that he had. The story of what happened when Bush, in defiance of all his own talk about the virtues of free trade, imposed tariffs on foreign steel coming into the US, tells us a good deal about what Tony Blair cares about – and what he does not.

Those close to Blair claim that the prime minister never quarrels in public with the US president. Instead, they say, ferocious debates go on behind the scenes, with Blair punching above his weight and changing American minds. The truth is more complex.

Blair could hardly avoid making some kind of public protest when Bush imposed tariffs on imported steel in 2002, threatening to wreck Britain's already crippled steel industry, and he did indeed do so, both in Parliament and at the Labour Party conference. But on this issue, his government's bark was far worse than its bite. The famous private exchanges did not live up to their billing.

The true story is that Blair failed in private to deliver a silver bullet, supplied courtesy of the British embassy in Washington, that could have caused Bush to make concessions that would have helped the British steel industry. Blair did not even try to make the case for British steel, and he cut the ground from under the feet of his ministers and his embassy when they tried to do so. As a result, jobs were lost in Britain and the tariffs remained in place while the issue was dragged through the World Trade Organisation.

The steel tariffs issue had been brewing since April 2001, when it became clear that Bush's determination to hold on to Republican seats in the mid-term congressional elections in November 2002 meant that he was desperate to offer concessions to key swing-voter states – in this case the old industrial rust belt around West Virginia and the Midwest. In the closely contested presidential election of 2000, the Bush-Cheney team had scored an unexpected victory in West Virginia by promising to support local steelworkers. Republican political strategists now believed that as many as six House seats – exactly the number the Republicans needed to retain control of Congress – hinged on Bush's decision over steel. Blair was warned that this was likely to mean the introduction of tariffs on steel imports.

The US steel industry had been in decline for decades, but its plight worsened after 1997 because of a rise in imports and a steep fall in prices. Around thirty steel manufacturers, mostly older companies such as Bethlehem Steel and LTV Corporation, had already gone bust, with the loss of 20,000 jobs. Foreign competition from Britain, the European Union, South Korea and China was rapidly making inroads into the US market. In 2001 steel imports were worth $25 billion, and the tariffs were aimed at putting prohibitive charges on some $20 billion worth of these imports – wiping out some 80 per cent of the competition.

Britain first raised the issue in Washington in July 2001, when Patricia Hewitt, secretary of state for trade and industry, and Baroness Symons, minister for trade, were there on a three-day visit. This coincided with a campaign launched by Corus, Britain's last major steel producer, who wrote to a hundred MPs after the loss of 6,000 jobs in Wales and Teesside because of the worldwide glut of steel. Sir Ken Jackson, then general secretary of the engineering union AEU, took a delegation to protest to the US embassy in London.

Documents obtained under the US Freedom of Information Act by *Guardian* journalist Rob Evans show that the US was determined to stick by its policy – even though it tried not to upset British sensibilities. A confidential memorandum to Alan Larsen, the US undersecretary of state for economic, business and agricultural affairs, prepared him to defend the plan vigorously at his meeting with Hewitt and Symons on 24 July. He was briefed to tell them that 'contrary to the belief in Europe', the US steel industry was highly efficient and had raised productivity by 300 per cent since 1980. It was being hit by 'massive intervention in the sector by foreign governments' which had been brought about by excess global capacity. The US minutes of the meeting show he was rather more emollient: he tried to play down the effect of the tariffs, blaming the media for highlighting the tariff issue at the expense of other multilateral diplomatic initiatives on steel by Bush.

Patricia Hewitt is recorded in the minutes as emphasising that 'the EU and the UK had, through restructuring, caused its steel industry to become significantly more competitive; the US should now do the same'. British embassy officials thought she would have done better simply to seek help and sympathy from the United States. Nevertheless, Larsen tried to assuage concerns. He promised that an independent investigation would decide whether the US industry had been 'seriously injured by imports'. 'Let's see what they come up with,' he told her.

Two months after the visit came the events of 9/11, but the steel tariffs issue rumbled on uninterrupted. Nothing happened to change US minds. As late as 19 January 2002, Melanie Johnson, parliamentary under-secretary of state at the Department of Trade and Industry, disclosed that Blair himself had not yet raised the issue with Bush – even though he was being pressed to do so by MPs, the unions and the industry. In a parliamentary answer she told Meg Mumm, Labour MP for Sheffield Heeley:

> The prime minister yesterday wrote to Sir Brian Moffatt [chief executive of Corus] to confirm that we take the issue very seriously. We are continuing to press our case at the highest level and he will press the case with President Bush at an appropriate time ... . The problems that are being experienced in the US are largely of its own making and we believe strongly that it should not seek to export those problems to the rest of the world. We will continue to register our strongest opposition to the proposals and I agree that the OECD and multilateral talks about how to deal with the problem on a global basis are the way ahead.

It was only on 5 March 2002, when Bush unilaterally went ahead with the imposition of tariffs, that Downing Street disclosed it had raised the issue with the US president at all. From the government's point of view, the Americans' unwelcome decision was made far worse because of a side issue. An astute researcher to Adam Price, the Plaid Cymru MP, discovered that the prime minister had written a letter to the Romanian government supporting the efforts of a Labour donor, Indian entrepreneur Lakshmi Mittal, to acquire a Romanian steelworks at a knockdown price. The story was undeniable because the Romanians – apparently believing what the West had told them about the virtues of 'open government' – put Blair's letter up on a website.

Blair defended his action by saying that he was backing British business – only to find that Mittal's company, LNM, was registered in the tax haven of the Dutch Antilles and employed fewer than a hundred British citizens. Calling the allegations 'Garbagegate', he claimed the name of the company meant nothing to him and that he had never met Mittal. This defence began to look rather thin when it was revealed that Jonathan Powell had removed from the draft of Blair's letter to the Romanians a reference to Mr Mittal as 'a friend' of Mr Blair. In a Commons debate on 5 March, Adam Price accused Blair of meeting Mr Mittal personally at a dinner for the party's fifteen top donors (Mittal had given Labour £125,000) at the London home of Lord Levy, the party's chief fundraiser, a few weeks before he approved the letter.

But worse was to follow when it was disclosed that Mittal – also a donor to Bush's Republican Party – had spent $600,000 (£422,000) on lobbyists to urge Bush to ignore British and European pressure to drop the tariffs – thus working completely against British interests. Of course, there was one exception: he wanted no tariffs imposed on Mexican steel, because he owned a plant there.

In the light of all this, it was no wonder that Conservative leader Iain Duncan Smith had a field day at PM's questions on 6 March. The exchange is worth recording in detail:

Mr Iain Duncan Smith: Given the wholly unacceptable decision of the United States to impose steel tariffs, will the prime minister stand by his statement of a few weeks ago, when he said of Mr Mittal's firm, LNM: 'I am delighted that a British-based company has succeeded.'

The Prime Minister: Of course, the British government stand by the policy that we have outlined, which is to oppose the tariffs introduced by the United States. They are unacceptable and wrong, and they affect not only Britain but the European Community and other countries throughout the world. In our view, the problems of the American steel industry are best solved by restructuring that industry, not by imposing arbitrary and unjustified tariffs.

Mr Duncan Smith: Well, of course they are, but we have a problem here, because the company that the prime minister celebrated as a British company spent $600,000 on lobbying the United States government to impose tariffs on steel imports. Those tariffs will, of course, affect the United Kingdom steel industry. As one chief executive put it this morning: 'The only measure we have had out of 10 Downing Street on steel is their support for a non-UK steel manufacturer.' It took the prime minister thirty seconds to write a letter supporting a non-British company producing anti-British policies, yet it takes him months to write a letter to the US president to stand up for British interests. Will the prime minister now apologise to the British steelworkers who may lose their jobs?

The Prime Minister: First, in relation to the British steel industry, let us take no lessons from a Conservative party that destroyed 100,000 British steel jobs while in government. Secondly, in relation to the American administration, this matter was first raised by my Right Hon. Friend the Secretary of State for Trade and Industry last July, and it has been raised with the American administration at every level of this government. It is important that, together with other European countries, we now pursue the right remedies through the World Trade Organisation.

Mr Duncan Smith: In case the prime minister has not noticed, he has been in power for almost five years, during which time nearly 400,000 manufacturing jobs have been lost. Ten thousand of those were steel jobs, so we do not need any lectures from him, either. When will he understand that his government's misconduct affects people outside Westminster? What he arrogantly dismissed as 'Garbagegate' some weeks ago will affect the lives and work of thousands of people who look to him for protection. It seems that the only mistake that the steelworkers and the steel industry made was not to give more money to the Labour Party, because we now know that the prime minister always puts the interests of his friends before the interests of the British people.

The Prime Minister: First, let me repeat that this is a decision by the American administration in respect not only of Britain but of imports into the United States from all countries. It is, therefore, absurd to suggest that it is somehow directed only against Britain. In respect of the decision, we have made representations at every level of government and will continue to do so through the European Union.

Downing Street briefed lobby journalists that Blair had taken action on US steel tariffs. A press spokesman said, non-attributably:

Mr Blair has protested both in writing and in speech against Mr Bush's determination to impose up to 30 per cent duties on steel from outside the North American free trade area. Last week he even broke into a transatlantic conversation about whether or not to bomb Iraq to make his point.

The Conservative Party could have made an even better case if they had known what had really been going on between Downing Street and the British embassy in Washington. The embassy had been marshalling their facts about the steel tariffs: they had discovered that many US companies were desperate to retain British imports of specialist steel because they could not get it from US sources. If they had to pay extra tariffs of up to 30 per cent, their own businesses would be at risk – just to save uneconomic steel jobs elsewhere.

But the embassy had a trump card to play. Bush was keen for more British support in Afghanistan. Blair was keen on stabilising the country

– particularly as he had promised the Labour Party conference the previous October: 'We will not walk away from Afghanistan, as the outside world has done so many times before.' Bush was more interested in pursuing Osama bin Laden and widening the war on terror than in nation-building in Afghanistan. But, either way, he wanted more British troops in the country.

While the steel crisis was coming to a head, the question of sending more British troops to Afghanistan was also at the top of the Downing Street agenda. Britain had committed marine commandos and paratroopers the previous December, and, now that the US wanted more help, the Washington embassy suggested that Blair had a unique opportunity to bargain. But he chose not to. A diplomat who saw the plan observed:

> Obviously it would not involve such a crude trade-off, nor be put in such a crude way. But it was perfectly possible to say at a time when the Americans needed our help, that perhaps they could be helpful to us. Blair could easily have explained Britain was in a really difficult position over the steel issue because it would cost British jobs.

But Blair would not even raise the issue; it was left to Patricia Hewitt to do so.

She did, in a diplomatic fashion, link Afghanistan and steel tariffs. Five days before their imposition, she wrote a private letter to Don Evans, the commerce secretary, released under the US Freedom of Information Act. She wrote: 'Unilateral restrictions would be particularly inappropriate at this time of growing international co-operation – notably the global coalition against terror.' But she was squashed on both sides of the Atlantic.

Hewitt was ignored because the White House would not have taken her seriously as a player unless they knew Blair thought the same. One can assume that Cheney would have immediately asked the British embassy the same question he asked when Straw raised a contentious point: 'What is Blair's view?' If Blair was silent on the matter, then the Americans would have known that her pleas could be safely disregarded. And Blair was more than silent on this matter – he went out of his way to tell Bush that he had no intention of using the 'Afghanistan card'. Downing Street said that it would be simplistic and wrong to make connections between events and issues that were totally separate. The two issues were not linked, said a spokesman.

Patricia Hewitt was forced into a U-turn by Downing Street and had to eat her private words in public, telling the Commons on 4 March:

It is important to understand that there is no connection between the action on steel and the global coalition against terrorism. We stand with the Americans and many other countries around the world in the coalition against global terrorism because it is the right thing to do and it is in our interests to do so.

Blair had one last chance to raise the steel issue in the context of Afghanistan, six days after Bush imposed the damaging tariffs, but he again failed to do so. On 11 March Dick Cheney was passing through London and Blair met him for lunch. The records suggest that Blair did not mention the subject of steel. This is all the more remarkable given the great fuss made over tariffs in the Commons a few days earlier, and given that Downing Street spokesmen were regaling lobby journalists with stories of Blair interrupting conversations with Bush on Iraq in order to discuss the issue. Eight days later, on 19 March, Defence Secretary Geoff Hoon gave the US what it wanted – 1,500 more troops for Afghanistan.

Blair had thrown away a good chance of at least saving some steel jobs. In his determination to play the 'world leader' role, he threw away his key bargaining chip. Foreign adventures counted for more than saving traditional smokestack industries.

He then poured cold water on Plan B. If the embassy could not get steel raised in the context of Afghanistan, it had another cunning trick up its sleeve. Britain could negotiate a separate deal with the US to exempt British steel from the prohibitive tariffs. Admittedly, such a move would mean stitching up Britain's European partners – but it would save British jobs and could be sold as one of the advantages of the 'special relationship'.

The idea had already alarmed Pascal Lamy, the EU trade commissioner. He insisted that Britain should stand behind the common EU strategy against the US tariffs, which involved taking the US to the World Trade Organisation for acting illegally. British diplomats knew that this would give Bush the period of grace he needed to safeguard American jobs until after the mid-term elections – and the US could accept an adverse ruling from the WTO a year later. But, in the meantime, competition to US producers from Europe would have been reduced, by plant closures in Britain and the Netherlands.

Blair decided that it was not worth annoying Britain's European partners either, so he ruled out a separate deal. Instead, he opted for Plan C – tortuous negotiations on a case-by-case basis to exempt specialised types of steel from the ban. This was the least effective option, so it was combined with a spin operation to convince the public, backbench MPs and the unions and manufacturers that Blair meant business. In this, it was largely successful. MPs from steel towns, the steel industry, and the steel union ISTC seem to have been convinced by the selective information they were fed that Blair was standing up for their interests.

As early as 10 April he told MPs, after meeting Bush at Crawford, Texas, that he condemned the tariffs. Questioned by Helen Jackson, MP for Sheffield Hillsborough, he said:

> The action that the United States has taken – against many countries, obviously – is now the subject of European Union action under the World Trade Organisation. I made it absolutely clear that we fundamentally disagree with the United States' decision, which is not good for anyone, including the US steel industry. The action undertaken by the WTO is important. If the WTO finds against the United States, I hope that it will abide by that ruling. The more free trade there is, and the fewer restrictions on trade, the better.

Ms Jackson says, in retrospect:

> As chair of the steel group we had meetings with Patricia Hewitt, meetings with Pascal Lamy, meetings with the US embassy. We raised it with Tony in Prime Minister's Questions because there was a heightened awareness of US/UK relations because of the build-up to war. He was very susceptible.
>
> Informally it was raised with Tony at the Parliamentary Labour Party meeting. We were able to push it there. He [Blair] certainly was [bringing it up with Bush] and I believe he did. Tony took the point and did raise it. It was a combined parliamentary effort.

Denis Macshane, then a junior Foreign Office minister and now minister for Europe, who represents the steel town of Rotherham in Parliament, believes his appeal to Blair convinced the prime minister of the need to raise the tariff question with Bush: 'I remember taking a delegation of steel MPs to his room in the Commons. They were all able to make their case and Tony listened to them.'

Ken Penton, head of communications at ISTC, the main steel union, was also satisfied, as the union had been consulted before the tariffs were imposed.

> We had meetings with the DTI, the Treasury and Number 10. It was something the prime minister took very seriously. It was only us, the prime minister and two other people in the room. This is the one issue on which the UK, from the prime minister down, took on the US. We were very pleased with the prime minister and Patricia Hewitt.

Diplomats attending the Blair–Bush Crawford summit in Texas – better known for the crucial talks on whether the US and Britain should invade Iraq – do not know whether Blair ever raised the issue with Bush, because there is no private, let alone public, record of their talks. When they did talk for a whole afternoon and evening, nobody else was present – not even Sir David Manning, Downing Street's foreign-policy adviser; all the advisers were sent off for a meal in a restaurant in Waco. So both Blair and Bush can claim the matter was raised – but only they can ever know the truth.

The only thing that reached the rest of the British contingent in their Waco restaurant was the offer of custom-made cowboy boots embossed with the Lone Star of Texas and the Union Jack, made by the personal bootmaker of Bush's adviser, Karl Rove. No one could accept the boots as a gift because of civil service rules, but Sir Christopher Meyer ordered a pair and was measured up for them on the spot.

The scale of the concessions negotiated between the US and Britain became apparent in July. It was not impressive. Papers prepared for Don Evans, the US commerce secretary, for a meeting with Patricia Hewitt in Washington on 31 July show how complex the negotiations had become. The meeting followed the closure of two steel plants run by Allied Steel and Wire with a loss of 1,000 jobs in Sheerness and Cardiff. These closures were directly attributable to the US tariffs.

The US documents show that Britain was more adversely affected than either Germany or France, since it exported 15 per cent of its steel to the US, compared with 7 per cent each for the other two countries. Each exclusion from the tariffs was for a specified tonnage of a particular product and, by July, the papers show that the British had been granted 88 exclusions out of a total of 498 exclusions conceded by the US – a higher number than had been given to either Germany or France. After 5 March, Patricia Hewitt had sent a list of 67 products for which she requested exclusions. Of these just 18 were granted, which sounds like a modest but significant success for the British. But – and it is a very big but – Hewitt's wish list of 67 exclusions mounted up to a total of 1,075,712 metric tonnes; the 18 exclusions granted covered just 7,592 tonnes.

The documents also make it clear that the negotiations were mired in considerable muddle and confusion. One application submitted on the Hewitt list related to a product that had already been excluded before 5 March; another was, in fact, a German exclusion request made on behalf of Saarstahl. Another company seeking exemption, Bromford Iron and Steel, did not exist – the US reclassified it as Bedford Steel. Yet other lists were submitted too late to be considered.

A telling paragraph in the US briefing documents records why the initiative was not a great success.

This has been a difficult and technical process requiring the analysis of an enormous amount of information about US consumer product needs and US production capabilities. The president's position is that no exclusion should be granted if it would undermine the steel safeguard. Accordingly each exclusion request has to be judged by this standard.

On 30 September Hewitt made another strong speech criticising the US, to the Labour Party conference:

We are internationalists – and we uphold international law. That's why we stand with our steelworkers and steel industry against the illegal tariffs imposed by the United States. With the ISTC and our steel communities and MPs, Liz Symons and I have made sure that 70 per cent of British steel is exempt from those tariffs. With our European partners, we are challenging those unjust tariffs in the WTO – and I have no doubt at all, conference, that we will win ...

But the figure of 70 per cent is not reflected in US documents and appears to be highly misleading – it may reflect the percentage of the requests for exclusions which had been granted by the US government, not the quantities of steel exported to the US.

It took over a year and the loss of another 1,150 jobs – this time at Corus – before the WTO ruled that the tariffs were illegal and Bush was forced to lift them. Hewitt told Tory MP Henry Bellingham on 16 December 2003:

UK steel exports to the US fell by 14 per cent in 2002 compared with the figure for 2001. The negative consequences of the US decision for the UK steel industry were reduced by our success in securing exclusions for UK products from the US safeguard measure. At the point when the safeguard was lifted, 74 per cent of UK steel exports to the US were free of safeguard tariffs. The government also supported the EU steel safeguard, which prevented any surge into the EU of steel from third countries diverted from the US market.

On 19 November, after the WTO had ruled the tariffs illegal but before they were lifted, Blair told Ashok Kumar, Labour MP for Middlesbrough South:

I will raise this issue with President Bush. Of course from time to time such trade issues come up in the relationship between Europe and America – I remember they did under the previous President of the United States as well – but let us not forget that in commercial and trading terms it is still an enormously important relationship for our two countries.

I just point out that, according to the latest figures, about one million people in Britain are employed by American firms. So it is a very good two-way deal, but we want it to become a perfect one. Obviously, it is in our interests, and we will argue very strongly for the WTO ruling to be obeyed.

Politically, Bush did well all round. He managed to hold onto most of the US rust belt in the mid-term elections – which was the main reason for imposing the tariffs. He did not have to give many concessions to his friend Tony Blair, and the prime minister was helpful in not pressing the issue at a time when the US needed British support in Afghanistan. Those who believed Blair had been tough in advancing British interests had simply been conned. And another 2,000 British steel jobs were lost in a highly competitive world market, while the so-called world leader on free trade was able to subsidise its own uncompetitive backyard.

On the morning of 11 September 2001, when the news of the dreadful events of that day began to come through, Tony Blair was in his room at the Grand Hotel in Brighton – the same hotel that the IRA had blown up during the Conservative Party conference in 1984, killing five people and injuring more than thirty. He was preparing to do one of the things he does best and seems to enjoy most – reducing the trade unions to impotent fury. His speech to the TUC that afternoon was to be a combative defence of the Private Finance Initiative.

The speech, of course, was never made. Blair made a brief, dignified statement to the TUC and then went straight to Downing Street to deal with the most serious international crisis to arise in years. It was not until the next day that he managed to speak to Bush, who was, Blair feared, not in complete control of events. He said he assumed Bush was considering an immediate military response. Bush said he was not going to 'pound sand with millions of dollars in weapons' just to make himself feel good.[7]

The strategy that emerged in the next few days was essentially Blair's. The Taliban rulers of Afghanistan were given an ultimatum to hand over Osama bin Laden and shut down his training camps or face a war. Both Iran and Pakistan, a military dictatorship and the Taliban's main ally, should be made into allies. Russia should be brought on side. Putin should be offered sweeteners: Blair and Bush would classify Russia's war in Chechnya as part of what was to become the 'war on terror' and give them a consultative role in NATO. A new effort should be made in the Middle East peace process.

Blair travelled the world to try to deliver these objectives, and less than a month after 9/11, British and American forces were in action in

Afghanistan. Kabul fell on 13 November, and in January 2002 the first of hundreds of chained and hooded people were herded onto a US cargo jet and flown to Guantánamo Bay. As we write, more than three years later, we are little nearer knowing what crimes they are suspected of committing, what evidence there is that they ever committed them, what methods have been used to humiliate them and extract confessions from them, or when, if ever, they will be released. We do know that some of them are British citizens, and that even their own prime minister does not seem particularly concerned about whether they will ever receive justice. His wife, the leading human rights lawyer, does care about these things, but she, as we saw in the last chapter, has been silenced.

Towards the end of that month, on 30 January 2002, in the first state of the union address after 9/11, Bush said that Iraq was part of an 'axis of evil'. Blair had always refused to rule out the possibility that the 'war on terror' might be widened to include other countries. But going to war in Iraq seemed to most people to be a distant nightmare. Most Labour MPs assumed that, if such a thing were ever contemplated, it would only be with the support of the United Nations.

As late as 23 July 2002, the prime minister chaired a meeting on foreign and defence policy at which it was noted that 'Iraqi capabilities were smaller in scale than those of other states of concern'.[8] Thus, months before the war in Iraq, Blair knew that the weapons of mass destruction (WMD) allegedly possessed by Iraq, his main justification for going to war, were certainly far less extensive and dangerous than those possessed by Libya or North Korea. North Korea was known to be close to having a nuclear bomb and was thought to be developing missiles capable of launching nuclear strikes on the US and Europe. And the country is also a prolific arms exporter, selling weapons to anyone who can afford them.

An even bigger danger was Pakistan, one of Britain and America's chief allies in the 'war on terror'. The threat which Bush and Blair most often talked up – that of WMD falling into the hands of religious fanatics – was most likely, and is still most likely, to be realised there. Pakistan is a military dictatorship with nuclear capability, under pressure from many of its own people because of its government's support for the West. Prior to 11 September it was the Taliban's biggest ally, and much of the northwest region of the country is controlled by Muslim fundamentalists who still support the Taliban and their ideology.

Nonetheless, it became increasingly clear as the year progressed that the American president and his advisers were set on a policy of 'regime change' in Iraq and that, in their minds, far from being a last resort, a full-scale war was the favoured means of achieving it.

Saddam Hussein, in response to the threat of war, invited the chief United Nations weapons inspector to Baghdad. On 7 September 2002 Blair met Bush at Camp David, where the press was told that he 'championed the role of the United Nations'. As often happens with Blair, the public report of the meeting bore little relation to what actually happened. Bob Woodward's authoritative book, *Plan of Attack*, claims that Blair looked Bush in the eye and said: 'I'm with you.' Blair was, claims Woodward, 'pledging flat out to commit British military force if necessary, the critical promise Bush had been seeking'.[9]

At the end of the month, Blair published the first of Downing Street's 'dossiers'. This document claimed that Iraq would be able to produce a nuclear weapon within one or two years if it obtained fissile material and other components from abroad and, most notoriously, that Iraq had chemical and biological weapons that could be ready for launch within forty-five minutes. UN negotiators and an Iraqi delegation met in Vienna to agree terms for resuming weapons inspections. In November the UN security council voted unanimously to back a US-British resolution requiring Iraq to reinstate weapons inspectors after a four-year absence. Saddam Hussein wrote to Kofi Annan, the UN secretary-general, accepting this, and the inspectors returned to recommence their search for WMD.

On 2 December, the British government published a dossier documenting human rights abuses in Iraq, which was attacked by Amnesty International for being 'opportunistic and selective'. Critics said it used longstanding evidence of human rights abuses to justify current military goals, ignoring US and British support for Saddam at the time of some of the worst atrocities. Soon afterwards it emerged that the Reagan administration and its special Middle East envoy, Donald Rumsfeld, now Bush's defense secretary, did little to stop Iraq developing weapons of mass destruction in the 1980s, even though they knew Saddam Hussein was using chemical weapons almost daily against Iran.

The following day, UN weapons inspectors sprung a surprise search on one of Saddam Hussein's Baghdad palaces – and the Iraqis co-operated fully. On 7 December, Iraqi officials in Baghdad presented the UN with a 12,000-page dossier disclosing Iraq's programmes for weapons of mass destruction, as demanded by UN resolution 1441. An initial evaluation was published by John Scarlett's Joint Intelligence Committee on 18 December, and Jack Straw was sent before television cameras to rubbish the Iraqi document. But, as the Butler Report later pointed out: 'Despite [the dossier's] importance to the determination of whether Iraq was in further material breach of its disarmament obligations under United

Nations Security Council Resolution 1441, the JIC made no further assessment.' Why, when so much had been made of the importance of Saddam's declaration, did the government not wish to analyse the document fully?

As the inspection team under Hans Blix continued to draw a blank throughout the months of January and February 2003, Bush and Blair ratcheted up the pressure to go to war. The Butler Inquiry team subsequently recorded their 'surprise that policy-makers and the intelligence community did not, as the generally negative results of UNMOVIC inspections became increasingly apparent, re-evaluate in early 2003 the quality of intelligence'.

For Tony Blair, there was one over-riding policy objective in those months: to get Britain into the coming war with Iraq alongside the US. It was now clear that, without a second UN resolution, this would cause enormous political turmoil, and he asked for Bush's co-operation in trying to get one.[10] In an effort to allay widespread misgivings in Britain, Downing Street released a second dossier on Iraq's WMD. Whatever support this may have gained for the government's policy quickly evaporated when it emerged that the document consisted, in large part, of an old PhD thesis downloaded from the internet and judiciously edited by mid-level officials in Alastair Campbell's office, or, in the case of some passages, reprinted word-for-word (which is what gave the game away). Even Jack Straw was soon forced to admit that it was a 'dodgy dossier'. Nor did it help when Hans Blix listed examples of Iraqi compliance with resolution 1441 to the UN security council and questioned the US intelligence on Iraqi munitions that Colin Powell had presented to the UN earlier in the month. A million anti-war protesters took to the streets in London on 15 February.

Nonetheless, there was a final attempt by Bush and Blair to obtain a second UN resolution. Their efforts had to be abandoned when the foreign ministers of France, Russia and Germany released a joint declaration that they would 'not allow' a resolution authorising military action to pass the UN security council. Meanwhile, Blair faced the biggest parliamentary revolt against a British governing party in more than a century: 121 Labour MPs voted against going to war on Iraq.

By early March, Bush was telling the American people that war was 'very close', while Blix was advising the UN that his work was not yet done and he could not say that Iraq had failed to co-operate. In Britain the intelligence reports that underpinned Blair's policy were unravelling, though this was kept from the public. In early March 2002, advice on Iraq given to key government ministers stated that 'Iraq continues to develop weapons of mass destruction, although *our intelligence is poor* [our italics]'.

Exactly how poor was not to become clear until the publication of the Butler Report in July 2004. Lord Butler found that the Secret Intelligence Service (SIS) had just five main sources in Iraq. Following the end of the war, the service's 'validation' of its sources revealed that only two had been reliable. The first, although accurate on some issues, had no first-hand knowledge of chemical and biological weapons. Instead, he reported what he learned from others in his 'circle of high-level contacts'. The second, though deemed reliable, often used a sub-source with links to opposition groups. Butler reported:

> post-war validation by SIS has raised serious doubts about the reli-
> ability of reporting from this new sub-source. We conclude that
> this stream of reporting that underpinned JIC assessments on Iraqi
> production and possession of chemical and biological weapons
> must be open to serious doubt.

A third main source provided 'significant assurance to those drafting the government's dossier that active, current production of chemical and biological agent was taking place'. However, in July 2003, the SIS withdrew the reports, deeming them unreliable.

Not a single source claiming that Saddam had a growing and danger-ous programme of weapons of mass destruction could be relied upon, it turned out. As to the claim that such weapons could fall into the hands of terrorists intent on attacking the West, Butler stated that the advice which the prime minister received in March 2002 'noted the judgement of the JIC that there was no recent evidence of Iraqi complicity with international terrorism, and thus no justification for action against Iraq based on action in self-defence to combat imminent threats of terrorism'.

Butler, of course, had the advantage of hindsight, but if the govern-ment ever made any serious effort to objectively assess the evidence avail-able to it, it would have had to accept that it was, at best, thin and inconclusive. It seems more likely, however, that no such effort was made and that most ministers chose to believe what Tony Blair wanted them to believe – including, apparently, Jack Straw, who proposed that the UN should set an ultimatum: Iraq would be invaded unless the country demonstrated 'full, unconditional, immediate and active compliance' with UN weapons inspectors by 17 March. The French made it clear they would veto such a resolution. Bush telephoned Blair and offered him a get-out clause if the resolution failed. He would, he said, understand if Blair couldn't commit troops. Three times during the course of the conversation, Blair politely declined the lifeboat on offer. 'I'm with you,' he said. 'I'm there to the very end.'

War was now very close. With China, France and Russia opposed to an attack, the US and Britain had to abandon any hope of gaining UN security council support for a second resolution authorising war on Iraq. They withdrew the resolution, blaming the French.

Former foreign secretary Robin Cook, now leader of the House, resigned in protest at the government's decision to back a war with neither 'international authority nor domestic support'. By this time, there were only two rebels left in the cabinet: Cook and Clare Short, the international development secretary. Earlier on, there had been many more. When the war was first mooted, says one cabinet minister, 'Most of us were against the war. Blair did not sum up; he started to put us right.' But apart from Cook and Short, the rest of the rebels had fallen into line by now. Short was expected to resign when Cook did but failed to do so, which fatally weakened their case. It is at least arguable that, had she come out with Cook, they could have made the war politically impossible for Blair.

At the time, there was much speculation about how Blair had handled Short. It turns out that she went to Blair to ask whether Chirac might agree to an invasion if Saddam was given a little more time to comply and still failed to do so. In such circumstances, with a short delay, it might be possible for UN approval to be obtained. Blair said that the French would never agree, ever. It was only after Short saw the actual text of the French statement that she realised the French might have agreed after another forty-five days. She felt she had been conned and now bitterly regrets failing to resign straightaway. By delaying her resignation, after she had threatened it, she fatally damaged her credibility.

On 18 March 2003, in a televised address, Bush gave Saddam Hussein forty-eight hours to leave Iraq or face invasion. Two more junior British ministers resigned, and after a parliamentary debate, the number of rebel Labour MPs voting for an anti-war amendment rose to 139. The war began two days later. After just three weeks of fighting, on 9 April US marines helped crowds to topple a giant statue of Saddam in the heart of Baghdad. Iraq had been successfully liberated. Before long, widespread looting broke out unhindered in the capital. At the time of writing, seventeen months later, what is happening in Iraq is a lot worse than looting.

Iraq was defeated and in ruins, but it was not at peace, and is still not at peace. Despite the best efforts of the specialist teams who had been sent to find them, and who now had the run of the country, no weapons of mass destruction had been found. The public started to suspect they had not been told the truth. A diversion was required. Blair turned his attention to one of the many enemies within: the BBC.

The great battle between Blair and the BBC had its roots several years before the Iraq war, in the era of Greg Dyke's predecessor as BBC director-general, John Birt, appointed under the Conservative government in 1992. Both Birt and the then chairman Marmaduke Hussey, who had been appointed after a single telephone call from Downing Street asking him whether he would like the job, considered the BBC they inherited to be wasteful, badly managed and complacent.

Hussey's former employer, Rupert Murdoch, is a key player in the government's battle with the BBC. Clipping the wings of the Corporation is very much in Murdoch's commercial interests, and his papers actively campaign for it. There is more than a suspicion that the row with the BBC was connected with Murdoch's longstanding support of Blair.

The courtship between Murdoch's papers and Blair goes right back to a *Sunday Times* article of 1992 about the 'leader Labour missed', which suggested that Labour would have done better to choose Blair rather than John Smith as its leader. Certainly we know that Blair was very careful to ensure Murdoch always understood that they were political soulmates. Chris Smith, Blair's first culture secretary, used to receive a briefing via telephone from Anji Hunter just before he was due to set out to attend Murdoch's annual summer party in his sumptuous apartments overlooking St James's Park. The gathering always attracts leading political figures. Lady Thatcher is a regular attender. So are Mandelson, Campbell and Hunter. Blair himself took care not to attend; any meeting he had with Murdoch needed to be at a more private occasion, where it would not leak into the gossip columns.

Anji Hunter never asked Chris Smith to make specific promises to Murdoch. Rather, it was a question of Downing Street telling him to create the right mood music. 'Tell him we are keen on deregulation and pro-market, don't be specific' would be the sense of Hunter's advice. Blair obviously did not want his independent-minded culture secretary to rock the boat by being too pro-BBC and didn't quite trust him to attend without a quiet briefing from his own close confidante. He need not have worried: Chris Smith never hung around for too long at Murdoch's parties. The sight of Margaret Thatcher was enough for him to make polite excuses and go home early.

Even so, Downing Street was not always on Murdoch's side. One of the most controversial issues to affect BSkyB was a potential decision by the BBC to offer to give its News 24 service free of charge to cable

channels. The BBC saw this as a good way to extend their viewing figures and get their round-the-clock news service better known. BSkyB
saw it as a commercial threat that would damage their subscription service and were outraged to think it was being financed by the licence fee.

The phone lines to Chris Smith's office soon became red-hot. News
International's Sam Chisholm was deputed to lobby Smith and persuade
him to intervene to block the BBC. But Smith thought the BBC's plan
was a good one, and would not be moved. Chisholm became enraged,
and the quietly spoken culture secretary was reduced to holding the
phone at arm's length as Chisholm shouted obscenities into the receiver.
Then Smith got a telephone call from Downing Street. It was James
Purnell – a man close to the BBC's director-general, John Birt – who had
responsibility for media in the policy unit. He is now minister for creative
industries and tourism. Smith was expecting the worst, because it was
clear that Chisholm had tried to lobby Downing Street. But Purnell was
not about to take the obvious line. 'It's your decision, you don't have to
take any notice of aggressive lobbying,' he said. The BBC got their way
and News 24 was made available to cable TV.

John Birt began his reign at the BBC by giving a speech to its employees
about the aspects of the organisation that needed to change. Many staff
members agreed with him. The trouble was, as Anthony Rendell, then a
senior BBC executive, puts it:

> He was the Man with the Plan. It was not enough that he had vision;
> others must be charged with blindness. This attitude killed off the
> modest reform movements which had been trying their best. It was as
> dangerous to have been a premature Birtist as an anti-Birtist. Revolu-
> tionary dictatorships normally kill off the moderate reformers. Not sur-
> prisingly, his distrust created mulish resentment, but he seems to have
> taken hostility as proof of his rightness.
>
> During his time at the top of the BBC, the management fashion was
> for the CEO-as-hero, the Man with the Plan, re-engineering the corpo-
> ration, transformation, revolutionary entrepreneurship, and all the rest.
> Management consultants arrived by the lorry-load.
>
> The BBC was deliberately de-skilled through outsourcing. In line
> with its privatisation philosophy, the [Blair] government required the
> BBC's transmission service to be sold off ... There was a period in the
> World Service when half a dozen senior producers had to go, crossing at
> the door with half a dozen new recruits, all business managers. When
> staff learnt that the BBC was no longer loyal to them, they withdrew
> their loyalty to management, while remaining loyal to their concept of
> the organisation's purpose.[11]

Blair heartily approved of all this. Never having managed anything in his life, he has an instinctive awe of private-sector managerialism. Birt's autobiography makes it clear how close he and the new prime minister became. When he first met Blair, they took to one another at once. 'I felt comfortable with Cherie too, for we were of the same stock,' he writes; like Cherie, Birt was born into a working-class Liverpool family.[12] The guest list at Birt's fiftieth birthday read like a roll call of the New Labour establishment: the Blairs, Scottish TV executive Gus Macdonald, Greg Dyke, Peter Mandelson, Polly Toynbee and cabinet secretary Robin Butler, among others.

Even as leader of the opposition Blair played a crucial role in supporting Birt. In 1996, after Hussey's resignation as chairman, Birt and the Conservative minister Virginia Bottomley wanted to appoint Sir Christopher Bland as the new BBC chairman. But they needed the opposition's agreement: with a Labour victory at the polls expected the next year, the appointment had to appear politically bipartisan. Bottomley, says Birt, 'telephoned me to ask me to do all I could to get the Labour leadership to accept it'. So Birt talked to Blair, and Blair fixed it for him. Birt was Blair's man even before Blair was prime minister.

Birt writes about how well his ideas matched those of Blair. They agreed about 'the value of markets and wealth creation and sound money, yet at the same time wholeheartedly valued effective public services too, run for the benefit of the citizenry and not for those who worked in them ...'. And: 'Once or twice over the years he had turned to me for personal guidance.'

To many Old Labour people, Birt's managerialism was not at all what public service broadcasting should be about. But Birt knew he had Blair's support: 'For many in New Labour, the reformed BBC was a model of a modern, well-run, efficient world-beater, devoted to public services.' Birt was delighted when his key aide James Purnell went to work for Blair in Downing Street: 'His appointment was a sign of the new political realities.' It worked the other way as well: Peter Mandelson was a key adviser to Birt.

When Birt left, Blair spoke at his farewell party: 'Your reforms at the BBC stand out as one of the success stories of public service reform of recent years.' Then, in 2001, Blair made Birt his personal strategy adviser. He gave him an office at 70 Whitehall, approached by an expensively refurbished spiral staircase which, civil servants said, Birt loved to use to avoid having to mix with the *hoi polloi*. 'Looking at Birt,' says Anthony Rendell, 'is one way of looking at some aspects of Blair,' adding that during his tenure, 'The BBC and the political parties

were much closer than normal. Birt did what Blair applauded and presumably wanted others to do – and Blair could easily have thought this
was real modernisation.'

So Blair had little trouble with the BBC in Birt's day. 'Birt was very
close to New Labour,' says Nicholas Jones, who had by now moved on
from being the BBC's industrial correspondent to being its political correspondent. Jones himself was deeply distrusted by New Labour; Peter
Mandelson once mused publicly about whether Jones was mad. Alastair
Campbell openly called him 'a nutter' and constantly complained that
Jones exposed Campbell's work to the public gaze in his books. Jones's
books, still the best detailed exposition of the New Labour spin machine,
angered both Campbell and Blair. Campbell besieged the BBC with letters demanding to know why a public service organisation was paying
Jones to write books. However, the BBC was not paying him to do so:
Jones, anticipating the line Downing Street might take, was always
scrupulous about taking unpaid, not paid, leave to write them.[13]

None of this mollified the Blair spin machine. During the 1997 general election campaign, Jones roused Blair's ire by reporting an industrial
dispute involving the Essex fire brigade. Campbell shrieked at him: 'So
that's the story, then, a trade union dispute. I just love the way you guys
in the BBC decide what the issue is.'[14]

Later, Blair and Campbell may have found a quicker way of getting
the media to deal with striking firefighters. At the height of another fire
dispute, a sex scandal involving Andy Gilchrist, general secretary of the
firefighters' union, was reported in the tabloids. As it happened, he was
due to meet the deputy prime minister later that day. When they met,
John Prescott said: 'I'm sorry about all that stuff in the papers, Andy.' The
embarrassed Gilchrist started to mutter something about it not being
Prescott's fault, but the deputy prime minister persisted. 'No, Andy, I
want to tell you that I'm sorry.' And they looked at each other for a
moment – perhaps one day we will know what both men were thinking.

One of Jones's crimes, in the view of Blair and Campbell, was to keep
drawing attention on air to the government's habit of leaking its most
important news to Rupert Murdoch's *Sun* instead of telling Parliament. In
2000, after one such leak, Jones mentioned the matter on the BBC's
Breakfast News – and then had to brave Alastair Campbell at the morning
press briefing. As the correspondents stood up to leave the briefing,
Campbell pointed a finger at Jones and shouted out, catching everyone's
attention: 'Hey, I was watching you this morning with one of my kids
and he said to me, "Dad, that bloke is obsessed with you." Even my son
can spot a nutter.'

With Blair's friend Birt as his ultimate boss, Jones had to watch his back. When, at a press conference, he asked chief whip Hilary Armstrong a question about New Labour's relationship with lobbyists, a complaint went straight to Birt. Birt immediately set up a full-scale BBC investigation and had an aide ring round all the other journalists at the press conference to inquire about Jones's behaviour. When another New Labour minister, Harriet Harman, complained about Jones filming outside her home, Birt instructed Jones to write a letter of apology to Harman. The letter was immediately leaked to the newspapers, Peter Mandelson saying this was legitimate because Jones had not put 'confidential' on it.

Blair was in a powerful position to intimidate Jones while Birt was in charge, and Jones's persistence is the hallmark of a courageous journalist dedicated to telling the truth. When Jones quoted Roy Hattersley's criticism of Labour's spin machine, Birt's admonition was relayed to him by his direct boss, chief political correspondent John Sergeant: 'Nick, you have been told before: your job as a BBC correspondent isn't to antagonise Alastair Campbell.'[15]

After Birt, Blair wanted a new director-general with whom he could have the same sort of relationship. He thought he had found the right man. He was accused, with some justice, of cronyism when he appointed his friends and New Labour sympathisers Greg Dyke and Gavyn Davies as, respectively, director-general and chairman of the Corporation. But Birt knew better than Blair the nature of his successor. One of his colleagues, Will Wyatt, tried to scupper the appointment by leaking to a newspaper a letter showing that Dyke had contributed funds to the Labour Party and was therefore not neutral.[16]

Birt's fears were fulfilled: Dyke went native. With a background in broadcasting news, he thought the BBC news programmes ought to be competing to break the best stories first, regardless of whom they offended. Investigative journalists like Jones found they had much more room to manoeuvre. Dyke, says Jones, 'gave BBC journalists a degree of freedom which had been lacking under John Birt'.

Each individual programme was also allowed to pursue stories independently of the main news operation. This is why, later on, Andrew Gilligan of *Today* and Susan Watts of *Newsnight* could find themselves chasing the same story about weapons of mass destruction in Iraq, using the same contacts, unaware of each other's activities – and, as it turned out, reaching very different conclusions about the information they were obtaining.

Richard Sambrook, the director of news, later told the Hutton Inquiry that Gilligan had become 'a particular sort of journalist' who uncovered 'stories that cause the government discomfort'. Gavyn Davies said Gilligan's style was to report in 'primary colours of bold colours rather than shades of grey'.

For the first time, Blair found the BBC intransigent. He started to threaten. The BBC was not like the Murdoch press: Murdoch could and would do what he pleased, whether the government liked it or not. But the government sets the level of the BBC licence fee, and Blair was not above suggesting that the BBC should remember that when it weighed up whether it was going to broadcast stories which might be unwelcome to government.

In November 2001, two months after the destruction of the World Trade Centre, when British troops were fighting in Afghanistan, the first shots were fired in another conflict closer to home. Alastair Campbell wrote a sixteen-page letter to the BBC's head of news, Richard Sambrook, complaining about the way the Corporation was reporting the war. He wanted to know 'when those covering the story post-September 11 had their specific attention drawn to the BBC's guidelines, and how they might relate to the coverage'. He knew, he said, that BBC policy was to refer difficult questions to heads of department, but he wanted to know how often had this happened. 'Who is responsible for the issuing of advice and guidance? I have been informed that nothing has been referred up beyond programme editor. Is this so?'

Campbell's particular target was the BBC's war reporter Rageh Omar, who was ranging free in Afghanistan, at considerable personal risk, to bring such news as he could get to the BBC. Campbell had already complained verbally about Omar and is said to have told a BBC executive: 'You've got to get Rageh Omar off television, he's gone native.' Now he put his antagonism in writing. Omar incurred Downing Street's wrath by reporting the human suffering caused by Allied bombing. BBC guidelines stated that correspondents are not allowed to give personal opinions, and therefore, said Campbell, Omar should not have been permitted to end one report with the words: 'The next generation of Afghans are now having to cope with the waste of another conflict.' Omar, reporting from a country which had been more or less permanently at war for decades, might have replied (if he could have spared the time between dodging bullets) that this was a straightforward statement of fact.

'I felt his report to be as pure a piece of Taliban propaganda as the Taliban and the terrorists they harbour could have wished,' wrote Campbell. He added the dreadfully serious – and entirely false – charge that Omar was knowingly broadcasting what the Taliban wanted him to broadcast in the hope of getting further access to information from them.

Defence correspondent Andrew Gilligan was the other major target of Campbell's ire. Asked on air whether neighbouring nations would fall into line with the coalition, he had said: 'I'd say Oman and Uzbeck will fall into line, after extracting massive concessions, a blind eye being cast on their immense human rights abuses.' This had obviously made Campbell incandescent. In fact, Gilligan's statement and prediction were accurate in every respect. In 2003 the US gave Uzbeck $500 million in aid, including $79 million to its police and intelligence services. These services, according to the US State Department, 'use torture as a routine investigation technique'.

Campbell went on at great length about the supposedly uncritical reporting of Taliban war claims. He ended: 'These are serious questions and I look forward to a serious, detailed response.'

Campbell appended to his letter what he called a 'catalogue of lies'. He cited twenty-three separate BBC reports: not one of them was inaccurate. Mostly they were instances in which the BBC had reported a Taliban claim that Campbell asserted to be untrue. But all the BBC reported was that these were Taliban claims. To call this a 'catalogue of lies' can only have been an attempt to intimidate by hyperbole.

Richard Sambrook's reply took up eleven pages. 'I do not recognise the description of our journalism that you provide,' he wrote. 'The BBC at all levels, including the Board of Governors, is proud of our coverage of this crisis.' He rebutted the charge of 'moral equivalence' between British and Taliban claims and the charge that he had claimed the BBC could do no wrong. He provided examples of reporting to back this up.

He wrote: 'As part of your general view that we have been "soft" on the Taliban you question the BBC's behaviour at the various Taliban news conferences held in Pakistan. Perhaps you are unaware that CNN carried some of these events "live" whereas we preferred first in each case to assess the material.' But, he went on, he had to insist that 'the Taliban claims are part of the story'. Sambrook refuted in detail Campbell's attacks on Rageh Omar, Andrew Gilligan and Fergal Keane. 'The BBC's independence and impartiality is under even greater scrutiny at times of war. I have to say that I do not believe a detailed critique from the government is helpful in preserving that independence,' he added.

But it was the Iraq war in 2003 that brought the simmering dispute to a head. On 19 March a five-page letter from Campbell to the BBC listed several bitter complaints. John Humphrys had asked impertinent questions of war office minister Mike O'Brien: 'We are all well used to the contempt Mr Humphrys displays to elected politicians (unless they are "rebels"),' wrote Campbell; and that was not all. Reporter Tom Carver had been unforgivably unimpressed by British manoeuvrings at the United Nations. Andrew Gilligan, the old offender, had said, 'Innocent people will die here in the next few hours.' (They did.) And the other recidivist, Rageh Omar, had quoted an ordinary Iraqi as suspecting that the British and Americans would bomb civilian targets. (They did.) Campbell asserted: 'Coverage on the legality of the war has been heavily biased toward stories asserting the war would be illegal without a second resolution ... I know you will try to justify this. You always do. But it is wrong.'

Unusually, Campbell felt it necessary to emphasise that he spoke for Blair (not that anyone had ever seriously doubted that) and that Blair felt just as he did; furthermore, he made a veiled but serious threat:

> You may be interested to know that the prime minister has also
> expressed real concern about some of the reports he has seen and heard.
> I feel strongly that if the BBC reporting continues as it is, this will
> become a public controversy, which I am sure neither of us particularly
> want.

Campbell was acting on behalf of Blair, and Blair had power over the licence fee. Of course, if the correspondence ever became public and it was found that the BBC had been threatened inappropriately, it would be Campbell, the prime minister's lightning conductor, who would attract the subsequent opprobrium.

Blair also enlisted the willing aid of Gerald Kaufman. Kaufman was chairman of the parliamentary culture, media and sport committee, which handled matters concerning the BBC, and which could make difficulties about the licence fee. Campbell showed Kaufman his letter, and Kaufman wrote the very same day to BBC chairman Gavyn Davies in much the same terms, ending with typical portentousness: 'I look to you, as a matter of high speed and urgency, to have this situation rectified. If I feel it appropriate to do so, I shall be in touch with you over the next few days with further examples.'

The very next day, Campbell complained of a report in the journalists' trade paper *UK Press Gazette* that said the BBC was to warn its correspondents of the dangers to their objectivity of being 'embedded' with British troops. Governments like embedded reporters because they can be controlled. The BBC was not the only news organisation to warn its journalists to keep a professional distance between themselves and the army units that were looking after them. Campbell's main complaint appeared to be that the BBC was reported to have pointed out Ministry of Defence regulations stating that the unit commander might censor the correspondents' reports: 'Would that you applied the same principle to your reports from Baghdad,' Campbell wrote – another dig at Rageh Omar.

The day after that, there was yet another four-page letter, mostly about Gilligan. Sambrook responded with the full text of Gilligan's latest report, which was far more balanced than the extract Campbell provided. Campbell complained that Gilligan and Omar were in Baghdad, where they saw what the enemy wanted them to see. But Sambrook pointed out that the BBC was emphasising, every time it broadcast Gilligan's or Omar's reports, that their freedom of movement in Baghdad was restricted. Campbell claimed that Gilligan had reported in a sympathetic manner a story about Saddam Hussein's son Uday. Sambrook reminded him that, in a part of the report Campbell did not mention, Gilligan had said: 'Uday has run his own private torture chamber, a place that was absolutely notorious as a place of real horror for the Iraqis.' The day after Baghdad fell, Gilligan further enraged the government by telling *Today* listeners: 'Baghdad may in theory be free, but its people are passing their first days of liberty in a far greater fear than they have ever before known.' He was, of course, correct.

And that's how it went on, day after grinding day. Frequently Campbell's letters would arrive on the same day as letters from Gerald Kaufman, saying the same thing in different words. Here are some extracts to provide the flavour.

7 April, Campbell to Sambrook: '[Gilligan's] sneering contempt for anything put out by this coalition was on display once more this morning when he said on the *Today* programme: "We don't know if they've got it under their complete control but for once I think we can believe the American claims that this could be it."'

8 April, Sambrook to Campbell: 'The fact that some claims have been made [by US and British official spokesmen] which have turned out to be premature or inaccurate provide the context for Andrew Gilligan's remarks ... He was speaking live as he watched events unfold before him ... What you see as a sneer at the end is not that – but a reflection of some of the problems with some of the briefings at an earlier stage of the conflict.'

11 April, Campbell to Sambrook: 'Even by Andrew Gilligan's standards (which are low) ... . It is hard to resist the notion that some journalists, having talked up what they predicted would be a failure, are now determined to present military success as a disaster. Mr Gilligan, and to a certain extent Rageh Omar, are among them ... . The nature of BBC reporting out of Baghdad throughout the conflict has done you little

credit, and it hope you will undertake an <u>honest</u> and deep analysis of
it.'

11 April, Davies to Kaufman: 'Thank you for your letter of 27 March,
previously unacknowledged, about BBC coverage of the war in Iraq. I
am sorry you feel this demonstrates a pro-Iraqi bias and reinforces your
view that the BBC should not operate under a Royal Charter and be
funded by the licence fee .... You seem to imply that the BBC should
not carry any items which question the conduct or objectives of the war,
whereas I believe it is part of its mandate to do so.'

15 April, Sambrook to Kaufman: 'I regret you felt our coverage on the
day Baghdad fell to American forces (9 April) was too negative .... You
compare our coverage of the anti-war demonstration in mid-February
with the coverage last Wednesday. I am not sure whether you think we
went overboard about the million people who marched in London. At
that time of course there was significant public and parliamentary opposition to the war .... I can assure you we have received letters and e-
mails from many who think we paid too little attention to it.'

Subjected to a prolonged course of this kind of treatment, it would be
a pretty shoddy editor who failed to defend his reporters from so powerful
a vested interest. And that was how Blair wrongfooted his old friend Greg
Dyke. 'This is one of a dozen rants I've had from Campbell in the past
two weeks,' Dyke is said to have grumbled. The trouble is that if you get a
dozen similar complaints in a fortnight, the only one of them that really
matters can easily go unnoticed. And that is what happened to Dyke.

The one that mattered arrived on 29 May. There seemed to be nothing special about it at the time; and, as it happened, just at that time Dyke
was dealing with a complaint that had come in three days earlier from
Conservative leader Iain Duncan Smith, who had produced a dossier
designed to prove that the BBC was too favourable to the government
and biased against the Conservatives.

On 29 May at 6.07 a.m., Andrew Gilligan told listeners to BBC Radio
4's *Today* programme:

> We've been told by one of the senior officials in charge of drawing up
> that dossier [alleging that Saddam Hussein had weapons of mass
> destruction and could launch them at forty-five minutes' notice] that
> actually the government probably knew that that forty-five-minute claim
> was wrong, even before it decided to put it in.

The claim was not repeated: it was dropped from Gilligan's subsequent
reports that morning.

The truth, as we now know, is that the claim confidently made by
Blair that Saddam Hussein had weapons of mass destruction capable of

being launched in forty-five minutes was entirely false. But – and this was the crucial weakness on which, after a few days' delay, Blair pounced – we cannot know for certain that Blair was aware of this when he made the claim.

A press release was issued from 10 Downing Street at 7.15 that morning: 'These allegations are untrue ... . Not one word of the dossier was not entirely the work of the intelligence agencies ... .The suggestion that any pressure was put on the Intelligence services by No. 10 or anyone else to change the document is entirely false.' There is no sense that anyone in government realised that, at long last, they had their old enemy Gilligan where they wanted him. The letter of complaint that morning did not come from Blair. It did not even come from Campbell, or even Campbell's assistant, Tom Kelly. It came from lower down than that: from Anne Shevas of the Downing Street press office, and it began: 'In the absence abroad of my colleague Tom Kelly ...'. It was worded in much less inflammatory tones than the letters the BBC was by now used to receiving from Campbell. In comparison with Campbell and Kaufman's usual strident demands for instant, honest, detailed responses, Shevas simply told Mark Damazar, deputy director of BBC News, that she would be 'interested to receive your comments on these issues'. The next day there was a low-key response from Stephen Mitchell, head of Radio 4, which ran to just two pages. Neither side yet saw this row as anything out of the ordinary.[17]

Nor did the press. To the few people who heard Gilligan's report, he did not seem to have said anything very different from what everyone else had been saying. By then, it was clear that Blair's claim that Saddam Hussein could launch chemical and biological weapons within forty-five minutes was rubbish. This had been the key factor that had led to front-page headlines like '45 MINUTES FROM ATTACK', 'BRITS 45 MINUTES FROM DOOM' and 'HE'S GOT 'EM, LET'S GET HIM'. Blair's insistence that British and American forces were going to find the promised weapons of mass destruction seemed increasingly laughable. Today, no one even bothers to make the claim any more.

The newspapers on the morning of Gilligan's broadcast were dominated by the announcement that there would be an inquiry into the WMD claim by the House of Commons foreign affairs committee. Blair had also had a spat with the BBC over its decision to show the bodies of dead British soldiers, members of the occupation forces in Basra. He claimed it was insensitive to the soldiers' families; he did not mention that it was politically inconvenient to him.

On the Sunday following the broadcast, 1 June, the *Mail on Sunday* published an article by Andrew Gilligan in which he repeated all the charges he had made on the *Today* programme, and added an extra charge: that Campbell personally had made changes to the dossier. This was much more serious, and Blair and Campbell constantly referred to it in the days ahead. Gilligan also used for the first time the emotive and inelegant phrase 'sexed up' to describe what he claimed Campbell had done to the dossier.

Yet, in all that followed, the government never mentioned the *Mail* article, for three reasons. First, the government had no power over the *Mail*. It could not threaten its revenue, as it could with the BBC. Bullies do not attack people they cannot hurt. Second, naming Campbell suited Blair: the more Campbell was in the frontline, the less the various accusations flying around would stick to Blair. And third, the *Mail on Sunday*, though anti-Labour, was pro-war. This, if proof were needed, shows that it was Blair, not Campbell, who called the shots; for Campbell loathes the *Mail on Sunday* and its sister paper, the *Daily Mail*, whose editor, Paul Dacre, he considers to be 'the most poisonous man in British public life'.[18] Left to his own devices, he would surely have wanted to go after the paper.

But, of course, the material in the dossier had been – let us avoid the term 'sexed up' – enhanced. Jonathan Powell made this clear himself in an e-mail sent just seven days before its publication, telling John Scarlett that the dossier 'does nothing to demonstrate a threat, let alone an imminent threat from Saddam'. As the Butler Inquiry subsequently discovered, every caveat, every 'maybe' or 'possibly', every mention of 'limited intelligence' was removed. In his foreword to the dossier, the prime minister declared that it 'establishes beyond doubt' that Saddam was a threat. The Butler Report stated: 'We conclude that it was a serious weakness that the JIC's warnings on the limitations of the intelligence underlying its judgements were not made sufficiently clear in the dossier.'

Robin Cook demanded an inquiry into the WMD claims. Clare Short claimed that Bush and Blair had privately agreed to go to war on Iraq back in September 2002. Blair called Clare Short a liar. Fifty MPs signed a call for the government to publish its full file of evidence about WMD. The whips whispered that the 'enemy within' consisted of Clare Short, Robin Cook and Frank Dobson. 'They really must hate us,' said whips in quiet, insinuating tones to gullible Labour MPs. The worst polls since Blair became leader showed the damage the Iraq war had done to his government.

The government then startled everyone by suddenly announcing that people in the security services were trying to discredit it. 'There have been uncorroborated briefings by a potentially rogue element or elements in the security services,' said John Reid, the leader of the House. 'I find it hard to grasp why this should be believed against the word of the British prime minister and the head of the Joint Intelligence Committee.' Chief whip Hilary Armstrong talked of 'skulduggery' in the security services.

None of this had anything to do with Andrew Gilligan's report. It would all still have happened if Gilligan had never spoken. Nonetheless, as private letters to the BBC make clear, the prime minister's press secretary had begun devoting a very great deal of his energies to Gilligan's report. By the time Campbell himself took over the correspondence, five days after Gilligan's broadcast, the decision had been taken in Downing Street that nothing less than Gilligan's head on a plate would do.

Blair and Campbell loathed Gilligan. He was independent; he did not hunt with a pack, as most other specialist journalists do, and could not therefore be partially controlled, as the House of Commons lobby could. Geoff Hoon made this point in a different way when he tried to stifle Gilligan's career by telling *Today* editor Kevin Marsh: 'One of the things about Andrew is that he is in with the wrong crowd. We are much more used to dealing with BBC correspondents who are well connected. He is not of the mainstream.' During the Iraq war, he brought the BBC a raft of embarrassing exclusive stories about faulty or non-existent equipment. Campbell called him 'gullible Gilligan', which, as Oborne and Walters rightly point out, was 'a classic piece of Campbell character-assassination'.[19]

Campbell's letter to Sambrook of 5 June, sent by fax, is a bitter, vindictive four-page tirade against Gilligan and all his works. Sambrook replied a little wearily on 11 June: 'I see no likelihood of our agreeing on this matter but I will briefly set out why I think your allegations about our journalism are misguided.' He added – and this is an indication that, at this stage, the BBC had no idea how far the government wanted to push this issue – 'You would not expect me to reveal the source (and I am gratified that you have not asked).' Sambrook was, of course, referring to Gilligan's source for his dossier story and was treating Campbell as a fellow journalist who would not dream of trying to force a colleague to reveal his sources. But Campbell was his master's voice; and his master had no interest at all in the ethical dilemmas of journalists.

Sambrook was soon to learn this harsh truth. Campbell replied the moment he saw the letter, on 12 June. 'Thank you for your reply of 11 June 2003. There are several outstanding issues you have failed to address, to which I would like responses.' These were spelled out in three further pages. They included references to 'Andrew Gilligan's obvious ignorance about intelligence issues' and much heavy sarcasm about 'Mr Gilligan's single uncorroborated source'. Campbell wanted to know whether the BBC would be 'conducting an internal enquiry into how one of its journalists could get it so wrong and be left unchallenged by his colleagues and bosses'.

The letter disabused Sambrook of the notion that he was not going to be put under pressure to reveal Gilligan's source. In his reply, Sambrook said defensively: 'As for your assertion that you know the source of Andrew Gilligan's information was "not a member of the JIC or directly involved in compiling the dossier" I make no comment.' Sambrook had been in journalism long enough to know a fishing expedition when he saw one.

While Campbell was writing to Sambrook, Blair himself was having a parallel correspondence with director-general Greg Dyke. But Blair managed to protect his own letters from the eyes of the Hutton Inquiry. There is a brief reference to Blair's letters in one of Campbell's letters. Once again, when it looked as though Blair himself might be exposed, Campbell interposed his person.

The BBC's chairman, Gavyn Davies, like the director-general, believed the BBC's independence would be at stake if it did not stand up to the government. So an all-out conflict was inevitable, and after a month of phoney war, with private and occasionally public letters passing more or less daily between Downing Street and the BBC, war was declared on 26 June. That day, Campbell gave evidence as scheduled to the foreign affairs committee. The committee was supposed to be inquiring into the evidence for those non-existent weapons of mass destruction. This was intensely embarrassing for Blair, and it was very much in his interest to have a battle with the BBC in the headlines instead.

The headline in *The Times* the next day was: 'Campbell accuses BBC of lying'. Campbell told the committee that both he and Blair had demanded an apology from the BBC, and would go on demanding one, over the allegation that the government had ordered the intelligence service to 'sex up' the dossier. He said: 'There was an agenda in large parts of the BBC, a disproportionate focus on the dissent, the opposition to our position ... Something has gone very wrong with BBC journalism.' But he admitted that he and Tony Blair had made 'drafting suggestions' on the dossier.

That same day, as soon as he was back in the office, Campbell wrote a public, press-released letter to Gavyn Davies and a private one to Greg Dyke. The private one was, by his standards, emollient, and his old friends in journalism may hold out the forlorn hope that it betrays his personal disquiet, as a former journalist himself, at what he had to do as Blair's emissary.

> I'm sorry that I had to say what I said about the BBC, but I'm afraid private discussions and correspondence about recent events have proved to be pointless ... Put to one side our complaint about the BBC's coverage of Iraq about which you were dismissive in your letter to the prime minister ... Our concern is that you are content to see BBC standards debased by agenda-driven journalism within parts of the Corporation. I think it's a big mistake. I also wonder whether listeners really think they need to see and hear as much about this story as they've been force-fed in recent days. I just ask you, as someone whose career and commitment I've always admired, to think about it. I am copying this letter to Gavyn Davies, and regard it as private.

For Dyke, it was now a question of the BBC either standing by its reporter or becoming the government's poodle. He said he would not bow to 'unprecedented pressure' from Tony Blair; and he accused Blair of adopting diversionary tactics to take the spotlight away from the admitted flaws in the dossier.

Blair himself upped the stakes. At a press conference after a meeting with Russia's President Putin, he pointedly refused to take questions from the BBC's Bridget Kendall, while taking questions from the Sky and ITN reporters. He allowed the deputy leader of the House of Commons, Phil Woolas, to release to the press a letter accusing Gilligan of lying to the foreign affairs committee. Labour MPs were told to bombard the BBC with complaints about Gilligan. A young and ambitious junior minister, Ben Bradshaw, was put up as the public face of the government's wrath, mainly because Bradshaw was a former BBC journalist and could fulminate about how standards had declined since his (and John Birt's) day. Bradshaw started making an almost daily contribution to the blizzard of letters which Sambrook and other senior BBC news executives had to answer, taking up obscure points in his frequent interviews with John Humphrys and demanding apologies for them, and fulminating about Andrew Gilligan.

Rarely, if ever, has a prime minister become so vengeful towards one journalist. The nearest equivalent is Harold Wilson, whose later years were clouded by obsessive hounding of journalists who he believed were plotting to discredit him, but even Wilson never worked himself up as badly as Blair seems to have done about Gilligan.

On 30 June, four days after Campbell's appearance at the foreign affairs committee, Bradshaw was writing yet another indignant letter to Sambrook. Dyke was meeting Conservative Party chairman Theresa May

to discuss her claim that the BBC's news coverage was unfair to the
Tories. Campbell was announcing an 'eight-day countdown to BBC
meltdown'– it was eight days before the foreign affairs committee reported and he had inside information that they would be critical of the BBC.
And Gavyn Davies was offering the government independent arbitration
by a leading QC. Everyone was talking about Campbell and the BBC,
and no one was talking about weapons of mass destruction any more. It
had taken the heat off the prime minister. Blair had not lost his touch.

Geoff Hoon picked up the baton. He agreed to do an interview with
Today about the current situation in Iraq, but only if the scope of the
interview was expanded to include the arcane matter of exactly what had
been discussed between Gilligan and the MoD press officer the night
before Gilligan's now-famous broadcast. The *Today* programme, perhaps
mindful of Campbell's injunction not to ram this stuff down their listeners' throats, refused, and the interview was cancelled. Campbell kept up
the pressure on the BBC to name Gilligan's source.

On 4 July, Downing Street learned that someone had come forward
within the Ministry of Defence and confessed to his superiors that he had
met with Andrew Gilligan. Campbell wrote in his diary that day: 'Spoke
to Hoon who said that a man had come forward who felt he was possibly
Gilligan's source, had come forward and was being interviewed today.
GH [Geoff Hoon] and I agreed it would fuck Gilligan if that was his
source … GH and I agreed to talk tomorrow.'

Hoon, Campbell and Blair talked, not only the next day but for most
of the next three days. Meanwhile, the foreign affairs committee report
was published, clearing Blair and Campbell of presenting misleading
information. According to Campbell's diaries, which he was later obliged
to hand over to the Hutton Inquiry, Blair appears, rather late in the day,
to have started wondering where all this might lead, but Hoon and
Campbell did not seem to have much trouble persuading him that the
only way was forward. And so, on 9 July, Hoon wrote to Gavyn Davies:

> So that you can establish whether the name of the person who has
> come forward is the same as the name given to BBC management by
> Andrew Gilligan, I am now prepared to tell you that his name is David
> Kelly, Advisor to the Proliferation and Arms Control Secretariat in the
> MoD.

That same day, Hoon had a crash meeting with Sambrook; he wrote
privately to him the next day that he was grateful to Sambrook for
changing his plans in order to meet him. The meeting and the letter all
concerned that issue he had been so determined to talk about on the *Today*

programme: exactly what Gilligan and the MoD press officer had spoken about the day before Gilligan's famous broadcast. 'I am disappointed that you are not now prepared to broadcast an apology,' he wrote. And then he added a handwritten postscript: 'I was sorry to take you away from your son's sports day. I hope that he did well and enjoyed himself. I hope that we can meet again under easier circumstances.'

Hoon, like Campbell and Mandelson, was becoming a lightning conductor for the prime minister, taking the blame for the messy war of attrition with the BBC upon which Blair had deliberately embarked, and it must have occurred to him that he was becoming one of the most disliked people in the country. It was Hoon, a lawyer by trade, who was delivering himself of lawyerly evasions in public. He lacked, and must have known he lacked, the charm that enabled the prime minister to deliver evasions that did not sound evasive. Hoon looks and sounds like a grey-suited lawyer-politician, with a stony face and an unseeing gaze. Blair, on the other hand, could say just the same thing and come across as a decent, straightforward chap.

Blair was willing the end and yet distancing himself from the means. He wanted the BBC to be utterly, humiliatingly defeated – but he wanted its blood to be on Campbell's and Hoon's hands, not his. That is the only explanation for the exchange he had with Gavyn Davies, two days before Hoon's letter to Davies:

> Blair: 'The story is totally wrong. You need to withdraw it.'
> Davies: 'Alastair has put us in an impossible situation.'
> Blair: 'I realise that, but I am trying to calm him down. He has a justified grievance but his behaviour has been too loud.'[20]

Of course, Blair was doing nothing of the kind. If he had wanted to change Campbell's behaviour, he could have done so instantly. Campbell was nothing, and knew he was nothing, without the prime minister's support.

The task to which 10 Downing Street now turned its attention was how to get Dr Kelly's name into the newspapers. It was Blair himself who came up with the ruse of asking the Commons intelligence and security committee if they might like to interview Gilligan's source. Blair contacted committee chair Ann Taylor, but she was having none of it. Campbell's diary records: 'TB came back and continued to try and sort out the source issue. He met Scarlett and agreed to try and resolve through letter to Ann Taylor. Word then came back she didn't want a letter on it. That meant do it as a press release.' Blair chaired no fewer than four meetings in two days at which this matter was discussed. The solution finally reached was to issue a press statement which gave enough information for well-informed journalists to work out the name of Gilligan's source. MoD press officers were told to tell the press that, while they were not going to name the source, they would confirm it to any journalist who could guess it. It did not take long.

The sad end to Dr Kelly's story is all too familiar. Following a public, televised grilling by the foreign affairs committee, on 17 July 2003 he went for a walk in the Oxfordshire countryside and killed himself. Blair, hearing about Kelly's death on a long plane journey from Washington to Tokyo, at once announced the setting-up of an independent judicial inquiry – and turned his mind to how this could be spun in Downing Street's favour.

Blair needed someone to conduct the inquiry who was not likely to cause him avoidable political damage. He turned for advice to two of his closest confidants, Lord Falconer, the new Lord Chancellor, and Peter Mandelson. Both came up with the same name – Lord Hutton – but for different reasons. Lord Falconer knew that in judicial circles Hutton had a reputation for independence but also a deep respect for the security services. Northern Ireland judges are loath to criticise the security services, for one simple reason – their lives depend on them. So he gambled that Hutton would be very unlikely to want to criticise John Scarlett, the chairman of the Joint Intelligence Committee, too severely. If Scarlett escaped serious damage, Blair stood a fighting chance. Lord Falconer disputes this – though Lord Hutton's views about the security services were undoubtedly helpful.

Mandelson provided another vital piece of intelligence to his embattled master. When he was secretary of state for Northern Ireland, Mandelson had noticed that Hutton was extremely careful when dealing with both IRA and loyalist terrorist cases to stick closely to the facts of the case and take into account (in such cases he was sitting without a jury) only that evidence which bore directly on the issue of the accused's guilt or innocence. In other words, he was a lawyer who could be trusted to stick rigidly to his brief. Hutton, Mandelson suggested, could be relied upon to steer clear of controversial issues, provided his terms of reference were strictly limited.

Blair took the point. Lord Hutton was asked 'urgently to conduct an investigation into the circumstances surrounding the death of Dr Kelly'. Hutton emphasised in his opening address: 'I do not sit to decide between conflicting cases – I sit to investigate the circumstances surrounding Dr Kelly's death.' The only other available candidate, Lord Hope of Craigugad, a former Lord Chief Justice of Scotland, had an equally conservative background.

Equally interesting was the choice of the secretary to the inquiry. Downing Street often likes a safe pair of hands in that job – since the secretary is the key to keeping the show on the road. The Lord Chancellor's Department was responsible for the appointment, and the decision seems to have been left to Lord Falconer. His choice, on the recommendation of Sir Hayden Phillips, permanent secretary at his department, was Lee Hughes. Hughes had impressed both Jack Straw and Derry Irvine with his competence and determination on the briefs he had been given. But he is very much his own man. He also had one quality that did not sit very well with the Blair court – he is an advocate of open government.

His appointment came after he had been involved in a long-running dispute between Irvine and Blair over whether the *Guardian* should be given details of ministers' official gifts. The dispute, which is detailed in the parliamentary ombudsman's report, had led to prolonged correspondence between Downing Street and the Lord Chancellor's Department; Downing Street was determined to block the release of the information, and Irvine, Hughes and Phillips argued just as strongly that it should be published.[21] So appointing Hughes to the sensitive job of secretary to the inquiry was a bold step by Falconer – particularly as Hutton had wide discretion over what information he would publish.

The result was a decision to publish all the evidence on the Hutton website – though neither Hutton nor Hughes would have known at the time how much information was going to be available. Campbell later got over his horror and told the Commons public administration committee that his experience over Hutton led him to believe that there was a case for open government. 'I have had a modest conversion,' he told MPs.[22]

One thing the Hutton Inquiry was not told was that the SIS 'withdrew' (that is, stated that the source was no longer considered credible) one of its five main sources in July 2003. Blair did not mention this at the time and now claims that he only heard about it when the Butler Report was released in July 2004. Did no one really tell the prime minister, for a whole year, that a key source providing the intelligence on which he took the country to war had turned out to be dodgy?

The Butler Report, which followed that of Lord Hutton, was an inquiry into the intelligence relating to those non-existent weapons of mass destruction. It concluded that the famous forty-five-minute claim was included 'because of its eye-catching character'. During the debate on the Hutton Report, Blair had maintained that he did not know the claim referred only to battlefield munitions, as opposed to long-range missiles that might be used to attack cities. This astonished Robin Cook,

who had been told by John Scarlett that it referred to battlefield munitions when he had requested a personal briefing. Did the prime minister
not ask his intelligence chief what sort of weapons the claim referred to?
The Butler Report, according to Blair, cleared him of blame. But it was
not an inquiry into the decision to go to war. As Blair said when he
announced the inquiry in February: 'We can't end up having an inquiry
into whether the war was right or wrong. That is something that we have
got to decide. We are the politicians.'

In fact, it is not at all clear that Butler 'cleared' anyone. The report
notes that Parliament, when asked to declare war, was not given the JIC's
assessments on which the dossier was based – it was only given the
dossier itself. Nor was the cabinet given these assessments. In the twelve
months leading up to war, the cabinet formally discussed Iraq on no
fewer than twenty-four occasions. Yet at none of those meetings were
papers ever distributed. The prime minister, foreign secretary and defence
secretary briefed the rest of the cabinet verbally. Butler expressed 'concern' that the 'informality and circumscribed character of the government's procedures' reduced the scope for 'informed political judgement'.

This informality is confirmed by a swift comparison of the number of
meetings held by Blair's informal clique of advisers, military officials and
key ministers, and the number of meetings held by the official ministerial
committee on defence and overseas policy. Blair's informal group met on
twenty-five occasions, naturally without taking minutes, while the official
cabinet committee, traditionally the forum at which such matters as war
and peace are discussed, did not meet once. Butler also noted a shift in
the government's decision-making structures that 'acts to concentrate
detailed knowledge and effective decision-making in fewer minds at the
top' – something that Butler, as a former cabinet secretary, was not at all
keen on.

These days, we do not hear anything from Blair about weapons of
mass destruction. He talks about the brutal nature of Saddam's dictatorship instead. It was indeed brutal, and many people had said as much.
Ann Clwyd MP, a supporter of the war, had been expressing her concern
for the plight of the Kurds and campaigning against Saddam's horrific
gassing of them for nearly twenty years. Jack Straw had himself been one
of the first to protest against Saddam's brutal treatment of the Kurds
when he was in opposition. But if Saddam's brutality was a good enough
reason to go to war, why were we told that the reason was weapons of
mass destruction? And why did Blair say that if Saddam would only
agree to be disarmed, he would not be attacked? A Saddam Hussein with
no WMDs would be just as brutal a dictator.

Is a brutal dictatorship reason enough to take British troops to war? Amnesty International's annual report for 2004 states that there are victims of torture and ill treatment by security forces and police in 132 countries. Extrajudicial executions were carried out in 47 countries. People were 'disappeared' by state agents in 28 countries. Armed groups have committed violent acts and killings in 34 countries. So why choose Iraq? Butler dismisses the claim from some in the anti-war movement that it was a war prosecuted, at least in part, for control of Iraq's oil supplies. He concludes: 'We saw no evidence that a motive of the British government for initiating military action was securing continuing access to oil supplies.' However, Butler also points out that this issue did not fall within the inquiry's remit, nor did they take evidence on it. Butler did not investigate, nor does he draw conclusions, on whether oil supplies contributed to the reasons for the United States (as opposed to Britain) going to war.

Butler is careful not to apportion blame or absolve anyone of responsibility – with one rather strange exception. Butler 'greatly hopes' that Scarlett will not resign from his new position as head of MI6. And yet in his conclusions on the work of the Joint Intelligence Committee, Butler states there is a 'strong case' for the next head of the JIC to be someone who is 'demonstrably beyond influence'. Why should the head of MI6 not also be such a person?

The Butler Report might have been the last word on the war, at least until the principal characters leave government and start writing their memoirs, had it not been for the curious affair of the legal advice.

It was known that the Attorney General, Lord Goldsmith, had been asked for an opinion on whether the war was legal. There are, fortunately, a good many people around with nasty, suspicious minds, who wondered why the text of Lord Goldsmith's advice had never been revealed, either to Hutton or to Butler. Was there something in it which the cabinet would rather we didn't see?

Suspicion was fuelled by the letter of resignation before the war from Elizabeth Wilmshurst, deputy legal adviser at the Foreign Office. She claimed that Goldsmith had at first shared her view that war without a new UN resolution would be illegal. She wrote: 'I cannot in conscience go along with advice within the (Foreign) Office or to the public or parliament which asserts the legitimacy of military action without such a [UN] resolution, particularly since an unlawful use of force on such a scale amounts to the crime of aggression; nor can I agree with such action in circumstances which are so detrimental to the international order and the rule of law.' Goldsmith, she wrote, had changed his advice twice to bring it in line with 'what is now the official line'.

By January 2005 there was a growing clamour for Goldsmith's advice to be made public, and the cabinet minister responsible for open government, the lord chancellor, Lord Falconer – Blair's old Scottish legal chum – announced that he was minded to make sure we never saw it – he could, and would, veto its release. We would have to make do with the parliamentary answer on 17 March 2003, the eve of the crucial Commons vote on the war.

But Goldsmith had told the Butler Inquiry that this statement was actually drawn up by Falconer himself, together with Baroness Sally Morgan, who worked in 10 Downing Street. 'I conveyed that view [that the war was legal] in the first place,' Goldsmith told Butler, 'in a meeting on that day on March 13 with Baroness Morgan and Lord Falconer, at which I informed them that I had formed the view that the interpretation of Resolution 1441 was that it was lawful to use force without a further resolution ... They shortly, of course, set out my view in the PQ [parliamentary question] which was published on the following Monday. That set out what my view was, of course.'[23]

And that brief parliamentary answer, it turned out, was all the cabinet had ever seen. If Lord Goldsmith had ever set out his full legal opinion and explained the reasons for his conclusion, members of the cabinet which voted for the war had never seen it.

Blair seems honestly to have believed that these arguments about what he called 'process' – the process of going to war – were a distraction from the big picture. Had he not, after all, overthrown a spectacularly evil dictator? Should that not be enough for all of us? Why did people have to go on worrying away at whether or not he had cut legal corners to do so? But the process mattered terribly – because he had not sold the war to Parliament on the basis of getting rid of an evil dictator. He had sold it on the basis of international law and of destroying Saddam Hussein's weapons of mass destruction. Richard Norton-Taylor summed it up powerfully in the *Guardian* on 25 April:

> The intelligence, though, was wrong, and anyway there was an alternative to war. [UN chief weapons inspector Hans] Blix and his inspectors could have stayed in Iraq, where they would have confirmed what is now admitted: Iraq had no weapons of mass destruction and was therefore – contrary to what Blair again claimed last week – in compliance with UN resolutions.
>
> The point here is the legality of the invasion. It seems clear that by spring 2002 Blair had, in effect, promised Bush he would join the US invasion. Thus everything had to be done to make the war legal. Blair, as he says, was 'desperate' for a new UN resolution. Only when it was

clear that they were not going to get it did Blair and Straw argue that it
was not needed after all. More significantly, so did Goldsmith.

Ministers dismiss any discussion about how the war came to be legal
by taking refuge in their mantra that they are concerned with substance,
not process. It is as if due process – whether it be the internment of suspects without trial or the lawfulness of military action – is of no importance. The end justifies the means.

That, Norton-Taylor argued, was why the full version of Goldsmith's
advice on March 7 ought to be made public – so that we could see 'the
precise words he used, and compare them with his brief but confident
statement of March 17'. If he had changed his mind, 'what happened in
those 10 days to make him change? All we know is that Sir Michael
Boyce, chief of the defence staff, asked for unequivocal advice from
Goldsmith that the war was legal. Blair cannot continue to rebuff questions by resorting to bland phrases about doing what he thought was
right. He has got away with it so far, but sooner or later his evasions and
omissions will catch up with him.'

By then, the 2005 general election was being fought – polling day, 5
May, was less than two weeks away. Blair still hoped to get through the
election campaign without revealing Goldsmith's full advice. But others –
opposition politicians as well as journalists – were equally determined
that he should not be allowed to do so, especially after newspapers
started to allege that Goldsmith had initially advised that the war would
be illegal, and had changed his mind. Ministers took refuge in attacking
an old, and now seriously weakened, enemy: the BBC. Deputy Prime
Minister John Prescott wrote to the new director-general, Mark Thomp-
son: 'You are determined to tell only one side of the story, the side that
fits the agenda that says the government took the wrong decision in
removing Saddam.'[24] This rather neat sentence, with its delicately crafted
spin in the phrase 'the wrong decision in removing Saddam', is not
Prescott's usual literary style, which tends towards the blunderbuss rather
than the rapier; and it is unlikely that Prescott himself, in the run-up to a
general election, could have spared the time from campaigning to craft it.
In a late change to a planned speech, he employed the neat alliterative
phrasing already used by Blair: 'The world is a better place with Saddam
in prison than [with] Saddam in power.' Removing Saddam was not, of
course, supposed to be part of our war aims.

So, on 28 April, with polling day just a week away, the government
agreed, with the worst grace, to publish the full advice. The announcement, in a press conference, was one of Blair's finest theatrical performances. The months of wriggling and evasion to avoid revealing it might

never have been. With a casual shrug of his shoulders, the prime minister simply told a press conference: 'As for the legal advice, well, you've probably got it already. Frankly, I see no reason at all not to publish it. Yeah, why not?' He insisted he had not forced Goldsmith to change his advice. Yet at the same time he once again implied that the war was about regime change: 'I had to decide whether we back away, leave Saddam immeasurably stronger, or remove him. I took the decision to remove him. These decisions are tough and that is what leadership is about.'

It was immediately clear why the government had tried so hard to suppress Goldsmith's advice (which we reproduce in our second appendix). It said, unequivocally, that regime change could not, in law, be an objective of military action. Regime change was by then the only justification being offered for the war – with ministers lining up to say, as Prescott had, that they had not taken 'the wrong decision in removing Saddam'. It said that British troops could only take such action as was necessary to get Iraq to disarm – an injunction that had clearly not been followed. None of this appeared in the much briefer statement drafted later for presentation to Parliament. It said that a legal action to stop the war, either in Britain or internationally, might succeed.

Even the cabinet had not been permitted to see the advice when they approved the war. Professor Peter Hennessy, historian and leading expert on Britain's unwritten constitution, went into a wholly uncharacteristic rage. This, he said, was 'the most supine cabinet since World War II'. He added: 'The whole thing reeks. Even if the prime minister wins handsomely on polling day this will stain him and his premiership as long as people remember it, just as Anthony Eden's name is forever associated with the Suez crisis.' The attorney general as well as the cabinet attracted Hennessy's scorn. 'I'm convinced that history will judge Lord Goldsmith as the most pliable attorney general in modern political history. Nothing changed in Saddam's behaviour between March 7 and March 17 to take away these reservations and caveats. All the warnings are in [Goldsmith's advice], all the elements of uncertainty are in there. The shift from that to the written answer he discussed with the cabinet on March 17 and relayed to the Lords later that day is enormous.'

It emerged that Sir Michael Boyce had sought from Goldsmith, and received, a written assurance that Saddam Hussein was still in breach of UN resolutions. When Blair provided this assurance, he had already been told of Hans Blix's statement to the UN that Saddam Hussein was finally cooperating with arms inspectors. And Sir Michael Boyce wanted an assurance from Goldsmith that his troops could not be charged with war crimes. Goldsmith's advice, seen only by Blair, was that they could be charged. Yet Sir Michael received his assurance. It was not just the heat of the election that led Conservative leader Michael Howard to say: 'What, or who, changed the attorney general's mind?'

Now, all this is, as Blair rightly says, process. It can even be made to sound like a lawyer's quibbling. It does not tell us whether going to war in Iraq was pragmatically sensible or morally justifiable.

But Blair, it should be remembered, is a trained and not untalented lawyer. He knew the meaning of Goldsmith's advice. He knew that his own attorney general was telling him a war fought for regime change was illegal, and he chose to keep this advice from everyone, even his own cabinet. He knows what war aims mean. His war aim was not regime change; and he now justifies the war only in terms of regime change.

There is no need to doubt his motives. He believed what he was doing was both sensible and morally right. He is a man of utter self-belief, and having reached this conclusion, he saw nothing wrong in cutting a few corners in order to be able to do it. He was sure that, once the war was won, no one would start worrying away at the way he did it. 'The victor,' Adolf Hitler once said, 'will never be asked if he told the truth.' Blair is, of course, not in any way at all to be compared with Hitler, but there is the sense over Iraq that this was what he believed.

And he was wrong. For the first time, the most accomplished politician of our time overreached himself. The questions will not go away, not as long as he is in power, nor as long as historians still take an interest in him.

Iraq was Tony Blair's war in a way that no other war in which Britain engaged during the twentieth century was the prime minister's war. Never before has a prime minister had both the self-belief and the political mastery to lead into a war a cabinet that did not demand the full facts, a party that disliked and distrusted the project, and a nation that was sharply divided. That is what is special about Tony Blair. Who is this man, what is his secret, and what has he done to our constitution? These are questions we will address in our final chapter.

CHAPTER SIXTEEN

THE FAILED COUP AGAINST GORDON

The war on Iraq and its aftermath was to have a major impact on Labour's fortunes in the general election that was eventually called for May 2005; this was something that most observers – except, apparently, Blair himself – expected. What was totally unexpected was Blair's eventual announcement that, if returned to power, he would step down at some point during his third term. The announcement had the immediate effect of refocusing attention on the relationship between Blair and his presumed heir apparent, Gordon Brown.

Ever since Blair was elected to the leadership in 1994 his relationship with Brown had been prickly. They were still friends and were both on the modernising wing of the party. But the rivalry between the two resurfaced in the autumn of 2003 – partly because of the fall-out from the Iraq war and partly because Brown was becoming increasingly worried that he would never succeed to the leadership because Blair would never stand down.

Blair's concern about his unpopularity over the Iraq war grew after the suicide of David Kelly, the UN weapons inspector, in July 2003 led to the setting-up of the Hutton Inquiry and events in Iraq started to unravel with the first attacks on the American and British forces.

Blair's pre-occupation with Iraq had always been more philosophical and religious than political. Cherie Blair is said once to have astonished her fellow partners at Matrix Chambers, the human rights law firm, by telling them during the Iraq crisis that 'Tony kneels down at the end of the bed and prays every night'.

So when it became clear that there could be long-term political repercussions from the war (at this stage Hutton had yet to report and effectively exonerate ministers), Blair – according to Brown's friends – became increasingly depressed. At the same time, Brown became increasingly belligerent, emphasising opposition to Blair's and Blunkett's ID card scheme and creating 'clear red water' between Blair and himself in a speech at the Labour Party conference that year.

Matters came to a head in November 2003 when John Prescott hosted a dinner for Brown and Blair at his Admiralty House flat. It is at this dinner, according to Tom Bower's biography of Gordon Brown,[1] that Prescott is said to have told him: 'Gordon, you should one day be leader of the party. I want you to be leader of the party. Many others do as well. But the one thing that will stop you becoming leader is if you continue trying to destabilise Tony. The party won't have it.'

At this point it is said that Blair and Brown agreed to patch up their differences, and Blair showed this publicly by revoking his ban on Brown's attendance at the Labour National Executive Committee and appointing Brown to once again head up Labour's election campaign.

But, more importantly, it was said – again according to Brown's friends – that Blair finally agreed he would stand down and pave the way for Brown to be his successor. Brown had a particularly happy Christmas and the truce between the two men continued for the next nine months. But the following June, Blair began to change his mind. Events in the interim had restored his self-confidence. The Hutton Inquiry – which reported on 24 January – turned the story into an inquisition on the BBC's handling of events and its relations with ministers, with the government and the security services absolved from any blame. There was a further inquiry under Lord Butler still to report – but the press had already discounted this as likely to produce a further whitewash. The government had also succeeded in passing its controversial introduction of university top-up fees – effectively reneging on election manifesto commitments.

More importantly, three key figures in his life had urged him to reconsider. Over Easter Cherie is said to have encouraged him to renege on any promise – on the grounds that he still had work to do and there was no reason to doubt his abilities. Lord Falconer, one of his oldest friends and political allies, also pressed him to stay and stand for a third term – emphasising that he had not completed his mission. Peter Mandelson, still in the inner circle despite being out of government, also pressed him to forget his past promises to Brown. Neither of the latter two would have had a political future if Brown had become prime minister.

So there was no summer changeover for Brown, and Blair was already having grave doubts about the need for any change at all. Robert Peston's book *Brown's Britain* quoted the chancellor as saying to Blair in the summer of 2004: 'There is nothing you could say to me that I could ever believe.'[2] People close to Brown actually contest that Brown ever said anything like that to Blair's face, but the quote is recognised as a phrase used by one of his aides.

Blair also received a major boost – again with the help of Brown – from the conclusion of the Warwick Agreement (named after the venue, Warwick University) with the unions in July. Effectively this meant that the unions agreed on an agenda for change with the government – including ministers meeting some of the unions' concerns over pay and conditions, holidays, and the basic minimum wage for young workers between eighteen and twenty-one – and secured a commitment that Royal Mail would not be privatised. More significantly, it meant that the Labour-affiliated unions were now committed to contributing to the party's general election coffers – essential after bad feelings between the unions and the government had led to a draining of support. Blair knew he would continue to get the cash.

In September, after Blair returned from his holiday, he took decisive action to secure his position and effectively to isolate Brown. He used the occasion of a reshuffle to bring Alan Milburn back into the cabinet and also raised no objections when Derek Scott, until recently his chief economic adviser, published a book full of searing criticisms of Brown. Both moves devastated Brown.

Scott's book, *Off Whitehall*,[3] depicted Brown as 'obstructive and deceitful' – refusing to give the prime minister the details of his budgets, being churlish about discussing joining the euro, and trying to block Whitehall appointments to Number 10, particularly that of Jeremy Heywood, a former Treasury man who became Blair's principal private secretary. Scott also criticised Blair for giving too much power and authority to Brown. 'The effect of giving too much power to Gordon is to create a messy and constant disorder. This started early in the first term and has continued,' he wrote.

While Brown was furious about the effect of the book's revelations in the short term, the return of Milburn threatened to be a much more serious, long-term setback to his ambitions. If the relationship between Brown and Blair was rarely on an even keel, the relationship between Alan Milburn and Gordon Brown was far more precarious. Milburn, one of the rising stars from the North East, had already clashed with Brown over the introduction of foundation hospitals. His resignation from the cabinet to spend more time with his family in June 2003 had appeared to remove him from the political scene. But Mandelson had other ideas. He saw Milburn as a potential successor. Milburn is a gritty Northerner brought up by a single parent, with a reputation for decisiveness and bluntness (privately bordering on aggressive bullying – as demonstrated by his clash with Dame (now Baroness) Fritchie, the commissioner for public appointments, as we saw in Chapter 11). He also possesses charm and appears, like Blair, to be 'a pretty straight guy' – a man of the people.

Mandelson's original plan had been that, after returning to the backbenches, Milburn should emerge, when the time came, as a fresh face untainted by any associations with his former government colleagues. But this idea was flawed. Milburn had to be seen playing a major role if he wanted to be leader – otherwise other challengers could emerge. There was no shortage of 'wannabe leaders': the candidates ranged from Charles Clarke and Peter Hain to David Blunkett or even Jack Straw. If it came to a fight, Milburn could easily find himself sidelined in the mêlée.

By reappointing Milburn to the cabinet as Chancellor of the Duchy of Lancaster (in charge of the Cabinet Office) and giving him responsibility for the forthcoming election campaign, Blair dealt Brown a severe and humiliating blow.

Faced with an infuriated chancellor, Blair is said to have told him, 'Gordon, I don't understand what you have got against Alan, he is very talented.' One of Brown's friends said: 'We don't know today whether this is what Tony really thought or whether it was another wind-up for Gordon.'

Whatever Blair's motives for reappointing Milburn, the signal to the Brownites was clear and was not lost on the press, which renewed its speculation about the relationship between Brown and Blair. For the next five months, newspapers repeatedly suggested that Brown might be finished. The fact that Milburn's return coincided with the sudden resignation of Andrew Smith, the secretary of state for work and pensions and a prominent Brown supporter, and with further promotion for John Reid, another prominent Blairite loyalist, fuelled the speculation. The *Guardian* commented that 'Mr Milburn is seen as one of those ministers Mr Blair consciously deployed to restrain his over-mighty heir apparent. Mr Reid, who is known to back Mr Milburn for his fellow Scot's job, is a similarly combative Blairite.'[4]

Then, at the end of the party conference, Blair revealed a change of heart. Repeatedly warned by MPs that the division and speculation could damage the party's chances at the next election, he seemed to recognise that it had gone on long enough. He decided to state clearly that, rather than following Margaret Thatcher's example and promising to 'go on and on', he would stand down sometime during a third term and would not fight a fourth election.

But even that did not end all the speculation. As late as the following January, Rachel Sylvester from the *Daily Telegraph* – a political journalist who, like her partner Patrick Wintour from the *Guardian*, had good sources among Blair's aides – predicted Brown's demise. In an article headed 'Brown may be sacked in Blair reshuffle'[5] it was claimed that Blair 'is preparing to conduct the biggest Cabinet reshuffle of his premiership if he wins the next general election in order to stamp his authority on a third Labour term'. She reported a senior Blairite adviser as saying that 'removing Mr Brown may have to be considered, despite the huge risk'.

This just added to the feeding frenzy. On 9 January 2005 Gaby Hinscliff in the *Observer*[6] raised the prospect of 'two campaigns' run by Blair and Brown with the two men making 'competing speeches about Britain's role in a troubled world at opposite ends of the country'. She concluded: 'The only thing on which both camps can agree is that the episode has been deeply damaging. Once again, the focus is on rifts, not policy.' Hinscliff's article also reported the desperation felt by Labour backbenchers about the situation. Eric Illsley, Labour MP for Barnsley Central, said the two most important men in the government were being 'bloody childish', while veteran transport committee chair Gwyneth Dunwoody urged both sides to 'shut up'.

In the end, however, it was neither overtures of peace from Blair nor dissatisfied Labour MPs that ensured that Brown would have a major role in the campaign. Instead, he was saved by two factors – Alan Milburn's capacity for self-destruction and proof of the huge lingering damage to Blair's reputation done by Iraq.

When the campaign began in January, Milburn was joined by Alastair Campbell on the strict condition that Campbell was confined to a backroom role (albeit an important one), had no direct dealings with the press and never appeared at briefings. The Labour campaign was to be different – no battlebus, stricter security surrounding Blair's whereabouts and 'a more conversational, more spontaneous and less scripted campaign'. There were no plans to highlight the strong economy – the ace in Brown's pack; instead, the emphasis was to be on the reform of the public services promoted by Blair.

The campaign got off to a less than auspicious start, with Blair and Brown speaking from different scripts, as the commentators had forecast. But the most publicised problems arose out of decisions taken by Milburn over campaign advertising. Two campaign posters – one depicting Tory leader Michael Howard as Shylock and another depicting leading Tories as flying pigs – had to be hastily withdrawn. Nobody seems to have realised that since Michael Howard and Oliver Letwin, the shadow chancellor, were both Jewish, such images could easily cause offence. In a party that preached tolerance and respect for other faiths and ethnic communities, the oversight was all the more glaring.

Milburn himself, while competent and professional in chairing press conferences, did not even appear to be in charge. According to researchers for a Channel 4 television programme that had planted a reporter inside Labour's campaign headquarters, Campbell appeared to be the dynamo – always in control and directing operations. More often than not Milburn was seen with his feet on the table reading the newspapers. Far from being Labour's new leader-in-waiting, he often appeared to do little and care less.

Luckily for Milburn, the Tories' own campaign had even bigger difficulties. It began with Michael Howard forcing Howard Flight, the Tory deputy chairman and longstanding MP for the safe seat of Arundel, to stand down as a candidate after he was secretly taped promising much bigger public spending cuts than had been endorsed by the leadership. The entrapment, which the Tories believed was part of a Labour-inspired 'dirty tricks' campaign, caused huge embarrassment and was an enormous distraction.

But Labour was hit in the middle of the campaign by a more devastating blow. They had employed opinion pollsters Yougov to do their private polling. Concern about the party's trust ratings led to them to ask the electorate some direct questions about the factors that might affect their voting intentions. The most direct question of the lot was simply whether Blair or Brown should lead the Labour Party. The results, presented under the heading 'Is Blair a liability?', were very disturbing.

If Blair remained leader, the pollsters forecast that Labour's lead over the Tories would shrink to just 4 per cent – Labour getting a 36 per cent share, the Tories 32 per cent and the Liberal Democrats 25 per cent. But when voters were asked their intentions should Brown take over, the figures were transformed. Labour leapt to 42 per cent, the Tories fell to 29 per cent and the Liberal Democrats dropped to 21 per cent. For a party whose guiding lights were focus groups and private polling, the figures were horrendous. Quite simply, if Blair remained in charge, the party would still get home – but with a much-reduced majority. If Brown took over as leader, it would get back with its third landslide victory.

Milburn was left in shock – it amounted to curtains for his campaign leadership. Blair was equally alarmed – the Iraq war had come back and bitten him hard. Campbell knew that the campaign would have to change dramatically and that all bets on dropping Gordon were off.

Campbell, according to friends of Brown, decided there were two alternatives.

> He could swap Blair for Brown, but nobody could do this in the middle of an election campaign so he did the next best thing – if Brown wasn't going to be the leader he could be given equal billing with Tony – the two could both be seen to be leaders.

Faced with the horror of ending his premiership with a potentially small majority – and with all the problems that John Major had had with right-wing Tory rebels, the famous 'bastards', being replicated by Labour's own awkward squad, the Campaign Group – Blair abruptly changed tactics. As one aide put it bluntly: 'He simply flip-flopped overnight.' From then on Brown was brought back centre stage – with Blair even being pictured buying him an ice cream. Clearly, Blair had been forced to recognise that his 'project' was doomed unless he could get a working majority.

Brown himself has been circumspect about his change of fortune. He had originally planned a separate campaign, appearing with trade union leaders at rallies. He alluded to the change after the election. During his address to the Amicus annual conference in Brighton – part of his post-election wooing of the unions – he jokingly boasted of working with 'a very important man', Derek Simpson, the union's general secretary, for the election campaign until he was called away to work with Blair.[7]

In fact, the final result was remarkably similar to Yougov's polling results – Blair was re-elected with a much-reduced majority. Effectively, Blair returned to government as 'a liability'. The margin was even smaller than the private pollsters had predicted: Labour got 35.26 per cent of the vote, the Conservatives 32.34 per cent and the Liberal Democrats 22.06 per cent.

With the election over, relations between Blair and Brown again returned to normality – the distance between the two men grew. But Blair was in no position to sack Brown from the cabinet – he was indebted to his chancellor for his contribution towards an election victory that had left him with a workable majority of 66. Milburn was no longer in pole position to challenge Brown. In fact, he was nowhere at all. He left the cabinet – his old friend, John Hutton, took on his job as Chancellor of the Duchy of Lancaster. Milburn's political future – if any – would be in cultivating outside interests, pursuing his links with the Labour lobbying company Sovereign Strategy.

Any others who harboured ambitions for the leadership crown also had to put any plans they may have had on hold. Peter Hain, newly appointed as Northern Ireland secretary, who is also keen on wooing the trade union vote, privately told one union leader, 'I don't think I could challenge Gordon for the leadership, I'm more likely to go for the deputy leadership.'

But any expectations that Blair would be reduced to the status of a lame-duck premier soon faded as once again events went his way. The prospect of a divisive referendum in Britain on the European constitution collapsed after the French and the Dutch voted down the idea. Brown and Blair shared credit for the G8 summit and the initiative on reducing poverty in Africa. The growth of the economy – Brown's strongest card – slowed down and the cost of public spending threatened to rise, enough for Brown to change the terms of his 'golden rule' – balancing borrowing and expenditure over a longer period to appear to balance the books.

But probably the biggest short-term boost for Blair came from the most unexpected quarter. The ugly appearance of Europe's first suicide bombers, killing over fifty people on London's tubes and buses, brought Britain into a fresh crisis. The horrendous attacks in London brought out the best in Blair – as a good communicator and a steadying hand as Britain stared into the abyss.

Once again, Blair was at the centre of events and on an international stage. The temptation to stay in power must be great. The latest joke doing the rounds among trade union leaders is that Blair's offer to Brown to stand down after this election was misunderstood: 'Oh no, Gordon, I meant after the fourth term, not the third, didn't you understand?' Frankly, after such a public statement it is almost inconceivable that Blair would change his mind again. But he can be very capricious and Brown could still have a long wait before it eventually happens.

As of July this year, Brown seemed content to bide his time – knowing that the present moment is not the best one. By the end of this year, the Tories will have a new leader – and a fresh chance to convince the public that the party could form a credible alternative government. Brown may again become restless. Blair may again feel his mission is not complete. Events could still change everything.

CHAPTER SEVENTEEN

WHO IS TONY BLAIR?

The first edition of this book was widely perceived as a relentless attack on the prime minister. Even Roy Hattersley, who is one of Tony Blair's most trenchant critics, complained in his review that we were too harsh. We were a little surprised, since we were certainly no harsher than Hattersley was in the long interviews he kindly gave us.

But perhaps we should put on record the good there is in Blair. And it's not negligible.

Tony Blair is the most accomplished politician of his generation. That may sound like a double-edged compliment – the word 'politician' has always carried an undertone of contempt – but most of us would rather live in a society governed by accomplished politicians than any of the alternatives so far invented.

He's sincere and courageous. When he says he cannot apologise for taking Britain to war in Iraq because he honestly believed it was right, he is telling the truth. Because he thought it was right, he was willing to live with the consequences. It made a political bed of nails for him to lie on. His party lost members in droves, and his relationship with Labour MPs suffered a blow from which it will never recover. The things he had to do to drag us into the war took all the gloss from his image and made him look shifty. The war reduced his parliamentary majority at the 2005 general election. He was forced to announce before polling day that he would not lead his party into any more elections. He accepted this pain because he believed the war was right. Of course, that sort of self-belief also has its downside – but we'll come to that later.

His near-recovery in 2005 has been that of a masterly political technician. First, he has seamlessly managed to turn a war that he fought for one purpose into a war justified by a completely different purpose. He fought it, he told us, solely to get rid of Iraq's weapons of mass destruction; he now justifies it solely on the basis that Saddam Hussein was an evil dictator. Second, since the 2005 general election, he has been able to bring home some triumphs. Against all the odds, he had a glorious political summer in 2005, as even Hattersley acknowledged:

> Whether or not his last-minute lobbying swayed the Olympic committee in favour of London, Blair's decision to make Sebastian Coe leader of the bid set the campaign on the course that led to victory … (His) reaction to the London bomb outrage [of July 2005] was near perfect. His response was entirely free of false sentiment and bogus patriotism. Then he squeezed every possible drop of progress out of the G8 summit. Almost as important, he resisted the temptation to claim more success than he had achieved.[1]

And the extent of his sincerity and self-belief is the more remarkable because it is not rooted in any definable political philosophy. It comes from within the man. In a forthcoming book[2] Robert Skidelsky writes that his missionary zeal 'is not attached to any concrete projects or doctrines. It is a generalised, unfocused urge to make the world better, to right wrongs.' So 'he has reconnected British politics to its radical, progressive, pre-Labour roots. And it has been his own lack of roots which has given him the audacity to do so.' Roy Hattersley, coming at it from the other side – Skidelsky from the right, Hattersley from the left – makes the same point. Remarking that Blair knows little about the history and philosophy of the party he leads, he calls the prime minister 'the soldier who crossed a minefield in confident safety because he did not know that the mines were there'. That is why, though Gordon Brown's views may not be much different from Blair's, he could never have moved the Labour Party anything like as far as Blair has done. Brown is an expert on Labour traditions and history, who as a young man wrote a biography of the legendary Labour hero Jimmy Maxton, of whom Blair had probably never heard until he met Brown.

Add all that to Blair's enormous personal charm and his fierce personal loyalty to those who give him loyalty in return, sometimes well beyond the point where it is politically expedient – witness the multiple reinventions of Peter Mandelson – and you have a remarkable and not unattractive human being.

But his strengths are also his weaknesses. 'One is tempted,' Skidelsky added, 'to write of him, as Keynes did of Lloyd George: "(He) is rooted in nothing; he is void and without content; he is an instrument and a player at the same time."' Not having a definable political philosophy makes him prey to every fashionable fad. He grasped at the cod management theories of the 1980s like a drowning man.

On a visit to the National Theatre in his first term as prime minister, Blair was introduced to an actor backstage. The young man probably hoped the prime minister would say something complimentary about his performance, but what Blair said was: 'I'm very pleased to meet you – I've read every one of your father's books.'

The actor's father is management guru-turned-religious philosopher Charles Handy, and it is very significant that Blair has read all his books. Professor Handy is in the wealthiness-is-next-to-godliness school of management gurus. He also offers a sort of simplistic piety which at one stage earned him a regular gig on the *Today* programme's godspot, and he has a reputation for management wisdom earned while teaching at the London Business School. So he presses all the right buttons for Blair: God; the moral worth of material success; the desirability of a society in which we are all watching for a chance to make a buck; and the magical powers of private sector management techniques.

Handy pours scorn on the idea of having a safe job, and urges us all to become business entrepreneurs. He holds up John Birt as a shining example. For the first six months of Birt's time as director-general, Handy points out, Birt was not employed directly by the BBC; instead, the BBC had a contract with Birt's private company. Handy thinks this was visionary.[3] Most people thought it was just greedy.

Perhaps it was Birt that Blair had in mind in February 2002 when he told an American audience through *Forbes* magazine: 'It's about creating the right enterprise culture in Britain, which we still haven't driven all the way down in our country, by any means at all. I want to see far more emphasis on entrepreneurship in schools, far closer links between universities and business, I want to see us develop a far greater entrepreneurial culture. We have only just gone beneath the surface of this so far.'

Birt, who, after leaving the BBC, became Blair's personal strategist, has given the prime minister a good many management tips. These range from the ludicrous to the blindly reactionary. At the BBC, as Anthony Rendell put it to us, 'all the currently fashionable management devices were tried, all at once, in a hurry'. Birt instituted a Big Conversation, as well as a Making It Happen initiative involving staff sitting around on red beanbags. Blair ran a Big Conversation with the electorate. The two 'conversations' had one essential element in common. Both were designed not as two-way discussions, but as occasions on which the management, or the government, could convince those lower down of the correctness of their view. Only one side was really expected to listen.

Being a man with no definable political philosophy, Blair turns lack of political philosophy into a virtue. In a private, and unreported, lecture to civil servants at London Docklands, he told his astonished audience that there is not a huge difference between the Labour and Conservative parties. It is more a question of management. Labour should sell itself on being more efficient than the Conservatives.

Blair's great skills as a political manager are the more remarkable because he came to Downing Street with less experience than any prime minister for well over a hundred years. Not only had he never been in government; he had never run or managed anything, not even a student union. So he gobbled up the theories of management gurus like Handy. And what they said to him was: tear down all the bureaucratic civil service structures, all the paraphernalia of meetings and minutes and consulting; do it like the business leaders we admire, on the hoof, in your shirtsleeves, latte in one hand and mobile phone in the other. Run Great Britain plc as though it were a City investment company. Get by on management jargon. 'Think the unthinkable,' as he told Frank Field when he appointed him to look at welfare (and perhaps we should be grateful he did not use the dreaded management jargon phrase 'Think outside the box' – though we are told he has been heard to use it on occasion). But when Field took him at his word, Blair fired him, because he thought the wrong unthinkable.

His former cabinet secretary, Sir Robin Butler, watched horrified as the structure of cabinet government was pulled down about his ears, but lacked the dynamism to do anything except protest ineffectually. 'Blair is a good chairman of cabinet,' one senior former cabinet minister told us. 'He is relaxed, permissive, lets colleagues speak. But it is not part of a decision-making process.' Butler once told Blair: 'Your trouble is that you have never managed anything.' Blair protested that he had managed the Labour Party, but Butler replied: 'You didn't manage it, you led it. That's different.'[4]

Under Blair, Parliament has become much less important, and the prime minister's private office much more so. The growth of the power of the prime minister's office goes back to David Lloyd George, who invented what was then known as the 'kitchen cabinet'. Since then, prime ministers have made growing use of their private office, and some of them – Harold Wilson and Margaret Thatcher in particular – have greatly increased its power. But right up to John Major's time, cabinet government still meant something. The story of the Iraq war suggests that this is no longer true. Under Blair, the power of the PM's office has grown to the point where Parliament and the cabinet are often treated as ciphers.

That is why, when the Blair court implodes, it matters. And, as we have seen, it imploded dramatically in 2003, under the dual strains of Iraq and the Blair family's embarrassment over the purchase of two flats in Bristol and their friendship with Carole Caplin.

It looked briefly as though Blair was willing to rein in his private office. He replaced three unconventional personal advisers, who could only have worked in a Blair-style court, with conventional political operators.

First there was Alastair Campbell's replacement. Neil Kinnock was one of many who thought right from the start that Campbell's appointment would be a disaster, both for Blair and Campbell; and old public relations hands could have told Blair that a PR who got to be as well known as his boss was a liability. But Blair wanted more than a PR: he wanted political cover. He wanted someone to do the dirty work, who did not mind being seen as more powerful than he really was so that it looked as though he, and not Blair, was dishing the dirt. Campbell was vain enough to do it. Campbell wanted to leave after the 2001 general election, but Blair persuaded him to stay, and Campbell took the arrows for Blair over the BBC.

In his place, and with reduced and far more conventional powers, Blair appointed the experienced conventional political PR whom the old guard would have recommended in the first place, David Hill. Blair still seems to demand absolute loyalty, though: Hill's old boss, mentor and friend Roy Hattersley says Hill has stopped returning his calls, presumably because of the unkind things Hattersley says about Blair.

Next there was Campbell's partner, Fiona Millar, hired to look after Cherie. This was never a meeting of minds. Millar is an atheist, Cherie a Catholic. Millar is steeped in political discipline, while Cherie is more of an instinctive and tribal Labour Party figure.

Millar imposed on herself, and tried to impose on Cherie, a fierce New Labour-style control. Imposing it on herself was as much of a strain as imposing it on her boss. Fiona Millar is, by background and temperament, an Old Labour type, who has used her recent freedom from the Blair court to campaign ferociously against some of Tony Blair's most cherished policies on health and education and is now one of the leading campaigners against city academies.

Millar's replacement was a much more conventional appointment: Sue Geddes, a career civil servant from an old English Catholic family. Geddes does not see herself as a gatekeeper in the way that Millar did, and friends who want to talk to Cherie no longer feel they are being interrogated before they are allowed to do so. Cherie is said to feel much more comfortable in the hands of someone who does not want to control her life, just run her diary.

Finally, there was Anji Hunter, Blair's oldest and closest female friend whom he met as a teenager, and his closest adviser in Downing Street. Until she joined Blair she had no strong political interests but vaguely right-wing political views, and no relevant experience, but her charm worked magic on vain male Labour MPs. Her replacement is the old Labour Party organiser, fixer and safe pair of hands, Sally Morgan.

The ship was righted. Or, as Blair's management books would probably have it, re-engineered.

On 1 August 2003, Blair flagged up an anniversary. On that day, he had occupied Downing Street for as long as Clement Attlee, Labour prime minister from 1945 to 1951. And he invited us to compare their records.

There are some personal similarities. Attlee and Blair were both products of public school and Oxford. As students, neither took an interest in politics. Both were trained barristers; neither practised much. But Attlee came to politics after seeing poverty in the East End of London and vowing to change the system responsible for it. Unlike Blair, he arrived in Downing Street with a political philosophy which underpinned everything he did as prime minister.

Attlee's achievements are reminders of what Labour government is supposed to be about, which is why Blair's creepier ministers try to diminish them. Attlee 'ran out of steam', they say; his government's Welfare State and nationalisation measures had faults; Attlee failed to win a full second parliamentary term.

But Attlee's government was, at its heart, about fighting the five giants identified in the 1942 Beveridge Report: Want, Disease, Ignorance, Squalor and Idleness. So there were family allowances and national insurance, the National Health Service, a vast new council housing programme, and the first universal system of free education, with a huge school-building programme and the raising of the leaving age to fifteen. As for Idleness, the government started with 10 million people in wartime jobs that were no longer needed, yet it managed to stop unemployment ever going above 3 per cent.

The difference this made to the lives of ordinary people was staggering. By the mid-1950s, almost all Britain's fourteen-year-olds went to school; twenty years earlier, only four in ten had done so. The dole queues of the 1930s ended, and those few who could not work no longer starved. NHS doctors reported seeing thousands of women with prolapsed internal organs that had been like that for years, and men with hernias and lung disease who had never been examined because they could not afford it. Before the NHS, people regularly died of curable illnesses because treatment cost money.

These measures shifted the balance of wealth and power away from the rich and towards the poor. Blair's government has done the opposite. The gap between rich and poor is wider now than in 1997 – though there have also been advances for the poorest, chief among them the national minimum wage.

Attlee's government nationalised the railways, which seemed like a revolutionary step at the time. This was not reversed until John Major's government botched the job. So Blair inherited a new privatised monopoly which everyone could see was not working – and still did not take it back into public ownership. Only now are ministers starting to confess that this may have been a mistake.

Attlee came to power in immeasurably more difficult circumstances than Blair. Britain was bankrupt, with a war-ravaged economy and infrastructure, made worse by the abrupt withdrawal of lend-lease by the United States and the harsh terms of the American loan. He faced a Conservative Party led by a national hero, Winston Churchill, which took the opportunity to renew itself in opposition. There were many who argued that a welfare state should wait until Britain could afford it.

New Labour has created little that is really new: it has tinkered with what it inherited. Foundation hospitals, city academies, specialist schools – all represent a restless need to take the springs out of the engine and put them in the other way round to see if that makes it go faster. As Robert Skidelsky writes, 'Despite Blair's personal passion for education, his government is unlikely to leave a mark on its structure as profound as Balfour's Act of 1902 or Butler's Act of 1944.'[5]

The press was bitterly hostile to Attlee from the start, because proprietors like Beaverbrook saw him (rightly) as a real threat to the status quo. No newspaper proprietor has ever seen Blair like that. And Attlee, unlike Blair, did not much care what the media wrote. When Attlee's press secretary Francis Williams brought him an especially unfair attack, he just grunted: 'Suppose they've got to say something. Circulation slipping, you think?' If Williams had had so poor a sense of priorities as to devote most of his working day to pursuing an Andrew Gilligan, Attlee would have fired him.

Attlee would have loathed the 'Call me Tony' style of unminuted decision-making in Tony's den – the 'denocracy'. For Attlee, minutes and constitutional behaviour helped preserve democratic government, and he insisted in cabinet that ministers referred to each other by their titles. In private he would talk to his old friend Ernie, but in cabinet he addressed Ernest Bevin formally as 'Foreign Secretary'.

Blair's July 2004 tirade against the 1960s was really a tirade against the Attlee settlement. For it was in the late 1960s – a period Blair enjoyed at the time and excoriated in retrospect – that the first generation grew up in Britain that was educated, and had never had to fear unemployment, near-starvation, or being unable to pay for their medical treatment. That gives people freedom, and Attlee would have approved. If the sixties generation used that freedom in unconventional and sometimes foolish ways, is that not what freedom is for? Labour is now led by a man who believes that the freedom from worry that his generation enjoyed is too good for the next generation. It is his generation (and that of the present authors) that has pulled up the ladder he and we climbed.

Neither Attlee's admirers nor his detractors are likely to think much of the parallel with Blair, except perhaps in the area of foreign policy, where Harold Macmillan offered a tribute to Attlee's foreign secretary Ernest Bevin that might well fit the Blair government: 'Bevin . . . has imposed upon an unwilling and hesitant party a policy of resistance to Soviet Russia and to Communism. A Tory Foreign Secretary [in the immediate post-war years] could not have done this.'[6] In foreign as well as domestic affairs, Conservative policies have been implemented by the Blair government far more effectively than a Conservative government could have done.

In personality and political style, Attlee and Blair are polar opposites. Attlee believed that if you wanted to bring in radical policies, you should sound as tame and unthreatening as possible. He had a personality that lent itself to this: he sounded like a suburban bank manager and could have left his audience yawning after announcing the last trump. Blair, on the other hand, believes in dressing up the smallest initiative in apocalyptic language.

Blair shares virtually nothing with Attlee: neither his policies, his radicalism, nor his personality. He does share a lot with Lloyd George, according to Robert Skidelsky, who says there is much more than their shared political rootlessness to connect the First World War premier with the Iraq war premier: 'Like Lloyd George, Blair has no sense of history, he does not read books. He runs a sleazy court, and he is an exceptionally gifted political seducer.'[7]

But for all Skidelsky's persuasiveness, we still think that the model for Blair was Ramsay MacDonald, Labour's first prime minister in 1924 and again in 1929–31 until he deserted his party in 1931 to lead a predominantly Conservative government.

Both were vain, handsome, charming men with theatrical talent. Both were idolised by their closest friends. Both were ruthless about firing people, but liked to get someone else to convey the bad news. Attlee, who was more ruthless about firing people than either of them, once said: 'You have to send for the man and tell him yourself. MacDonald used to get someone else to do it.' In the early days, Blair's bad news was conveyed by the luckless Nick Brown.

Both were ridiculed for their deference to the rich and titled. 'Tomorrow every duchess in London will want to kiss me,' MacDonald exulted when he left Labour to lead the National Government. Blair is impressed by royalty and the landed gentry, but even more by the very rich and powerful. Rupert Murdoch is worth a dozen duchesses to him.

Both wanted to lead a national consensus that was above politics. Both yearned to gather other parties under their leadership into a 'big tent'. MacDonald dreamed throughout his 1929–31 government of taking the Labour Party with him into a coalition with the Conservatives. He was not able to achieve this, and eventually settled for second best, leaving the Labour Party to lead a National (essentially Conservative) Government. Blair has been more successful: he managed to take the Labour Party with him in his lurch rightwards.

MacDonald left behind him a political landscape that was badly broken, but able to renew itself. Blair's legacy is an entirely altered political landscape.

Most prime ministers spend their time tugging the centre of political gravity a little in their direction. They cannot pull too far, or they will lose the middle ground entirely. But they tug it as far as they can. Attlee tugged the centre of gravity towards the things that Labour stood for, so successfully that much of what Labour did became the new political consensus for nearly thirty years. Margaret Thatcher tugged the centre of gravity in her direction, again very successfully – we still do not know when the consensus she created will be challenged, but it has not happened yet.

Blair did the opposite. He did not pull the centre of gravity; he pushed it. Electorally, it was brilliant. It left the Conservatives struggling for space. They have to find more and more outlandishly right-wing things to say in order to have some ground of their own. There is, since the 2005 election, no evidence that they have found another way forward. But people who have been voting Labour since Harold Wilson was prime minister are left wondering what they waited eighteen years for.

Lack of political roots – a set of beliefs which guide your actions – is in some ways an advantage to a prime minister. It gave both Lloyd George and MacDonald the ability to manoeuvre quickly, and to lead cabinets consisting overwhelmingly of their political opponents. Lloyd George the Liberal leader and Ramsay MacDonald the Labour leader both ended up leading Conservative-dominated cabinets.

The fact that Blair comes entirely unencumbered with roots is apparent from a glance at the nearest thing we have to a statement of his beliefs – a book published in 1996 whose title compressed the largest number of feel-good words into the smallest amount of meaning: *New Britain – My Vision of a Young Country*. It's full of headings that repeat those words. We opened the book at random and all these headings hit us at once: 'A young country that wants to be a strong country', 'Modern public services for the people', 'Strong Britain', 'Democratic Britain'. (We hit on pages 50–1 if you want to check.)

The main ideological thought in it seems to be that we should re-define socialism as what Blair calls 'social-ism'. This, Blair claims, means 'we can regain the intellectual confidence to take on and win the battle of ideas'. He does not explain what battle is to be fought with which ideas.

Since there are no coherent written statements of what Blair believes, we have to work it out from his day-to-day pronouncements and his actions. From these we can see that he believes there is nothing the public sector can do that the private sector can't do better; that trade unions are at best a burden on business and must be kept firmly in check; that there are few economic problems which cannot be solved by the creation of a market; that the best hope for the world is the pax Americana, and Britain should hug America close and not be seduced by either our European neighbours or dangerously idealistic talk of international action through the United Nations; and that Britain, America and Christianity can between them create a new and better world order.

All these views and values are quite respectable, and Blair shares them with millions of his fellow countrymen. There is even a mainstream political party that shares them. It is called the Conservative Party.

Once Labour adopted these ideas too, we lost our democratic choices. Compare Britain with Spain at the time of the Iraq war. Both countries had prime ministers who supported the war. But when the Spanish people wanted to show they were against the war, they could vote for the opposition – as they did in a spectacular political upset on 14 March 2004. In Britain, there is no such choice.

Suppose you think that the public sector is better at running public services than the private sector, or that the railways ought to be nationalised, or that higher education ought to be free, or that schools ought to be non-selective, or that taxes on the rich should be raised well above 50 per cent to improve the Welfare State, or that labour laws should be designed to help trade unions bargain on behalf of the workforce, or that foreign wars ought to be sanctioned by the United Nations. These, too, are perfectly respectable things to believe, but there is no longer a party you can vote for that believes them and has any prospect of power.

Voters in most other European countries have a choice between competing ideologies. In Britain we do not, not any more.

In 1945 the Labour Party had a million individual paid-up members. The total published in 2004 was 248,294, and that figure was considerably inflated by including lapsed members and those who had already left because of the Iraq war. The real figure is thought to be less than 200,000.

Membership of all political parties has been declining steadily since 1945, for several reasons. But Labour's decline as a mass party has gained momentum in the Blair years, partly because, when political party membership is so rare, people only join a party if its stance is one they strongly believe in (unless, of course, they want a political career).

People have mostly joined the Labour Party because they think it is instinctively on the side of the underdog. They are less likely to join when it is led by a man who gives the impression that his first instinct is always that the rich and powerful are likely to be right. Blair is instinctively supportive of private companies and dismissive of the public sector, and he has tried to run the government as though he were the chief executive of Great Britain plc.

You would have thought that a leader so fundamentally at odds with the deepest instincts of the members of his party could not last long or achieve much. So why has Blair been allowed to take Labour so far, so fast? For that, you have to start from the circumstances of his election as Labour leader in 1994. The 1992 general election was traumatic for the Labour Party. After eleven years of Thatcherism, they at last thought they were coming back and the tide of Thatcherite policies could be stemmed. But after the election, whatever the polls said, most of Labour's top brass still secretly thought they could lose next time too.

That's why the Parliamentary Labour Party was such fertile ground for the seeds of discontent so assiduously sown by Tony Blair and Peter Mandelson during John Smith's brief leadership. The spectre of the Bennites and the spectre of a fifth defeat gave Blair his victory in the leadership election of 1994 – even though the Bennites were a spent force and the Conservatives were busily making themselves unelectable.

Blair feasts on the Bennite spectre, just as Thatcher did. So long as you can still frighten the children with the names of Tony Benn and Arthur Scargill, so long will Blair continue to thrive.

Once elected, he was allowed his own way with Labour's policies because his famous threat was real: 'The choice is not between the Labour government of your dreams and this Labour government. It is between this Labour government and the Conservatives.' Any other choice, he was saying, died with John Smith. Get used to it.

Anji Hunter has said Blair enjoys winding up television interviewers and watching them get angry while he stays calm. He also enjoys doing this to the party he leads. He's hated, as no previous Labour leader was ever hated, in his party. In trade unions, once a candidate for office is identified as a Blairite, his or her chances are finished. His old friendship with Roy Hattersley ended on the day that Blair twitted Hattersley about wanting to go back to the policies of 1983, for Hattersley knew that he, and not Blair, had fought to free Labour from the policies of 1983. Neil Kinnock struggles to stay loyal, and is privately appalled by much of what goes on – he believes that his position as a former Labour leader means he cannot say credibly what he feels.

Yet Blair has managed to make himself pretty well impregnable. This is partly because of what he has done to Labour's constitution. He has ensured that getting rid of a leader cannot be managed without a bitter internal battle, which could cause fatal damage to the party's electoral prospects. And it is partly because Labour politicians have power at last, and are not going to turn on the man who has led them to it. The more ideologically inclined, people like David Blunkett and John Reid, were once intolerant members of the left; they are now equally intolerant Blairites. The Blairites, like the Bennites, police ideological purity strictly. So long as Labour remains in government, Blair, more than any of his predecessors, is able to go at a time of his choosing.

The distance Labour has travelled under his leadership is amazing. On almost any subject – the structure of the health service, the way state education should be organised and its relationship with private education, the nature of the special relationship with the United States, the role of the trade unions in industry – the debate is on completely different ground to what it was ten years ago. There is no longer even much pretence that Blair simply carried on the reform work started by Neil Kinnock, more a sullen acceptance that he has created a different party from the one Kinnock led.

Where Clement Attlee slayed the 'five giants' identified by Lord Beveridge – Want, Disease, Ignorance, Squalor and Idleness – Tony Blair slays the giants inside his own party: the trade unions, the public sector, socialism. Are there more left-wing giants to slay? Probably only one, and we were put onto it by a senior and experienced British operator in Brussels.

A Labour government led by either Neil Kinnock or John Smith would have moved swiftly closer to Europe, lessening Britain's dependence on the

United States. They would have gone into the euro early, without a referendum. They would have gone into the European constitution without a referendum, and France would have followed suit. For most people in Britain, the European issue would be settled by now, as much yesterday's news as the Falklands war. The world would have found what Kinnock or Smith might just have been tempted to call a Third Way.

In May 2004, the Luxembourg prime minister, Jean-Claude Juncker, visited 10 Downing Street to discuss the Luxembourg presidency of the EU, due in the second half of the year. The Christian Democrat Juncker said he wanted to go some way to meeting the European TUC's call for a charter of fundamental human rights, and Blair said: 'That's the most Old Labour speech I've heard in Downing Street for a long time.' Soon afterwards, Foreign Secretary Jack Straw gave a promise to a Confederation of British Industry dinner that Britain would block Juncker's proposals. 'We're not going to change Thatcher's laws and we're not going to let Europe change them,' he said.[8]

In May 2004 Chancellor Gordon Brown made a private and unreported speech to several big City players, including News International's Rupert Murdoch. He said that Europe was a failed experiment, and he extolled the virtues of the United States.

There were already many in Europe who believed that from the moment Blair announced that Britain was to hold a referendum on the European constitution, instead of ratifying it through Parliament, the writing was on the wall for Britain in Europe. That, they suspect, is at the root of the talk of an 'Anglo-Saxon' model of Europe. Blair and Brown have both been fascinated by the USA, and it has always been the north star of Blair's foreign policy. The word among Brussels-watchers was that Blair would find a way of stopping the European constitution, and, like the Eurosceptic wing of the Conservative Party, that he sees Britain's future as drawing even closer to the Americans.

Blair's announcement that Britain was to hold a referendum forced President Jacques Chirac of France to announce that he, too, would hold a referendum – a referendum which Chirac duly lost.

The former Conservative chancellor Kenneth Clarke, a convinced European, once recalled privately that when Prime Minister John Major announced that he would not agree to going into the euro without a referendum, and Blair as opposition leader was obliged to match the pledge, Gordon Brown said to Clarke: 'You've probably ensured that Britain will never join the euro.' In the same way, they say, Blair ensured the death of the European constitution.

In mid-2005, Blair, on Britain's behalf, took on, for six months, the rolling presidency of the European Union. By then, the EU constitution was dead, having been rejected by the French and the Dutch. In many European capitals, its demise was greeted by genuine dismay, but in London one very quickly sensed that ministers were looking at a silver lining. Blair made his entry as president with a speech to the European Parliament which was generally acknowledged to be a tour de force, judging exactly the mood of the moment. Meanwhile, his spinners were as busy in the corridors of the European Parliament as they traditionally are in London. What the PM means – they said – is that the Franco-German model of Europe is dead; long live the Anglo-Saxon model.

It looks as though the pure Atlanticists have won, just as they did under Thatcher. Blair is proving a secret but thoroughgoing Eurosceptic. These days, French politicians talk darkly about 'America and its little helper Britain', and John Monks, general secretary of the European Trades Union Conference, has written a careful letter to Blair. The prime minister is right, he says, to be trying to map out a new role for Europe in the world. But it needs to be a Europe that is not a pale shadow of the US.[9]

Monks has appeared earlier in this story, when he ran the British Trades Union Congress, and will always be remembered as the man who said that Blair saw Old Labour people as 'embarrassing elderly relatives at a family gathering'. He was the first general secretary of the TUC ever to face the problem of dealing with a Labour prime minister who neither liked nor understood the unions.

Blair found a role for the unions in the New Labour scheme of things. But it was the strangest and most humiliating of roles. Unions, he discovered, could be used as voting fodder – so long as you forgot all the fine words you once spoke about how they should be made to use their power democratically.

The result was a shameless trade union fix, an attempt to make Frank Dobson mayor of London instead of Ken Livingstone, and Alun Michael leader of the Welsh assembly rather than Rhodri Morgan. Both the Labour Party and the electorate greatly preferred Livingstone and Morgan, and Blair tried to deny them their chosen leaders by the use of the trade union block vote.

In the end, but only after a titanic struggle, the people of London and Wales got the men they wanted. But why did he risk so much – especially in Wales, where Rhodri Morgan, though well to the left of Blair, did not have Livingstone's long history of being a thorn in the side of the 'modernisers'? It is, again, that almost superhuman certainty Blair possesses.

In Wales there was probably an additional factor. Alun Michael is a pillar of the Church. As a student at Keele University at the end of the 1960s, he was the leader of the campus Christians, and no candidate for student union president could be elected without Michael's support, for the Christians, who normally took little interest in student politics, voted the way he told them to. At election time he would interview all the candidates about their policies, morals and attitude to Christianity, and place his imprimatur on one candidate, who was usually elected. Blair would have approved.

For his God is far more important to Blair than his politics. He is a Roman Catholic, but an eclectic one, open, as we have seen, to all sorts of ways of finding God.

And this helps to give him his unshakeable certainty. It was a truly remarkable personal decision to take Britain to war in Iraq, requiring almost superhuman certainty and self-belief. Leave aside for a moment whether it was the right decision; just look at the circumstances in which it was made.

Of course prime ministers have to lead their countries into war sometimes, and, as Neil Kinnock put it to us, if you are not willing to take that on your shoulders, you should not go for the job. But Blair's decision to take Britain into war in Iraq differed in quality from that of any previous twentieth-century prime minister. In other wars – Asquith and the First World War, Chamberlain and the Second World War, Attlee and Korea, Thatcher and the Falklands, John Major and Iraq, even Anthony Eden and Suez – there was something of a political consensus, at least in the prime minister's own party, around the need for war.

Blair took his country into Iraq knowing that most of his cabinet opposed it (they voted for it, for the alternative was resignation, but they opposed it when it was first mooted); the overwhelming majority of his party opposed it; even close members of his court (probably including his wife), the people on whom he most relies, opposed it personally, though their first loyalty is to whatever Blair decides. If the Labour Party leader had been anyone else – any of the people it might have been – we would not have fought in Iraq. And he was even deprived of the support of his faith – the Pope was against it, and told him so forcefully.

So Iraq was Blair's war in a way that no other war has been the prime minister's. The decision, and its consequences, are as personal as that. The grieving parents whose children died in Iraq can say, with more truth than the parents of those who died in other wars, that the blood of their children is on the hands of one man.

You could argue that his reasons were good, and that, if he had decided differently, people would still have died. That is true; but *those* people would not have died (and fewer people would have died). That is what Blair must live with. Not many people, even prime ministers, have to live with that sort of knowledge. It would crush most people. It does not crush Blair. That is the measure of the man's certainty and self-belief.

It is also a measure of his uncanny political touch. Britain went to war in Iraq because Blair said there were weapons of mass destruction there, and Saddam Hussein had links with al-Qaeda. No one even bothers, today, to deny that these things were untrue; and that Blair (to put it at its mildest) could not have been sure they were true when he asserted them. So far, the people who have lost their jobs as a result are a BBC journalist who claimed at the time that these things were untrue; the chairman and director-general of the BBC, who supported the journalist; and the editor of the *Daily Mirror*, Piers Morgan.

Morgan is at least partially to blame for his own downfall. Morgan had a longstanding feud with the Blairs, and – it has to be said – behaved very badly, both publicly and privately, taking every opportunity to pillory Cherie. On one occasion, at a *Mirror* lunch, he jeered at Blair for earning less than he did and threw a £20 note on the table, saying: 'Here, Tony – give the kids a treat.' Alastair Campbell, unexpectedly dignified, quietly folded it up and gave it back, suggesting Morgan give it to charity. Cherie Booth, leaving the lunch, looked at Morgan for a moment and said: 'You're such a boy, Piers. When will you grow up?'[10]

She had, however, frequently urged *Mirror* executives to fire Morgan. And when Morgan printed pictures of British soldiers torturing Iraqis that turned out to be fake, his fate was sealed. 'The trouble with Piers,' according to one of his rivals, is that, 'his balls are bigger than his brains.'

Nonetheless, it's instructive to compare Morgan's fate, as well as that of BBC director-general Greg Dyke and BBC journalist Andrew Gilligan, with that of Tony Blair. Gilligan was right – Blair's claim that Saddam Hussein could launch weapons of mass destruction against Britain in forty-five minutes was quite false. Morgan was right – British troops were torturing Iraqis. Gilligan and Morgan did not survive in their jobs. Blair did.

When, in July 2005, bombs exploded on the London Underground and a London bus, killing more than fifty people, it quickly became the height of bad taste to link these deaths to the Iraq war. They were simply murders, committed by evil men. And so, of course, they were. That is a simple truth. But another simple truth became something one could not say in polite company, and only John Pilger – the Blair circle's most hated journalist – put it into words. Pilger wrote that without the war 'the

Londoners who died in the tube and on the number 30 bus almost certainly would be alive today'.[11]

That doesn't prove the war was wrong. Blair took a decision, which he defends to this day, and there are still those who argue that it was the right decision. Neither does he deny that the deaths of Britons in Iraq are the result of his decision. But his response to the London bombings, despite its sure-footedness in other respects, contains something very curious, which suggests that he may, perhaps, have allowed a flicker of uncertainty into his mind.

The man with the extraordinary self-belief which took us to war would surely have said: these bombs are part of the price we pay for doing the right thing. Instead, Blair has denied flatly that the war in Iraq had anything to do with the London bombings. Even Jack Straw was forced to admit the next day that the government could not possibly know for certain that what Blair said was true.

You do not have to agree with Pilger about the war to see that he must be right about this. Before the war, the Joint Intelligence Committee told Blair that war would increase the threat of terrorism in Britain. A leaked CIA report says that the war has turned Iraq into a major al-Qaeda centre, when before the war al-Qaeda had virtually no presence there. A Chatham House report in July 2005 said the war had boosted the al-Qaeda network.[12] Suicide bombing was unknown in Britain before the war. It might have found its way here eventually, but without the war those fifty-two people in London would be alive today.

A right-wing commentator, Robert Skidelsky, sums up the Iraq war in words that the left-wing John Pilger could only applaud. 'It is clear,' writes Skidelsky, 'to any unprejudiced observer that there was no defensible casus belli for the joint Anglo-American invasion of Iraq either in terms of national interest or international law. Saddam Hussein had no weapons of mass destruction, and the most that could be justified was a continued policy of surveillance and pressure to make sure he did not develop or acquire them ... It is now also tolerably clear that Blair agreed to back George W. Bush in a war to overthrow Saddam when the two met in Crawford, Texas, in April 2002. The only problem was to manufacture a plausible casus belli, since the object of regime change could not be openly avowed.'[13]

If you believe in yourself that strongly, then you believe you matter enough to sacrifice anyone else's reputation to save your own. Alastair Campbell and Peter Mandelson have done well enough out of Blair – Mandelson is European Commissioner, and Campbell is as saleable a commodity as publishing knows – but they have both had to spend years placing themselves between the guns and their master. And so has Cherie Booth.

Cherie introduced her husband to the Catholic church, as well as to the Labour Party, and understands both institutions far better than he does. We are inclined to agree with the many politicians and friends of the Blairs who have told us that she has had a thoroughly raw deal, pilloried by the press as a surrogate for her husband; but they miss one crucial point.

They are right to complain of the cruel and sometimes vindictive coverage she gets in the media. They are right to say that her friendship with Carole Caplin has been grossly misrepresented. Robin Cook, who frequently saw Caplin in Downing Street, offered us an antidote to the usual picture of Cherie's friend and lifestyle guru.

'She talks with great confidence and has good clothes sense. She is a pleasant, attractive woman with a vigorous personality. Her style is to make friends and seek influence. Her only real problem is that she is not someone who ages gracefully.' And he added, significantly: 'Holding onto her friendship with Carole was for Cherie one way of showing defiance.'

In the early days, when Blair was a parliamentary hopeful and then a young backbench MP, Cherie was known and respected on the left of the Labour Party: a good, clear, logical public speaker with clear views and principles. 'She cannot have found it easy to live in her husband's shadow,' says an MP who knew her in those days.

But the point they miss is the role of her husband, and her husband's staff, in making her position far harder. Dealing with an office that lives on media manipulation, as Blair's does, you cannot always say: the press did this, and it was not fair. As often as not, what happens is at least partly the result of a steer given to journalists, or an attempt to manipulate what they write. And so it is with Cherie.

No primeministerial consort has ever faced Cherie's problems. The nearest equivalent was Denis Thatcher, who had a successful career of his own. But he did not have her fiercely analytical mind; his career was drawing to an end when his wife became prime minister; his politics were vaguer than Cherie's, and more in tune with those of his primeministerial partner; and he was a man, and so did not face the same obsessive interest in what he wore.

Blair's wife wanted nothing so much as to carry on being Cherie Booth QC, successful and much-sought-after barrister. She had already given up any thought of a political career so as to help her husband's; she did not wish to give up her legal career too. But, as John Edmonds says:

'She was persuaded against her better judgement to take a prominent role in Blair's public life. She would rather have concentrated on her legal career. Peter Mandelson and Philip Gould told her that her husband needed her, she must for example be on the platform with him after his conference speech. They wanted her for the family image. She was being effectively blackmailed by people saying, if you are not there you are letting him down. And once she says anything, she pleases no one.'[14]

She did not want to be sidelined into the role of political wife. She went along with it at first, out of loyalty but also because, as one friend has put it to us, 'she believed he had a mission'. And no doubt she was all the things people say she was: a bit too greedy for the trappings of power, for the access to freebies it gave her, perhaps too conscious of the status of the prime minister's wife.

But when she started to rebel, it was not just the press that turned on her. It was the relentless Downing Street New Labour machine as well. The awful process of trashing Cherie over her friendship with Caplin and the purchase of two flats in Bristol – Cheriegate, as it came to be called in the press – which we describe in Chapter 14 had one objective. 'My job is to protect the prime minister and I don't care what it takes,' said Alastair Campbell at the time.[15]

New Labour spin doctors started to talk darkly of Cherie as a potential liability much earlier than that. A journalist in a position to know insists that the drip-feed of damaging stories about her friendship with Carole Caplin well before Cheriegate was at least in part instigated from Downing Street. It concealed the fact that Caplin was as much Tony Blair's friend as his wife's friend, and that the interest in New Age religion at least as much his as hers.

Tony and Cherie were once very much in love, and perhaps they still are. But the behaviour of her husband's staff, supported by her husband, during Cheriegate if not earlier, would kill trust in most marriages. Roy Hattersley complained that this suggestion of ours was 'tasteless', and so it may well be, but we are more interested in truth than taste; and the truth is that her husband turned his spinners loose on her. That cannot be easy to forgive. Like Mandelson and Campbell, but less willingly, she had become a lightning conductor for Blair, stopping bullets for him.

And while she certainly believed in her husband's mission in 1997, she is now alienated by some of his policies. Her careful, thoughtful recent lectures, described in Chapter 14, need to be read remembering that this is the prime minister's wife, who knows that any overt criticism will be ferreted out by the press. Even in the circumspect form in which she makes them, the government would rather she didn't, but cannot stop her; Foreign Office officials have privately admitted as much.

She has chosen to move her legal practice away from her first interest, in employment and family law, and into the much more politically sensitive area of human rights. As a human rights lawyer she is horrified by George Bush's America. She has spoken out forcefully against its use of the death penalty and its refusal to support the international court, and more obliquely against human rights abuses in Abu Ghraib and Guantánamo Bay. Privately, she is thought to have opposed the Iraq war, by far her husband's biggest project in his second term as prime minister.

One day, perhaps, Cherie Booth QC will have a story to tell.

APPENDIX I

ST. JAMES'S PALACE
LONDON SW1A 1BS

From: The Office of HRH The Prince of Wales

3rd April 2001

Dear Prime Minister,

I have been reflecting on our conversation this morning and on the point you made to me about the need for wider public support for a vaccination policy. For what it is worth, I do feel that much of the resistance within the farming community is based on ignorance and fear. For instance, I have seen an NFU advice note which says that 'Ring vaccination still requires the slaughter of all vaccinated animals'. It is little wonder as a result that the farming community is not in favour. If I may suggest, it might be worth the Government dispelling these myths in as clear and forthright a way as possible. I am sure that would help change the attitude to vaccination overnight.

I thought it might be helpful if I set down the key worries which farmers have and, as I have been advised, the answers to them:

1. All vaccinated animals must be slaughtered.

No. Vaccinated animals can and should go into the food chain. The only exception is where vaccinated animals show clinical signs of the disease, which they will do if they were infected before vaccination. These animals would, obviously, have to be slaughtered.

2. Vaccinated animals will become carriers.

This is not so. According to Gareth Davies, the epidemiologist who I understand was at your meeting yesterday morning and who has now been invited to join the Government's Foot and Mouth scientific advisory committee, the carrier frequency is similar in infected non-vaccinates as in infected vaccinates. And of course, there is no question of a non-infected animal becoming a carrier because it has been vaccinated.

3. The vaccine is not safe and might not work.

FMD vaccine contains killed virus and provides immunity lasting some 6 months. Immunity is induced within 10–14 days, but what is called 'High Load Antigen' vaccines induce immunity in as little as 4–5 days. And, again according to Gareth Davies, the present generation of vaccines is 'safe'.

4. Can you tell if a vaccinated animal is infected or not?

Yes you can. There are tests available which will reliably distinguish between infected and vaccinated animals. I am told that the Pirbright laboratory is preparing for mass testing.

5. What are the consequences of vaccination for the UK's disease-free status?

Even with the current slaughter policy I have not heard a scientist willing to predict when the disease will be over and therefore when the UK will achieve disease-free status again. But we do know that the UK could regain disease-free status twelve months after the last clinical case of the disease and/or the last animal has been vaccinated. If vaccines are used now to contain and cut short the outbreak, it must bring forward the date by which disease-free status can be claimed again.

6. Are there sufficient quantities of the vaccine available?

Yes, Pirbright has 500,000 doses of High Load Antigen vaccine. Beyond this there are 8.5 million doses of suitable vaccine in the EU vaccine banks. Cattle require one dose each and sheep one third of a dose.

Apart from these concerns, farmers are also worried that vaccination will mean that they will have problems selling produce from vaccinated animals. Certainly, the EU has laid down some conditions, for instance that within 30 days meat and milk from vaccinates must be kept separate from other meat and milk and identified and subjected to certain treatments. These problems worry farmers, particularly when set against the generous compensation available if their stock is slaughtered and against a background of such difficult times recently. But if the Government were to extend the compensation package to cover farmers suffering any shortfall as a result of vaccination, this problem could be overcome too.

Finally, I do think that the permission which the EU has given to the UK to allow vaccination only in Cumbria and Devon, and only on cattle, is short-sighted and unmeasurable. The permission must surely be extended to any holding where there is a legitimate reason for vaccinating, such as rare or native breeds, or organic farms. I know this may prove difficult to secure in Europe, but I do believe that it is essential.

I am sorry to go on pestering you in this way, especially as I am sure that you are receiving copious quantities of briefings on the subject, but I cannot tell you how important I believe it is to start a policy of vaccination urgently. Time really is of the essence. Every day pedigree and organic herds and flocks, and rare breeds are being lost – most urgently, as we have discussed, the Herdwick sheep in Cumbria. The situation will only become worse when cattle are put out for summer grazing onto fields which might have held infected sheep at some point. Farmers will have no choice but to do this because winter fodder will have run out. And then the infection could begin all over again.

The long-term devastation which delay is wreaking is almost beyond price. My own strong view is that if you were to make public the answers to these key questions, with all the force and reassurance of the Government's authority behind them, opinions could change quickly and allow you to introduce a vaccination policy. But, in the meantime, I have the awful feeling that a vaccination policy will only be introduced after further delay, during which thousands of animals will have been sacrificed needlessly and too many farmers' livelihoods lost forever.

I hope that these thoughts are helpful. I am so grateful to you for being prepared to converse with an interfering busybody during this immensely difficult time.

With kindest regards, as ever,

Charles

APPENDIX II

The legal advice given to Tony Blair by Attorney General Lord Goldsmith on the war in Iraq, 7 March 2003: Lord Goldsmith's summary.

SECRET
PRIME MINISTER
IRAQ: RESOLUTION 1441

Summary

26. To sum up, the language of resolution 1441 leaves the position unclear and the statements made on adoption of the resolution suggest that there were differences of view within the Council as to the legal effect of the resolution. Arguments can be made on both sides. A key question is whether there is in truth a need for an assessment of whether Iraq's conduct constitutes a failure to take the final opportunity or has constituted a failure fully to cooperate within the meaning of OP 4 such that the basis of the cease-fire is destroyed. If an assessment is needed of that sort, it would be for the Council to make it. A narrow textual reading of the resolution suggests that sort of assessment is not needed, because the Council has pre-determined the issue. Public statements, on the other hand, say otherwise.

27. In these circumstances, I remain of the opinion that the safest legal course would be to secure the adoption of a further resolution to authorise the use of force. I have already advised that I do not believe that such a resolution need be explicit in its terms. The key point is that it should establish that the Council has concluded that Iraq has failed to take the

final opportunity offered by resolution 1441, as in the draft which has already been tabled.

28. Nevertheless, having regard to the information on the negotiating history which I have been given and to the arguments of the US Administration which I heard in Washington, I accept that a reasonable case can be made that resolution 1441 is capable in principle of reviving the authorisation in 678 without a further resolution.

29. However, the argument that resolution 1441 alone has revived the authorisation to use force in resolution 678 will only be sustainable if there are strong factual grounds for concluding that Iraq has failed to take the final opportunity. In other words, we would need to be able to demonstrate hard evidence of non-compliance and non-cooperation. Given the structure of the resolution as a whole, the views of UNMOVIC and the IAEA will be highly significant in this respect. In the light of the latest reporting by UNMOVIC, you will need to consider extremely carefully whether the evidence of non-cooperation and non-compliance by Iraq is sufficiently compelling to justify the conclusion that Iraq has failed to take its final opportunity.

30. In reaching my conclusions, I have taken account of the fact that on a number of previous occasions, including in relation to Operation Desert Fox in December 1998 and Kosovo in 1999, UK forces have participated in military action on the basis of advice from my predecessors that the legality of the action under international law was no more than reasonably arguable. But a 'reasonable case' does not mean that if the matter ever came before a court I would be confident that the court would agree with this view. I judge that, having regard to the arguments on both sides, and considering the resolution as a whole in the light of the statements made on adoption and subsequently, a court might well conclude that OPs 4 and 12 do require a further Council decision in order to revive the authorisation in resolution 678. But equally I consider that the counter view can be reasonably maintained. However, it must be recognised that on previous occasions when military action was taken on the basis of a reasonably arguable case, the degree of public and Parliamentary scrutiny of the legal issue was nothing like as great as it is today.

31. The analysis set out above applies whether a second resolution fails to be adopted because of a lack of votes or because it is vetoed. As I have said before, I do not believe that there is any basis in law for arguing that there is an implied condition of reasonableness which can be read into the power of veto conferred on the permanent members of the Security Council by the

UN Charter. So there are no grounds for arguing that an 'unreasonable veto' would entitle us to proceed on the basis of a presumed Security Council authorisation. In any event, if the majority of world opinion remains opposed to military action, it is likely to be difficult on the facts to categorise a French veto as 'unreasonable'. The legal analysis may, however, be affected by the course of events over the next week or so, e.g. the discussions on the draft second resolution. If we fail to achieve the adoption of a second resolution, we would need to consider urgently at that stage the strength of our legal case in the light of circumstances at that time.

Possible consequences of acting without a second resolution

32. In assessing the risks of acting on the basis of a reasonably arguable case, you will wish to take account of the ways in which the matter might be brought before a court. There are a number of possibilities. First, the General Assembly could request an advisory opinion on the legality of the military action from the International Court of Justice (ICJ). A request for such an opinion could be made at the request of a simple majority of the States within the GA, so the UK and US could not block such action. Second, given that the United Kingdom has accepted the compulsory jurisdiction of the ICJ, it is possible that another State which has also accepted the Court's jurisdiction might seek to bring a case against us. This, however, seems a less likely option since Iraq itself could not bring a case and it is not easy to see on what basis any other State could establish that it had a dispute with the UK. But we cannot absolutely rule out that some State strongly opposed to military action might try to bring such a case. If it did, an application for interim measures to stop the campaign could be brought quite quickly (as it was in the case of Kosovo).

33. The International Criminal Court at present has no jurisdiction over the crime of aggression and could therefore not entertain a case concerning the lawfulness of any military action. The ICC will however have jurisdiction to examine whether any military campaign has been conducted in accordance with international humanitarian law. Given the controversy surrounding the legal basis for action, it is likely that the Court will scrutinise any allegations of war crimes by UK forces very closely. The Government has already been put on notice by CND that they intend to report to the ICC Prosecutor any incidents which their lawyers assess to have contravened the Geneva Conventions. The ICC would only be able to exercise jurisdiction over UK personnel if it considered that the UK prosecuting authorities were unable or unwilling to investigate and, if appropriate, prosecute the suspects themselves.

34. It is also possible that CND may try to bring further action to stop military action in the domestic courts, but I am confident that the courts would decline jurisdiction as they did in the case brought by CND last November. Two further, though probably more remote possibilities, are an attempted prosecution for murder on the grounds that the military action is unlawful and an attempted prosecution for the crime of aggression. Aggression is a crime under customary international law which automatically forms part of domestic law. It might therefore be argued that international aggression is a crime recognised by the common law which can be prosecuted in the UK courts.

35. In short, there are a number of ways in which the opponents of military action might seek to bring a legal case, internationally or domestically, against the UK, members of the Government or UK military personnel. Some of these seem fairly remote possibilities, but given the strength of opposition to military action against Iraq, it would not be surprising if some attempts were made to get a case of some sort off the ground. We cannot be certain that they would not succeed. The GA route may be the most likely, but you are in a better position than me to judge whether there are likely to be enough States in the GA who would be willing to vote for such a course of action in present circumstances.

Proportionality

36. Finally, I must stress that the lawfulness of military action depends not only on the existence of a legal basis, but also on the question of proportionality. Any force used pursuant to the authorisation in resolution 678 (whether or not there is a second resolution): must have as its objective the enforcement of the terms of the cease-fire contained in resolution 687 (1990) and subsequent relevant resolutions; be limited to what is necessary to achieve that objective; and must be a proportionate response to that objective, i.e. securing compliance with Iraq's disarmament obligations. That is not to say that action may not be taken to remove Saddam Hussein from power if it can be demonstrated that such action is a necessary and proportionate measure to secure the disarmament of Iraq. But regime change cannot be the objective of military action. This should be borne in mind in considering the list of military targets and in making public statements about any campaign.

NOTES

CHAPTER ONE

1. *New Statesman*, 2000.
2. John Rentoul, *Tony Blair: Prime Minister*, Little, Brown, London, 2001.
3. Doreen Gibson to authors.
4. Rentoul, *op. cit.*
5. Robert Philp, *A Keen Wind Blows: The Story of Fettes College*, James & James, London 1998.
6. Nick Ryden to authors.
7. Nick Ryden, *Observer*, 27 April 2003.
8. Gordon Dowell to authors.
9. David Kennedy to authors.
10. Ryden to authors.
11. Dowell to authors.
12. Rentoul, *op. cit.*
13. *Ibid.*
14. Robert Roberts to authors.
15. Robert Philp to authors.
16. Roberts to authors.
17. *Fettesian*, 1969.
18. Lindsay Clubb to authors.
19. Rudyard Kipling, *Stalky and Co*, 1899.
20. Alastair Macdonald to authors.
21. Roberts to authors.
22. Kennedy to authors.
23. *Ibid.*
24. Ryden to authors.
25. Roberts to authors.
26. *Ibid.*
27. *Ibid.*
28. Rentoul, *op. cit.*
29. Robert Roberts, *Worm's Eye View*, Pikestaff Press, Devon, 1995.
30. Roberts to authors.
31. Ryden to authors.

CHAPTER TWO

1. Rentoul, *op. cit.*
2. Friends Reunited website.
3. Professor Mark Freedland to authors.
4. Laura Mackenzie to authors.
5. Roy Hattersley to authors.
6. Anthony Seldon, *Blair*, Free Press, London, 2004.
7. Dr Sarah Hale, *The Third Way and Beyond*, Manchester University Press, Manchester, 2004.
8. Clifford Longley to authors.
9. Hale, *op. cit.*
10. John E. Costello, *John Macmurray: A Biography*, Floris Books, Edinburgh, 2002.
11. Clement Attlee, *The Social Worker*, G. Bell & Sons, London, 1920.
12. Hale, *op. cit.*
13. Mary Riddell, *Daily Mirror*, 26 September 1996.

CHAPTER THREE

1. John Kampfner, *Blair's Wars*, Free Press, London, 2003.
2. Tony Booth, *Labour of Love*, Blake Publishing, London, 1997.
3. Rentoul, *op. cit.*
4. Nick Ryden to authors.
5. Rentoul, *op. cit.*
6. *Ibid.*
7. *Ibid.*
8. *Ibid.*
9. Michael White, *Guardian*, 26 April 2002.
10. Anthony Seldon, *Blair*, Free Press, London, 2004.

CHAPTER FOUR

1. John Carr to authors.
2. Seldon, *op. cit.*
3. Carr.
4. Rentoul, *op. cit.*
5. Carr.
6. Rentoul, *op. cit.*
7. *Ibid.*
8. *Ibid.*
9. Harold Frayman to authors.
10. Paul Tyler to authors.
11. Frayman.
12. *Ibid.*
13. *Ibid.*
14. Rentoul, *op. cit.*

CHAPTER FIVE

1. Rentoul, *op. cit.*
2. Keith Proud, *The Grit in the Oyster*, Northern Echo, Darlington, 2003.
3. John Carr to authors.

4. Neil Kinnock to authors.
5. Michael English to authors.
6. John Burton to authors.
7. Brian Gibson to authors.
8. Alan Meale to authors.
9. Rentoul, *op. cit.*
10. David Watkins to authors.
11. Proud, *op. cit.*
12. *Ibid.*
13. Rentoul, *op. cit.*
14. Gibson.
15. *Ibid.*
16. *Ibid.*
17. *Ibid.*
18. *Ibid.*
19. *Ibid.*
20. *Ibid.*
21. Jim Innes, *The Journalist*, July 1983.
22. *Ibid.*

CHAPTER SIX

1. Lord Hattersley to authors.
2. Rentoul, *op. cit.*
3. Seldon, *op. cit.*
4. Rentoul, *op. cit.*
5. *Ibid.*
6. *Ibid.*
7. Lord Hattersley to authors.
8. Roy Hattersley, *Who Goes Home?*, Little, Brown, London, 1995.
9. Lord Hattersley to authors.
10. Martin Westlake, *Kinnock: The Biography*, Little, Brown, London, 2001.
11. Neil Kinnock to authors.
12. Westlake, *op. cit.*
13. Bob Worcester to authors.
14. Kinnock papers at Churchill College, Cambridge.
15. *Ibid.*
16. Neil Kinnock to authors.
17. Westlake, *op. cit.*
18. *Ibid.*
19. Bob Worcester to authors.
20. Kinnock papers, *op. cit.*
21. Nigel Stanley to authors.
22. Bryan Gould to authors.
23. Stuart Bell, *Tony Really Loves Me*, SpenView, London, 2000.
24. Lord Hattersley to authors.
25. Rentoul, *op. cit.*
26. Seldon, *op. cit.*
27. Lord Hattersley to authors.

CHAPTER SEVEN

1. Bob Worcester to authors.
2. Bryan Gould to authors.
3. Peter Oborne and Simon Walters, *Alastair Campbell*, Aurum Press, London, 2004.
4. Rentoul, *op. cit.*
5. *Ibid.*
6. Rentoul, *op. cit.*
7. Bryan Gould to authors.
8. *Ibid.*
9. *Ibid.*
10. *Ibid.*
11. Derek Draper to authors.
12. Michael Meacher to authors.
13. Colin Byrne to authors.
14. Rentoul, *op. cit.*
15. Kinnock papers, *op. cit.*
16. Kinnock papers, *op. cit.*
17. Worcester to authors.
18. John Booth to authors.
19. John Booth, 'Why I had Mandelson's life pulped', *New Statesman*, 2 August 1999.
20. *Ibid.*
21. Larry Whitty to authors.
22. Roger Pope to authors.
23. Neil Kinnock to authors.
24. Kinnock papers, *op. cit.*
25. Meacher to authors.
26. Byrne to authors.
27. Meacher to authors.
28. Roy Hattersley, *Fifty Years On*, Little, Brown, London, 1997.
29. Roy Hattersley to authors.
30. John Edmonds to authors.
31. John Monks to authors.
32. Byrne to authors.
33. Rentoul, *op. cit.*
34. Nicholas Jones, *The Control Freaks*, Politico's, London, 2001.
35. Barry Clement to authors.
36. Jones, *op. cit.*
37. Nicholas Jones to authors.
38. John Burton to authors.
39. Westlake, *op. cit.*
40. Kinnock papers, *op. cit.*
41. John Underwood to authors.
42. Byrne to authors.
43. Westlake, *op. cit.*
44. Underwood to authors.
45. Kinnock papers, *op. cit.*
46. Westlake, *op. cit.*
47. *Ibid.*

48. Kinnock papers, *op. cit.*
49. Westlake, *op. cit.*
50. Rentoul, *op. cit.*
51. Sir Menzies Campbell to authors.
52. Worcester to authors.
53. Kinnock papers, *op. cit.*

CHAPTER EIGHT

1. Neil Kinnock to authors.
2. Bryan Gould to authors.
3. Rentoul, *op. cit.*
4. Seldon, *op. cit.*
5. John Carr to authors.
6. Seldon, *op. cit.*
7. *Guardian*, 30 September 1993.
8. Kinnock to authors.
9. Roy Hattersley, *op. cit.*
10. Roy Hattersley to authors.
11. Richard Rosser to authors.
12. Denis MacShane to authors.
13. Larry Whitty to authors.
14. Andy McSmith, *John Smith*, Verso, London, 1993.
15. McSmith, *op. cit.*
16. John Edmonds to authors.
17. Edmonds to authors.
18. McSmith, *op. cit.*
19. Neil Kinnock to authors.
20. McSmith, *op. cit.*
21. *Daily Mail*, 6 January 1993.
22. Colin Byrne to authors.
23. Edmonds to authors.
24. *Guardian*, 13 April 1992.
25. Byrne to authors.
26. Kinnock to authors.
27. McSmith, *op. cit.*

CHAPTER NINE

1. Rentoul, *op. cit.*
2. Roger Pope to authors.
3. John Carr to authors.
4. Rentoul, *op. cit.*
5. *Ibid.*
6. John Burton to authors.
7. Carr to authors.
8. Peter Kilfoyle to authors.
9. Burton to authors.
10. Larry Whitty to authors.
11. Richard Rosser to authors.

12. Derek Draper to authors.
13. John Edmonds to authors.
14. *Ibid.*
15. Nick Cohen, *New Statesman*, 23 October 2000.
16. Carr to authors.
17. Tom Clarke to authors.
18. Quoted by Colin Leys in *The Socialist Register*, Merlin Press, London, 1996.

CHAPTER TEN

1. *Sun*, 17 March 1997.
2. *Daily Telegraph*, 27 March 1997.
3. *Daily Telegraph*, 22 April 1997.
4. Labour MP to authors.
5. *Daily Telegraph*, 24 April 1997.
6. John Burton to authors.
7. *Daily Telegraph*, 2 April 1997.
8. David Clark to authors.
9. *Ibid.*
10. Briefing released under US Freedom of Information Act.
11. Michael Meacher to authors.
12. Roger Pope to authors.
13. Derek Foster and Roger Pope to authors.
14. Derek Foster to authors.
15. Tom Clarke to authors.
16. *Ibid.*
17. *Ibid.*
18. *Ibid.*

CHAPTER ELEVEN

1. Rawnsley, *op. cit.*
2. Derek Draper to authors.
3. Jonathan Glancey and Ewan MacAskill, *Guardian*, 14 June 1997.
4. Interview with *Cafod*, the Catholic overseas aid magazine, 1997.
5. Rentoul, *op. cit.*
6. Rawnsley, *op. cit.*
7. A hint of this is given in an article by Frank Kane and Rupert Steiner, *Sunday Times*, 8 June 1997.
8. *Ibid.*
9. National Audit Office report into the commissioning of the Dome, 9 November 2000.
10. *Ibid.*
11. *The Times*, 20 June 1997.
12. Department of National Heritage press release, 27 June 1997.
13. *New Statesman*, 12 December 1997.
14. Nigel Morris, *Daily Mirror*, 25 February 1998.
15. *Today*, 1 January 2004.
16. Derek Draper to authors.
17. Kampfner, *op. cit.*

18. Oborne and Walters, *op. cit.*
19. An Evening with Alastair Campbell, Hoddesdon, 1 July 2004.
20. Oborne and Walters, *op. cit.*
21. Neil Kinnock to authors.
22. Oborne and Walters, *op. cit.*
23. An Evening with Alastair Campbell, *op. cit.*
24. Rentoul, *op. cit.*
25. John Cruddas to authors.
26. *Ibid.*
27. John Monks to authors.
28. Graeme Brady, *Daily Telegraph*, 11 April 1999.
29. David Hencke, *Guardian*, 8 July 1999.
30. 'Public Appointments to NHS Trusts and Health Authorities', OCPA, March 2000.
31. Second report from the Commons public administration committee: *Appointments to NHS Bodies: Report of the Commissioner for Public Appointments*, 19 July 2000.

CHAPTER TWELVE

1. Hugh Pym and Nick Kochan, *Gordon Brown: The First Year in Power*, Bloomsbury, London, 1998.
2. Rentoul, *op. cit.*
3. Peter Wilby to authors.
4. Jonathan Haslam to authors.
5. Roger Pope to authors.
6. Rentoul, *op. cit.*
7. Hansard, 5 July 1999, quoted in Rentoul, *op. cit.*
8. Matthew Parris and Kevin Maguire, *Great Parliamentary Scandals*, Robson Books, London, 2004.
9. David Hencke, *Guardian*, 2 March 2002.
10. Kampfner, *op. cit.*
11. Rawnsley, *op. cit.*
12. Paul Brown to authors.
13. Evidence to Anderson Inquiry, 2002.
14. Sir Ben Gill to authors.
15. Evidence to Anderson Inquiry, 2002.
16. Evidence to the Commons public administration committee, 22 June 2004.

CHAPTER THIRTEEN

1. Donald Macintyre, *Mandelson: The Biography*, HarperCollins, London, 1999.
2. *Ibid.*
3. Dispatch from US Ambassador Maputo to Secretary of State Madeline Albright, Washington, January 1997. Released under US Freedom of Information Act.
4. Rawnsley, *op. cit.*
5. Released under the US Freedom of Information Act to the *Guardian*.
6. Sir Tom Shebbeare to authors.
7. Rawnsley, *op. cit.*
8. *Prospect*, June 2004.
9. *Spectator*, 26 June 2004.
10. Rachel Sylvester, *Daily Telegraph*, 23 September 2000.

11. Peter Kilfoyle to authors.

CHAPTER FOURTEEN

1. Oborne and Walters, *op. cit.*
2. Guy Black to authors.
3. An Evening with Alastair Campbell, Hoddesdon, 1 July 2004.
4. *Washington Post*, 18 November 2003.
5. *Tablet*, 7 February 2004.
6. Lecture by Cherie Booth QC at the Reform Synagogues of Great Britain, 11 February 2004.
7. Oborne and Walters, *op. cit.*
8. *PR Week*, 20 June 2003.
9. Oborne and Walters, *op. cit.*
10. *Ibid.*
11. *Observer*, 8 December 2002.
12. Guy Black to authors.

CHAPTER FIFTEEN

1. Kampfner, *op. cit.*
2. *Ibid.*
3. *Ibid.*
4. Peter Riddell, *Hug Them Close*, Politico's, London, 2003.
5. Jef McAllister to authors.
6. Kampfner, *op. cit.*
7. *Ibid.*
8. Butler Report, 14 July 2004.
9. Bob Woodward, *Plan of Attack*, Simon and Schuster, London, 2004.
10. *Ibid.*
11. Anthony Rendell to authors.
12. John Birt, *The Harder Path*, Time Warner, London, 2002.
13. Nicholas Jones to authors.
14. Jones, *op. cit.*
15. Jones to authors.
16. Will Wyatt, *The Fun Factory: A Life at the BBC*, Aurum Press, London, 2003.
17. Most of the letters quoted are in an annex to the Hutton Report, 28 January 2004.
18. An Evening with Alastair Campbell, Hoddesdon, 1 July 2004.
19. Oborne and Walters, *op. cit.*
20. *Ibid.*
21. Sixth report of parliamentary ombudsman: Access to Information, July 2003.
22. Evidence to Hutton Inquiry, 11 May 2004.
23. Richard Norton-Taylor, *Guardian*, 24 February 2005.
24. Tania Branigan and Michael White, *Guardian*, 26 April 2005.

CHAPTER SIXTEEN

1. Tom Bower, *Gordon Brown*, HarperCollins, London, 2004.
2. Robert Peston, *Brown's Britain*, Short Books, London, 2004.
3. Derek Scott, *Off Whitehall: A View from Downing Street by Tony Blair's Adviser*, I. B. Tauris, London, 2004.

4. Kevin Maguire and Michael White, *Guardian*, 7 September 2004.
5. Toby Helm, Rachel Sylvester and Brendan Carlin, *Daily Telegraph*, 8 January 2005.
6. Gaby Hinscliff, *Observer*, 9 January 2005.
7. Gordon Brown, Speech to Amicus annual conference, Brighton, 18 May 2005.

CHAPTER SEVENTEEN

1. Roy Hattersley, *Guardian*, 18 July 2005.
2. Robert Skidelsky, *The Blair Effect 2001–5*, to be published by Cambridge University Press.
3. Charles Handy, *The Elephant and the Flea*, Arrow, London, 2002.
4. Oborne and Walters, *op. cit.*
5. Skidelsky, *op. cit.*
6. Peter Caterall (ed.), *The Macmillan Diaries 1950–57*, Macmillan, London, 2003.
7. Skidelsky, *op. cit.*
8. John Monks to authors.
9. *Ibid.*
10. David Seymour to authors.
11. John Pilger, *New Statesman*, 25 July 2005.
12. *Ibid.*
13. Skidelsky, *op. cit.*
14. John Edmonds to authors.
15. Oborne and Walters, *op. cit.*

INDEX